IT STARTS WITH TROUBLE

It Starts with Trouble

William Goyen and the Life of Writing

CLARK DAVIS

University of Texas Press

AUSTIN

Requests for permission to reproduce material from this work should be sent to:
  Permissions
  University of Texas Press
  P.O. Box 7819
  Austin, TX 78713-7819
  utpress.utexas.edu/rp-form

♾ The paper used in this book meets the minimum requirements of
ANSI/NISO Z39.48-1992 (R1997) (Permanence of Paper).

LIBRARY OF CONGRESS CATALOGING-IN-PUBLICATION DATA

Davis, Clark, author.
   It starts with trouble : William Goyen and the life of writing / Clark Davis. —
First edition.
     pages   cm
   Includes bibliographical references and index.
   ISBN 978-1-4773-1067-0 (pbk. alk. paper)
1. Goyen, William.   2. Authors, American—Biography.   I. Title.
   PS3513.O97Z46   2015
   813'.54—dc23
   [B]   2014031607

doi:10.7560/767300

In memory of Martin Pops

What starts you writing?
It starts with trouble. You don't think it starts with peace, do you?

GOYEN, *TRIQUARTERLY* INTERVIEW (1982)

Contents

List of Abbreviations

AR   Goyen, William. *Arcadio*. New York: Clarkson Potter, 1983.

BOJ Goyen, William. *A Book of Jesus*. New York: Doubleday, 1974.

CR   Goyen, William. *Come, the Restorer*. Evanston: TriQuarterly Books and Northwestern University Press, 1996. Originally published 1974.

CS   Goyen, William. *The Collected Stories of William Goyen*. New York: Doubleday, 1975.

FS   Goyen, William. *The Fair Sister*. New York: Doubleday, 1963.

GAE Goyen, William. *Goyen: Autobiographical Essays, Notebooks, Evocations, Interviews*. Ed. Reginald Gibbons. Austin: University of Texas Press, 2007.

HHM Goyen, William. *Had I a Hundred Mouths: New and Selected Stories, 1947–1983*. New York: Clarkson N. Potter, 1985.

HLC Goyen, William. *Half a Look of Cain: A Fantastical Narrative*. Evanston: TriQuarterly Books and Northwestern University Press, 1994.

HOB Goyen, William. *The House of Breath*. Evanston: TriQuarterly Books and Northwestern University Press, 1999. Originally published in 1950.

HRC William Goyen Papers, ca. 1923–1984. Harry Ransom Humanities Research Center, the University of Texas at Austin. Box and folder numbers are cited where available.

IFC   Goyen, William. *In a Farther Country: A Romance*. Evanston: Tri-Quarterly Books and Northwestern University Press, 1995. Originally published in 1955.

SL   Goyen, William. *Selected Letters from a Writer's Life*. Ed. Robert Phillips. Austin: University of Texas Press, 1995.

WP   Goyen, William. *Wonderful Plant*. Palaemon Press, 1980.

WRC William Goyen Papers, 1937–1978. Woodsen Research Center, Fondren Library, Rice University. Box and folder numbers are cited where available. Goyen's family correspondence is in WRC 3.7 through 4.13; his correspondence with William Hart is in WRC boxes 1–3. Quoted material courtesy the Woodson Research Center.

IT STARTS WITH TROUBLE

Introduction

I remember Marian Anderson was my first experience with what truly was a spiritual moment. Suddenly when she sang she was purely an instrument for the spirit, pure spirit. Through her mouth, here was this blessed moment, the light and the fire were on her, way beyond her training or the song itself. I was sixteen; I identified thoroughly, purely, with her. "That's where I belong, I come from that," I said. "That's why I feel so alone, because I belong to whatever that was."

WILLIAM GOYEN, *TRIQUARTERLY* INTERVIEW, 1982

Unlike Truman Capote, William Goyen matured without betraying his sensitivity, he became stronger without surrendering the qualities which made him both human and subtle, able to handle overtones in relationships without destroying them in the process. The balanced, harmonious maturity of sensitiveness is a rare quality in our culture, for it usually does not have the endurance to survive.

ANAÏS NIN, *THE NOVEL OF THE FUTURE*

William Goyen is a unique and lonely figure in American literature. Though praised and recognized as a remarkable talent, particularly early in his career, he never felt welcome in the literary world. When asked in 1975 if he saw himself as part of the writing generation that included William Styron, Truman Capote, and Norman Mailer, he admitted that he "felt immensely apart. . . . I still feel apart and, well, I *am* apart from my contemporaries. And they don't know what to *do* about me, or they ignore me. I am led to believe they ignore me" (*GAE* 96). This isolation was partly the result of a fundamental feeling of estrangement—from home, family, from most forms of community. In part it was a function of his commitment to an idea: that the artist is his only subject and art a sacred act of finding a form for the soul's disorder. For Goyen, writing was never simply a matter of self-expression, nor was it a kind of economic manufacture; it was a struggle to stay alive, to wrest a blessing from the angel. "I've limped out of every piece of work I've done," he revealed in a lecture just before his death. "It's given me a good sock in the hipbone in the wrestling. My eyes often open when I see a limping person going down the street. That person's wrestled with God, I think. . . . Work, for me—writing, that is—has been that renewal through wrestling, that naming, that going home, that reconciliation with old disharmony, grief, grudge" (*GAE* 66).

In her 1983 introduction to Goyen's final collection of short stories, Joyce Carol Oates attempted to capture the wounded Texan's unique place in his country's literature, calling Goyen "the most mysterious of writers. He is poet, singer, musician as well as storyteller; he is a seer; a troubled visionary; a spiritual presence in a national literature largely deprived of the spiritual" (*HHM* vii). The description is apt and perceptive. Yes, Goyen remains a mysterious, almost elusive figure; his obsessive, worried stories do indeed live in the spaces between music and narrative; and his language, though dramatic and insistent in its way, pushes at clarity, hoping to see through the skin of the real. And yes, there's trouble—lots of it: deep disturbance and unspecified desire that push his lonely characters to tell their haunted stories.

But how exactly is Goyen a "spiritual presence"? And how can American literature be thought of as spiritually deprived?

It might have been more obvious to suggest that spiritual concerns have dominated American literature, particularly in its early phases. Literary historians often speak of the biblically soaked language and mindset of American writing at least until the Civil War, and it's difficult to see the Transcendentalists, for example, as nonspiritual, whatever their other attributes. But to recognize a religiously derived culture or an Old Testament style is not to identify the spiritual itself as a mode or content of the writing. And one of Goyen's primary goals for his fiction was precisely this—the embodiment of spirit in language, the evocation through colloquial music of a real, human presence. In an interview conducted near the end of his life, he tried to explain how a story, through the discipline of style, can create a heightened form of personal encounter:

> Something happens to me which changes my attitude toward . . . you. What is that? It's not that you've given me a lot of money, or bought me a house, or given me a reward. What changed my attitude toward you? Something, I say, came from outside me. And I see as I say this that I tend to look up, because we've been told that heaven is above us, though it may not be at all, it may be quite lateral, I don't know. But it has come from beyond me somewhere, it is not anything I have learned, been taught, or even done. So that the *spirit* is involved in the change of feeling between me and you.
>
> Style, then, is directly related to that experience. So that style is a spiritual manifestation of the experience of the story, for me. My stories *are* spiritual. (*HHM* 256–257)

It's important to recognize that Goyen's sense of spirituality is grounded in the face-to-face encounter, the emotional exchange between two people. And by style, he tends to have in mind a musical but dramatically *present* speech (present in the sense that it is directed intimately toward the other person), an ordinary language pushed to the limits of the ordinary, edged toward the inexpressible. In a review of Goyen's *Collected Stories* in 1975, Richard Rhodes suggested that to experience a Goyen story "is to read as if through a layer of fire-darkened mica. He is not deliberately obscure, but he is writing about qualities of memory and feeling, shifts in loyalty and love, that ordinarily function or occur outside any frame of words."[1] These shifts of feeling—or the occasion through which they are registered—emerge from a staged (that is, deliberately intensified) moment of speaking and listening. Through a technical elision, the reader becomes the listener, the intimacy of the speech reaches across the page, and the usual filters of literary form, language, and time seem to break down. It is as though the fictional speaker had turned directly to face us, and in that facing made an instant and unavoidable claim not just on our attention but on our lives.

The critic George Steiner has written of art's demand on the reader or listener as a form of "answerability." The reader is responsible for, *answerable to* the claim made on her attention. The work of art is not a distant object to be contemplated by a protected consumer (a Grecian urn in a glass case); it is a "real presence" that demands "vital welcome and habitation." We must make room for its voice, and this displacement of our own satisfaction and selfhood is fundamentally uncomfortable. "Embarrassment" is the term Steiner relies on to describe this sense of breached decorum. Goyen's originality stemmed in large part from his ability to raise such emotional claims to the level of method, and yet this very quality assured that his audience would always be limited. In a century increasingly devoted to the ironic investigation of a listless materialism, his work could seem backward or out of step. Though a modernist, his style was not pruned or pared down; a self-proclaimed rhapsodist, he directed his language not toward effusion but seductive invitation. He risked everything: the charge of sentimentality, the vulnerability of directness, the awkwardness of sincerity. Indeed, he now retrospectively resembles the post-ironic, future "rebels" imagined by David Foster Wallace in his 1993 article "*E Unibus Pluram*: Television and U.S. Fiction"—those who "eschew self-consciousness and fatigue," who are "[t]oo sincere," "[c]learly repressed": "Backward, quaint, naïve, anachronistic. . . . The new rebels might be the ones willing to risk the yawn, the rolled eyes, the cool smile, the nudged ribs, the parody of gifted ironists, the 'How banal.' Accusations of sentimentality, melodrama. Credulity. Willingness to be suckered by a world of lurkers and starers who fear gaze and ridicule above imprisonment without law."[2]

As Oates implies, writers devoted to so bare an emotional exposure *are* rare in American letters. Walt Whitman comes immediately to mind, but very few others. In recalling his early reading, Goyen admitted an attraction to what he called "singing people," a category that included poets like Whitman and a very few fiction writers: "And when I read 'Song of Myself' for the first time, again I was given voice, resounding in the little Texas room: 'Salut au Monde!' '*O take my hand, Walt Whitman! Such gliding wonders! Such sights and sounds!*' I was given freedom to speak of myself out of long isolation and out of the captivity by my own family" (*GAE* 58). Along with William Saroyan and Thomas Wolfe, Whitman offered a lyricism that gave voice to the exile's longing for contact. He spoke directly to an audience conceived as an ally or friend. The gesture that ends *Song of Myself* suggests the isolated longing and deliberate address so characteristic of Goyen's fiction:

Failing to fetch me at first keep encouraged,
Missing me one place search another,
I stop somewhere waiting for you.

The faith in organic unity that underlies this invitation appears with less certainty and optimism in Goyen's work, but the delicate mixture of the forlorn and the possible caught in Whitman's last line is an important part of Goyen's inheritance. "Waiting" is the exile's stance, a way of establishing desire while tending to the self's fragile but necessary separation.

When Goyen's first novel, *The House of Breath*, was published in 1950, the critical reception was mostly warm, at times effusive, and yet many critics had difficulty placing him. For a majority he seemed another of Faulkner's cast-off children, grouped with the "decadent" set of Capote, Carson McCullers, and Tennessee Williams. The mistake was easy enough to make. Goyen counted all three as friends and rivals, and he shared their shaded but daring approaches to sexuality. But he rejected any attempt to label him or his work as "southern." He considered himself southwestern, a modernist grounded in the emotional terrain of East Texas but not limited to the colorist aesthetics of regionalism. Subsequent reviews of his novels, short stories, and plays often recognized the strangeness and difficulty of his writing—its combination of folk storytelling and lyric intensity, its wedding of myth and aria—but more often than not the response was confused or impatient. As a result, Goyen lived on the edges of literary celebrity, occasionally honored but seldom rewarded, quietly admired by readers and writers attuned to his gifts, overlooked or forgotten by the rest.

Perhaps this oblique, uncomfortable relationship with U.S. letters accounts in part for Goyen's greater welcome in Europe. His intensely poetic style, often counted as a failure of clarity in America, found a receptive audience in France and Germany in particular.[3] The great scholar-translator Ernst Robert Curtius, for instance, considered Goyen one of the finest American writers of the mid-century in part because the author of *The House of Breath* seemed one of the few Americans attuned to European models: "From the American novel we expect brutality and cynicism; intellectual over-refinement but also primeval eruptions; morbidity and neurosis. In William Goyen's book we shall find very different elements: substantive poetry . . . ; harmony with the deepest simplicities of existence; reunion of sexuality with love; but also an artistic discipline that is more reminiscent of Flaubert, Proust, Joyce than of Melville, Wolfe, Faulkner."[4] Goyen's precise attention to lyric states of feeling attracted French intellectuals raised on the symbolists; unlike other American writers of the 1950s, he sought to register refinements of consciousness rather than the bump and hustle of postwar life. The phenomenologist Gaston Bachelard was so taken with *The House of Breath* that he included a brief account of its central image in his influential *The Poetics of Space*. To Bachelard, Goyen was one of the "poets and dreamers" who "find themselves writing things upon which metaphysicians would do well to meditate." By "overlaying our memory of the childhood house with daydreams," he continues, Goyen "leads us to the ill-defined, vaguely located areas of being where we are seized with astonishment at being."[5]

In other countries, particularly those with a tradition of fabulism or oral storytelling, Goyen found and continues to attract fervent admirers. (To give but one example, the only edition yet produced of Goyen's complete stories is a Spanish translation published in 2012 by Seix Barral. It is both startling and shameful that no English edition of his complete short fiction exists.) Again, the devotion to the spiritual— to "the music of what happens," as Goyen once put it (*CS* x)—may explain these disparate attentions. The American ironic mode diagnosed by Wallace as a feature of postmodernism, and of television in particular, is protective, an armor against illusion, and therefore suspicious and intolerant of the oracular or prophetic. The validity of such roles seem reserved for writers who emerge from alternative cultures, from traditions new or ancient enough to be allowed their clarity and innocence. Both despite and because of his upbringing—isolation, the simplicity and at times poverty of country life—Goyen claimed this intensity of vision as his own: a voice for the isolated, impoverished self, a prophetic speaking that ignores the protective gestures of sophistication in favor of an art of feeling. To reclaim him, to make a place for him in American letters, is to acknowledge, despite our jadedness, these unusual, or simply unfashionable, virtues: the idea of art as a direct encounter between selves; the notion that what passes beyond the physical, even beyond articulation, is vital to human connection; that telling one's story is a deep inner demand, an undeniable responsibility that cannot be shirked through ironic shielding or intellectualism; that writing is living, is being alive, and is a form of finding recognition in the world, of fundamental encounter with an other, a form of love, of being.

It Starts with Trouble emerged out of a basic desire to gather and present the facts of Goyen's life as they relate to the production of his art. Goyen has been fortunate in attracting very good criticism, but the efforts of the relatively few commentators devoted to his work have necessarily been partial and introductory. Robert Phillips, a close friend and important promoter of Goyen's work, produced the first book-length guide, including a short biography, in 1979. This was followed by Reginald Gibbons's *William Goyen: A Study of the Short Fiction* in 1991 and Patrice Repusseau's *William Goyen: de la maison vers le foyer*, published in Paris the same year. Repusseau's account, based on his earlier master's thesis, covers Goyen's formative years through his time at Rice. Though unfortunately never translated into English, it remains one of the most thorough accounts of Goyen's childhood and youth and is particularly valuable for its investigation of Goyen's student writings. The publication in 1995 of a selection of Goyen's letters, edited by Phillips and chosen to highlight Goyen's writing career rather than his personal life, provided the first close look at this writer's deeply thoughtful and passionate attempts to find and maintain his idiosyncratic vision.

Relatively few independent critical articles were published during the later years of Goyen's life and the period since his death in 1983, but there have been notable attempts by literary journals to solicit and publish a range of important materials, including critical readings. In France, Repusseau oversaw a special edition of *Delta* in 1979 that included French and American criticism, some of Goyen's letters, and one of his most revealing late interviews. The *Mid-American Review* assembled its own Goyen issue in 1992, collecting several new and important critical essays and publishing excerpts from manuscripts and remembrances by an array of friends and colleagues. This tribute issue provided material toward the publication of *A Goyen Companion: Appreciations of a Writer's Writer* in 1997, a volume produced by the editors of the *Texas Review*, another journal, along with *TriQuarterly*, that has been consistent in its devotion to Goyen studies.

Despite this steady if periodic level of interest, no complete study of Goyen's life and work has been produced, and it is arguable that further critical exploration of his writing has been handicapped by a general lack of information.[6] *It Starts with Trouble* is meant to fill this gap and to be a starting place for scholars, critics, and general readers who want to know more about this unusual and deeply affecting writer. In this sense, the book serves the traditional purpose of a literary biography but does so, I hope, with a more than usual sensitivity to the limits of the genre. Journalistic life writing as it is currently conceived and frequently practiced, despite disclaimers to the contrary, leans heavily on the conceit of exhaustiveness. While all biography intends to give shape and wholeness to the welter of facts that constitute personal history, there is something to be said for reminding ourselves of the brokenness of individual experience, particularly for a writer who saw the fragment as a fundamental feature of reality. Goyen understood the essentially tragic nature of existence as a function of our inability to gather what we have lost. He saw the wonder and hope of life in our determination to save what remained nevertheless, to bring order to the salvaged remnants of time and remembrance. Such arrangements, like the quilts sewn by his mother and women like her, were acts of salvation in the face of loss, ways of making that did not and could not reclaim everything but made something new out of the broken. All lives, literary or otherwise, are similarly piecemeal. All archives are metaphors for how memory speaks to us through both presence and absence, through the remnant and the space between what remains. And so the biography, no matter how assiduously it wrestles to find a communicable form, should always do so within the shadow cast by what is missing or lost.

In Goyen's case, many aspects of his early life do remain in the shadows. We have only a limited sense, for instance, of the background of his extended family, the Goyens and the Trows, who inspired many of the characters in *The House of Breath*. Likewise, only hints and indirect suggestions remain that can tell us what this wider family thought of his writing, his style of living, and his refusal to settle in Texas. Goyen's early relationships, particularly romantic attachments, are especially veiled, and his romantic life in general, outside of his major relationships, is often more the stuff of rumor than reliable fact. As a consequence, much of the information about Goyen's early years is limited to what the writer himself chose to share, an absence of perspective that appears to reflect, at least partially, an embarrassed reluctance among surviving family members to speak of his life and work. Goyen's nephew Don Gerrard indirectly suggested Goyen's reputation within his family when he explained that his mother, Goyen's sister Kathryn, had once told him that he could do anything he wanted with his life, "Just don't be like your uncle Bill."[7] The attitude may have been justified; Goyen was often both an emotional and financial burden to his family and could be so consumed with his own trials that he failed to tend to others'. But it also indicates that his sense of exile was not a figment of his imagination: there was resentment and disapproval beneath the politeness of family interaction, and some of that chill may survive to this day, if only as a socially conservative culture's distrust of its own complexity.

Was this strategy of avoidance a family attitude that led to Goyen's own penchant for secrecy? Possibly. The habit of not speaking can be difficult to break, particularly when the bonds of affection are intensified by absence. Whatever the case, Goyen was often sharply protective of his personal information. Despite the very large collection of materials housed at the Harry Ransom Humanities Research Center, his archive is by no means exhaustive, and in some instances he clearly preferred to avoid a document trail. When it comes to information regarding sales of his books, for instance, he could be defiant against requests for statistics, particularly later in his life when editors tied approval of new publications to evidence of past revenues. In gestures that were both aggressive and defensive, Goyen worked very hard throughout his life to maintain control of his image. A letter to the bibliographer Clyde Grimm provides a brief glimpse of this sometimes intense vigilance. After answering Grimm's long questionnaire in detail, Goyen concluded with this caveat:

> It's very important that it be clear that this is only information that I'm giving you. Please do not quote me in my own words. I can't give you my approval to do so. In other words, I am not writing these things for the pamphlet or for you to quote. Thanks for understanding this; and I ask you to write to me telling me that you will give me approval of the manuscript when it is finished and before it is published. I'd also like the right of approval of proof before the pamphlet is finally printed.[8]

Such an eye to his public persona might be considered merely prudent and less than fearful if it weren't for the regular secrecies and omissions of Goyen's correspondence over the years. Many of these elisions issued directly from attempts to conceal his sexuality, though more generally they seem motivated by a desire to avoid bad or upsetting news when writing to his parents. The impulse to hide—to avoid trouble and create private spaces for protection and dreaming—was fundamental to his personality. And he knew it. Working through his past to understand his alcoholism in the 1970s, he identified his "creative being" as one associated with "hiding": "1. Blanket over chairs— hidden world, exquisite aloneness. Self-pity, abasement, secretiveness. 2. What is 'reality'? I said. 'And *whose* reality? Who wants *that* reality. Let those others have that. I'll make my *own* reality'" (HRC 29.6). To make a secret space and construct there your own imperium may suggest a childish retreat, but it was also Goyen's way of nurturing a self that could hold out against the hostility and misunderstanding of his upbringing. One of the triumphs of his art was the recognition that the hidden always remains; writing was not confession but a way to gather emotions made stronger by confinement and repression.

Describing his second book, *Ghost and Flesh*, to his editor Robert Linscott, Goyen insisted that the artist is not only isolated, cut off, an outcast "longing for the whole" but

> a kind of magnet that attracts and carries about, seeks for, heavily loaded with it, the enormous burden of humanity's ghosts—and that in this sense he exists in a kind of twilit graveyard world surrounded by the ghostly part of everything that ever had flesh or blood or light in its face and upon its limbs—he is laboring to make the epitaphs for all things dead and so keep them alive, to return life to them. It is, then, a divine project that he is about, and a very human one, too; for with one hand he is handling and caressing life and with the other he is warming death.[9]

The project slowly formulated by the boy hiding under the blanket— initially perhaps little more than an emotional response to loneliness— became the idea of rescue, salvation: to save, not as a minister might in

a church but as an exile can when burdened with the task of remembrance. To be devoted to this province of spirit is to be separate, but it
is also to understand more keenly how physical desire drives the need
to recover. The "handling and caressing" of life is always shadowed by
the ghost's burden, the sense that what is held and loved is momentary,
spectral, already lost.

   William Goyen chose—or was chosen—to give his life to this task.
As a consequence, each story he wrote was a kind of trial, less an occasion for a display of sharpness or wit than a test of devotion. How can
one possibly "make the epitaphs for all things dead" and come out
whole or happy? How can art that asks so much not take from its creator some of the shine of his living?

Prologue
The Drowning

The bridge from Trinity, Texas, to the nearby town of Riverside is like any other on a modern rural highway—a twin span of concrete sliding low and flat over dark water. In the early 1920s, however, this important link between the two small towns was made of a combination of wood and steel, and it creaked and groaned to such an extent that Emma Goyen, the young mother of William Goyen, was afraid to cross it in the family car. To her husband's exasperation, she made him pull off the road before they reached the river. Then she got out, let the car pull away, and walked. Many years later, her son would write of the strange sight of his mother moving fearfully across the beautiful but unstable bridge: "My sister and I peered back at the small figure of our mother laboring darkly and utterly alone on the infernal contraption which was her torment. I remember my father getting out of the car, on the other side, waiting at the side of the road, looking toward the bridge, watching my mother's creeping progress. When she arrived, pale, she declared, as she did each time, 'I vow to the Lord if my sister Sarah didn't live in Riverside I'd never to my soul come near this place'" (CS 284).

The Goyen story that contains this brief but significant anecdote is called "Bridge of Music, River of Sand." It concerns a man's return to the town of his birth and the site of a family legend. The narrator, a slightly off-center, not entirely stable personality, is searching for signs of his past, scraps of memory. He drives to the river a mile or so outside of town, out onto the decayed bridge now slated for demolition, and just as he himself begins to feel his mother's terror ("the whole construction swayed and made such a sound of crackling and clanking"), he sees something extraordinary: a naked man, "diving from the old railroad trestle" into the moist sand of the dry riverbed. Horrified, he makes his way off the bridge and out of his car, hurrying to where he can still see the body, "a figure on its knees with its head buried in the sand, as if it had decided not to look at the world any more. And then the figure began to sink as if someone underground were pulling it under. Slowly the stomach, lean and hairy, vanished; then the loins, thighs. The river, which had swallowed half his body, now seemed to be eating the rest of it. For a while the feet lay, soles up, on the sand. And then they went down, arched like a dancer's" (CS 281–282).

The narrator has no idea what to do about the fallen man. He climbs onto the railroad bridge, as though to see what the man has seen. He finds no evidence, no clothes or footprints; he isn't even sure he saw it happen now that the body is gone. He wonders if he's suffering a "kind of bridge madness" or from hallucinations brought on by "going back to places haunted by deep feeling." Then he remembers his mother's fear and through that memory a related story, barely mentioned, repressed actually, but essential to the vision. It is his sister's voice that prompts it, making clear a family ritual:

> "Mama," said my sister, trying to pacify the situation. "Tell us about the time you almost drowned in the river and Daddy had to jump in and pull you out."
>
> "Well, it was just right over yonder. We'd been fishing all morning, and . . ." (CS 284)

We don't hear the rest of the mother's story; the narrator moves on, casually dodging the hidden center of his own telling. But Goyen did tell the rest, and more than once. In an interview conducted not long before the publication of "Bridge of Music," he explained the significance of this spot near the bridge:

> I was in my mother's body when she almost drowned in that very river . . . and she was with . . . the terrible thing was that she was with another girl friend . . . they were just seventeen . . . young things, and the girl drowned, and it was she whom they pulled out and rolled over a log— the way they did Otey [in his first novel, *The House of Breath*], so you see my mother witnessed that and my father pulled them both out, and it was hideous, for poor country people. . . .[1]

Some childhood stories have, or attain, a defining force. This pre-natal scene of death, drowning, and near-drowning—as though the one girl might be the other's double—seems already mythic. Its frequent repetition ("They told me this so early—they kept telling me this story, and for years . . .") often in the context of his mother's understandable fear of water, set firm its significance.[2] Orphanage. This was the word Goyen eventually chose for the sense of isolation and loneliness he had felt since he was a child: "it's not physical, it's not material, it's truly spiritual. I have always had it from a tiny boy, lying on a pallet. I had a sister and a brother. But that permeated most everything. I was the oldest. . . . My mother was an invalid most of the time, and so I took care of my sister, and took care of her, she was always in the bed."[3] And it isn't difficult to picture a young boy able to imagine his own mother's death by drowning, able to feel in some sense connected to it, possibly responsible, somehow the product of both rescue and loss.

The idea of the unborn child saved from drowning surreptitiously feeds and haunts the story's naked figure drowned in sand; his slow ab-sorption is a birth in reverse, a more intense sterility unmaking the past. But true to Goyen's deeply probing, oneiric method, the story never un-packs these burdened signs. They remain integral, fully charged, thick with unspeakable feeling. The narrator has returned to his sacred place, the site of birth, death, and fear—the site of crossings, transitions, a gateway both dangerous and destabilizing—to see in his blurred con-dition a vision of himself, of his own disturbed seeking, a telling suicide of the bared self pitching forward into dryness.

PART I ∽

The House in the Bitterweeds

CHAPTER ONE

Trinity

1915–1922

O Charity!

THE HOUSE OF BREATH

E ast Texas is a pine barren. Across its densely forested, slowly
swelling hills the soil is sandy and poor, and though it produces admirable kitchen gardens of tomatoes, okra, and mustard greens, the only crop that grows in true abundance is the pine
tree. Virgin forests of ancient longleaf pine brought large numbers of
people to the region in the late 1800s. Across the American South, some
230,000 square miles of *Pinus palustris* once stood in what historians
describe as vast "open parklike stands, where travel was easy and a person could see a long way. The reddish-brown longleaf trunks were huge,
often exceeding three feet in diameter and soaring fifty feet to the first
limb."[1] At the turn of the century, lumber companies moving west from
Alabama and Mississippi discovered this region of cheap and abundant
"stumpage" and invaded in force, building towns and mills and railroads and systematically cutting all the old growth in a period that extended from approximately 1890 to 1930. When the towering stands of
ancient yellow wood were gone, many of the sawmill towns went with
them, reclaimed by weedy thickets or left to fade into slumping, rusty
ghosts.

"Little goodbye villages," Goyen once called them in a magazine
article that never made it into print. "They were once towns of the
Depot (the train is gone), the Railroad Hotel, the Drugstore as meeting-
place, the General Merchandise store. . . . Where there are big, honey-
comb-like houses, they are tree-sheltered and stand alone and wide-
faced, and there is a generous gallery flowing half-way round them.

Some vine is usually climbing on strings on the front porch, the swing behind; there are ferns in green-glazed jardinieres or in washbuckets on the front steps. . . . Or there are little 'Shot-gun' houses with a cap-like porch; or flimsy, tilted, boxy houses with swept dirt yards." The people go to church twice a week. "Their faces are lean, their ears usually large for their small heads, and they are small-boned. In times past, the womenfolk's hair was generally long and pulled round to a loose knot in back. They were slumped from carrying children on their hips; their dresses were straight-down." When forced to leave these "deep nature-towns, hazy, moist, viney, dreamlike under great brethren trees," the small country people grieve in their city neighborhoods, holding "fast, for a time, to an old romance way that is lost. They were, for a time, forever talking of 'goin back to Bedias' (pronounced Bead-eyes) or of 'when we go back home to Groveton,' and they lived in city neighborhoods like country people, one foot forever trying to find home again" (HRC 27.2).

It was in a town like this, Trinity, that Charles William Goyen was born on April 24, 1915. His father worked at the local sawmill. Members of his mother's family painted houses, did repairs for the railroad, and ran the town post office. The small community—in 1914 the population was roughly 1,800—relied on the lumber industry and the freight lines that linked the mills to Houston, 85 miles south. The Trinity River, brown and turning in its sandy banks, touched its outer limits; it had once seen small river boats carry cotton bales from central Texas down to the Gulf Coast, but when the railroad arrived, commercial river traffic ceased. By the time Goyen was born, the town consisted of a main street of essential shops up against the train tracks, a small graveyard fenced and planted with cedars and crepe myrtles, and a scattering of bungalows and shotgun houses tucked into the shade off hard-packed dirt roads.

The oldest of three children, Billie Goyen was an isolated, emotional, and even strange child.[2] His health was poor; his birth had been difficult, a breech presentation, and he wasn't expected to live through the night. Perhaps as a result he was perpetually thin, thought to be epileptic, and subject to sudden and prolonged spells of crying. An unpublished story written when he was a teenager describes the childhood of an unnamed character whose emotional fragility is his defining characteristic: "When he had been a child he would suddenly break into tears and crying that was inexplicable to those around him. His mother was consternated by this strange enigma; she feared a serious abnormality. The doctor was mentioned and he was shut up, tight, like a locked door. But he would go to some quiet place and cry, alone. He spent his first thirteen years like that: crying and fearing doctors and knowing he was abnormal and enigmatic."[3] In the Old Red Building, as the little elementary school was called, he experienced more than the usual measure of childhood slights and taunts. Years later he sketched the typical, humiliating scene:

> He could not play ball. When the class chose sides, the girls against the boys, he would hear his mates, one by one, being chosen. And when the number unchosen grew smaller and smaller, he felt himself grow-ing deathly sick, sicker and sicker, because he knew in the end he would be left sitting there at his desk, alone and unchosen, with all the others lined up against the blackboard in front and around him, proud and secure and chosen. Then there would be a big laugh and the teacher would be a little embarrassed and say that he would go on the side that had the least number. Someone said that day that he should play on the girls' side; their side had the least number. When they said that he felt himself tear all up inside, like a hairspring unravelling.[4]

As might be expected of a hypersensitive child, Goyen was closer to his mother than to his father, especially during these early years in Trinity. Described by one of his grandsons as "macho as hell," Charles Provine Goyen, known as Charlie, was a tall, handsomely square-jawed lumberman who had gone to work in the mills when he was thirteen and who came to represent a way of life and an idea of masculinity that his young son instinctively rejected: "[W]e were separate," Goyen later told an interviewer. "He played baseball professionally on the town baseball team; and he hunted; and I didn't; that's where it stopped."[5] The difference of sensibility is clearest in Goyen's 1964 story, "The Thief Coyote." When a "red coyote" is seen running through Cranestown with a turkey in its mouth, Mark Coopers, a wealthy farmer, organizes a posse to hunt for the robber. The party includes his young son, Jim, a quiet boy who prefers gathering pecans to hunting. "Other boys around Cranestown had made some little fun of him because he picked pecans instead of killing hogs and branding cattle, and this seemed to hurt him more now than it ever had" (*CS* 234). Jim quietly opposes his father's world and secretly identifies with the thief coyote, hiding in his silence a different vision, both ecological and aesthetic: "For he had, in some way, already made up his mind, alone in grove and orchard, that his real and loving work was to collect quietly what the earth had made and had fallen, yielded to him upon the ground, and store away a quiet gathering-up of small, dirt-grown morsels and meats" (*CS* 235).

As in many of Goyen's stories, the principal character emerges not so much as an autobiographical stand-in but as a mouthpiece for an artistic project—the "gathering-up" of home-grown myth and memory. Or, as is here the case, as a sacrifice that establishes the virtue of this opposition. For not only does Jim die on this ill-conceived expedition; he is killed, accidentally, by his own father: "They saw for a magical instant the limp and folded shape of a coyote lying over the snowy leaves. But when the hand of Lazamian touched the shape and the light he held was lowered to show the features of the captive, there was the figure of Jim lying on the ground with a string of blood beginning over his eye and curling down his cheek" (*CS* 237). Jim's interest in the small and earth-born is what dooms him. His cracking of pecans in the woods spooks the hunters more than once and eventually brings on his death.[6] A judgment is passed on the father for his suspect values, elevating the withdrawn and isolated boy to the position of savior—a self-justifying fantasy, to be sure, but no less evocative of a boy's loneliness and his tender, passive hostility.

After Charlie Goyen died, in 1968, Goyen wrote of his father with great gentleness: "[You were] one [of] those young men come up out of a large poor family in a poor place, lumber people in your case, Mississippi in your case, that moved from work place to work place: mill towns. . . . When your family moved to East Texas for a sawmill at Trinity, you found my mother there (she had been born there, her father was Postmaster there and her brother and sister worked in the Trinity Post Office . . .)" (*GAE* 42). In a manuscript from the same period called "The Belleek Swan," Goyen meditated on the contrast between his father's world and "a precious little swan of painted china" found among Charlie Goyen's possessions:

> I took from my father's house and for his memory the Belleek Swan and nothing more! Why? The swan is an imperial creature of grandeur

and refinement. Had I looked for something from his house to represent him absolutely, I might have taken a crude boll of cotton that had burst roughly into a ball of doughy white, which he had picked from a field near his birthplace in Mississippi, near Hattiesburg, where he once made a return—finally, after swearing to do so for some years. Or a piece of yellow pine—a staunch, splendid tree, which he sold for many years. (Think of a man selling trees!) . . . My father was a man of simple realities: hard days' work, providing family needs. He was a man of simple generosities and deep unselfish affection for friends and kin. He was a man of woods and earth. What had he to do with this elegant and aqueous bird? (*GAE* 4)

The swan is small and feminine—"so small," he wrote, "that I can cup her in my hand"—and seems to represent Goyen's choice to remember the tenderness of a man associated with harsh, masculine realities: "In my memory of my father the swan glides before me as though it were conveying my true Father back to me." The interpretation is almost willful, stubborn, an emotional claim made by a son intent on reimagining his father's inner life as a way of recovering him after death. The distance is both measured and erased, setting the son apart while positing a secret bond with a father from whom he was always emotionally separated.

There was no such awkwardness with Emma Goyen, whom her son consistently cited as the source of his own creative voice: "As a literary person I truly am the offspring of my mother and women like my mother. . . . Hers was a singing way of expressing things, and this I heard so very early that it became my own speech; that's the way I write" (*GAE* 89). The image of the very young Billie watching and listening to his mother as she went about her daily tasks appears frequently in his early work, particularly in the unfinished novel, *Christopher Icarus*. Here Mary Ganchion, an early version of Malley Ganchion from *The House of Breath*, yearns for a fuller emotional and aesthetic life but keeps her desires restrained, filtered sadly through her sewing and singing: "Always there had been some unfinished, unfulfilled thing in her, something not come to bloom, tight and held back. She went about containing it, lidded down. It was in her singing and in her sewing that some of this incompleteness came out of her. Christopher knew even at an early age that this singing was not ordinary mother singing; it broke his heart and made him weep."[7] In one instance recounted in the novel, the young Christopher is so lonely for his mother while at school that he rushes out of the classroom and runs home in the middle of the day: "He found her in the yard, digging with her hands and a little spade around some hollyhock sprouts. How warm and content he felt upon finding her again, as though he had imagined her to be in danger and had fled to her protection. She turned, a little startled to see him beside her so unexpectedly and asked what had happened at school. He had no reply, no reason at all to give her. Then, quickly sensing it all, she said 'A little worm is eating my hollyhocks,' trying to let him know she understood."

Because of his mother's persistent illnesses, her eldest son came to think of himself as both her caretaker and confidant, and in *Christopher Icarus* as in *The House of Breath*, sorrowful and sometimes sickly mothers and their emotionally complicated sons maintain a resistance against a father who is unable to share their sensibility. Here Malley Ganchion, addressing her son Berryben, captures the tension and tone of the conflict:

> "But Walter Warren [her husband] would never save me from anything of fear or any nightmare. The world he gave me was cold; and so I waited for you, Berryben, to grow up and make the world warm and save something for me.
>
> "Walter Warren would never let me swank. When I had my hair bobbed (was one of the first of Charity to do it, sittin on a crate on the back screenporch), Esther Crow came over to do it and I was so excited, trembled and giggled and I screamed so and we all got so tickled (somethin terrible happened) and me screamin so, 'Oh! oh! oh!', that it scaired little Berryben half to death and he cried, 'Mama! Mama!' and thought they were hurtin me and ran and hit Esther Crow and tried to pull her away from me to protect me and Walter Warren was mad and trembled too and went away to set on the front porch sayin 'I'll be damned, Malley'; and little Berryben ran cryin out to the chickenyard.
>
> "Then Walter Warren would grumble about my long gloves I'd wear at nights over my coldcreamed hand and arms to keep them white—for him, but he never cared. But he cared enough to make me have Jessy, me in my condition that never should have had another child and she

was born so hard and mangled and nearly killed me; that's why she died so young, because she never should have been born.

"'That's all right,' I would say to Walter Warren, lyin with his back to me in the night, 'wait till Ben grows up, we'll never have to depend on you for anything.'

"And I'd lie there and hear the tune in the shutter and feel cold and alone and want to die except for Berryben, my salvation, in the next room, sleepin with his little sickly sister Jessy.

"It was waitin and waitin, through these cold years. And then, when it was time, Berryben just turned and went away and I cain't even call him back. It was Walter Warren drove him away, that meanness in him; called him a scoundrel once, always criticized him and fought with him at the supper table, made him vomit up all his supper, is why he was always so thin." (*HOB* 81–82)

No doubt there is exaggeration and distortion here. After all, this is a dramatic passage from the first novel of a young man bent on revealing what he thinks of as the hidden truths of his background. But what rings true nonetheless is the almost musical scoring of emotional interplay. A young mother of fragile health resentful of a distant, somewhat hardened husband struggles over a hypersensitive child overtly burdened with her expectations. The familial mise-en-scène recurs with surprising regularity in Goyen's writing, and there is no reason to doubt its essential truth.

The Ganchions

At least some of this tension within the immediate household reflected larger differences between the two extended families, the Goyens and the Trows. Again and again in Goyen's fiction, his father's family (the Ganchions in *The House of Breath*) supplied many of the wild, wandering, adventurous, and sometimes cursed characters. Their patriarch is an alcoholic lumberman from Mississippi who had followed the timber cut west to Texas. In the story "Old Wildwood," the grandfather offers a family history: "'We all lived in Missi'ppi,' was the way he began, quietly, to speak. 'And in those days wasn't much there, only sawmills and wildwoods of good rich timber, uncut and unmarked, and lots of good Nigras to help with everything, wide airy houses and broad fields. . . . Your granny and I moved over out of Missi'ppi and into Texas, from one little mill town to another, me blazing timber and then cutting it, counting it in the railroad cars, your granny taking a new baby each time . . ." (*CS* 143–144).

Though this brief account could describe the lives of thousands of southern families during this period, it accurately follows the turn-of-the-century movements of the Goyens. The family had originally migrated from South Carolina to Mississippi in the early 1800s, often spelling their name "Goings" until around 1860 when William Walter Goyen—a good-looking, blond-haired schoolteacher who died in the Civil War battle of Brice's Crossroads—changed it. William Walter had married Sarah Martha Bell in 1851, and they had four children, of whom William Smith, Goyen's lumberman grandfather, was the youngest. Census records and death certificates verify that W. S., or Billy, Goyen brought his family from Mississippi to Texas between 1894 and 1896, settling first near Groveton in Upshur County and moving south to Grayburg in Hardin County in 1910 before settling in Trinity. And from 1890 until 1910, his wife, Katie, had nine children, one every two years or so, the third of whom was Goyen's father, Charles.[8]

"Old Wildwood" offers an extensive portrait of "the little old grandfather" with "the animal grace and solitary air of an old mariner, though he was a lumberman and purely of earth" (*CS* 141):

> The grandfather was an idler and had been run away from home, it was said, by his wife and children time and time again, and the last time for good; and where did he live and what did he do? Later . . . the grandson's mother had confessed that she knew her husband went secretly to see his father somewhere in the city and to give him money the family had to do without. It was in a shabby little hotel on a street of houses of women and saloons that his father and his grandfather met and talked, father and son. (*CS* 142)

This secretive meeting between Charlie Goyen and his father is repeated, along with Emma's disapproval, in the small story "Right Here at Christmas," published in *Redbook* in 1977. In both pieces, the grandfather is a figure of shame to the narrator's mother, who sees her husband's family as deeply and embarrassingly flawed. In the Christmas version, the grandfather shows up at the family's house "with whiskey on his breath":

> That rankled my mother. Later she would draw my father, whose breath now had the same smell, gotten from his father's hip pocket, where a half pint always traveled with him, onto the sleeping porch and tell him that he would have to take his father (who had walked twenty blocks from a cheap mission hotel in town) home if he drank any more.
>
> "Hell, Mary, it's Christmas," my father would protest, almost apologetically.[9]

The father's other relatives are no more welcome as far as the mother is concerned. "Other kinfolks arrived, all trouble for my mother, all her mortal enemies—my father's city family. Hers remained in the little town she grieved for, a shady, piney-woods place on the banks of a soft river."[10] The new arrivals are "three women, three sisters and not a one of them with a current husband. . . . Two of them had on dresses—red and white—of starched cotton, hard as boards. The young one, May, a Texas pathfinder, wore green slacks. Though my father always protected his young, wild sister, he had little patience with her, still in her twenties and already married twice and her second husband long gone. My mother had no patience with May at all, and at the sight of the tight slacks, her face turned hot red."[11]

Although Goyen's primary emotional allegiance was to his mother, his father's family fascinated him deeply. As he told Robert Phillips in his 1975 *Paris Review* interview, *The House of Breath* is essentially about the Goyens, the wandering aunts and uncles who seem to represent both the attractions and dangers of a life outside the small town world his mother cherished.[12] A disconcerting if exciting mixture of unsettled desire, booze, material ambition, and sex seems to drive those characters who return obsessively in his work. The grandfather, for example, is more than just an inveterate drinker; he embodies a taste for sensuality that Goyen presented as a family trait, made manifest in this case through the old man's "crooked foot": "His left leg was shorter than his right, and the left foot had some flaw in it that caused the shoe on it to curl upwards" (CS 141).[13] Remembering a fishing trip to Galveston, the boy narrator tells of secretly watching as the old man sneaks a woman into the beach cabin:

Something began between the two, between the grandfather and the woman, and the grandson feigned sleep. But he watched through the lashes of his half-closed eyes as through an ambush of grass the odd grace of his grandfather struggling with the woman with whom he seemed to be swimming through water, and he heard his grandfather's low growl like a fierce dog on the cot, and he saw his grandfather's devil's foot treading and gently kicking, bare in the air, so close to him that he could have reached out to touch it. And then he knew that the foot had a very special beauty and grace of moment, a lovely secret performance hidden in it that had seemed a shame on his person and flaw upon the rock. It had something, even, of a bird's movements in it. It was the crooked foot that was the source and the meaning of the strange and lovely and somehow delicate disaster on the bed; and it was that shape and movement that the grandson took for his own to remember. (CS 148)

As a recorder, a *savior* of memory, Goyen positioned himself both within and outside his family's world; he was the watcher learning something incommunicable about the relationship between sex and loss, about his grandfather's very human weaknesses. That a "lovely secret performance" could transform the crooked foot into something peculiarly expressive, rich, and real makes clear just how important sexuality would become to his reading of his own family, his origins, and ultimately to his own artistic motivations.

The House of Breath's most haunted characters often seem to elicit these opposing feelings: an admiration of their wandering independence, their unruly desire, mixed with a fear of their self-consuming sensuality. Christy, the wayward and secretive uncle, has perhaps the greatest resonance, making clear the tragic link between forbidden knowledge and displacement, pent-up desire and ranging violence:

They said around Charity that he did the thing that would make you crazy if you did it too much; they said he was a niggerlover; they said he was a KuKlux; they said he was adopted by Granny Ganchion and was a no-good Peepin Tom whose parents were probably foreigners or Jews or thieves in the Pen; and some of this was true and he was bad. . . . He would say whispered things about animals: udders, the swinging

sex of horses, the maneuvers of cocks, bulls' ballocks and fresh sheep—
he was in some secret conspiracy with all animals. He fought game and
Cornish cocks with the Gypsies and the Mexicans, and often he would
clink in his hand some dangerous-looking tin cockspurs that he used
for his fighting roosters. But after a roosterfight with the Mexicans or a
hunt in the woods, Christy would be quiet and then sit all day close to
Granny whittling little figures; and once he carved a perfect ship and
put it in a bottle. (*HOB* 148–150)

Christy is the initiator, teller of secrets, a trapped, animalistic, sexual
being who serves simultaneously as an object of desire, emulation, and
admonition. His position as sexual secret-keeper is strengthened by his
ties to Folner, or Follie, his brother, whom he raised "like a mother": "I
was Folner's mother all those years, makes me part woman and I know
it and I'll never get over it" (*HOB* 149). Folner is openly and flamboy-
antly effeminate, a cross-dresser who runs away with a traveling circus because "it was the only bright and glittering thing in the world he
could find. Of all the ways and things in the world, he chose a show,
with acrobats and lights and spangles" (*HOB* 113). He later commits suicide "in a hotel in San Antonio" and is buried in Charity. The narrator
describes the scene in direct address to his dead uncle: "At your funeral
there was a feeling of doom in the Grace Methodist Church, and I sat
among my kin feeling dry and throttled in the throat and thought we
were all doomed—who are these, who am I, what are we laying away,
what splendid, glittering, sinful part of us are we burying like a treasure
in the earth?" (*HOB* 116).

In a French interview published in 1979, the interviewer, Rolande
Ballorain, asked Goyen about the family sources of these characters:

RB: Is that pattern Boy, Ben Berryben, Jessy, Walter and Malley—was
that your family? Your brother?
WG: Mixed up a little. My family and yet not my family. It's a
reconstruction.
RB: And an uncle?
WG: An uncle, very much so. But a reconstructed one.
RB: An illegitimate son.
WG: Yes.

RB: And Follie—how about Follie?
WG: Follie, yes, was in my family. And truly died. So that there's a lot of that that's true, you see.[14]

As with most writers' pronouncements on character sources, we should take this information with considerable skepticism.[15] Though Goyen did consistently note the presence of homosexuality in his father's family, there is little specific evidence—and even less remembrance among surviving family members—of verifiable links between these characters and the Goyens or the Trows. What such "reconstructed" characters do suggest most clearly are versions of Goyen himself, partially modeled on family members but also built out of his own experiences. As mythic forebears, the two symbolic uncles offer possible genetic explanations, a tracing of character through blood, that may have helped Goyen justify his own identity and behavior.

That said, such meditations on family figures—real or imagined—can still tell us a great deal about the young Billie Goyen's place within his extended family. A nervous, epileptic boy in East Texas who was no good at sports and hated hunting, who preferred a sullen withdrawal, a furtive listening to family stories, would undoubtedly be suspected of abnormality, even in the absence of other signs of extremity such as fits of crying. For that same boy to emerge in a family filled with complex and sometimes troubled personalities would simply heighten suspicions—theirs and his—that he had inherited some of these traits. Perhaps the family's temptations would become his. At the very least, the struggles and repressions he witnessed would define the world he lived in and the choices he would eventually face.

"A medieval world of terror"

Mark Coopers of "The Thief Coyote" seems to have only circumstantial resemblance to Charlie Goyen (whom his son later termed a "gentle man"), but the somewhat pasteboard character does encapsulate a reading of East Texas male culture that Goyen never relinquished. Its primary note is violence. Speaking of the late story, "Had I a Hundred Mouths," he stressed this darker side of the country boy's idyll: "You know it *was* like that, to me; as a child I really felt that. I lived around all of that. There was a man preaching the salvation of my soul in a tent across the road from my house, but up on the hill beyond there the Ku Klux were burning their crosses and I saw them run tarred and feathered Negroes through the street. I saw them running like that, twice. Aflame" (*GAE* 122).

It's a mood, and reality, captured in the story "Figure Over the Town," in which a flagpole sitter—mysterious, attractive, disturbing— appears unexplained, high above the Methodist church. The story, re- lated as a memory from the narrator's childhood, is set in a time of war:

> Everywhere there was the talk of the war, but where it was or what it was I did not know. It seemed only some huge appetite that craved all our sugar and begged from the town its goods, so that people seemed paled and impoverished by it, and it made life gloomy—that was the word. One night we went into the town to watch them burn Old Man Gloom, a monstrous straw man with a sour, turned-down look on his face and dressed even to the point of having a hat—it was the Ku Klux Klan who lit him afire—and above, in the light of the flames, we saw Flagpole Moody waving his cap to us. (*CS* 287)

Flagpole Moody becomes a figure of the artist for the boy whose story this is, an isolated watcher, both of the town and apart from it. Like the straw man (and its biographical analog, the immolated black man on the streets of Trinity), Moody is an all-purpose sacrificial object, gathering the region's religious intensity and evangelism with its darker tendencies toward xenophobia, racism, and vigilantism. At first loved, the flagpole sitter gradually absorbs the town's suspicion and hatred simply by refusing to explain himself, by holding himself at a distance: "Apparently he had nothing to sell, wanted to make no fortune, to play no jokes or tricks; apparently he wanted just to be let alone to do his job. But because he was so different, they would not let him alone until they could, by whatever means, make him quite like themselves, or cause him, at least, to recognize them and pay *them* some attention" (*CS* 291).

Isolation, sacrifice, the sensitive figure at the center of a rough, sus- picious, and superstitious country—the arrangement appears repeat- edly in Goyen's fictional worlds; it is primarily an emotional truth but has its roots in general fact. The Ku Klux Klan was very much an active presence during the years of Goyen's Trinity boyhood and just after. Regional historians note that "during the early 1920s, the national spread of the 'Invisible Empire' of the Ku Klux Klan brought the KKK into the [lumber] company towns, where the Klan seems to have focused its attentions on social irregularities associated with the quarters—domino halls, 'barrel houses,' illegal alcohol, gambling houses, prostitutes, and Anglo-American seekers after these diversions."[16] In one incident in 1921, a doctor from Beaumont thought to be under indictment for abortion was kidnapped, beaten, and tarred and feathered. Other white men were punished for cheating on their wives or associating too closely with neighboring blacks. Lynchings, whether specifically carried out by the Klan or not, occurred often enough in various small towns to form an established part of the cultural and emotional landscape. In the town of Sour Lake, often mentioned in *The House of Breath*, a black store owner named Henry Cade was shot and hanged after an eight-year-old white girl accused him of assaulting her. This, too, was in 1921, a year before the Goyens left Trinity for Shreveport and later Houston, and it lends a simple if terrible weight to a boy's haunting memories: "Yet above your bottomlands, River, like a hill of terror, rose Rob Hill in its shaggy old pelt of scrub oak and crowned by burning crosses, where the Ku Klux Klan met and burned a Negro to remind them all along you [sic] that they were Negroes" (*HOB* 26–7).[17]

As Goyen himself suggested, these episodes of communal terror were juxtaposed—astonishingly to a young boy's eyes—with the evangelism of the tent preachers and revivalists. In the 1960 story "Rhody's Path," the flagpole sitter appears again, this time less as an unknowable artist than as a religious advertisement, an intriguing East Texas combination of sideshow attraction and stylite mystic:

> The hooded flagpole sitter was a part of it all. He had come in advance as an agent for the Revival and sat on the Mercantile Building as an advertisement for the Revival. He had been up there for three days when the grasshoppers come. Twas harder for him than for anyone, we all imagined. The old-timers said he had brought in the plague of hoppers as part of prophecy. They raised up to him a little tent and he sat under that; but it must have been terrible for him. Most thought he would volunteer to come on down, in the face of such adversity, but no sir, he stayed and was admired for it. (*CS* 166)

The story magnifies an incident that Goyen witnessed as a child when a snake-handling revivalist came to town and the rattler he pulled from its cage was apparently in no mood to play along: "The handler fell dead, and the people fled, and the snake got loose. They hunted the snake all night and found it and killed it, which was a terrifying thing to see."[18]

Repeatedly, in stories and interviews, Goyen described this tent revival as taking place in Baily's pasture "across from the house." In *The House of Breath*: "Now, ruin (of childhood) returning to ruin, come, purged of that bile and gall of childhood (into the empty purity of memory), come through the meadow called Baily's Pasture that is spun over with luminous dandelions like a million gathering shining heads, through random blooming mustard and clover and bitterweeds, over the grown-over path that was a short-cut to town when there was no circus or revival tent there" (*HOB* 42). Goyen's visual method layered picture on picture: circus over revival tent, hooded flagpole sitter over Klansman; intermingling religion and showmanship, salvation and sacrifice, threatening display and spiritual ceremony: "Once the Ku Klux Klan interrupted the sermon on Sunday to come marching down the center aisle in their sheets, terrifying the congregation who did not know who among them they might be coming after—but they had come in only to make a demonstration in favor of the preacher, of whom they approved, and to give a donation, wrapped in a white handkerchief, to the church" (*HOB* 117). Or, as Folner explains to Boy Ganchion:

> "When the circus came to Bailey's Pasture, I knew this was my chance. Remember how you and I and Aunt Malley went and what we saw and did, the yellow-skinned grinning freaks in their stalls with the sawdust floor, twisted like worms the freaks grinned and ground in the sawdust; and the screams of the animals in the menagerie and the sad, exciting music of the calliope? . . . Remember when I lifted you up on that big elephant, you little scared thing perched on that enormous back, you shook and cried and got so excited you almost fainted and Aunt Malley had to run to buy some lemonade and throw it in your face." (*HOB* 131)

To a boy's mind, these various shows or spectacles (good or bad, uplifting or appalling) gather into a single tonal perception—of a world more dramatic than rational, more symbolically driven (by faith, fear, or superstition) than subject to analysis. "A world that was folk drama," as Goyen himself put it. "I remember them lined in their chairs on the front porch at dusk, some womenfolks in the swing, talking of kinfolks and farms and nearby towns, of the fortunes or failures of sawmills and roundhouses and packing stands, of weal or woe of carpentry, small-crop gardening, road-building and timber cutting, of crises of drought or gulleywasher" (HRC 27.2).

Goyen's East Texas seems forever lost or left behind, not just quiet or underdeveloped but forlorn, its deeper sections mixing rural poverty with a still-untamed suspicion. The area known as the Big Thicket, which extends from just north of Beaumont to Nacogdoches and from the Sabine River to near Trinity in the west, has had a reputation since the nineteenth century for mystery and lawlessness. Since the early 1800s, its dense undergrowth and palmetto swamps have also provided shelter for anyone who hoped to escape the law or other discomfiting aspects of civilization. Some of this historical isolation may have resulted from the Neutral Ground Treaty between the United States and Mexico. At the time of the Louisiana Purchase, the two countries failed to agree on a new border between U.S. and Mexican territory in what is now Louisiana. The area between the Arroyo Hondo (near present Natchitoches, Louisiana) and Sabine rivers, adjacent to the thicket, was claimed by both governments but controlled by neither. According to one local historian, "this strip of land naturally became a haven for desperadoes and renegades of all sorts. Travel became so hazardous for traders and others who ventured through the neutral strip that in 1810 and 1812 both governments were compelled to send armed expeditions to expel outlaws."[19] Though the dispute was eventually settled in 1819, the area retained its aura of territorial disorder for generations after.

This history of unsettled and unruly independence helped lend the region its air of isolation and penchant for legend. Much of Goyen's work—in fact, his entire literary sensibility—draws upon a need to transform the unknown and slightly forbidding landscape of his childhood by combining regional tales with mythic-religious story forms. The most direct example can be found in "A Shape of Light" collected in *Ghost and Flesh* (1952). Here a figure named Boney Benson follows "a scrap of light rising like a ghost from the ground" (*CS* 100). His pursuit of the light becomes a tortured personal quest, a quasi-religious and artistic calling: "He had to *follow*, hard and in hardship and torment, he had to give himself wholly, unafraid, surrendered to it" (*CS* 101). And this devotion to the task excites the narrator to form a story of the light's origin, a legend rather than a history, an invented response to a disturbing, questioning presence. In this reconstructed "record"— described as "a shape of light in the darkness, a lighted shape of dust"— we learn that Boney Benson has reacted to the death of his wife and unborn child by mutilating himself and burying his severed genitals in the grave: "The tale is told that the child was born in the grave, delivered itself of its tomb within tomb and, mole-like, began a life of its own underground, rising at nights when the Mexicans who lived in the Mexican houses round the edge of the graveyard were playing their mandolins and harmonicas and singing their passionated luted summer-heat songs in the pallid summer nights, to wander phantom over the countryside" (*CS* 119–120).

Though overlayered with Goyen's distinctive concerns—the artist as saint, transforming the burdened self through sexual self-violence— the story's starting point is the local legend commonly known as the Saratoga Light. On "Old Bragg Road," a graded dirt byway that was once a train line that ran from the oil fields of Beaumont, witnesses have long reported seeing a ball of white, yellow, or sometimes red light that seems to move unpredictably, sometimes toward, sometimes away from pursuers but never close enough to determine its source. Though typically explained as an emanation of swamp gas, the light has produced its share of ghostly etiologies, from the decapitated railroad worker who searches for his lost head to the Spanish conquistadores who supposedly buried their treasure deep in the thicket and left a supernatural flame to mark its location.

When Goyen wrote of the region's tendency to dream and wonder, he very probably had in mind the persistence of such tales: "This East Texas landscape, unnoticed by outsiders except where it has become oil-boom, is one of deep nature-towns, hazy, moist, viney, dreamlike and timeless under great breathren trees. A poetic and melancholy Gaelic air was over it, over shadow glen and warm lake and mossy riverbank. It produced a singing folk of living legend and active superstition and slow ironic wit, a folk of seasoned woods wisdom" (HRC 27.2). No doubt every rural region has its similar spooky tales, but Goyen understood the history of East Texas as a potent source of story and myth, a place whose history and geography made possible the resilience of legend.

River of Sand

Hauntings follow curses. In part because of his personal experience, Goyen imagined the region of his early childhood to be under a sort of malediction, particularly when the delicate pastoral of dirt road and river began to yield to oil wells and dams. Though many of these changes took hold only after his family had left Trinity, the discovery of oil in East Texas and the sudden sprawl of mid-century Houston played an important role in the way Goyen came to mythicize East Texas in his fiction. The tone of loss that characterizes so much of his work from *The House of Breath* to *Arcadio* issues not only from the family's relocation—and his mother's subsequent longing for the life left behind—but from the deeper understanding that what had been (geographically, ecologically, culturally) no longer existed.

In Goyen's version of this small-town paradise lost, the discovery of oil in the region at the turn of the century was partly to blame. From the boomtown atmosphere of the 1901 Spindletop gusher near Beaumont to the subsequent discoveries of rich fields at Sour Lake, Saratoga, and Batson's Prairie, East Texans suddenly found themselves surrounded by, and part of, a new, frenzied, and corrupting economic force. In an essentially impoverished region, a very few people found sudden, unexpected wealth while, at least in Goyen's eyes, despoiling the quiet land of his childhood. The portrait of Wylie Prescott in *Come, The Restorer* (1974) offers perhaps the most forceful, and stylized, version of this indictment. Like a demon, Prescott begins his fabled career as a Red Adair–style fighter of oil well fires: "He emerged from the fiery depths of the golden opening in the earth that was like the throat of a large bloom that spewed forth mud, rock, salt water, and shining leathery black oil, demanding a percentage of what he had rescued. Thus he rose up out of burning holes to become a man of power and wealth . . ." (*CR* 153–154). He subsequently turns wildcatter and developer, drilling wells and clearing land with the same hellish fury and avarice:

> He became the first independent oil-well driller in East Texas. He leased land and he bought our leases. He now knew oil as he knew fire. He had gone after fire with his very hands, fondling it; he physically handled it, in hand-to-hand intimacy, like a snake handler, a broncobuster, a lion tamer, a crocodile wrestler. Now he went after oil with the same sen-

suality. . . . He was accursed with the sense of destruction, marked like
Cain, by the natural gift, the ancient instinct for devastation. . . . He
was a walking Plague, a pestilence, locust, frog, grasshopper, tree moth,
a devourer, worse than any chemical spray or poison, a devastator. He
took away from Nature its pure self, its forces, and did not put back anything, but he added fake stuff—chemicals, preservatives, coloratives.
His factories murdered rivers, spoiled freshness, soured and embittered
sweetness, withered green. He was the first, the leader, the beginning
of the generation that poisoned itself, that spoiled its own, that ate its
own poison. (*CR* 155, 156)

The most damning of these accusations is surely the phrase "murdered rivers," for if there was any one symbol of what Goyen's early
life meant to him—and what gathered in one idea everything beautiful, strange, and mysteriously enriching about Trinity—it was the river
itself, the "little taffeta ruffle" that "scalloped round" the hem of Charity
in *The House of Breath*, itself a *speaking* character in that novel. The
river is nothing less than the soul of the book, a source of natural and
sexual power, good and evil, fertility and death, which is why its pollution and partial disappearance so outraged Goyen's memory. In "Bridge
of Music" the narrator witnesses what he takes to be an act of suicide—a naked figure diving into a dry riverbed: "Into a nothing river.
'River'! I could laugh. I can spit more than runs in that dry bed. In some
places is just a little damp, but that's it. That's your grand and rolling
river: a damp spot. That's your remains of the grand old Trinity. Where
can so much water go?" (*CS* 280). The question is more psychological
than physical. The Trinity River still flows by the town of Goyen's childhood, though it may have been diverted from channels that he knew as
a boy.[20] But the river's apparent absence makes clear his long-standing
feeling that the country of his birth has been ruined, its old way of life
emptied, missing.

The naked diver seems compelled by the same impulse as the narrator: to seek, even to his own death, the lost vitality and regenerative powers of a condemned world. "The feeling of something missing
haunted me: it was the lost life of the river—something so powerful that
it had haunted the countryside for miles around; you could feel it a long
time before you came to it. In a landscape that was unnatural—flowing
water was missing—everything else seemed unnatural" (*CS* 281). The

diver remains stuck headfirst in the sand and then disappears, sucked into the river bottom. His vanishing is a type of burial but also a birth in reverse, the body reabsorbed into the once-fertile bed, a reading reinforced by the family legend of his mother's near drowning that is nothing less than Goyen's personal creation myth. Birth, death, the forbidding power and possibility of the river, the logic of sacrifice, the pattern of peril and rescue, of loving and appalling sacrifice—the mother's story seems to contain everything that might have been and that was.

CHAPTER TWO

Merrill Street

1923–1931

In those days (1923–24) Woodland Heights was like a soft woods with little houses in close rows on dusty streets. There were few cars; we played in the street. Merrill Street was a little street that ran nine blocks long, east to west, and it was a neighborhood of shy immigrants from small towns, like us.

"WHILE YOU WERE AWAY," 1978

It can be difficult to register the full force of Goyen's ties to Trinity without seeing them as part of a fundamental feeling of dislocation and loss. If the house in Trinity—the house of early childhood—was "the place," Houston, where the family ended up in 1922 after a few months in Louisiana, was a nonplace, a dark exile, the antihome:

> What caught me up so early and made me feel that I had to be a voice for it was the sense of exile, misplacement, the poverty, spiritual and material, of city living, the growing hell of automobiles, the loss of open nature of woods and rivers, the simple lyric yearning of people out of place. This was the lament I heard from these gentle uprooted people in their singing speech, their poignant outcry (my mother's joined them, often led them): "When we go back one day to Red River"; "When we all go home to Polk County." Or to Honey Grove, or to Lovelady, Tyler, Big Springs. Houston in those early days seemed to me a place of the half-lost and the estranged, even the persecuted. (*GAE* 44)

But these small-town people exiled to the city almost never did return. The lumber boom was over; in the roughly thirty years since companies had begun buying pine timber in East Texas, the great stands of untouched forest had all but disappeared. By the early twenties, most of the mills were closed or downsized, putting large numbers out of work. As historians Thad Sitton and James H. Conrad explain, the effect on Trinity County was typical: "Only the fact that the mill closings had been extended over several years' time kept Trinity County from bankruptcy. The Josserand Brothers mill at Josserand closed in 1909; and a town of 900 vanished. In 1911, Thompson and Tucker Lumber Company closed down Willard (population 1,200), and in 1919, Saron (population 1,200) closed. With the closing of the West mill at Westville (population 1,000) in 1921, only the lumber operations of the Trinity Country Lumber Company at Groveton and the Rock Creek Lumber Company at Trinity remained."[1] In the East Texas sand hills, there were few alternatives to cutting timber. When the last pine fell and the mills went silent, many of the little towns simply melted away.

This regional depression and migration—or its emotional echo— became one of the deep, almost mythic sources of Goyen's writing. He returned to it repeatedly, as in the story "Zamour, or A Tale of Inheritance," in which the residents of "Hines Street" in Houston are described as "migrants from little towns" or from the mythical Red River County, one of Goyen's stand-ins for Trinity: "These people had changed their style of living and slid into the pattern of the city," all except Princess Lester, who "went on living as if she were still in Red River County. . . . She seemed the last carrier of the bred-up aspects of a played-out species of large ears, small neat heads, faces no bigger than a coffee cup, dainty claws of hands with which to shell peas and bean, to cup a chick, to gather eggs one at a time and not to break any, to hand out small washings, dip one dipper of well water but not to draw a bucketful" (*CS* 187–188). Lyric detail can be a response to loss, not only in the fine observation but in the phrasing, the saved language of a missing world: "bred-up," "cup a chick," "washings." There is more than a little of the seven-year-old here, refusing to budge, defying change, hanging on grimly and with considerable pleasure to the little things children see and touch. Goyen's memory often seems to return to this age (and to this time, 1922), overriding acceptance and maturity in favor of a ritual self-attention.

Why else set out this childhood path in the opening sections of *The House of Breath*? Its awareness is distinctly liturgical:

To get to the house, Charity, if I had been in town, I would just start walking toward the sawmill, down Main Street (which was really on the Highway named this for the short time it ran through you and became a little piece of you) under all the Charity trees. I would pass the only stores you had, looking across Main Street at each other; and ahead of me would stretch the Highway, going to pretty close little towns like Lufkin and Lovelady, and behind me it wound to faraway places, huge and full of many people, like Dallas or Santone. Then I would turn off at the twisted cedar, in whose branches I had been as often as any bird, that had a forked limb like a chicken's wishbone, where once I slipped and hung like Absalom until Mrs. Tanner came running to save me; then there would be the sawmill, where my father worked (the men urinating in the lumberstacks)—and came home with sawdust in his pockets and shoes—that had a long, legged sawdust conveyor sitting like a praying mantis. And next would come the graveyard, nothing but names and dates and enormous grasshoppers vaulting over the graves; and the little Negro shacks next, with black faces at the windows or some good old Negro children playing in the mudpuddles, and a rooster crowing somewhere, after the rain. Finally I would take the sandy road, my feet barefooted and glad in it, stand by the Grace Methodist Church where it always seemed I could hear the voice of Brother Ramsey inside saying "Blessed are the peacemakers, for they are the children of God," and then if I suddenly looked up, after thinking into the sand what peacemakers were, I would see the house, looking at me like a face of a sleeping bird (the cisternwheel would be its tail over it), and calling me back to it, home. (*HOB* 11–12)

To recover this animated pastoral—things humanized, objects transformed into welcome animals—the speaker must inhabit distance and speak from a place of loss. Like the mournful refugees from other small East Texas towns, this retrospective voice from *The House of Breath* is not merely home- or place-sick; it is resentful and grieving, and its pained sense of loss fuels an increasingly moral argument. The range of connectedness that produces this passage's animism is impossible to maintain in the city. For Goyen, the countryside of East Texas *as seen from the exile of the city* became the source of a premodern clarity—mythic, legendary—an imagined world that fed dreaming.

Woodland Heights

Despite its more recent reputation for sprawl, Houston in the 1920s was a relatively small and old-fashioned city. Dallas, San Antonio, and even Birmingham, Alabama, were larger, and Houston was just beginning to spread out from its traditional, brick-faced and awning-lined Main Street into new, remote neighborhoods like River Oaks. An extensive streetcar system brought businessmen and shoppers in from nearby neighborhoods, but the city was also in the early stages of its passion for the automobile. In his 1978 lecture "While You Were Away" (addressed to his father), Goyen emphasized the shift from walking in Trinity to being driven around Houston in Charlie Goyen's newly acquired company car: "But car-less in the sawmill town, we had walked to church through the fields or strode along on sandy roads to neighbors and kin, back up somewhere in a clearing. You walked the railroad tracks to the sawmill, walked through pastures to the store in town, walked me to the little doctor's office, walked me with my mother to Trinity school. Transferred to a new place, you were my driver, my conductor, chaperone to my early simple journeys . . ." (*GAE* 42).

The family had lived in two separate duplexes in Woodland Heights before buying the two-bedroom wood-frame house at 614 Merrill Street. Like so many dwellings in the yet-to-be-air-conditioned city, it had a sleeping porch and an enormous attic fan that, as Goyen explained, "rumbled and roared and brought in bug-studded cool air" but was so loud that conversation was impossible while it was running (*GAE* 43). The smell of natural gas from the nearby reservoir hung both inside and out, replaced later by the pervasive sourness of the local paper mill. The houses had just been built, and only a few newly planted saplings lined the bare streets. For Goyen, the tight, working-class neighborhood became both a comfort and a trap, a gathering of exiles huddled against the new and the strange. At each end of the street was a school, Travis Elementary on the east and James S. Hogg Junior High on the west. From the age of eight to fourteen, Goyen made the daily journey up and down Merrill Street; in his later recollections, it was this sense of living in an enclosure, of being on a restricted path that both bound him and urged him outward. As always, the longing for what had been, imbibed through his mother's plaintive repetitions, defined him:

By the time my daily walks to the eastern end of Merrill Street had ended and I began my way toward the other end, to my junior high school, I was able to express a little of these feelings I had now taken on for myself, which had been given to me, indeed had been mine, too, from the very start, now I knew. And I was beginning to write down these feelings of homesickness, of loss of place, reveries of my beginnings, of a countryside that now seemed like the Garden itself, like a country of Paradise. . . . The city grew rawer, harsher. When a girl from our Sunday School at Woodland Methodist Church was knocked down by a car on Houston Avenue and lay dying in the Church vestibule, I cursed the city and wept for the peace of my town and vowed I would run away. (*GAE* 46)

This sort of emotional response is probably not uncommon in many children, but Goyen's tendency to dwell on such moments and to assign overwhelming significance to the feelings they produced—to navigate primarily by emotion rather than thought—became a consistent feature of his life and work.

The story "A People of Grass" is one of the few based in these early years in Houston, and it conveys an almost florid sensitivity to social failure in a boy who sees himself as the inheritor of a family burden. The plot is relatively simple: a homesick Texan, alone in Rome, comes upon a group of schoolgirls playing in the Borghese Gardens. It is May, and the girls have decorated themselves with flowers ("early poppies") and grass buds. The narrator, who gently suggests Actaeon spying on Diana, lies in the grass and watches, only to be taken by a memory of his own childhood, of the "Grammar School May Fete" in "faraway Texas." The internal narrative is essentially tragic: the boy, called "the brother," is cast in the school pageant as the "king of flowers," and the sister is costumed as a poppy, in a fragile dress "all of crepe paper, crimson and green," with "a little cap of an inverted poppy bloom with the green stem on it" (*CS* 175). When the program begins, the boy's role is to touch with a wand each of the flower girls, "folded" as though in bud, and "bring them up to bloom" (*CS* 176). When he comes to his sister, however, his touch seems to bring on disaster; as she rises, the sister steps on her dress and falls "as if he had struck her with a burning rod." In retrospect at least, the moment becomes an emblem of family failures and of the burdens the brother seems unable to shoulder: "Yet he had not been able to help his sister come to flower, as he or nothing in this world could help his mother make the proper stem; and in that moment he knew certainly that no one ever could mend certain flaws, no mother's hands or brother's wand but some hand of God or wand of wind or rain, something like that, beyond the touch of human hands" (CS 179).

There are several important elements to take note of here: the mother's anxiety as projected through the son ("Once the mother even wept with despair over the stem and said, biting her lip and looking out the window, 'I just cannot make it right'"), the brother's conviction that *he* is the focal point and designated savior of the family's dignity, and the subdued but nevertheless clear sense that this is a moment of sexual maturation that the brother comes to see as a disaster. The boy may have his "very first" adult suit of clothes, but he can't perform the role given him—either the masculine part of "bringing girls to flower" or the symbolic role of family redeemer. What he finds years later in Rome might be called the gift of tragic distance: seen from "his alien room of ancient floor, round which the denouncing cry of the demon swifts whirled" (CS 181), the small failure becomes a sign of life's bitterness, its stigma lifted by a larger myth of fallenness.

More simply, "A People of Grass" can be read as a story of humiliation, suggesting that the strongest of Goyen's youthful feelings, particularly in the new environment of Houston, was a combination of loss and shame. This is not to say that Merrill Street didn't prompt its own obsessive gathering of detail. As Goyen explained in a brief tribute to George Williams, the longtime professor of creative writing at Rice, "[Williams] knew from listening to what I was writing that I hungered to get away, to flee, so that I could experience and write about it, make art of it, something true and lasting. Later, when I began, at last away from there, to write, what I wrote about, obsessively and tenderly, with no anger, was Merrill Street in Woodland Heights—what I had fled— one long block of little wooden houses that became for me, away from it, a whole rich and human world" (GAE 172). But the general tone of these reminiscences has little of the elegiac, pastoral longing that often colors his tours of Trinity. Instead, bits and pieces, salient facts and observations seem gathered defensively, critically, as signs of their observer's intelligence and power. Goyen may be right about an absence of anger in his depictions of this period of his life, but there is no lack of suspicion and fear, of protectiveness, as though memory is a sign of quiet, personal assertion and, ultimately, of artistic will.

This desire to control the details of his past is clearest in the one story partially related to Goyen's experiences at school, "The Grass-hopper's Burden." The title alludes to Ecclesiastes and carries a vaguely apocalyptic tone, suggesting the presence of failure and death ("and the grasshopper shall be a burden, and desire shall fail") like a shadow, over the "days of thy youth." The school building itself is a threatening presence "like a great big head with flat skull of asphalt and gravel and face of an insect that might be eating up the young through its opening and closing mouth of doors" (CS 60). It contains, according to the brief prelude, "a world," and the story seems designed to give us a tour of its inhabitants via the movements of Quella, a prissy, self-concerned girl eager to play her part as a "Royal Princess" in the annual May Fete. As Quella moves through the school on her way to the pageant rehearsal, the narrator provides short but finely detailed portraits of a variety of students and teachers. (From an earlier typescript version, it is clear that the story began as a numbered series of personality sketches based on Goyen's brief stint as a middle school teacher in California in 1947.) There is Miss Morris, the social studies teacher, with her "puckered mouth just like a purse drawn up" (CS 60); Billy Mangus, who is "fat and white and whined a lot" (CS 62), who put Red Hots in the girls' hair and could wiggle his false tooth with his tongue; and Quella her-self, preening, bored, nosey, her self-assurance dependent on a strict sense of privilege. The attention to detail is precise but largely exter-nal, and through Quella's hard-edged selfishness, the narrator sounds coolly hostile, the tone precise and brittle.

Enter George Kurunus. As Quella makes her way through the empty halls (classes are still in session), she encounters the "writhing and slobbering and skulking" form of a disabled student:

> He was shuffling closer. She stood up and pressed against the wall and watched him, hating him. It was said that if he ever fell down he could never get up unless somebody helped him, but just lie there scram-bling and waving his arms and legs, like a bug on its back, and mutter-ing. His little withered left arm was folded like a plucked bird's wing and its bleached and shriveled hand, looking as though it had been too

long in water, was bent over and it hung limp like a dead fowl's neck and dangling head. But he could use this piece of hand, this scrap of arm quickly and he could snap it like a little quirt and pop girls as they passed him in the hall. Here he came, this crazy George Kurunus, a piece of wreckage in the school. What did *he* want? She looked to see if *he* had a pass in his hand. No. Certainly he was not going to practice for any May Fete. Why should *he* be in the halls and without a pass? (CS 68–69)

Most Goyen stories contain a surrogate for his central concerns, a character around whom a specific, almost obsessive, rhetoric emerges. Generally speaking, these characters are set in opposition to the world; whether obviously so or not, they are exiles, loners, kept apart less by a conscious rebelliousness than by an innate but often inexpressible difference. Unlike the satirically observed students, George Kurunus is granted a seriousness of presence that suggests a different register of being, both more adult and, at the same time, more meaningful as a sign of tragic "breakage."

To Quella, George is a threat to her idea of a perfect social world as exemplified by the Kings and Queens of the May Fete. In her mind, privilege is a result of beauty, and the class structure of student life has no place for the misshapen. She is offended by his inability to speak properly: "He couldn't even hold a word still in his mouth when he said it, for it rattled or hopped away—this was why he was in Stuttering Class, but it did him no good, he still broke a word when he said it, as if it were a twig, he still said ruined words" (CS 67). George is a figure of ruin but with an air of deliberate anarchy about him: "But at the end of a straight marching line he twisted and wavered like the raveling out of a line and ruined it, even then; he was the capricious conclusion and mocking collapse of something all ordered and precise right up to the end" (CS 67–68).

But what is disorder to Quella is a kind of salvation for the narrator, who presents George as the symbol of a different attitude toward life, his brokenness the sign of his modernity: "But if you live among breakage, he may have reasoned, you finally see the wisdom in pieces; and no one can keep you from the pasting and joining together of bits to make the mind's own whole. What can break anything set back whole upon a shelf in the mind, like a mended dish? His mind, then, was full of mended words, broken by his own speech but repaired by his silences and put back into his mind" (*CS* 67). As a retrospective reading of his own artistic development, this statement—and it is just that, a personal statement that rises up out of the fictional world that prompts it—may provide the clearest emotional map of Goyen's school years in Houston. The vision is both philosophical and aesthetic; to decide, in other words, that you live "among breakage" is to enter into a dialogue between fracture and wholeness. To see this struggle taking place in the province of speaking is to believe that language, both because of and despite its silences, can be the agent of rescue, of salvation. George Kurunus may be broken, but he is also a figure of strange vitality, the energy to remake the world—his and the school's—through a kind of mending that refuses to hide its fissures.

He is also a figure of anger and resentment, of a fantasized revenge on the social order. He appears during the rehearsal, his face "like a grasshopper's" in the glass window of the auditorium door. And later, when the fire alarm rings and the school empties, Quella seems to see him everywhere. Asked by a teacher to run back into the building to shut the windows, Quella finds what she imagines are the traces of George in the Homemaking class: "But some hand or finger had been in it all, in all the cups and pans, who had been meddling in Homemaking?" (*CS* 72). Strange writing has appeared on the chalkboards, a "curious disheveled chaos of giant and dwarf runaway shapes, tumbled and humped and crazy" (*CS* 73), and when she looks into the auditorium again, George is sitting "on the King's Throne like a crazy king in a burning building. On his head was the silver crown and in his ruined hand the silver wand" (*CS* 73). In the end, it isn't clear whether Quella has seen these things or only imagined them, but when the fire drill is over, she seems touched by some unnamed knowledge, both a gift and a threat.

It is curious that the two stories most directly related to Goyen's school years involve the May Day celebration. The first is based on a traumatic memory and is an attempt to exorcize it. The second proposes a more symbolic set of relationships filtered through a thin gothicism. (Quella's vision of George on the May King's throne with the flames around him evokes the grisly conclusion of Poe's "Hop Frog.") In both, the sensitivity to social shame concentrates on the ceremony and drama of the ritual pageant; there is a sense that Goyen's youthful traumas are overtly staged, that his feelings demand an extravagant exposure even as they shrink from it. These traumas of early adolescence seem to be making way for—and perhaps retrospectively justifying—a more overt rebellion to come.

The Cardboard Piano

Daily paths, ritual journeys are common in Goyen's fiction and recorded memories. "While You Were Away" provides a sadder, more qualified tracing of paths than the child's walk through Charity that begins *The House of Breath*:

> Our destination was my high school, Central High, soon to be changed to Sam Houston Senior High. Our trip to school led us over a low-lying road along the bayou that was often flooded, once so disastrously that the markets and warehouses along its side were water-wrecked ruins for some years after. We passed the S.P. Hospital, passed a structure whose sign read "Bemus Bag," rode by the shantytown built of fruit-crates and towsacks in the bayou bottoms shaggy with weeds and lush with trumpet vines, honeysuckle, blooming morning glory. "Lots of Cottonmouths in there," you told me. "Coming home some nights I've seen 'em crossing the road." We crossed a bridge over the muddy bayou and arrived at your Building on the corner of Main Street and Franklin Avenue. . . . We crossed Main Street and saw the old City Hall and when you got to Louisiana you turned on that and went on, in the stinging tropical heat of early morning through a city sprouting up out of its own castaway like a new plant, past boarded-up facades, empty buildings under renovation. (*GAE* 46)

On one occasion mentioned here, father and son drove silently past Goyen's skid-row grandfather, "the silent and defiant little man with the crooked foot and the Roman head and a pint in his back pocket, selling *The Houston Post* on that very corner, sitting on a nail keg . . ." (*GAE* 46).

In this brief memoir, Goyen emphasizes the early stages of Houston's astonishing growth—and his deeper incompatibility with its transformation. His father is given the voice of urban optimism, while the son dreams "of escape, release, brightness, dazzle—some un-known, unnameable beautiful thing" (*GAE* 46). The contrast is clarified by Goyen's description of the streetcar that he rode home from high school each day:

> The afterschool ride home on the Watson streetcar in the early Nine-teen Thirties has been a part of my sleeping dreams for many years. We rocked along on narrow streets so close to the little houses on either side that we could see in the poor kitchens and shabby bedrooms. Two brothers drove the Watson streetcar and they were the riders' and the neighbors' friends. The little car made its way to noisy Washington Avenue then to wide Houston Avenue until somewhere near Luna Park it turned into a neighborhood of poor houses with tin roofs and clothes-line washings and barking dogs running along with us, roosters crow-ing. (*GAE* 47)

But the simplicity and smallness of the streetcar suggests a time quickly fading, giving way to "street jams of trucks and cars, of beginning traf-fic lights in places, and accidents." And as is frequently the case with Goyen, the perception of loss created a desire to escape and at the same time to save what he was leaving behind. The city was growing and his father was urging him to take advantage of new opportunities, so he sought refuge in "a wilderness of thick woods and cliffs" near his neighborhood: "It took me no more than thirty minutes' bicycle ride to get to this wild place. There I took my notebook and wrote fantasti-cal passages."

Despite the measured but determined warmth with which he evokes his father in "While You Were Away," Goyen consistently presented his adolescent turn to art as a defiance of his father's demands and wishes. By the end of his high school years, this meant not only secretly writ-ing in the "wild place" at the end of Eleventh Street, but, with the help of his mother, taking music lessons at the Houston Conservatory of Music. It was an important period for the often sullen teenager, full of small but decided rebellions, and Goyen told and retold these forma-tive moments in interviews throughout his life. In the *Paris Review*, he explained to Robert Phillips the secrecy required to evade his father's control:

My foremost ambition, as a very young person, was to be a composer; but my father was strongly opposed to my studying music—that was for girls. He was from a sawmill family who made strict a division between a male's work and a female's. (The result was quite a confusion of sex-roles in later life: incapable men and over-sexed women among his own brothers and sisters.)[2] He was so violently against my studying music that he would not allow me even to play the piano in our house. Only my sister was allowed to put a finger to the keyboard. . . . The piano had been bought for her. My sister quickly tired of her instrument, and when my father was away from the house I merrily played away, improving upon my sister's Etudes—which I had learned by ear—and indulging in grand Mozartian fantasies. In the novel *The House of Breath*, Boy Ganchion secretly plays a "cardboard piano," a paper keyboard pasted on a piece of cardboard in a hidden corner. I actually did this as a boy. My mother secretly cut it out of the local newspaper and sent off a coupon for beginner's music lessons. I straightaway devised Liszt-like concerti and romantic overtures. And so silent arts were mine: I began writing. No one could hear that, or know that I was doing it, even as with the cardboard piano. (*GAE* 74)

As in "The Thief Coyote," the father opposes the son based on an idea of what men should do or be. As in *The House of Breath*, the mother abets the son's ambitions, joining him in a secret bond against the father. The image of the cardboard piano gathers all these tensions and more: here is the desire for expression silenced but surreptitiously fed; the need for performance, for display, driven inward. In many respects, the paper keyboard becomes the emblem for Goyen's reading of his own adolescence and artistic development. It helps explain why he later spoke of himself as a singer: "I've cared most about the buried song in somebody, and sought it passionately; or the music in what happened" (*CS* x). The silent piano is the sign of the *buried* song, expression that emerges through and out of a perceived repression. No wonder then that Goyen became a writer of arias, at first literally—one of his teenage musical compositions was an opera entitled *The House of Malvenu*—and later indirectly, inspired by William Saroyan and Thomas Wolfe.

And yet, for as much as Goyen portrayed himself as a revealer of secrets, he was also adept at repressions of his own, and the cardboard piano serves equally as the figure for what remains buried in him and his work. Implicit in his father's prohibitions is the fear that the son might be homosexual. Secreted in the image of the piano—and the various recountings, fictional and autobiographical, of this period of early self-assertion—is the same thought, indirectly revealed but never directly confronted. The buried song, then, is in part the secret of his identity, and this powerful combination of revelation and secrecy—of performing that identity and hiding it at the same time—consistently feeds Goyen's writing for most of his life. We can see it in his obvious attraction to imagining and writing about houses or enclosed spaces, in his need for containment, and in his idiosyncratic fictional method, which he once described as "a thawing process . . . as though the whole were a block (or circle or triangle) of something frozen—and I had to put *back* together the thawed parts of it" (HRC 7.8). A glance at his manuscripts makes clear just how much remained unthawed as he pursued the unspoken story within and beneath these images.

Goyen did have moments of open defiance, however. An astonishing example of the angry, exultant possibility of resistance appears in his most direct piece of autobiographical prose, the fragments that make up the unpublished *Six Women*. In one section, addressed to the stage director Margo Jones, Goyen provides a highly stylized account of his teenage infatuation with the local vaudeville theater:

> I told you about the dancing shoes hidden in my closet on Merrill Street in Houston when I was fifteen, about the magical makeup box of grease paint that smelled in the Texas humid nights, hidden there, too. And of the afternoons I rode around the city of Houston with the top down, in the convertible, between shows, in our makeup, with the Vaudevillians from the *Metropolitan* Theatre, Johnny Tap, the fastest tap-dancer in the world and beautiful Carmelita the Spanish dancer, Queen of Castanets, the dancers and the singers, people of enchantment, four-a-day people. We rode past Central High School that I was absent from most days that year to hide backstage in the shadows of the wings in my colored makeup, that I had on even now, in the daylight, in the convertible, and looked out at the drab building of Central High School that I had fled, past my father's office building, drab sober building where he was earning his poor pay that couldn't move us from our little house on Merrill Street, where my tap shoes were hidden and my grease paint and my secret cardboard piano that no one could hear when I played

it—hello Dad, look at me, I'm something glorious, all golden and rosy and purple-eyed and brilliantine slicking back my hair; hello Dad this is how I am, something marvelous, to hell with your Texas yellow pine and cheap clothes and your poor low-down family from the Mississippi sawmills, they won't break my heart anymore, why have I cried for them in the night, a boy crying for a whole family, for the doomed generations, wondering how on earth he can even save them from sickness and poverty (he ought to be thrashing with a young hard-on and jacking off to the promise of life); yet "Oh my people!" I heard that voice in me utter, "Oh my people, I will make it all right, you'll see! Lean on me, I will make it all right and give you beauty for ashes, joy for the oil of mourning." In my makeup, riding along Main Street of Houston in the open convertible in the company of wonder people, I ached with guilt for my secret and whispered I'm forsaking you, my father, I'm abandoning you, my family, I'm departing you, my little drab house that smells of collard greens and oil cloth, I've got my suitcase packed, *I'm leavin*. (*GAE* 27–28)

This moment of hurt self-assertion was just one of a series of usually hidden attempts to find a form of expression that would relieve the restraints imposed by his father. From his high school years through a part of his undergraduate career at Rice, Goyen repeatedly sought creative outlet in formal music, singing, and dance training—most of which he concealed from his family. The music lessons took place during his second year at college on Saturday mornings at "a funny, old dank house" on Caroline Avenue, otherwise known as the Houston Conservatory of Music. For a few dollars a week, money he got on the sly from his mother, Goyen studied composition and harmony and began piano lessons. Since he wasn't allowed to use the piano at home, he made do with the paper keyboard or snuck away to the piano in the basement of Woodland Heights Methodist Church. A year or so before, at the Lamar Hotel Ballroom, he had secretly begun voice training with Mrs. John Wesley Graham, an event described in "While You Were Away": "I had to walk all the way across a shining slippery waxed ballroom floor to arrive at her, positioned at her Grand, flounced out in an organza evening gown with a large Gladiola corsage bristling under her chin" (*GAE* 48). The "hoarse but tender voice of Mrs. Graham" told him that he had "a singing talent" but that a bad operation on his tonsils had left a small obstruction "like the tip of an asparagus" in his throat. In a similar fashion, he had pursued dance lessons, possibly at the same time as the flirtation with the vaudevillians described in "Margo," and studied tap in a class that included the young Ann Miller.

Typically, these secretive attempts at self-display brought a corresponding discovery by the father who fiercely disapproved. In "While You Were Away," Goyen explains the pattern:

> If you'd known this, or could have seen me there by the palm trees in the Lamar Ballroom, singing in Houston, age fifteen, what on earth would you have done? Nothing, I guess; but I'd have surely quit Mrs. John Wesley Graham's singing lessons and let the left-over tonsil have its way if you'd asked me to. Just as I did in the case of my secret music lessons . . . when you discovered my music book of Chopin Preludes (I had had about six lessons on the "Dewdrop," still can play about six lessons of it). It hurt you so, it was just—I said so, much later—the kind of thing you could not comprehend. . . . You sat away from me for a long time, we were strangers for some days and nights; I was already entering a world you could not comprehend; you had no words for anyone. "Why's your daddy grieving?" my mother came to me to ask. I simply could not say. The morning I asked you to drive me to the Houston Conservatory of Music to turn my music in to Miss Tree, my piano teacher, and to tell Dr. Hoffman, the Director, that I would have to quit my composition class and he said, "It's too bad, Billy, because you have a lot of talent," that changed you. After that you were all right. (*GAE* 48)

The relation of these moments has a definite shape, set by this anecdote that appears in most of Goyen's accounts of his personal development: the secrecy of the lessons, the enthusiasm of the teachers, an emphasis on a hidden talent, followed by his father's discovery and the repression of that talent, the reimposition of silence. In this case, his father refused to speak to him until he gave up the music lessons; in the case of the singing and dancing, the reaction remains unspecified but is fairly predictable. The dancing classes, for instance, culminated in the typical year-end recital. To avoid discovery, Goyen had his name listed on the program as "Billy Martin," but a member of his church saw him and told his family.[3] The singing instruction prompted yet another moment of exposure, one more comic than the others, perhaps, but no less significant. As Goyen explained to an interviewer, "One of [the vocal exercises] was to break a match stick and put it between your teeth and go aaaaaahh, like that. Well, guess who found me doing that? My father. 'What the hell are you doing?' he asked me. And I couldn't get the match stick out to *tell* him."[4]

In what appears to have been the most dramatic revelation of all, detailed in "Margo," there is a very public and embarrassing scene at the end of Goyen's infatuation with the traveling theater troupe, one that may have been responsible for heightening his father's vigilance when it came to his son's ambitions:

> The Vaudevillians were drinking out of a bottle now, not much, a swig here and there, but I smelled the terrifying fumes of whiskey that had crazed my grandfather and killed my uncle Ben and one time my own father kicked out a window on a half-pint, we saw him praying on his knees by his bed, kneeling in the broken glass, and I was afraid. . . . It was on one of those afternoons, Margo, that I kept the bottle and did not let it pass me by, and turned it to my mouth. . . . Out of me flared up a wild and thrilling being, a grand and wild and ready being of flesh and heat; and I didn't care, I let go, I was ready to go. . . . When they saw that I had brought my suitcase and was ready to run away with them, with the Show, they brought me home, passed out; and when I came to in my glaring makeup, with all the neighbors and my parents gathered around me, I called "Johnny Tap! Carmelita!" and saw on the floor my forlorn suitcase. (*GAE* 29)

"Margo" sometimes has the air of fiction—or of a kind of emotionally distorted remembering—that makes its details slightly suspect. Even so, the strongest traits of Goyen's autobiographical myth-making are here: the need for exposure, the understood tension between home and away, between the church where he vowed to be a missionary to China and the glittering, unfettered world of the theater. ("I wanted even to be a minister, a preacher," Goyen told Patrick Bennett in 1979. "I planned to do that when I was about fifteen; I was so tormented by everything, sex and art and music. I thought the only thing to do was to renounce it all, before I had even begun it.")[5] In fact, church and theater, opposites yet fundamentally allied, tend to structure his imaginary world from this point on, giving force to what will become the persistent and fertile divisions of his work. The haunting and haunted evangelists that emerge in stories set in Trinity have their roots in the revivalists who set up their tents in the field across from the family house. The vaudevillians are their obverse, offering self-display and sexual freedom rather than theology as the path to salvation. In a retrospective note-book entry, Goyen recognized the division and the deep ties between the two: "I knew the neurotic Texas, guilt-laden Texas, black, Mexican Texas, Southern Texas. My dreams were vaudeville fantasy; (I wrote out of that) theatrical, melancholy, were sentimental, romantic in the way Noel Coward was . . . . But there was also the Christian missionary in me, even the gospel Evangelist—for the poor, the afflicted so that my life in Texas (1915–1940) was one beset (if not tormented) by the schism . . ." (HRC 7.8).

CHAPTER THREE

Rice Institute

1932–1941

That was when I was about eighteen and very lost, very starry, very imprisoned in my father's house, on my neighborhood street, imprisoned in my city, imprisoned in my state of Texas, imprisoned in myself.

"DEAR GEORGE: THE SALT? THE WRATH? THE SALVATION?"

In 1932 at the age of seventeen, Goyen entered Rice University, then Rice Institute, "a quiet awesome place of only three buildings standing in a meadow on the edge of town" (*GAE* 49). The university itself was relatively young, opened in 1912 with just 77 students and 12 faculty. It originally charged no tuition, having been founded with the fortune of William Marsh Rice, a former Houston merchant who became rich trading cotton and investing in railroads. Though now a thickly wooded campus with an array of Neo-Byzantine buildings set around a majestic quadrangle, in 1932 the campus was indeed a "meadow," often a muddy one, with only a few scraggly saplings to line the drive leading to the sally port of Lovett Hall. The new university was near what was then the end of Main Street. As Goyen himself later described it, "there was Bellaire Boulevard, and beyond was prairie and mud roads," and across the street was Hermann Park, a 278-acre tract of woods donated to the city by George Hermann in 1914.

Frustrated in his attempts to find some form of artistic expression, Goyen showed no enthusiasm for Rice. A picture taken at the time shows a thin-faced, handsome young man, with the somewhat prominent ears of many Scotch-Irish Texans, a long, straight nose slightly flaring at the nostrils, and dark, wavy hair. He is dressed for the portrait in what looks like a new sports coat with a wide collar, but despite the sharp clothes and just-right grooming, the dour face can't hide its recalcitrance. Goyen associated Rice with Houston, which he wished to leave, and with his father's idea of what he should do or become. Consequently, he skipped quite a few classes as a freshman, hanging around the park until it was time to make his way back to Woodland Heights and Merrill Street. In "While You Were Away," he adds truancy to his many confessions: "You never knew that most every day after I saw your automobile drive away, I turned away from that cold campus and went back on the gravel path, in flight. In the empty park I sat under trees or wandered through the empty spaces. It was usually raining, soft Gulf rain, warm and melancholy. From the little zoo a couple of lions uttered a forlorn roar" (*GAE* 50). If Rice was what his father wanted for him, he would attend only under protest, as he later explained to Rolande Ballorain: "It was an extremely rich school and a whole lot of snobs around, and again there I was, very withdrawn and very afraid, and all, and secret, and it was just a terrible place."[1] A summer job at Humble Oil only added to the sense that he was following the wrong path:

> Why is it that I go through such agony here? I like to think that it is because working in such a place cramps my creative powers—and I think I am right. I feel that I shall never be satisfied working in an office; my experience this summer has shown me this. I seem to feel sick and crammed full inside; but once I get out of this place, I feel better. I don't hate this particular place; the people are nice to me, and I have nice work, but still I feel that it isn't the place for me. I dream of the things I've always wanted to do while I work—every minute, and that isn't right. Even though I know that I have only a week more to work, I feel, every day, that I can't even stand it that much longer. At my desk, while I work, I am constantly writing or calling up ideas. That is all I want to do. I feel that I am out of place, and that if I had to work in a place like this, or any office, I should rather die first. The psychiatrist told me that I shall travel a great deal—and that's what I want to do; she told me that I would have very good success with music and writing—and that's what I want to do. Maybe it's because I want to believe these that I do believe them, but she gave me encouragement and a little more confidence. (*GAE* 143)[2]

In a basic sense, there is little unusual here; artists of all sorts have chafed at office work and found it creatively disabling. But Goyen displays a few stylistic ticks that suggest more at work than just youthful boredom: the repetition of "I feel," for instance, confirms the tendency to follow emotions that he couldn't always understand or control. And because these feelings are opposed to the wishes of his family, the whole entry has a highly constrained stiffness, as though this is a young man trying to convince himself and, eventually, those around him that the life they imagine for him is fundamentally opposed to his personality. From his family's point of view, the job at the oil company was a great opportunity, a chance to cash in on Houston's wild growth. But for Goyen the oil industry became, along with the automobile, the symbol of everything new and forbidding about the city, the sign of a voracious culture of money and chemical waste. And at least in the beginning, Rice Institute was at the heart of all this—his family's plans for him, the city's new devotion to engineering and petrochemicals. He probably got the summer job because he was a student at Rice, and to work at Humble Oil or to imagine himself in any such position was to surrender to his father's control, to give up music and writing and become a part of the city he hated.

On one of the lonely truant days during his first year at Rice, Goyen was hitchhiking on Main Street, trying to get back downtown, when a big Cadillac pulled over and a tiny woman stepped out from the driver's side and told him to get in. She was a local oral surgeon, Mary Jane Rauch-Barraco, who served as a sort of sponsor for young artists and those interested in the arts in Houston. "And we just drove around," Goyen explained in an interview, "and she said, 'I'm going to tell you something. You keep yourself in there.' She said, 'You see these people walking around here? They don't know what you're going to know if you stay in there. You see these people digging around? They don't know what you're going to know.'"[3] The two soon became friends, and as Goyen began to discover other confidants during this period, it was Rauch-Barraco, called "Doc" by her circle, who helped organize musical evenings for her young protégés: "For the first time, I heard classical music," Goyen recalled for a *Houston Post* reporter. "Beautiful recordings that seven or eight people would just lie on the floor and listen to. I wasn't a group guy, but I knew this was my one escape."[4]

Perhaps because of Rauch-Barraco's pep talks, Goyen's attitude toward Rice slowly began to change. "I don't know how I got through that freshman year, but by the second year I was just hooked. . . . Just a survey course in English literature was a whole new world to me. I just *devoured* it."[5] This was probably George Williams's "Modern British Poetry," an introduction to twentieth-century poets (Ezra Pound, T. S. Eliot, W. H. Auden) that, according to Patrice Repusseau, "marked Goyen profoundly."[6] Williams emphasized the musical aspects of poetry—sound, rhythm, and voice—more than content, an approach that helped Goyen see writing as an alternative or complement to his thwarted musical ambitions. Now instead of morosely wandering the park, he haunted the book stacks at the library. His need for escape and self-expression responded dramatically to the creative urgency of the poetry he was reading: "Studying late at night in the room on Merrill Street, I heard the sound of the freight trains haunting the quiet neighborhood. It urged me, as the distant roar of the lions had stirred me. And as I learned and grew and matured, I saw my peers training for commerce in a growing city of opportunity; I felt estranged; I had found, in the library and classrooms of my university, poetry, words of feeling, what seemed like salvation for me" (*GAE* 50).

He began to study French and Spanish and took an interest in the theater. A job as an usher at the City Auditorium allowed him to see "from aisles, from the back of the house, from high balcony seats" the "San Carlo Opera Company, *La Bohème, Madame Butterfly, Tosca,* and the Ballet Russe de Monte Carlo! *Les Sylphides, Giselle, Gaîté Parisienne*" (*GAE* 50). If Rice had been his father's idea and Goyen's acceptance of it a kind of surrender to his father's wishes, his interests were another form of rebellion, a way to dream himself out of Houston. The theater fed his fantasies, gave them a shape, serving as a substitute for the tent shows and revival meetings of his childhood: "When the performance of Danilova and Eglevsky was over and they had departed, I wandered through rainy Houston in a trance, feeling forsaken, as if lovers had left me. Their world would be my world. What was Houston? What was Rice, Merrill Street? A city of automobiles and oil, a neighborhood of sadness and drabness. (But both had given me my feeling—and both were giving me, day by day, now, my freedom)" (*GAE* 50).

With these more intense artistic experiences came people to talk to, sympathetic friends like Rauch-Barraco and the widely read and opinionated Bill Hart. Goyen met Hart in 1935 at the Houston Public Library where they both worked during the school year. Hart introduced his new friend to more modern poetry and provided a sounding board for Goyen's ambitions and anxieties. According to Goyen's later recollections, "[Hart] was one of those prodigies, *enfants terribles*, that materialize in small towns, young men bearing a sense of art and poetry and life as naturally as others bore the instinct to compete and to copulate. He had a great deal to do with my early enlightenment and spiritual salvation in a lower-middle-class environment in an isolated (then) Texas town, where a boy's father considered him a sissy if he played the piano, as I've said, and questioned the sexual orientation of any youth who read poetry" (*GAE* 93). Hart was from a poor family. An autodidact with no more than a high school education, he impressed Goyen with his wide reading and energetic desire to learn. He sometimes went along to Goyen's literature classes at Rice: "He knew more than the professors did sometimes—he really did . . . about Elizabethan drama, and medieval romances. He knew these things" (*GAE* 94). Goyen and Hart remained close friends for years, corresponding regularly and, at times, intensely between 1937 and 1973.

Though the friendship had overtones of a romantic relationship, particularly on Hart's side, it was predominately verbal, literary, and intellectual, fed by voracious talk and writing. Goyen's response to his new confidant was so intense and manic that he wrote letters to Hart even while they both lived in Houston and worked together at the library. "He suffered, and he wrote about these torments," Hart later explained to Patrice Repusseau. "He sent me letters in the mail and brought them in person to the library. On the telephone his voice was often catastrophic and desperate."[7] Sometimes these letters contained what appear to be carefully disguised references to Goyen's romantic relationships with other young men; more often, they address less specific emotional crises. A sample from 1937, dated "Tuesday evening/Ten minutes to eleven" catches the tone:

> It's almost unfair that some of us were made different from the general run of people. It hurts deeply; it's a wound that's always fresh and certainly not self-inflicted. But wounds can be healed. Have you ever seen a dumb cat or dog humbly lick his horrid wounds for hours after someone has inflicted that wound with brutish hatred or ignorance?

Those wounds have healed. Yes, there are scars always left, but, oh, I had rather be one of those kind, not so dumb as even cats or dogs, who strive assiduously to heal their wounds, silently and alone in some dark secret place, than to be as some who never allow their wounds to heal. Those kind keep their wounds open and raw. They expose them to the dull wind and to passersby, shouting to them, "Here, I have a wound; it stings, it bleeds!"

And what's so crazy about the whole business is the fact that we are not compelled to do a thing. It's up to us to do as we like, or choose. That's where intelligence comes in. Perhaps that's where religion plays a part, also.

All of which says that I, too, am fighting Indians every day, just as you, Bill. But it's not going to be a blind fight if I have anything to do with it, and most certainly I do have very much to do with it. We've got to know where we are going, know what we would have ourselves be, and then go after it with all the power and madness that's in us. And think how much greater a victory it will be when we have achieved something, even with our petty handicaps and frailties! It's something glorious that can be fashioned out of something crawling and hideous. I'm going to see what my hands can make out of it.[8]

There are two important, enduring elements in this early letter: the talk of wounds and the idea that the wound can become the source—that is, provide the energy for—creation, a process which in turn can heal the artist. Goyen had already formed an image of himself not only as a kind of martyr, the hurt saint at odds with a broken world, but also as a writer obsessed with self-healing, with the conception of his own wounds as central and meaningful, as both real and capable of symbolic transformation. And this is why Hart's friendship—and the sponsorship of Rauch-Barraco—were so necessary to his survival and development. Here was a young man whose stark need for expression had been continually suppressed by his family and who, as a consequence, developed a sense of himself as someone rejected, unheard, as silent as the cardboard piano in his closet. It was essential that he find sympathetic listeners—and almost predetermined that his closest friends would be those who could play this role, to whom he could confess and rail and lecture with all the pent-up energy of the newly liberated.

"The Seadowns' Bible"

Though he'd been writing since his teenage years, pouring "fantas-tical passages" into his notebooks, it was at Rice that Goyen converted his teenage desire to perform into a more serious devotion to literary work. As he did for many student writers, George Williams provided the first real validation of Goyen's efforts to get his strong but undisciplined feelings onto paper. The quiet, skinny undergraduate approached the popular professor in his sophomore year but wasn't allowed to enroll in his creative writing class because it was already overcrowded. Instead, he was invited to participate in the meetings of the Writing Club, a less formal gathering where students shared their work. Williams remem-bered a reserved, studious young man showing up one evening at Autry House, the student center just across Main Street, to read a short piece later published in the undergraduate magazine: "I was much impressed (bowled over, actually) by the extraordinary promise the little piece showed. Until then I had no idea Billy could do anything like that."[9] Goyen later explained how vital this first chance to share his work had been for him. "I lived for those meetings where I sat in a dark place and when asked to offer what I had written, found, terrified though I was, the very first open release, the window I searched for. In the living room of somebody's house, somewhere in Houston, among fellow students who've long ago gone their way and left me few names to remember, I gasped out my dreams and songs from Woodland Heights" (*GAE* 172). Williams was a sensitive teacher who understood that the sometimes dour teenager from the Heights had buried his anger and resentment and "needed roiling." His advice, the first of many such responses to the vulnerability of Goyen's writing, was to turn sadness into anger: "The world's going to have to shake a little salt on your wounds, Billy. You need anger, venom, some meanness. Your writing is too gentle and melancholy" (*GAE* 170).

"Merrill Street reveries" was how Goyen himself described the frag-ments of short fiction he produced during his student years. Overall they tended to be short, intensely felt but mournful, often the fictional equivalent of his mother's homesick longing for the lost life of Trinity. In "The Children," for instance, a short story published in a student journal, the father of a family has died, forcing a move to the city where the mother has to take in laundry to make a living. One of the children is hit by a car, echoing Goyen's traumatic memory of the accident in his Houston neighborhood; another dies from an illness. The narrator, one of the surviving children, is a mouthpiece for Goyen's anger at the cold, dangerous city and longing for the small town he has left behind. In the end, the narrator tries to walk away, out of the city and back to the quiet country, but can't find his way home.

In the more developed "The Seadowns' Bible," written during Goyen's sophomore year, the central character and storyteller, Joe Edward Marks, does return to the small town of his youth, this time to visit "an old man and a woman," family friends who had read the Bible to him when he was very young. Significantly, he reenters this home-like place as a stranger: "It was my old town. No one knew me now except in the way a town feels a stranger walking up and down in it and is uneasy with him in it, and curious (and wants to spew him out or take him closer to it and ask him questions)."[10] But soon the town's geography revives his memory, and the narrator takes the same path Goyen would later describe in *The House of Breath*:

> I walked toward the Seadowns' hill, past the Tanners old place with the cedar tree that still had a forked limb, like a chicken's wishbone, where once I slipped (and fell) and hung like Absalom until Mrs. Tanner came running to save me; past the sawmill, still, now, and like the ghost of a sawmill, and past the graveyard with the same enormous grasshoppers still vaulting over the graves in it, and down the sandy road where I used to walk barefooted, coming home with some fryers or summer squash from Mrs. Larjens.
>
> And then I saw the Seadowns' house. It was still there on the hill and it was the same, although the shutters had fallen and had not been moved from where they had fallen.[11]

The couple are still alive but very old. Mr. Seadown walks shakily with a cane, and his wife is immobile, "lying like a shriveled bean in her bed." Joe asks Mr. Seadown to read the Bible to him the way he used to, but the old man's voice is like "the noise an old door makes when the wind opens and closes it," and the passage he reads is from Ecclesiastes: "And the almond tree shall flourish, and the grasshopper shall be a burden, and desire shall fail: Because man goeth to his long home, And the mourners go about the streets." Joe's reaction is a kind of confession: he sees his life as empty; he lives with a woman he doesn't love; his job is meaningless. He goes back to the city, haunted by the experience, but soon forgets and falls back into his routine. Several years later he returns to the town to find the Seadowns dead, their house occupied by someone else. But he notices the Bible on a table and decides to buy it from the new owner. He takes it home and tries to read from it but can't: "[I]t would sound dry and forced like a lot of words from a catalogue or like the numbers from a calendar." The Bible no longer speaks without the Seadowns' voices to give it life, and Joe never opens it again.

In an interview conducted in 1975, Goyen offered his own reading of the story:

> [B]ut again it's a search and it's a young man who is bound and in a way kind of cursed, bound, and in darkness, and who is trying to find a vision that will save him—the vision will come. He remembers that he had it once and threw it away. It was the Bible itself which is the symbol of that vision of light and escape, I mean, well, of freedom, of liberation, of deliverance is the word. . . . and what he remembers is the house, these things are always—isn't it odd that the house could so often contain the means of deliverance? Or so the boy, so the person, thinks, so the person is forever trying to return to that place.[12]

As he notes in this interview, it's remarkable the extent to which "The Seadowns' Bible" anticipates not only *The House of Breath* but also what is certainly the central concern of his life and work: the wounded searcher's return to a healing source. In other words, already at the age of nineteen he had begun to assemble the memories and shape the feelings that would move him toward his first successful novel. A great deal of technical maturity would follow, but Goyen's sense of both the subject and purpose of his fiction was essentially determined at least from his time at Rice. He was a writer of sensibility from the beginning, compulsively returning to the same subject year after year, digging deeper, certainly, and improving the manner of his telling, but always looking inward at the mystery of his early exile.

Playwright and Audience

As brooding as he could be, Goyen was not necessarily as antisocial at Rice as he might seem in retrospect. As he became more comfortable with college life and more interested in academic subjects, his involvement with other students and organizations increased significantly. He was president of the Methodist Student Union in 1936–1937 and treasurer of the French club, Les Hiboux. Perhaps most significantly, he took part in a variety of student theater projects, both with Les Hiboux in short plays presented in the language and with other organizations that mounted productions at the residential colleges. The first of these was probably *Weakness for Nurses*, in which he had a role in 1935, followed by parts in *Twelfth Night*, in which he played Sir Andrew Aguecheek, and in Clifford Odets's *Waiting for Lefty*. He was also writing one-act plays like *The Antiquarian*, in which he also had a role, and which caught the eye of Margo Jones, the Texas-born theater producer. Goyen and Jones soon became close friends, and Goyen joined the Houston Community Players while she was director to continue working with her.[13]

But greater exposure to others and increased opportunities to feed his desire for self-display didn't erase Goyen's essential adolescent plaintiveness. According to one classmate, he often seemed oppressed by personal dramas that appeared trivial to others. Though tall and handsome, he was nervous and mannered, walking with his feet turned out like a ballerina's and constantly pushing his hair back from his face. (His young cousin Nan remembered this "adorable forelock which came tumbling down" his forehead.)[14] He needed approval so badly that he often mistrusted even a favorable response to his writing.[15] His letters to Hart during his senior year and his two years of graduate study maintain a tone of high drama and purpose; they are quarrelsome and relentlessly self-centered, full of grand ambition that might be absurd if it weren't for the intense energy and intelligence they display. Perhaps most significantly, they anticipate Goyen's fictional method by combining an almost excessive level of nervous tension with what often seems a central repression, as though all these words poured out so passionately in response to others could never find what truly needed to be said.

A remarkable example written during his graduate school years deserves to be quoted at length. It tracks Goyen's emotional state while on a family trip to the Texas Hill Country:

Dear Bill:

We have arrived to find it practically winter here, and quite stormy. Tonight I am sitting down here in a little room, beneath the house, writing by the hot light of a strange sort of lamp that boils and rumbles as if it were going to erupt momentarily—like a volcano. I have no peace yet; when will that eruption come?

The house is situated on the edge of an exquisite river that does not flow—it simply moans below me, as if boiling and seething in some wild agitation. The landscape is wild and nervous-like; behind me are huge, torpid hills which are crazy and jagged and surprise you with wild springs and streams pouring out from the sides. The sky is black and low and lightning flashes periodically. There is no peace here—yet.

Imagine placing me here against all this turbulence. When I stand at the edge of the falls it is as if they were moaning at me and I stand there moaning, screaming back in response. It is so far a mad, brutal fight.

Tonight this place is eerie. We have had an invasion of a strange species of insect—a sort of spider-like thing which is horrible to look at—with long, spiny legs (about six of them). They have come in quiet hordes and move in the weirdest gyrations—a sort of mechanical, wooden hop that frightens me awfully. They are literally hundreds, everywhere, and I am upset by them; I feel them creeping, hopping all over my body. . . .

I have been in the throes of this acute *agitation* (I know no better word) for almost three weeks now. I say acute because this turbulence is always with me, inside me; but sometimes I am relieved awhile by some manner of false (usually false) pacification. But this is a chronic malady and so, sometimes a conversation, a thought, some lines in a book, a face, some music, excites it to an acuteness that is maddening.

What is all this? Why do I suffer this? . . . I have a bad conscience. I feel guilty. As Mann wrote: "I am rather a dreamer and a doubter who is hard put to it *to save and justify his own life*." That is why I tell you that driving down Main Street upsets me; that working at Humble Co. tears me up, that coming into a room filled with people and listening to them talk does something to me, annihilates me, makes me dumb and pent up. I am trying to *save myself*; to *justify myself.* That is why I am sitting down here, away from my family, weeping inside because I cannot go up to them and laugh with them and live with them, as one of them. Once I justify myself to *myself,* I inevitably justify and save myself to and for other people. That is why I told you I have always wanted to get my family, my puzzled friends in a room and say to them, "Listen, I am the victim of something; I want to understand it; I want you to understand it. Help me."[16]

As with many of Goyen's letters from this period, it's difficult to discover a specific source for this nervous tension. He hints at personal relationships gone wrong, at slights or arguments, but the more general impression is of a young man perpetually on edge, easily upset and a trial to his less anxious friends and family. The natural world doesn't comfort him; his isolation seems to transform the scene into a variety of emotional threats. Is this nervousness real, affected, or some combination of the two, as though this were a young writer trying on styles of agitation that are nevertheless genuinely threatening? (His letters to Hart often have this double quality of genuine confession and theatrical display; at times, the two friends seem almost to compete with one another for emotional attention.) Whatever its deeper context, the writing emerges as though on top of a submerged and unexplained source of distress. Words pour out but never seem to find their way to a direct expression of their subject. He confesses, in other words, without revealing.

That Goyen felt his identity to be under pressure had been true for several years, perhaps since he was a boy, but much of the high tension in this eight-page outpouring may be due to the more acute question of what he was going to do with his life. He was working toward his master's degree in English and serving as a teaching assistant at Rice, but it wasn't clear whether he had the temperament to teach full time. At the time of his graduation the year before, he had complained to Hart of his uncertainty:

Well, exams are over and school is finished and I wish I could relax. But that is impossible for me, ever. Now it's the worry about what to do after next Monday when I have received my diploma and everything is over for good. Humble Company rises up in the immediate future like an indomitable spectre; I really don't know of any place else to go, I am so incapable of doing anything specific other than teach and I am not fully equipped even for that (I lack required "Education" courses to teach in Texas!) And you know that there is nothing else in this city except monstrous office buildings and corporations.[17]

He had once considered working in theater, but he confessed to disillusionment with it by the time he entered graduate school. That left university teaching: "I believe that teaching will allow me to progress in the desired path," he wrote in a journal in May of 1939. "It concurs with and admits of my current ideals and convictions. I must create, interpret, and record—enlighten and beautify" (*GAE* 147).

Goyen received his master's degree in 1939 after completing a thesis titled "Playwright and Audience in the Elizabethan Drama." Though the topic was conventional and tailored to satisfy requirements, the essay does contain some hints about his interests and subsequent development. First is the attraction to drama itself. In the later years of his undergraduate study, theater was Goyen's primary obsession, not simply a corollary to writing poetry and fiction but a way of conceiving his work that was central to his developing vision of himself. The earlier flirtation with vaudeville and its negative link to the church career his mother wanted for him suggest that contemporary theater offered a satisfying solution to the need to "save" and "justify" himself, as he wrote to Hart. The theological language implies that performance, particularly the speaking voice addressing a listening audience, could affect a kind of salvation, even if (or perhaps because) it wasn't the sort of justification his family had in mind.

In this respect, Goyen's thesis was important because it showed interest in audience and in the relationship between the author and those attending the plays. "It is the aim of this paper," he wrote, "to show how the Elizabethan drama in its evolution and development was the creature of the people who supported it, and was conditioned by their dramatic tastes. We shall attempt to define the tastes of the playgoer, and to show how these tastes were formed, resulting from certain foreign and native influences. We shall then investigate the attitude of the playgoer toward the theatre, the demands he exacted of the playwright, and his reaction to the plays he witnessed."[18] What was the audience thinking, in other words, and what "demands" did it make on the writer? The last line in particular comes closest to foreshadowing Goyen's unique interest in the specific drama of telling stories. Such an approach avoids positing an author as a purely self-expressive individual but instead considers the writer as part of an interpersonal, interdependent social encounter. The implication is that the playwright has a responsibility to the audience, or, conversely, that the audience has a claim, via its attention, on the production of the writer. And yet, within this mutually demanding relationship, the artist strives for freedom: "In order to fulfill its function and realize its destiny, art demands freedom; it will not allow bondage or restriction."[19] Thus as he traces the necessary interaction between Elizabethan playwright and audience, Goyen interjects his own romantic notions of personal and artistic freedom in opposition to a society that demands conformity.

With the MA in hand, the next logical step was the PhD, and in the late summer of 1939, Goyen took the train north from Houston via Dallas and St. Louis to Iowa City, Iowa. Despite his stated aversion to Houston, he was terribly homesick. On the way through Texas, the train passed Trinity and Palestine, and he had to resist the urge to get off at his old hometown and go back to Merrill Street.[20] But his stay in Iowa City was short. His financial situation was precarious; instead of a fellowship, he was offered a job in the library at thirty cents an hour. By September he dejectedly wrote to Hart of his decision to return to Houston: "I believe I have learned something about myself, about universities, and about my place. As I see it now, I shall not return to Humble, but enroll in Houston University and prepare myself for a high school at least for a while. My belief in writing kills all enthusiasm and interest in a university curriculum—and I cannot subscribe to such a career wholeheartedly. I will not compromise here. Not yet."[21]

In a letter written after the war, Goyen explained that he had "locked horns with the theories of Norman Foerster, was utterly discontent, [and] left within a month."[22] In the late thirties, the well-known New Humanist Foerster must have seemed considerably dated to the temperamental, homesick graduate student, while the newly formed University of Houston was comfortably familiar and welcoming by contrast. By early 1940, Goyen was classified as an "Assistant Instructor," teaching five courses a semester, including Modern Poetry, Creative Writing, Romantic Poetry, and Sophomore and Freshman English. It wasn't the ideal job; more than anything, he wanted to write, but he had yet to find the courage and chance to free himself completely. He understood the limitations of the scholar's life—and the institutional hostility to creative writing at the time—but hoped, at least half-heartedly, "that the universities and the teaching chairs offer the greatest and most fruitful opportunity for action."[23]

This slightly stilted phrase appeared in a letter written in response to Archibald MacLeish's pamphlet *The Irresponsibles*, published in 1940. Outraged by the war in Europe and concerned about American isolationism, MacLeish had attacked writers and scholars in the United States for their isolation, on the one hand, and their scientistic detachment on the other. Fresh from his own entanglements with graduate studies, Goyen generally agreed—enthusiastically enough to write a précis of his recent experience in the form of a letter to MacLeish. Admiring neither the scholars with their "cold dry lecture notes" nor the contemporary writers who "are rooted in nothing deeper than their own shallow ambience," he imagined a new man of letters such as MacLeish seemed to be calling for: "And we shall look for men of letters among those like some of ourselves who have sought escape from the universities in order to keep scholarship alive in order to feed scholarship with art and life and so flower into a reunion that will produce men of letters; among the courageous and stubborn aliens living in strange out-of-the-way places and engaging in incongruous means of livelihood." The letter may never have been sent, but its purpose was clear. Goyen might teach for a while, but his eye was on something else: a way out toward work and struggle, "touching life now, moving among men of our time."[24]

PART II ∾

Song of Leaving

CHAPTER FOUR

Ulysses

1942–1945

The boy who dreamt of the great world in an East Texas pasture, the boy who had played the cardboard piano and heard the unfinished symphony under a quilt, who secretly danced at the Hallie Pritchard School of the Dance and held his mouth open with a matchstick according to Mrs. John Wesley Graham's instructions so that the little bubble would one glorious day rise in his throat and burst full of song: these beings were now hidden in a lanky young man in disguise in the uniform of a U.S. Naval Ensign who marched straight-backed out of those dreaming, shy, solitary and secret-ridden beginnings in a back-town of Texas.

UNDATED MANUSCRIPT FRAGMENT

Goyen was not to be a war writer, but his experiences from 1942 to 1945, mostly aboard the escort carrier *Casablanca*, were crucial to his development. The frustration and delay of the war—its combination of fear and wasted time—ultimately did more than anything to convince him that he couldn't return to Houston; he had to find a place free enough from old influences to allow him to speak his mind. Separated at last from his parents and their controlling if comforting world, the increasingly angry Naval officer slowly developed a deeper moral and personal intensity. His survival of the war came to represent—and to validate—his survival of early trials, and this forced confrontation with his own terrors gave him the right, as he saw it, to stand clear of family demands.

Before these hard lessons could be learned, however, his service got off to an awkward and embarrassing start. A few years out of Rice, Goyen was teaching at the University of Houston when his draft notice came. In a parade of conscripts, he marched down Main Street and was put on the train to San Antonio for processing. What happened next is tangled in multiple retellings and a bit unclear. In an interview conducted in 1977, he explained that he was told to go home because he was a "professor": "And they said, 'Man, you better get out of here *fast* because you're going to be carrying a broomstick. This is a *broomstick* army,' they said. 'All these guys out here are going to be killed because we don't have rifles for them yet. We don't have guns. These are farm boys,' they said, "and you're not, and we'll let you go if you'll enlist in the Navy and get to be an officer.'"[1] In an earlier *Austin American-Statesman* story from 1973, Goyen is described as having undergone "a month of indoctrination" before returning to Houston, but in his own autobiographical notes, he sketches the scene somewhat differently:

> I left Houston in early 1940 for the war (but was conscripted in 1939, marching down Main St. to the Railroad station, which? Union sta?, bound for Induction Center in San Antonio. In San Antonio—"rejection."
>
> Back in Houston—mother in bed, prostrated by my leaving. Now suddenly returned, I ran to her, who thought she was dreaming, or dead from grief. My students, who had hailed my farewell, the present of books, now cheered my welcome home. But I had only a few months. Enlisted in the Navy. Yeoman 2nd Class. In old P.O. Bldg.—Recruiting Office. (HRC 20.7)

It isn't clear what caused this momentary reprieve, but it seems likely—based in part on his worries about his weight and other health issues—that Goyen failed his physical. Given his consistent boyhood anxieties about masculinity, the return to Houston would have been difficult to accept or explain without some sort of redeeming cover story. What is clear is that his recollection of the timing of his enlistment was generally incorrect. According to Naval records, he did join the Navy in February of 1942 and worked in the recruitment office in Houston for about six months before being sent to San Diego for processing and on to the first stage of officer training school in Indiana, at Notre Dame University.[2] The step down from college instructor to common seaman was apparently a mild source of embarrassment at the time, and it may be that in retrospect Goyen preferred to gloss over the awkward circumstances of his draft rejection.[3]

The relatively easy work at the recruitment office did little to pre-pare him for his eventual training. The officer school at Notre Dame required drills, strength training, and exercise as well as classes in sea-manship, gunnery, naval customs, and math. Goyen worried almost constantly about failure but quickly surprised himself with his ability to keep up. His almost daily letters to his parents are not exactly boast-ful of his progress, but he does seem determined to do his best, despite worries that he isn't big enough (though nearly six feet, he weighed just 139 pounds on arrival), strong enough, or good enough at math to suc-ceed. (It was because of a failed math course at Rice that he took more than the usual four years to graduate.) He passed his first strength test and physical, delighted that the doctor had failed to notice his hem-orrhoids. And his aptitude scores placed him eighth out of the com-pany of 100. But the math remained the sticking point. "It is getting pretty tough," he wrote to his father. "The math is really hard and I am not doing as well as I want to."[4] Ultimately, his departure for advanced school would be delayed several weeks so that he and others in his com-pany could have extra time to improve. Other than the short stay in Iowa, the months at Notre Dame were the first Goyen had spent away from Texas and his parents. The pressure was intense, particularly for an already highly strung young man responding to demands that ran counter to his sensibility.

But if math was simply a hard subject to be complained about to his parents, in his letters to Hart it became a symptom of something larger and more sinister. "They are trying hard to make fools of us, and the engineers, the mathematicians and the reasoners have their day and we are forced to walk on our heads with our feet in the air." Eager to succeed outwardly and still preserve a hidden artistic self, Goyen raged to Hart to the same degree that he sought to soothe and encourage his parents. "I want to know what you do and if you feel. I don't—except rarely, and then it is unbearable. I am such a vacuum these days, try-ing so hard to become assimilated and fighting so hard to stay on the outside (or way down deep inside)." It is a strategy of repression that was certainly not new to him but that the war and his life in the Navy would intensify. Its counterpoint was a dream of release, a moment of complete expression, unrestrained by family or war-time necessity: "Re-member, remember . . . the great dreams and the music—and the *word*, Bill, the *word*, which will not, finally, fail us. Let us hold on together from the West to the East and *dare* them to shatter our grasp. And when we ultimately speak—oh my God, my God!"[5]

The distance from Texas highlighted Goyen's role as caretaker, or at least principal worrier, when it came to his mother's physical and mental health. As subsequent interviews make clear, Emma Goyen's illnesses defined much of her son's childhood and his relationship to her and the family. The letters from Notre Dame bear this out: he regularly exhorts his mother to eat more (just as he assures her that he is eating well and gaining weight), to visit the doctor regularly, and, perhaps most indicative, he writes separately to lecture his father about the kind of care and attention she needs: "You must keep her feeling well and prevent her from thinking about herself too much. Don't you and Jim stay away from her too much at nights, for she gets lonesome and gets too tired of the monotony of the house. She has always had the hardest job of all of us, and her life has been full of pain."[6] Money is likewise a constant concern. Hardly a day goes by that Goyen doesn't encourage his parents to use his Navy pay to cover bills or buy a new coat for his mother. No doubt much of this is simply the natural reaction of a responsible eldest child in difficult times, but the strain of worrying about his family is also directly related to his vision of himself as a threatened, restricted artist. To Hart he casts himself as "Ulysses," the wandering, heroic figure prevented from achieving his goals by a hostile fate: "We have all gone under the hill and there will be no dancing on the hillside for a long time, my Telemachus, and we must bear it, oh we must bear it."[7] It is perhaps Tennysons's "idle king"—a loner almost ravenous for adventure and movement but prevented by circumstance from following his path—that best fits this somewhat self-important but entirely earnest allusion.

By late August Goyen had survived the initial training program and moved on to New York, but the change of scene did little to relieve the intense pressure to prove himself. In fact, the midshipman school at Columbia University significantly increased the strain on his nerves. Math-heavy navigation classes again caused the greatest academic concern, but it was the atmosphere of the place and the constant demands of duty that made him doubt his ability to complete the training. "Mom," he wrote in October, "I am so tired and in such a strain, don't be surprised if you hear I am coming home week after next. For I am on the verge of cracking up. It's almost too much for me—the strain and the rush, not the work. . . . You know I go crazy under stress and strain. I am not counting on failure, of course, but nevertheless, let's be prepared."[8] To Hart he complained more fully about "the little officer game" and his inability to play it: "But he [Ulysses] is still here, vascillating [sic] inconclusively, never being sure of whether to continue to compromise his 'spirit' or end it abruptly and asking himself so many times, night and day until he has almost gone wild, whether one should concern himself with 'spirit' in these times."[9]

One potential remedy was New York's cultural life. Between his arrival in August and his exams in late October, Goyen was fortunate enough to hear Toscanini conduct Berlioz's *Romeo and Juliet* and Shostakovich's Seventh Symphony; to see *Porgy and Bess* and *Blithe Spirit* and a play by Emlyn Williams, *The Morning Star*. He had been to the Museum of Modern Art and to see the Ballets Russes production of *Rouge et Noir*, but still he complained to Hart of a feeling of falseness about it all: "So N.Y. is keen, but I feel as I walk about through it that I have all my senses numbed, my ears muffled and my eyes partially blindfolded. I just didn't bring *myself* here, a weird ungainly somebody is parading N.Y. in a uniform and he is not, *really*, getting much from what he sees. How, in God's name, do you doctor the deadness inside you? And God when I do feel something, it's like a torrent; I get so wild that I really become embarrassed. It has made me more child-like emotionally." And once again this apprehensive sense of repression— verging on claustrophobia and fed by the uncertainty of his immediate future after training—gave way to an ever more intense vision of a future release, a bold, uncompromised revelation of all that was now being forced into silence: "*But one thing has come*: I am even more determined to write the hell out of all of this one day. Let them shoot off ears, fingers, arms, *testicles*, if I can only *remember* and *recall* and *see*, I'll have my victory. There will be an explosion, for too much has been too closely packed too far down inside."[10]

Despite these possibly overdramatized worries, Goyen received his officer's commission in November 1942 in a ceremony held in Riverside Church. He had hoped to be assigned close to home (at one time trying for a post in Corpus Christi, Texas), but his initial orders sent him to Panama and the Canal Zone. In a letter to Hart written before he left New York, he explained that he would be doing "some kind of Intelligence or attaché work there and thereabouts" with "Local Defense Forces."[11] As usual, he was upbeat to his parents and poetic and ominously pessimistic to Hart. In part, the tone of the family letters was due to a conscious strategy to spare his mother and father as many worries as possible. (In fact, Goyen and his mother seemed to have a mutually deceptive relationship, with each variously accusing the other of withholding unpleasant information.) To his parents he praised the cool nights of the tropical climate and told of outings to nearby beaches and cocktail parties at the Navy base. He explained that his primary duties consisted of teaching training classes and serving as Education Officer as well as the occasional job translating documents from Spanish. To Hart he wrote cryptically—during this time, Goyen served as a military censor and taught censorship classes—of "going out" to sea and its potential dangers, though he says little about what this duty entailed or what sort of ship he was assigned to.

These unspecified missions were among Goyen's first experiences on the open ocean, and in Panama he had begun to think about the relationship between the quiet and emptiness of the water and the processes of memory: "What does the sea do to you?" he asked Hart.

> It is so strange what it does to one. I am afraid of it, yet already I feel its urge. There is a great calmness on the sea which breaks me loose from so much; the sea detaches you from real things so easily. Out there all the world seems to lie far away and there is a life full of beauty and terror. . . . And then there is the giant loneliness the sea brings. It floods in upon you and you are absolutely drowned in it. Nothing, nowhere can you touch, nothing but remembering. And oh what a delicious, voluptuous luxury is remembering out there.[12]

The conjunction between forced isolation and the urge to memory had struck him most forcefully on the voyage down to Panama from Norfolk, Virginia. In addition to riding through his first storm, or perhaps because of the intensity of this experience, he had begun to write again, intuiting a method for gathering and arranging emergent material:

> The most miraculous thing has been happening in my mind since that day I left for the sea: words have flowed so torrentially that I have scarcely been able to find enough paper to catch them on. Something

has been tapped. . . . During these times [of cold isolation] my mind has performed such beautiful things: long, continuous "movies" of remembering; the fingers of my mind have been performing such delicate patchwork, piecing together the fragments of past days. And there is a pattern to it all, Billy, although now our world is such a shambles and so ruined.[13]

(Goyen was fond of repeating the story of the genesis of his first published novel, *The House of Breath*: "Suddenly—it was out on a desk in the cold—I saw the breath that came from me. And I thought that the simplest thing that I know is what I belong to and where I came from and I just called out to my family as I stood there that night, and it just . . . I saw this breath come from me and I thought—in that breath, in that call, is their existence, is their reality" (*GAE* 77). Given the description of his "movies of remembering" sent to Hart, it is more likely that this experience took place on this winter trip down to the Canal Zone than during his time aboard *The Casablanca*, where he typically placed it. There is no other reference in Goyen's wartime correspondence to a similar shipboard epiphany.)

The discovery of this relationship between memory and ocean is an important one and raises several compelling questions about Goyen's complex and contradictory attitude toward water. It remains unclear, for instance, why he chose the Navy in the first place.[14] In interviews conducted later in his life, he often referred to his lifelong fear of water ("I have been terrified of water all my life. I would have fits when I got close to it") (*GAE* 77). Given the ritual repetitions of the story of his mother's near drowning—not to mention his own emotional interdependence with Emma—such terrors were understandable. But why choose a path that was likely to lead him into greater contact with what he feared? There are practical considerations, of course, and in his desire to avoid danger he may have thought the Navy one of the safer options. But it seems just as likely that for all his apprehension he was also powerfully drawn to the sea, just as he was deeply attracted to the dangerous but fertile river of his childhood. In an interview in 1979, Goyen revealed that his first sexual experience occurred as a result of contact with water, a scene he later reconstructed in *The House of Breath*. And now he found himself on a ship for the first time, surrounded by nothing but ocean. It isn't surprising that this atmosphere would produce a new urge to write and a deeper grasp of his aesthetic and moral purpose. If he thought of himself as nurse or caretaker to his distant family, he could also become the savior of memory, his and theirs, countering the stress and stimulus of a threatening sea with acts of "delicate patchwork" and recovery.

USS *Casablanca*

"Ulysses is on the way again!" Goyen wrote to Hart in mid-February 1943. After only a few months in Panama, he was off to the Seattle area to begin training and organizational work before the launch of one of the Kaiser Shipyards's new "Baby Flattops." Rumors had reached him about the new line of ships designed to be cheap and expendable, though at the time of his redeployment he had no idea he would be assigned to the very first of these. According to a 1944 *Time Magazine* article, "Kaiser's Coffins," as the *Casablanca* class came to be called, "were bow-heavy; in even moderate seas they corkscrewed like cooch dancers; they sprang leaks along welds; pumps and auxiliaries broke down; hot water heater tubes burned out; stanchions and hooks cracked off; flight decks extended so far forward that heavy seas rolled up under them and in the case of at least one ship carried the forward end of the flight deck away."[15] But by the time he settled in to the Receiving Station at Bremerton, Washington, it was all still just scuttlebutt, a vague foreboding that his service was about to get more dangerous. Yet again he withheld this sort of information from his parents, telling Hart that he would "beautify the whole picture" for them.[16]

For the next several months, however, until the commissioning of his ship in July, there was more monotony than threat to Goyen's existence. His primary tasks involved organizing and training new sailors coming into the base, but he had time to go to the movies most evenings and to the officer's club a few blocks from his barracks. He helped the educational officer administer the tests for admission to Officer's Candidate School and on his day off joined outings to the countryside, including a day on Mount Rainier. As was customary by this point, he regularly worried about his mother's health and reported to her about his own; constipation and hemorrhoids were high on his list as well as some new sinus trouble he thought might be contributing to the headaches he had suffered since he was a boy. And he now had time to write, not just the several personal letters every few days but new fiction meant as a weapon against the "dullness" that threatened him.[17]

In March of 1943, Goyen told Hart that he had "been trying to write" and had produced "a few typewritten pages of a hard, concentrated core of something as a result."[18] The untitled story included with the letter concerns a young man, David, who lives with his family in a small house in a sweltering, stagnant city. Like many of Goyen's surrogates, David is moody and restless, "a youth who could not sit down, for misery had stung his soul and put a wandering in his blood and there was a bitter beauty caged like a bird in his mind."[19] His mother watches over him, but she is less a caring figure than a type of emotional vampire, who has "parched or burned out all the beauty and urge to nobility in those of this house except for the few little flowers and crystals of it which her prey had managed to secretly hide away, like beasts of winter, in some occult place." She is allied to the "huge wooden cross with the Savior hanging, nailed through his hands and feet, from it" that dominates the house. The father, presumably one of these victims, has been declawed like an "ancient cock without his spurs," and the two sisters, Martha and Anna, are violently at odds: one openly sexual, the other cold and disapproving.

David is an artist just coming into maturity, a stifled romantic who needs desperately to escape the confining house: "This house, then, could not hold him; it was no cage for one who knew what he knew. He belonged in some great place. He was urged to it, for he felt himself strange and primitive and he did not want yet to be discovered. . . . Who in this house could understand this?" He fantasizes about saving Anna—the repressed, lonely sister—but finds her dead in her room, and she quickly becomes his mirror image, taking on his secret burden: "Had she loved someone, silently, all these years? What had wasted her life away? . . . He realized, too late, that Anna would have been the only one he knew to whom he could have given his secret." Shortly thereafter, Martha brings "into the house a strong dark man" and announces her pregnancy. The man, whose face "had all the colors of [David's] paint pots in it," carries "a power or magnitude . . . which dwarfed the family to weaklings and made them pale and weak-voiced." As though in response to this new power, David then finds the determination "to bend [his] knowledge to some cause and some end: to paint it or write it or sing it or dance it out to the world."

In the strictest sense, the story seems related to Goyen's time in Houston between assignments. In an earlier letter to Hart, he had written vaguely about "those strange days at home": "I have learned to benumb myself so that many times it is as though I walked in a dream. This I especially have to do while at home, for it would have been too much had I allowed myself to feel."[20] But in the accompanying letter, he suggests other, deeper sources: "I think it has been Raymond trying to get written down. Or perhaps Sterling, I am not clear."[21] The reference is to two of Goyen's prewar male passions, both relationships having since ended, though he kept track of Sterling Price III throughout the war and sometimes corresponded with him or his mother. The comment, elliptical as it is, is characteristic; in other words, he realized that these emotional turbulences were at the root of his work, but he wasn't necessarily sure which wound was the source that was now groping toward dramatic clarity. It also makes clear the relationship between Goyen's hidden homosexuality, his own conception of his role within and against his family, and his self-determined mission to be an artist, the one who tells. It is the repression of the household and David's inability to tell his secret—particularly to the dominating, religious mother—that creates his prophet-like burden. In other words, for Goyen, writing about his sexuality did not involve revealing it. Instead he let a charged silence push against the surface of his stories in a way that produced dangerous but still buried tremors of feeling.

That he had long since acquired the habit—and taken on the psychology—of living a double life is obvious but important to keep always in view. From his earliest sense of himself as an exile to his adolescent traumas of rebellion and silence, Goyen had developed not merely the ability to think of himself as divided but also the determination to claim self-division as an artistic mark, a sort of destiny. As often as he pounded his fist about revelations to come and the need for a recovered wholeness, he worked diligently to avoid exposure and, in his writing, sought to keep the tension of secrecy alive, avoiding or incapable of analysis. Sexuality was both root and branch of this emotional isolation, and the letters to his family and to Hart during this stage of the war provide some of the most striking evidence of Goyen's ability to live two delicately joined but mutually repellant lives. To Hart he is all passion, decrying his loneliness or revealing a new, apparently overwhelming crush. "I have found my Christopher and my Icarus," he wrote in May. "He has come here, out of the sky, and I have never been so disturbed in all my restless life. . . ."[22] The Icarus in question was William E. Velte, a Pennsylvania carrier pilot of German background who was in Bremerton awaiting a court-martial for breaking Navy regulations by flying under a bridge. In an effusive letter to Hart, Goyen poured out a new version of his prewar romantic history with other men: "Oh S. P. III was a young beautiful fool, a cheap and a passing, bitter beauty; R. W. was a Walpurgis-Nacht and a Michelangelo's cherub, but here, here is a human being, full blown, who has his hand on the reins and sees . . . all, all of it, the misery and the beauty."[23] Velte was more mature and better educated than Goyen's Houston attachments, an aspiring writer who read Chaucer and wrote drafts of a play during his house arrest. He had studied in Germany and played the cello, and planned to get an MA in English at Columbia after the war. His letters suggest an almost overwrought aesthetic sensibility undiminished by his membership in the Grumman Hellcat Fighting Squadron 10, and it isn't surprising that Goyen would find him a welcome presence in the dull wartime atmosphere. However, the relationship had little time to develop. Velte, too, was soon at a distance, off again on combat missions on the USS *Enterprise*, leaving Goyen to idealize him in memory while continuing to chafe and yearn against his isolation and boredom.

To his parents he wrote only of a new friend who "likes books and music."[24] Of his straight love life, Goyen was vague when writing his mother or father, speculating at times on what it would be like to be married but always eager to assure Emma in particular that he wasn't serious about anyone yet. A good deal of this talk revolved around a young woman from Houston he had been seeing at least since he joined the Navy. Nell Schedler worked as a clerk at the University of Houston and was a friend of the family; for a time during the war, she shared an apartment with Goyen's sister Kathryn and her two young children. Though it isn't clear whether Nell was Bill's first steady girlfriend, by the time he left for Notre Dame they were clearly a couple. He corresponded with her regularly through 1944 and spoke on occasion to his mother and father of the possibility of marriage. In late 1944 these discussions increased in frequency and seriousness. In part, Goyen was responding to the example of the many married friends around him, Navy buddies and their wives who played a large part in the *Casablanca*'s social life. He knew there were advantages to being married while in the Navy (toward the end of the war, he complained bitterly about the extra points toward discharge granted to married officers), but even more, he seemed eager to show those around him that he was serious about this long-described girlfriend. His monotonous duties in Puget Sound had also made him more and more depressed and desperate; talking about marriage may have been a way of dreaming himself forward into some more preferable reality.

What he didn't expect, at least initially, was his parents' strong objections. For reasons that remain unclear—or at least unspecified— Emma Goyen was hurt by her son's hints of marriage, prompting a contrite letter home that nevertheless tried to make a case for the practical value of the match: "I feel like Nell is a person I could spend the rest of my life with, and that she will give me so much that I need to continue what I have to go through now and after the war. And more than that, I feel that she is so close to you; she loves you like her own mother, and I know you love her."[25] Part of what worried the Goyens were plans for Nell to visit Bill over Christmas. Emma and Charlie were alarmed that the two might secretly marry without involving the family. They may also have had their doubts about Nell, who was nine years older than Goyen and had been widowed in 1932. Perhaps even more relevant, she had recently faced a serious health problem, possibly tuberculosis. Even so, Goyen's response to Merrill Street indicates that his mother was also quite simply jealous, afraid of losing the affections of a son she had come to rely on for emotional care.

Whatever the doubts and concerns emanating from Houston, in December Nell took the train north and spent the holidays with Goyen and his Navy friends. "She is such a strange little thing," he wrote his mother, "so honest and simple and different from all the rest." She impressed them all, particularly the other wives, with her quiet friendliness, and for a time, at least, Goyen seemed grateful for her presence and convinced of his need for her. He continued to make the case to his mother: "I just can't do without that little girl and she cannot exist without me. I never really knew her before, but now I do, and I know that I could never find anyone else like her. I would be a fool to give her up."[26] Emma was unconvinced, however, and it may have been this resistance coupled with an increase in candor on Goyen's part that finally induced a confession of sorts:

> Mom, I do love her, in a funny sort of way. I just feel like she somehow belongs to me and to all of you. But, Mom, I'm going to tell you some things that must always be just between you and me. I know you are the only one in the family who can really keep things to yourself, and I want you never to tell this to anyone. It'll always be just for you and me. Mom, Nell and I will never be married, we both know that. You see, we learned that up here. Because, somehow she is just not quite for me. There's something about her—her age or her health or her strangeness that just keeps me from feeling sure of her or right about marrying her. I believe that she feels someday, somehow we might go ahead, but deep down inside she knows we cannot. We do love being together, and I feel so free and at ease with her, as I have never felt with any other woman, but there's just something there that keeps me from going all the way. She knows this now, but we agreed to keep it always a secret from all of you.[27]

The letter is an important document in Goyen's history of near-revelation and secret sharing. Almost pressured into marriage—and half willing to go along—he was able both to free himself from the obligation and to present the break to his mother almost as a kind of gift, a renewed bond of intimacy between them. It was a given that he was unable to say more of the causes of his ambivalence, though the underlying silence can at times seem like the primary condition of an unspoken compact between mother and son.

In *The House of Breath*, Nell appears as Evella Sykes, rival to Malley Ganchion for the affections of her son, Berryben. "She was older than him," Malley explains in her monologue, "and had had one husband who died in Charity, and she was a kind of mother to him, I know, loved him and wanted to help him all she could" (*HOB* 85). And later, Berryben himself describes an autumn in a "fantasy land" that sounds very much like the Puget Sound area where he and Evella end their relationship: "'The luminous wind was binding the autumn to the glistening world, blowing it round through trees with the sound of the breaking sea, and the sun was driving the summer away,—all love is a turning on a spit, toward, through, and away from flame—and we were like sleepwalkers. . . . With Evella I could never see myself, only hold up a mirror for Evella to see herself; and thus I became unreal'" (*HOB* 107).

That he let himself come close to marriage was more than anything an indication of how tired Goyen was of the Navy and how eager to get on with his life. From his arrival in Bremerton in early 1943 until his first Pacific voyage in August of 1944, he had been either in training for the initial launch of the *Casablanca* or training others on cruises in the Strait of Juan de Fuca north of Seattle. As the first of its class off the line, the *Casablanca* served as a test of the new design, and the problems encountered during its sea trials and after helped alert the builders to the need for improvements.[28] At first, the shipboard activity was interesting and exciting for Goyen. As Second Division Officer, he commanded a battery of 20 mm antiaircraft guns and stood "top watch" on the bridge. According to the historian Barbara G. Jones, the overall training schedule for visiting crews on the *Casablanca* was rigorous: "Training for each pre-commissioning crew began with drills, including all hands at abandon ship, man overboard and the training at each position within a man's specialty, fire drills, calls to general quarters, and muster on stations. Then, drills would be added, including gunnery or assisting with landing and takeoff of aircraft, engineering, radar, radio, ship maneuvering, and any other skills necessary to run a ship and conduct flight activities."[29] But gradually the repetition of these instructional missions began to wear (the *Casablanca* trained crews for all forty-nine of the CVE class ships in two-week increments from July 1943 to July 1944), and the sense of uselessness and wasted time became increasingly depressing.

Later in the summer of 1944, Goyen's mood lightened when the carrier finally moved down the coast to San Francisco to pick up supplies and eighty-eight aircraft to ferry to Manus, the largest of the Admiralty Islands in the South Pacific. A key staging area for the impending invasion of Leyte Gulf, Manus had four airfields and a massive base built by the Americans and Australians after they took the island from the Japanese in May 1944. Relieved at finally participating in the war, Goyen wrote home enthusiastically about his first real wartime voyage, particularly his initiation as a "shellback" when the ship crossed the equator. The thrill didn't last, however. By October, the *Casablanca* was back in Puget Sound training again, and Goyen was once again tired, angry, and unhappy with his daily existence.

Over the next year until the end of the war, the ship made several trips from the West Coast to the South Pacific, ferrying men and supplies to Pearl Harbor and Guam and then operating as a supply and support vessel between Samar, Manus, and Palau. The *Casablanca's* cabins and below-deck areas were sweltering most of the time, and the duty was monotonous, though there were sights and incidents destined to produce lasting traumatic effects, particularly for someone with Goyen's emotional fragility. In February of 1945, the poorly designed ship ran into a major storm while en route from Bremerton to San Diego. The waves were so large that the stern was lifting its props out of the water as they topped the crests, and the flight deck fractured when the bow dug awkwardly into a massive wall of water. The storm went on for two days, the ship shaking ominously each time it plunged through the swells, making almost all of the crew violently seasick. On a different occasion, Goyen was officer of the deck while cruising in the dangerous waters between Pearl Harbor and Guam when the convoy's destroyer escort USS *Gilmore* made submarine contact. Though the alert was soon lifted, the tension of constant zigzagging and general quarters alerts remained high, particularly while the *Casablanca* ferried supplies from Manus to Samar in April 1945. Even Tokyo Rose, the infamous Japanese propagandist, singled out the *Casablanca* by name and described it as a known target for enemy submarines.

Though explicit war scenes seldom appear in Goyen's work, the story "Children of Old Somebody" contains a brief anecdote that hints at the emotional cost of these months inside the combat zone:

> For they had lately put me down from the ship into the waters in a little leaf of a boat and sent me to wait upon the spot where a plane had fallen into the sea, to hover at the rim of the broken waters to watch when a body would rise from the depths, and capture it. I waited on the leaf, at the spot of the destruction, and behold he came rising up like a weed, the drowned sailor. I, whose hands had named and shaped and blessed this sunken shape, dipped my hands into the water and lifted it from it and brought back the salvaged shape lying across my knees, sea-boy lie light on my body, to the ship. . . . (CS 81)

The situation itself is quite real, of course, though it's unlikely that Goyen himself carried out this kind of recovery mission. However, the description does suggest the memory of an accident that occurred during a training mission off Whidbey Island Naval Air Station. While practicing carrier landings on the *Casablanca*, the pilot of a Grumman F4F Wildcat, Vernon Wilbur Spalding, approached the flight deck at too low an angle and was waved off. But before he could regain altitude, his tail hook caught part of the arresting cable and the plane hit the crash barrier and went over the port side of the ship. Spalding's parachute apparently caught on the plane, and he was pulled under as the aircraft sank. The body was recovered by a trailing ship, called the "aircraft guard," and brought aboard the *Casablanca*, where Spalding was pronounced dead by drowning. Though no record attests that Goyen was on duty during this incident, he may have witnessed the crash and almost certainly heard about the incident from others.[30]

Naturally these voyages had bright moments as well, often brief excursions to small islands where Goyen as "public relations officer" was charged with scouting locations for a "club" (usually just a Quonset hut or clutch of tables beneath some coconut trees where beer was available). He had also formed a strong friendship with Gunnery Officer Walter Berns and was helping his fellow lieutenant with his French in their off-duty time. Nevertheless, his letters home grew more and more despondent, particularly about what he considered the lost years of the war and his increasingly desperate need to start his career as a writer. He no longer wanted to teach and was beginning to prepare his parents for the possibility that he might settle somewhere other than Houston: "I feel as though I must get started on what I really have to do as soon as I am free again. You know I feel like an old man now, and I have a horror of getting old without accomplishing my ambitions."[31] During his time in the Navy, it had become clear that he had lived too sheltered a life thus far. The college and graduate school years had been useful preparation, but after three years of service, with most of the last two on the same ship, he felt near panic at reaching thirty without having begun an independent, adult life. Though he had written consistently to his parents about coming back to Texas to live with them—even fantasizing about buying a little place in the country for all of them—he now demanded their support for his intention to devote himself single-mindedly to his work: "Before, I was a kid and you weren't sure of me and you felt you had to guide me in what you felt was the right direction. Now, I have broken away (or have been *torn* away), I am matured, and I've got to take the chance. Four years out of an eager, alive and active fellow's life is a big chunk. I've got a lot of time to make up, and I *know* I can do what I want to do if I can just keep my spirit up, and keep my faith in myself."[32]

This combination of bitterness and determination was not entirely new; it was present from Goyen's earliest sense of himself as an exile and caretaker within his family. But his willingness to repress or silence his own thought and temperament for the sake of his family and the demands of the Navy had finally worn thin. Never sympathetic to the wartime mentality, he now became more and more opposed to what he considered the increasing barbarism of the conflict. He refused to be optimistic after the bombing of Hiroshima and Nagasaki and told his parents that he was "neither happy over nor proud of the new 'scientific' means of annihilating 60% of a city and its inhabitants."[33] For the most part, he kept his thoughts to himself, but at times in this final year, he raged at those around him, unable to contain himself any longer. (A later inventory of his rebelliousness describes his being confined to quarters for telling his captain that he was "full of shit."[34] He also apparently told George Williams that he was once so seasick that he flatly refused an order to board a small boat pitching in heavy seas.[35]) To Hart he described, in terms that may be exaggerated for heroic effect, the final scenes of his shipboard mania: "I think of myself during these last few months as something livid, as firebrand, as demon, as saint, as prophet, as blackguard. God I was mean, Bill; I was pure evil, I was the Devil. People fled before me. And one man, so much like Velte, who was searching—not for something to believe—but for something to feel, felt something. I saw him crumble down on a table and weep and thank God for his tears."[36] The familiar migraines intensified and became more frequent, and the combination of physical pain and psychological stress increased his sense of futility: "For a long time now I have been, for all practical purposes, useless," he wrote his parents. "My service has been negligible and I want to be honest about it. It is a farce and I have almost lost my mind over it. I shall see it through to the end, the better to judge it and to do all in my power to see that others are not caught in and corrupted by the same destruction."[37]

On September 21, 1945, more than a month after the Japanese surrender, Goyen left the *Casablanca* at the Treasure Island dock in San Francisco for Oak Knoll Hospital in Oakland, transferred there on recommendation of the ship's doctor. His migraines were the primary trouble, though he was clearly suffering from stress and fatigue as well. After a full range of tests, doctors found no physical cause for the headaches, and he was transferred to the Naval Hospital in Medford, Oregon, to make room for newly released prisoners of war. Though he was concerned about what his family and others back home might think about his mental state, he enjoyed the relaxation and was already making plans for his new, postwar life. To Hart, he ticked off the "possibilities": "1) Hollywood—(you will shrink at this)—mainly its theatre. . . . 2) New York. You have no doubt heard of Toni Strassman's attempts to help me. Through Flora I got some stuff to her and she has had some encouraging success with the seven stories of mine. . . . 3) Teaching—which is a very weak third. It is a compromise, I feel, and I cannot allow it to drain me as it once did."[38] It is indicative of Goyen's intense ambition that he had managed, with the help of the Yorkshire-born but Texas-raised Flora Armitage, to find a literary agent while still hospitalized and was already writing the long, sometimes hectoring letters that would characterize his relations to agents for years to come. And to Bill Hart, back from his own war experiences and dealing with readjustment to civilian life, he was fiercely and grandly self-concerned, through with compromise and ready to cut all ties if the success of his work demanded it:

> I tell you I have waited long enough. And I don't give one good god damn what you or your fine prattling friends have to say from their nests of security and silky comfort. Have to say about my actions, my deeds, my ambiguous experiments, my violence, etc. I should know what I am doing by this time, and if not, then I do not ask for your grappling hooks to pull me out. Let me go under, Bill, let me go under, but for God's sake let me *move move move*.

CHAPTER FIVE

El Prado

1945–1948

*It is true that there is a feeling, alternately fierce and gentle, which
one gets up there. It is some ten thousand feet up, you are on the top
of a mountain and you look down over miles and miles of sweeping
uninhabited desert and mesa, all brown and ghostly blue. . . .
Through three huge open windows I could see the night and hear the
wind in the pines, and wild creatures of every kind ran, scrambled
over the roof, gnawed, screamed and skittered; once, what must
have been a whole herd of quarreling coyotes fought for five minutes
in a nightmare of a battle. Some were apparently wounded, for
they screamed like women; others were vicious and they moaned
and whined and howled. Then in a flash they were stilled, and not
another sound.*

LETTER TO BILL HART, JULY 15, 1946

In 1946, after the war, Goyen was determined to break away from
Texas. With his shipmate Walter Berns, he hatched a plan to
move to the San Francisco area and write. On a frosty January
morning, he left Houston and drove to Lubbock, where he met Berns,
who had come down from Chicago by train. They meant to drive to
Albuquerque and then north to Santa Fe and Denver before turning
west toward San Francisco, but Berns was ill, and they were forced to
find a doctor in Albuquerque. After a day of waiting for test results, they
moved on to Santa Fe and Taos.[1] "It really was like an Arthurian situation," Goyen later told Robert Phillips. "I couldn't leave. It was beautiful and remote, like a Himalayan village, untouched, with the adobe
color that was ruby-colored and yellow, all the magical colors of mud.

It's not all one color. It's like Rome. Rome looks like that. And the sunlight and the snow . . . just about everyone on foot . . . a few cars . . . high, 7500 feet" (*GAE* 81). By the beginning of March, Goyen was writing to Bill Hart to explain that he and Berns had rented "a little adobe apartment—quite primitive and quite large—for a month" and wanted to stay if they could.[2]

How much Berns's illness played a part in the decision is difficult to gauge. It is clear that a large part of New Mexico's appeal to Goyen was in the landscape—and in the feelings it evoked in him. He wrote to another shipmate, Emmet Riordan: "Out here we are certainly not removed from 'reality,' as people call it; indeed it seems to me that the realest reality is everywhere about. This land stuns me every time I take a look at it: Most of all I like its untouchedness, its refusal to be anything more than mountain, desert and sky. It does much to me, and so long as it does I shall remain in it."[3] What it did to him, as is so often the case with Goyen's intuitive reactions, remains unspecified, but several factors help explain the attraction to a place seemingly untouched, sparsely populated, and relatively remote. Though by now almost thirty-one years old, he had spent all his life in Texas, mostly in Houston, and continued to live on Merrill Street with his parents until he entered the Navy in 1942. For the three years of service during the war, he had moved from Illinois to New York to the Panama Canal Zone before being sent to Bremerton, Washington, prior to joining the *Casablanca* in mid-1943. Now, for the first time in his life, he had, with great self-determination, left his family and Houston to find a place of his own. The emotional challenge of such a break can be measured by an anecdote he later told about this period just after the war. It was during one of his mother's frequent illnesses. As Reginald Gibbons explains, Emma Goyen had been hospitalized, and during her recovery

[Goyen] had become more and more apprehensive about staying in Texas; he really could not bear it and had to get out. What would evoke in him his artistic work was elsewhere; what she and Houston then evoked in him was oppressive and stifling. On the day when he brought his mother home from the hospital . . . she saw, as soon as the two of them entered the front door, Goyen's small cardboard suitcase standing in the front hall. Containing the very little that he owned, it was packed, and he was ready to leave. "What is that?" she had asked. "I'm leaving," he replied. "If you leave, I'll die," she said. And he replied, "If I don't leave, I'll die." (*GAE* xvii–xix)

In an interview in 1974, Goyen was asked whether his family had been "oppressive": "No, they weren't oppressive," he replied, "it was just an abundance of love and affection and of devouring—you see, Southerners do that too; Southern families eat you up with love, closeness."[4] Combined with passages from *The House of Breath* that emphasize the burden placed on the son, Berryben, by his family, particularly by his mother, such a comment suggests a basic need in this intense, always emotionally charged young man to seek some ground swept clean of familial emotion. Whatever its other attractions, Taos—and particularly the outlying village of El Prado—was a small, quiet place, uncluttered by the daily demands of family and memory. In many ways, Taos seems to have been both an echo and a repudiation of East Texas, a small town like Trinity, untainted by Houston's bustle but set in a New Mexico landscape that was spare and simple and dry—the antithesis of the tangled thickets of East Texas. There is little doubt as well that Taos suggested a relatively calm retreat after more than two years aboard the *Casablanca*. Even before he was discharged from the Navy, Goyen had essentially decided to make his life somewhere other than Texas. "I should like to live there [San Francisco] or in Southern California for awhile," he wrote to Bill Hart in September of 1945. "But the family— you know all that. However, I have them somewhat prepared, if that is possible. Jimmy [his brother] is away at school now, and they call to me in every letter. But I am strong now, virile and all my own, and I must keep it that way."[5]

In later years, Goyen strongly denied any prior interest in the literary and artistic associations of Taos. "I didn't know anything about the Lawrence legend," he told Robert Phillips. "Had I, I might not have stayed at all" (*GAE* 81). But he and Berns did need to find jobs, and while working as waiters at the Sagebrush Inn, they soon met what was left of D. H. Lawrence's aging circle:

The whole Lawrence world came to dinner there: Dorothy Brett and Mabel Dodge, Spud Johnson, Tennessee Williams—he was living up at the ranch. They all came to my table. And then the owner of the Inn had to come out and say, this young man is just out of the war and he wants to be a writer. The *worst* thing I wanted said about me; it almost paralyzed me. Well, of course, Tennessee thought, oh, God, who cares about *another* writer. But Frieda said, you must come and have tea with me. She said it right away. I went and from that moment . . . we just hit it off. It was almost a love affair. It was the whole world. (*GAE* 81)

Frieda Lawrence was then sixty-six, and though to some she remained the legendary and sometimes scandalous figure of D. H. Lawrence's biography, to Goyen she seemed a "luminous" maternal or grand-maternal presence. She befriended the two Navy veterans, "the boys," as she subsequently referred to them, and welcomed them to her house in El Prado. "She would have high teas," Goyen later explained. "In Texas we had a coke. But here it was the first time I met someone who baked bread, you know? She made a cake and brought it out. . . . It was wonderful. She wore German clothes, like dirndls, and peasant outfits, and an apron. She was a kitchen frau" (*GAE* 81). To Bill Hart, he wrote with a kind of breathless excitement that suggests both discovery and validation: "Oh Billy, she is a grand old woman, like a peasant Queen, a marvelous smiling face and deep husky Germanic voice, and she answers every question with a lusty and throaty, 'Ya!'"[6] And again a few months later he described his and Berns's first dinner with Frieda and the painter and Lawrence confidant Dorothy Brett:

Then—last Thursday we found as we were washing our breakfast dishes, a quaint little note plastered to our kitchen window screen. It was from Brett, who had come stealthily and quietly, and an invitation to supper with Frieda Lawrence that night. We were ecstatic. We went, had a simple little peasant-like meal in her kitchen, Frieda powerful as a lioness, really just a sort of gross old German peasant woman, but ah! her face! Like a little girl's, and so beautiful and full of life. She talked incessantly about "Lawrence." We were shy about the subject, but she went on and on, once tears were in her eyes when she said in the indescribable husky voice of hers, "Oh, those were wonderful days." Brett sat in a dream, so quiet and faded. Then she asked if we would like to look at some of the Lawrence manuscripts. We sat in the living room with D.H.'s notebooks, immaculate and clear, in our hands—*Kangaroo, The Trespasser*, some of the plays, and *The Woman who Rode Away*. Frieda Lawrence was really inspired several times; and once, as a kind of valedictory, she leaned her head back, looked up toward the ceiling and said, "And now . . . I am old and you are young. I say to you that you must fight and refuse to compromise, refuse absolutely to compromise. I lived with a fighter and I know what it is to fight. . . ."[7]

She asked about the war, the Navy, what it was like to live on a ship, and she ended by offering to let Goyen and Berns stay the weekend in the newer of the two houses at Kiowa Ranch, about twenty miles northwest of Taos on Lobo Mountain: "It sits right next to the humble little cabin that she and Lawrence lived in. And she asked us to go into Lawrence's chapel and replace the greenery with fresh cedar and pine boughs."[8] They spent the night on the windy top of the mountain, listening to the coyotes howl and fight in the darkness. Soon after, Goyen recorded the experience in a poem, "Lawrence's Chapel at Kiowa":

> Through the wide windows we watched the giant night, deep blue,
>   the blue of depths,
> And the forest lying vast and raucous under the night.
> Once a band of coyotes mutinied somewhere,
> Flocked together in a cannibal herd and turned suddenly upon each
>   other, wild and screaming terror
> Like murderer and murdered.[9]

By Christmas, Frieda had given Goyen and Berns "a gorgeous hunk of land . . . about two acres" on her lower ranch on which to build a house. The small, flat-roofed structure made of adobe was finished by the end of May 1947. It cost just $500, about all the money the two veterans had left, but they had done most of the labor themselves, learning from a local Indian how to make adobe bricks and making do with furniture donated by friends or cobbled together by Berns. "Walter has proved a genius of a carpenter," Goyen wrote to Emmet and Anne Riordan, "has made a great cupboard, two very fine desks, thousands of shelves, etc."[10] The house meant a great deal to Goyen; it was in many respects the symbol of his independence, the first place that seemed truly his own, built from the ground up on his own terms and imagined not merely as a shelter but as a foundational space free from the repressions of family—a "place of telling," like those that appear again and again in his stories. In his 1955 novel, *In a Farther Country*, a New York apartment in an industrial building is reimagined as an otherworldly "house" that attracts the lonely and obsessed and, by its very nature, grants them the freedom to tell their stories.

> This house is not in the town you speak of, it is far beyond, it is not within the town limits, it is a house unto itself, at the far end of the road and against the mountain; it has nothing to do with other houses in a place called the town that lies so far beyond. There is no strife here, except the strife of the human heart that is forever trying to pacify itself and in many ways. Those many ways of pacification of self-strife make the climate of this house. It is a speaking place and a joining place. . . . (*IFC* 126–127)

Goyen's use of the word "tell" often carries a double meaning. Although it clearly evokes the drama of oral storytelling, it also suggests a child's determination to reveal a secret. The small house at El Prado was to be the space in which Goyen and Berns were allowed to tell what they knew. In their mutual case, this meant writing together about their experiences aboard the *Casablanca*. But for Goyen, it implied more: the chance to say what could never be said in Texas—about himself and about his family. It also very likely included the fantasy of making a home with Berns, still another way of showing the world that Bill Goyen could be and do and *say* what he wanted.

Section Two

In Goyen's story "Tenant in the Garden," published in 1962, the narrator describes a child's playhouse in which a nervous junior high school teacher, Mr. Stevens, has—strangely, stubbornly—chosen to live: "It was a playhouse of an earlier style with one little room, a tiny porch with two columns, and one small step. There was a gable and, in it, two eye-sized dormer windows" (*CS* 218). Mr. Stevens is a printer as well as a teacher and comes from the southwest where he had worked "at his little hand press" in his small shop in the desert. Eventually he is forced out of the little house because it is unapproved for habitation, but while he lives there the small structure, a space of imagination that feeds imagining, seems to attract lonely people. It becomes a "meeting place" to which people are drawn to tell their stories.

The story is based loosely on Goyen's own experience teaching junior high school in Napa, California, in the fall of 1947. He and Berns had always meant to get back to San Francisco, and after more than a year in Taos, they decided to try their luck in Northern California. The move was by no means permanent, but it offered the chance to see other country and possibly find some work that would finance their next year in New Mexico. They found a "little flat in the basement of a bourgeois little house," and Goyen took the teaching job against his better judgment; he lasted about a month.[11] "It was wrong, wrong, a betrayal," he wrote to Hart after the fact, "a kind of crime, great abuse. I could not stand it."[12] If Mr. Stevens is in any way an accurate self-portrait, the former college instructor had little ability to control his unruly students: "They seemed to want to chip off pieces of him like a little clay kewpie, by throwing chalk and spit wads at him when his back was turned." And so Mr. Stevens, who "was meant to sit quietly in some place, alone," retreats to his little house, followed by his students, all boys, who ridicule him for living in "a girl's playhouse."[13]

Goyen had a tendency to create self-defenses in his stories—particularly against those who questioned his choices about how and where to live. Mr. Stevens's playhouse is clearly a version of the small adobe house in Taos built deliberately by Goyen and Berns as both a retreat and an outpost of privileged expression. From the beginning, Goyen spoke of it as a sort of monastic space, devoted to an idea of work removed from the world and thereby intensified to the point of spiritual commitment. His rejection of teaching, even as a temporary money-making activity, served to reaffirm the kind of radical dedication he cultivated at the end of the war. Following Frieda Lawrence's advice with intensity, Goyen absolutely refused to compromise, and if his calling required that he hide out in what others considered a childish way or place, so be it.

One of the first and direct products of this determined, self-protective spirit was a novel about his time aboard the *Casablanca*. Goyen had begun *Section Two* in the latter months of 1945, but in El Prado he and Berns began to work on the manuscript together. Laid out in scenes more consistent with a play than a novel, the manuscript is difficult to summarize, but it loosely collects incidents from Goyen's life on board the ship during the final year of the war. He is Daedalus, a sensitive, philosophical, quietly rebellious figure who, like the rest of his watch—the "Section Two" of the title—opposes the world of the "idiot men." A "kind of maker of wings for people," Daedalus suffers from "bursting headpain" and carries a "secret misery."[14] His principal friend and ally, a mythicized version of Walter Berns, is known as the "Golden Giant": "He was big, really huge as a giant; and because of a golden glimmer all about his face and the red-goldness of his body, those in Section Two called him The Golden Giant. He had a pink-red face all full of light, and his hands were white and fair with big graceful swollen fingers pointing out from the round palm-like star." The relationship is close, potentially intimate, though the bond appears to be primarily intellectual and fraternal with hints of unrequited longing on the part of Daedalus: "Poor Golden Giant, he did not know the agony that ran through the streets of Daedalus's soul like a lion. He did not comprehend the secret misery that ate at him, because he did not understand his own misery. He would not recognize it, he would not be still and let it come face to face with him, because he was afraid. (But very soon Daedalus taught him)."

Around this seemingly mythic pair, the other members of the watch revolve in a highly stylized series of portraits and theatrical set pieces. The character list includes "The Great Black Monk," a "black-headed, black-skinned Jew" named Morisky, who is slow and obsessive, repeating whatever is on his mind like a paddle-baller "flinging the rubber ball at you until you were as frenzied as he"; and "Little Stamps," a former signalman who had been moved to the ship's post office. With the other members of Section Two, they form a small band of somewhat rebellious comrades critical of most of what they see around them. Other officers are indicted as too dull or conventional to be changed by the war or to feel deeply the madness and brutality of the system that produced it: "You have capered through a war, a *war*, mind you, and you have come out unchanged; the alchemy of war has not transmuted you. There is no real metamorphosis possible in you, Idiot Man; only the specious change of the chameleon on his momentary bough." Much of Goyen's own frustration and anger at what he perceived as the falseness of the officer class emerges with little real disguise. A senior officer, "Mr. Fallius"—self-important, paternalistic—is attacked for adultery and hypocrisy, while the other officers' wives, following the ship's movements in a group, are scorned as silly and immature: "To them, the war was just a prolonged sorority party. It was really great fun. Somewhat awkward not to be able to accompany their mates when the ship went to sea, but not unlike their school days even, for the departure of the ship recalled the adieus at the sorority house door at curfew time, when the men departed and the girls flocked upstairs to discuss their dates of the evening."

The manuscript has the quality of a private revenge, a chance for Goyen to say what he'd always wanted to about his frustrations with the Navy—and with life in general. There are moments of heated rhetoric, often still-forming philosophy aimed at recovering a truer experience from a world defined by its superficiality. Daedalus is usually the source: "I believe that's what we need now," he sermonizes. "Not delusion or the betrayal of illusion, none of that—but the hard reality that lies hidden in the myth. Seems we've lost that in our time; it's all gone out of us, replaced by cynicism and the snarling face of 'reality.' That kind of cocktail lounge casualness, that derogation of the unbelievable." From the perspective of El Prado, Goyen could lay out as a sort of statement not only his rejection of war-time values—including the treatment of black sailors as servants on board—but his emerging sense that such values must be opposed by a self-attention that would produce its own moral vision:

> In dream—not illusion or delusion—lies the highest reality, out of which comes a new and heightened consciousness of one's self and his place in the cosmos, and from there—the "dream" or "vision"—begins one's responsibilities—to the dream. It seems to me that the evolvement of a true human morality breaks out of the "vision." A kind of self-examination results, we are driven to look straight at ourselves and know our weakness, our foibles and flaws and failures thoroughly.

The bridge of the ship serves as the book's only stage. Most events are reported, like the moment of crisis when a storm damages the forward compartments and forty-millimeter ammunition gets loose in the passageways. Even the death of The Black Monk is related by an off-stage witness: "A sailor messenger came to Daedalus on the bridge, said 'Mr. Daedalus, Mr. Moriskey he is dead at Number One Battery,' and that was all." What plot the text has depends upon the anticipation of the end of the war, "Le Jour de la Gloire" as Daedalus christens it, echoing "La Marseillaise": "The day when a man will return whence he came, when he will have his life in his hands, all his own to wrestle with in his way, when he can go where he will, and be what he chooses." In one strange scene, the day itself appears as a humanized, hallucinated glow on the sea and speaks to the watch. In another, more realistic moment, the narrator tells what it was really like the day they learned the war was over:

> It was like this. They told the skipper on his radio and then he told all of us over the loud speaker . . . "All hands. . . ." We were riding up and down when they told us over the radio, some reporter from Guam or Frisco, they were telling us. Although we had been waiting for it, it was a shock, it was like a knock in the head, you just couldn't believe it. You went away to be alone and tell yourself yes it is really over it is ended this is the Golden Day, Le Jour de la Gloire. . . . And in a minute you scratched your head and said wait a minute . . . God IS it over, and how will I act and what do I do—I want to go home. It's like taking a squirrel out of his prison fly-wheel. But something keeps going round and round, it's hard to stop it.

Scenes such as this have the clarity and straightforwardness of truth about them, which is not to suggest that *Section Two* is a wholly realistic account of Goyen's time in the Navy but rather an occasion for retelling and recovering important moments of his final and most difficult year in the service. The storm the *Casablanca* experienced off the Oregon coast in February 1945 is clearly the source for the similar storm in the book, and the surreal scene in which the "day of glory" speaks to Section Two appears to be based on an incident of April 3, 1945, in which crew members spotted "three unexplained yellow lights" appearing "in the early morning hours, one after the other."[15] There also seems little reason to doubt that the book's concluding scene, in which Daedalus is loaded into an ambulance waiting at the dock, describes Goyen's final exit from the ship:

> They went below, down the ladder, tenderly and wordless, to the quarterdeck. Daedalus looked through the open hatchway through which he would walk into the world. There lay the great land-locked world, lying so strong and with such a feeling of permanence, the great treed, earth-world of soil and vegetation, of house and drugstore and bank, of street-car and alley, of morning newspaper and the saltless

windless odor, framed in the hatchway. And there, in the frame of the hatchway, sat a shining white limousine with a red cross on its side. "This is to take me away," he thought.

For a moment Daedalus reacts to the sight with near panic and the impulse to hide. "He would live in the frames of the ship like a spider, or cling to its side like a barnacle." But the ambulance is not only the vehicle of his escape, his transition out of the ship and water world; it is also the sign of his bruised sensibility, the wounded and docile—but, deeper down, angry—self emerging from a long isolation and nightmare confinement to seek out a voice, to tell what he had seen.

Ultimately, Goyen could never find a publisher for *Section Two*. Though it was considered at several houses, it failed to find readers open to its odd combination of static drama and declamation. He took this reticence as fear of the book's angry, satirical edge, but it seems much more likely that the lack of a clear, conventional narrative precluded any chance of acceptance by the larger publishers. The tentative efforts his agent Toni Strassman made at the time to push him toward more marketable writing were often met with angry, idealistic resistance: "Let's get this straight: I am a mature man, one grounded in literature and things written creatively, I have fought like hell to get that way, I have a little aesthetic integrity, and, put this down, NOBODY IS GOING TO TELL ME WHAT TO WRITE. That's the first point. The second is, NO ONE, NO ONE, IS GOING TO TELL ME HOW TO LIVE. And I take the consequences of these two statements."[16] More than anything else it is this attitude—absolute, intense, desperately self-protective—that is the true product of Goyen's war experience. His chosen life in El Prado—its location, as well as his deliberately provocative though ambiguous partnership with Berns—suggests a simultaneous defense against those who misunderstood him and an offense against a world too practical or too mercenary, in his view, to permit unfettered expression. This high rage would characterize his relationship to the world of letters for many years to come. It feeds through his work in a variety of ways and accounts for both his major difficulties with agents and publishers during his career and for his moments of powerful, unique expression. For better and worse, by 1946 Goyen had found his place and his role, his vision of himself as a teller, alone for the most part, intensely grounded, ready to have his say.

CHAPTER SIX ∾

Christopher Icarus
1948–1950

*"For my time and my strength, as things stand with me, can have
but one task, but this one: to find the road on which I shall come
to a quiet, daily work in which I can dwell with more security and
stability than in this uncertain sickly world that is collapsing behind
me and before me does not exist."*

RAINER MARIA RILKE TO LOU ANDREAS-SALOMÉ, NOVEMBER 3,
1903, COPIED INTO GOYEN'S NOTEBOOK CIRCA 1947

Section Two was not the only product of Goyen's wartime experiences. In late 1945 while recovering in Naval hospitals in
California and Oregon, he began to gather and rework a number of manuscripts, some written during his time in the service, some
during his college and graduate school years. Among the latter was
a story called "The Crimes of Mirensky," a brief but intense dramatic
sketch that echoes the family dynamics of the untitled piece he sent
to Bill Hart in 1943. In the first version (the manuscript is dated 1933–
1934) the title character, Steve, comes home to his family's apartment
one evening and begins to argue with Maranna, the pregnant wife of his
brother Nick. Her sister Sophie, with whom Steve has been having an
affair, is leaving for Chicago to care for her ailing mother, and Mirensky
goes into a rage, telling Maranna he hopes her baby is born an idiot.
The outburst prompts an angry speech from Sophie, who appears to
speak for the entire family when she calls Mirensky a "ruthless thief":
"Little by little you have stolen everything they have in this house—
their laughter, their joy, their goodness. In a month I have seen you take
everything they could get in their hands to give you. Everyone serves
you. Help me help me you cry. And they come running. Who are you? A

king? A messiah?"[1] Steve does not respond, except to say that he will go away "and send them money," though the story ends with a blending of the voice of Mirensky and the narrator, blaming art for his selfishness: "It will rob everyone for its own coffers. . . . How can a man continue, every day, every hour, even, to believe in himself as an artist, what will keep his vision from blurring; what? . . . O I am full of tricks. I cheat and I embargo, I exploit, I force bargains."

Considered as an early dramatization of family conflict from Goyen's college years, the sketch allows us to see him imaginatively trying out justifications for his own behavior. Whether such scenes occurred or not, the guilt of the son who pursues art while his family—again in this case a weak father and a nervous, invalid mother—suffers for it is strong enough to have brought Goyen back to the manuscript after the war. The second version is dated 1944–1945 and is written on stationery from the U.S. Naval Hospital. Again Mirensky is the selfish son, taking all that the family can give and offering nothing in return, but this time Goyen permits him more of a voice—and a fuller argument for his commitment to his art:

> He said to them all: "I am guilty, you are all of you right. I am unkind to the point of ruthlessness; I am intolerant; I am a beast, making experiments upon the passions. I feed you bread while you ask for my own flesh to be served up. It is not my goodness you ask for, but my heart. It is not my body, but my soul. You want claims to it: you want my life, like a child, to shake its ragged head and tell it how to live. I am full of tricks; I trump up, cannily and craftily, I trump up. Because you harness your life and cage it in these little rooms, you cry madman! at me because I flog it and flog it and beat it into senselessness, for I will not have it as you have it. I am cruel, because you are all poor and I work at music for twenty dollars a week when I could get fifty at a clerk's desk. I am selfish because I make all things, all men and women, serve me and my wild cloven-footed art. I am merciless, violent and pitiless and full of malice. I am guilty, guilty, guilty! Do you hear? And now that I am honest and admit my guilt, you cannot judge me for the crimes I shall commit."[2]

The guilt so loudly proclaimed was no doubt real enough: it is clear, for instance, that Goyen could have worked at Humble Oil and made enough money to significantly improve his family's prospects. (Indeed

Goyen's lack of a steady income and occasional reliance on his parents for emergency funds was to remain a source of guilt and inner conflict until he took a job in publishing in the early 1960s.) But real, too, is the desperate plea for distance and self-sufficiency, for the chance to build an identity separate from the all-consuming emotional requirements of a depressed and dependent Merrill Street. By the end of the war, these demands had increased rather than diminished, but Goyen's will to break free had reached an almost unbearable intensity. Though this is precisely the sort of writing he continued to hide from his family, it is a measure of his new determination that he allowed himself this passionate rehearsal of a speech he may never have made.

Here, then, is a combination of roles and feelings. Goyen sees himself as both criminal and victim, selfish and sacrificed. He is full of self-concern because the claims on him are so great—the family asks too much. Having thought of himself as his mother's caretaker for so long, he pushes that sacrificial role into the idea of himself as a savior, artistic rather than economic, a recorder of memory and a teller of truths. The implied martyrdom is, in large part, a response to his biggest dilemma, his inability to speak openly of his sexuality. Without that possibility before him, he takes what he can: the idea of himself as a person through whom others can speak, an exile whose self-imposed punishment brings him the attention he desperately requires.

All these elements were in place relatively early, as the first version of "Mirensky" suggests, but it was the war—and later Goyen's time in New Mexico—that catalyzed his conflicts into a productive artistic vision. The coalescing of materials and methods can best be seen in the manuscripts of *Christopher Icarus*, an unfinished novel that was Goyen's primary concern for many years both before and immediately after the war.[3] As the title suggests, the main character is connected to an idea of self-sacrifice: he is both Christ-like and a young man longing to escape. Like the Daedalus of *Section Two*, Christopher is an earnest truth-seeker who sees himself as a spiritual and moral mentor to those near to him.[4] In a synopsis of a later version of the story, Goyen calls him "a youth and man who struggles to be alive and moving, to feel life honestly and faithfully, and to make the effect of his life felt. His struggle is the fight of a sensitive human being to be alive, explore life, to understand men and help them understand themselves and particularly the potential within themselves, what they can *become*, soar into, out of their own ashes." But this impulse to help others ultimately leads them away from Christopher: "He 'builds wings' for two great people only to watch them fly away from him and he remains solitary" (WRC 5, 6).

Constructed in a sense out of and on top of the guilt described in "Mirensky," this conception of himself as the daedal helper—or nurse or troubled saint—runs persistently through Goyen's writings from his earliest work through at least the mid-1950s novel *Half a Look of Cain.* For someone who had been silenced as a teenager in his desire for expression and attention, the role of the heroic scapegoat offered an aura of theatricality combined with self-erasure that allowed him to be the center of attention while still seeing himself as an outcast or exile. It was a kind of negative heroism that he found attractive and available in Flaubert's "La légende de St. Julien l'hospitalier," one of the famed *Trois Contes* that Goyen consistently cited as a favorite. Here the titular figure, "someone marked out by God," does penance for an insatiable blood lust. He hunts and kills animals so wantonly that he is cursed by a "great stag" with sixteen antlers and "a white tuft of beard": "One day, savage heart, you will murder your father and your mother!" He does, of course, in an accident that leads to his exile and mendicancy. Eventually, Julien serves humbly as a ferryman and is translated into heaven through the strangely erotic embrace of a leper who turns out to be Jesus in disguise.

Christopher Icarus owes much to Flaubert's story and to Goyen's adoption of the role of the "erotic saintly figure," as he once put it. But the versions of the novel he worked on in New Mexico after the war also show the marked influence of D. H. Lawrence or, more accurately, of Frieda Lawrence filtering both her own and her late husband's ideas. Though Goyen frequently preferred to distance himself from Lawrence the writer, a summary of the manuscript demonstrates how in the years immediately following the war, he eagerly grafted Lawrentian themes and attitudes onto his own self-mythologies. The narrative is set in New Mexico and Oregon, reflecting Goyen's movements in the years immediately following the war. In the village of Caudillo, Dederick Ganchion and his wife Mary live with their son, Christopher. The three are recent transplants from "the prairies of western Texas" where they shared with their extended family "thirty acres of cattle ground called The Acre." The Ganchions—like those of the same name in *The House*

of Breath—are listless and cursed, the brothers and sisters "like fragmentary branches on a tree that had been stunted by the same blow or
scar." Dederick, though the steadiest, has inherited his mother's "cos-
mic fear" and imposes a quiet repression on his wife and son. His symbolic role as the restrictor and restrainer of life is made obvious by his
attitude toward the family's bull, Christian. Despite warnings that the
powerful animal cannot be kept confined in a small corral, Dederick
refuses to release him into the pasture because he is afraid the bull will
damage something: "Dederick kept things locked to hold them from
waste or theft. He wore always a big ring of keys at his waist. He did not
want a thing to go out into the world, to be let go where it would." Allied
with his mother, another sensitive soul trapped by his father's containment, Christopher defiantly releases his animal surrogate and watches
in horror as it kills his father. His mother dies soon after, and Christopher moves to Oregon, where he develops two important relationships.
Emily Johnson is a "frail intense girl who is suffering from an incur-
able blood malady" and who dies soon after their time together ends.
Christopher then befriends Waldo Harrison, a young man who follows
him back to Caudillo but who eventually moves away from Christopher,
both despite and because of the fact that Christopher has created "a
new world" for him.

Although a first step toward *The House of Breath*, this outline is
possibly more important as Goyen's first lengthy attempt at a form of
spiritual autobiography. The correspondences to his early life are easy
to recognize: the portraits of his parents in Dederick and Mary; the relocation of the house in Trinity ("The Place. We called the house 'the
place.'") to "the Acre" in western Texas; the rough equation of Emily
Johnson to the similarly "frail intense" Nell Schedler; and the almost
undisguised appearance of Walter Berns as Waldo Harrison (*GAE* 92).
The Icarus myth allowed Goyen to inhabit the sacrificial, tutorial role
he had claimed for himself, while the oedipal action gave him license
to work out his anger at his father's attempts to contain him. The symbol of the rutting bull, as overt and clumsy as it is, enabled him for the
first time to introduce sexuality as a driving force in his own life and,
along with its accompanying Lawrentian vocabulary, to think toward a
unique and self-justifying fusion of sexuality and spirit. In the synopsis
that introduces the outline and chapter samples, Goyen dares this more
coherent and abstract expression of his personal dilemma:

Is not the tragedy of our modern man that he is afraid to take life because of the suffering it entails, as in Christopher's life; or, because of the labyrinthine, tomb-like structure of his society, he has lost the courage or the will to build himself wings with which to escape into a personal freedom and an abundant life? And has he not lost the sense of the unknown and the unknowable in his life, does not even care; frequently willfully blasphemes it and sins against it? We must return to the mystery in our beings and in the earth. There is a higher reality, a reality-beyond-reality; it lies in legend and symbol and fantasy and mystery, all of which must be penetrated by our lives in the world, like a ray of light through a seemingly solid object. As Christopher says to Waldo: "We must give ourselves up to the land and its mysteries. . . . It is all ritual and legend, man's life. And we cannot find the secret anywhere but in ourselves, by opening ourselves all up, unfolding, then go deeply digging for it; and by living close with the earth, sun and rain and river and field. By not caging and locking up a *spontaneous* thing in ourselves." (WRC 5.6)

That the "spontaneous thing" is a fusion of creativity and sexuality becomes abundantly clear when Christopher extends the oedipal action by sleeping with his mother's sister.[5] Like the escaped and dangerous bull, Christopher's sexuality (and Goyen's guarded homo- or bisexuality) must be released in order for him to emerge as a fully formed human being. By uniting with his aunt/mother, Christopher is declaring an allegiance to the world of his mother's singing, to her penned-in sadness, her identification with birds, and to the need for release and flight that she inspires in him.

"The White Rooster"

Despite the Lawrentian notes in *Christopher Icarus*, it is possible to overestimate the influence of Lawrence on Goyen's work in general. Goyen encountered Frieda Lawrence at a crucial moment in his development, and there is little doubt that in the years immediately following the war, the hand of D. H. Lawrence was heaviest and most evident in the stories he was hoping to publish with the help of Toni Strassman, his first agent.[6] His first real success—and perhaps the most directly Lawrence-structured of all of his short stories—was "The White

Rooster," a tale based to a degree upon the figure of his grandfather, portrayed in *Christopher Icarus* as a man who "had long had pulled out whatever spurs of intrepidity and courage he might have sported in his youth. Like an emasculated cock, he simply went about the Acre without any power. He was a little quiet man who waited on the Acre, unquestioningly, for the fall of doom foreboded by his wife." Grandpa Samuels in "The White Rooster" is similarly trapped, confined to a wheelchair and the rooms of his son's house, but his spirit is less bowed than the elder Ganchion's. He wheels from room to room, gleefully tormenting his daughter-in-law, who sees him primarily as an unacceptable domestic disturbance: "Marcy, as she often told Watson, simply could not stop Grandpa's mouth, could not stop his wheels, could not get him out of her way. And she was busy. If she was hurrying across a room to get some washing in the sink or to get the broom, Grandpa Samuels would make a surprise run out at her from the hall or some door and streak across in front of her, laughing fiendishly and shouting boo!" (*CS* 2).

Grandpa's avatar is the scrawny white rooster who invades Marcy's flower beds, scratches up her pansies, and crows defiantly throughout the day. Like Grandpa, the bird is an outcast, "thin as some sparrow, his white feathers drooping and without luster, his comb of extravagant growth but pale and flaccid, hanging like a wrinkled glove over his eye. It was clear that he had been run from many a yard and that in fleeing he had torn his feathers and so tired himself that whatever he found to eat in random places was not enough to keep any flesh on his carcass" (*CS* 4). The life force continues in both, and when Marcy plots to capture and kill the rooster, it comes as no surprise that Grandpa makes common cause to fight the stifling and unsympathetic domestic order of the housewife. When Watson, Marcy's stolid husband, builds a trap to catch the bird, Grandpa sneaks up behind her, and as she springs the trap from inside the house, he stabs her in the neck with a hunting knife. The rooster escapes, and the old man wheels madly around the house, laughing and destroying everything he can get his hands on. By the time Watson comes home, both Grandpa and Marcy are dead, she still holding the string that sprung the trap, he in his wheelchair, blood bubbling from his throat.

In at least one respect, the story is a kind of revenge fantasy on behalf of Goyen's paternal grandfather. The old man who appears in

Christopher Icarus and *The House of Breath* and who is described more fully in "Old Wildwood" suggests a caged spirit, dominated by his wife and weakened by addiction and desire. Here, though confined to a wheelchair, his put-upon wildness is given one last expression, a triumph denied the club-footed alcoholic who appears in later stories. But if the old "man of timber" provided the template for Grandpa Samuels, the pairing of the almost emasculated man and the similarly diminished bird may have been suggested by the late Lawrence story "The Escaped Cock," a reimagining of the life of Christ after the resurrection.[7] Lawrence's "dandy rooster" is owned by peasants who tie him up out of fear that this particularly virile bird will fly off in search of more hens. When the "man who had died" appears at the peasants' house, he quickly attaches himself to the rooster, attracted to "the short, sharp wave of life of which the bird was the crest."[8] Later he buys the cock and takes it on his journey as a sort of talisman of the newly wakened physical life he struggles to understand.

The pattern of the animal of pure vitality tied or caged by others who wish to control it appears frequently during this period of Goyen's writing. Christian the bull in *Christopher Icarus* seems to have been the first version but was soon seconded by the white rooster, and both are repeated in the better known "roadrunner" for sale in Woolworth's in the 1955 novel, *In a Farther Country*. Given Goyen's fervent intention to free himself from the domination of his family, it isn't surprising that he was drawn to this formula of captivity and release. The essential conception of *Christopher Icarus*—that the title character sacrifices himself so that others can "fly"—may also owe a considerable debt to Lawrence's reborn man, who says to himself, "I tried to compel them to live; so they compelled me to die. It is always so, with compulsion. The recoil kills the advance. Now is my time to be alone."[9] What was unprecedented about "The White Rooster" was that for the first time, the caged figure becomes violent in his opposition to family conformity. Typically, this rebellion had remained passive; as in "The Crimes of Mirensky," for instance, repression had always led to exile and self-sacrifice. But Grandpa Samuels strikes a blow, and the effect is jarring to the comic surface of the story. It is as though the old man is released from the strictures of the domestic short story itself, wrecking the house (and the lightly sketched, stereotypical housewife) with a kind of anarchic joy.

This strange explosiveness, as though erupting through the surface of the fiction itself, was an important development for Goyen. If it suggests, on the one hand, a release of long-suppressed emotion, on the other it signals a dissatisfaction with the tidiness of contemporary fictional accounts of everyday life. In interviews on several occasions, Goyen expressed a dissatisfaction with the modern realistic short story and an abiding interest in the turbulent underside of daily life, its "spiritual deformity": "Since I am *not* writing Zola-istic realism, then everyday reality, the detail of it, is obviously not going to sustain itself for me, forever. I'm not Dreiser, I'm not interested in that at all. I'm aware that there is no everyday trivia in itself; that beneath it, or going on within it, there's always some slight deformity of thought or action. It's the hidden life I'm talking about" (*GAE* 125).

The deformity in the case of "The White Rooster" did not go unnoticed by the editors at *Mademoiselle*, who bought the story in January of 1947 but eventually rewrote it to remove the mayhem. The actual sequence of the editing is somewhat cloudy, but the incident itself is important because it helped confirm Goyen's suspicion of commercial publishing at a time when he was already inclined to see himself as an isolated, uncompromising artist. In a letter to the *Mademoiselle* editor Margarita G. Smith, he agreed to address her argument that both the rooster and Grandpa should survive the story. After its publication, however, he felt the editors had "cut [the story] up so badly" that he convinced Stephen Spender to print the original version in *Horizon* in 1949. The differences between the first and second versions are striking. The *Mademoiselle* text not only completely rewrites the ending to avoid most of the violence but also removes large chunks from the body of the story, often in an attempt to soften the language and regularize Grandpa's character.[10]

Though elated at finally placing a story in a national magazine, Goyen chafed violently at Toni Strassman's advice to make himself more commercial by adapting to the tastes and audiences of the slicks. "If I have to write 'the kind of stories as such-and-such a magazine *requires* or *wants*,' then I'll simply try to make my living by other means," he wrote only a few months after "The White Rooster" had been accepted. "I have little respect for your client who decides not to write what he must and 'slants' towards *Good Housekeeping*. He is a whore; on every page of the *New York Times Literary Supplement* is the story or picture of a literary whore, all the women with three names, all the sickly, craven, slick plots—they are dross, nothing; they amuse, entertain the sloppy and the half-alive. Such is not my mission. . . ."

Four American Portraits

In the early summer of 1948, Goyen was back in Taos after his unsuccessful attempt at teaching junior high school in Napa and a brief but enlivening spring reading scripts in Dallas for Margo Jones.[11] His list of publications was growing. James Laughlin, the publisher of New Directions who had visited Frieda a few months before, accepted "A Parable of Perez" for the New Directions annual; the *Southwest Review* had begun to take a few small prose pieces; and the little magazine *Accent* had agreed to publish sections of his newest project, described to Laughlin as "a collection of pieces on East Texas."[12] The small successes were encouraging, but Goyen was still trying to figure out how to survive on the small amounts of money he could scrape up either from writing or from odd jobs that didn't take too much time or energy. If his "mission," as he put it to Toni Strassman, was to write what he wanted and nothing less, it was also to live in opposition—economically and socially—to a society that he increasingly portrayed as corrupt and spiritually bankrupt.

The biggest challenge yet to this deliberately separatist mode of living came in May in the form of a bitter letter from his mother. The spring issue of *Accent* had been delivered to Merrill Street, and Emma Goyen's reaction to the East Texas pieces, titled "Four American Portraits as Elegy," was swift, cutting, and unambiguous:

> Bill, when we came back your magazine (ACCENT) was here, and Jim looked for it in Dallas so he could not wait of course to read it, and me to [*sic*] as for that, but am sorry to say am really disappointed in your work, and if that is the kind of literature you are going to write, I hope you never succeed (and you won't). I have all ways [*sic*] felt like you will write the highest and most cultured things and the good of the world, and be a help to mankind, instead of the nasty, vile, and sinful part. You know who you want to be like and I do to [*sic*], and have known it, but would not let myself believe it for one moment, but you have proven it now, so I can't be with you in that sort of work. No wonder you did not

ever want to see any of your old friends, I don't blame you, I will never leave Taos if I were you, that is where you belong, where you can live your own morbid selfish life, and you haven't gotten like this alone no, no as I have told you before. You have had plenty of leadership. I have prayed and hoped so long, for you to be what you were intended to be, but as I have told you before, You were not. So my hopes are all gone, for I can see your type of writing now, so I think it best for you to have all your mail and magazines such as *Accent* sent there for I don't want to ever read anything else you write. And far as your adobie [*sic*] melting away, I hope as you put a brick it will fall through, and it will, it may not right now but you can't succeed where you are and what you are, now I am really hurt worse than I have ever been in my life, such hope and confidence in you, I hope I don't live to see you write a book like D.H. has written, and that looks like your type. I hope this hurts you as badly as it hurts me. May God Bless you and help you to see the way you should. This is all for now.

Love

Mom

Now add this to one of your books, it will be wonderful that your Mother has lost hope in her Son.[13]

There is, of course, more here than just anger and embarrassment, though the primary, visceral reaction seems to have come from seeing people she knew, friends and relatives, turned into examples of a fallen, broken-down world. These early versions of the portraits that would fill *The House of Breath* are tied together by a more directly critical, even slightly vengeful attitude that blends uneasily with the loving impulse to remember: "Oh you Charity, Texas! You've done no good to any of these, but they can't forget you if they tried." Those in question are primarily Ganchions and Starneses, the two families brought together by the marriage of Boy Ganchion's (the narrator's) parents but kept apart by deeper differences of character and temperament. The four portraits—of the town itself, Aunty, Folner, and Granny Ganchion— explore not only these tensions but also what were quite clearly embarrassing family failures: ruined marriages, aimless children, and the darker thoughts of mothers whose dreams had never materialized.

But the section devoted to Folner—the overtly gay, cross-dressing uncle who joined a show "with dancing women and lights and spangles" and left Charity only to return in a coffin—may have been the catalyst for Emma's larger condemnation of both the writing and Goyen's life in New Mexico. Folner is equally a tragic figure, burned out by waste and sin, and, in Boy's eyes at least, a beloved and rebellious victim of the town's narrowness and violence. His voice runs closest to the thematic center of the four pieces ("'Nothing is made right around here, Boy,' you said"), and it seems likely that Goyen had put into Folner many of his own thoughts about being trapped in Houston as a teenager: "You wanted tinsel and tinfoil and spangle and roman candle glamour, to be gawdy and bright as a plaster ruby and a dollar diamond. Was that right? Of course not. Wrong? Wrong, wrong. Who has a *choice*, really? All of it was wrong from the beginning, from the corrupted foetus, the poisoned womb, from the galled cradle (endlessly rocking for you and me, for you and me)."[14] It is possible that Emma read this as an explanation or argument on behalf of her son's current living arrangements. Though there is never any mention of his attractions to other men in letters to his mother, exchanges between them often convey the impression that they share an unspoken understanding about his preferences, even if the reality was something she could never face. The portrait of Folner, in addition to reopening a family wound, may have been too close to the surface, an almost brazen attempt on Goyen's part to declare himself. A letter to his old Community Players friend Zoë Léger gives a clearer sense of just what was being said in Houston, whether by his immediate family or just by friends, about the choices he had made after the war: "P.S. To hell with Houston and all its god damned talk. Either I was married to Nell and turned queer or am living in sin with Walt. I'm too busy to worry over it. I have work to do. Let them prattle!"[15]

But he couldn't so easily dismiss this "deep and galling hurt," as he described it to Hart.[16] His response, written the same day he received the letter, is as remarkable for its intensity as for its clear-sighted maturity. He acknowledged his mother's hurt feelings but offered no apology. Instead he set out a careful defense of the right to his own understanding of the world:

> This has been my greatest and most valuable principle so far in my life—to take the responsibility for my choices and for my actions. If I could enlighten others at all, it would be to this end. Too many of us are

cowards in this world; we are afraid to say what we mean, we compromise. Has it occurred to you that what *I* see in life and in people may
not be *at all* what you see? I have the right to my own perceptions, and
I am striving as honestly and as clearly and as unmercifully, when it is
necessary, as I can to put those things down as writing and as art. . . .

I must write as I feel; honestly, I try not to tell lies—I don't believe I
have in these pieces in *Accent.* Underlying all that I have written there I
believe you will find a profound sympathy and love for the people presented there.[17]

He is equally vigorous, if less direct and honest, in defense of his
chosen style of living. Attacking head-on the implication that Berns
had led him into a "morbid selfish life," Goyen accuses his mother of her
own kind of selfishness in demanding that he be "there to give my all
to you."[18] He argues forcefully but deceptively that Berns "never knows
what I am writing" and that *he* has influenced his friend, or tried to, and
not the other way around: "When you blame him you are blaming the
wrong person. Blame me and I can take it and will try to understand;
but when you blame him it is something like a sin and I am sorry for
you." Ultimately, Goyen sets out as clear a statement as he apparently
can of his right to make his own decisions, regardless of what his family
may think:

As for my living with Walter, that is my choice. If I want to go and live
with a bull, that will be my choice and I have the right to do so. I have
committed no crime, I have done nothing evil or sinned against all of
you or society. But I simply won't justify it to any of you again. And as
for my writing, let me tell you that I shall go on putting down what I
believe I must, and God help us all to bear it if it is not nice or sweet or
any of that.[19]

As stirring and legitimate as this defense of his artistic and personal
rights may be, it is nevertheless less honest, or less candid, than it appears. In fact, Goyen was in love with Berns, and though he presented
their friendship as a high-minded comradeship against the corrupting
world, he fervently wished it could be more. Journal entries from 1948
through 1950 make clear not only his deep attachment to his former fel-

low officer but also his sense that the match he imagined was already tainted with its own sense of failure:

Kiowa—July 21, 1948

Is it clear now? That I do him harm—that he is *écarté* by me? That I have flung him into a world whose environment may be in too many ways foreign to him and that he copes so courageously but awkwardly? And I leave him floating, sort of unmoored, except to me, for whom his love is so great that he doesn't really know its scope and intensity—and that if he loses me—by a parting or etc.—he will, indeed, be left dangling or floating. It is in this light that he seems pitiful and we both seem doomed. (*GAE* 152–153)

This same note is struck somberly in the account of the relationship buried in section five of *The House of Breath*, when the narrator/Boy blends his own and Christy's experiences at sea. Goyen and Berns met on board the *Casablanca*, and this stylistically masked version hints at an initiatory sexual encounter as the ship "plowed and plunged through the water": "*Oh he was bright and I was dark and I gave him all my darkness on that ship; but we joined, for all good things in the world, and to find somethin together; and loved, I never knew I could do it and was afraid; and on the bow of the ship that night he said, 'What have we done Christy?'*" (HOB 35). Given that this passage is rendered through Christy's voice as remembered by the narrator, it is perhaps as likely to be a fantasy as it is an account of real events. (To Hart, Goyen had explained that Berns had "stood by my bunk and held my body with his giant's hands when I was pretty goddamned ill and almost out of control. He *stood* there *one* complete night, and I don't know how many other hours of other days and nights. . . . And, my friend, he is no lover (to use the vernacular); he is—have you ever really *known* the definition of this word?—a comrade.")[20] But once the book's voice switches back to the narrator, the story follows the shape of Goyen's postwar years with Berns. The two leave the ship, the crucible of their initial relationship, and while the others on board turn "their backs upon the enchantment as though it had been only [a] joke played upon them . . . we, nameless pieces, pieced ourselves together into each other and went away, off the ship, into a world of magic and witchcraft whirling in the twilight glimmer of hope and hopelessness" (*HOB* 36). They wander from city to desert, worlds of the nameless and lonely, as though searching for the lost isolation and intensity of ship and water. The desert, like Taos, ultimately fails them: "We felt all of bone and rock and metal, we could no longer melt together but stood apart hard as bone and rock. What ruined us? We yearned for water" (*HOB* 37–38). Though the friendship would continue at a distance after the early 1950s, Goyen's hope for something more intimate gradually faded between early 1948 and the end of 1949. In a notebook entry dated December 14, 1950, with the heading "Walter," he wrote: "A homosexual fell in love with a chubby little Naval Officer. They made the mistake of putting two lives together that never could touch anywhere. It's like a man marrying a woman because of her sexual attraction to him, later losing it, yet going on. The incomprehensible thing of it is, to me, *why you go on*" (HRC 20.7).[21]

To Goyen's parents and family in Houston, the source of this emotional torment remained buried—or, at the very least, unacknowledged. The reaction from Merrill Street to the "Four American Portraits as Elegy" was not entirely unexpected, but when it did arrive it confirmed Goyen's personal and artistic direction. He had struck a very significant nerve at the center of the family, and the pain he both dealt and received told him he had found his subject. In a letter to Zoë Léger, he stated his mission clearly: "You've no idea what a stink the 'Portraits' aroused in Houston. . . . Zoë, she [Goyen's mother] was outraged, to say the least; and there came a letter from her last week which I think I never want to read again. She just couldn't take what I said there, and, bless her, I understand why; but it hurts just the same. However, I go on with the work, nothing can stop me, it must be said."[22]

Stephen and Dorothy

In personal terms, the year and a half leading up to the publication of *The House of Breath* was both exhilarating and increasingly complex for Goyen. Perhaps most significant, professionally and personally, in June of 1948 he was introduced by Frieda to the poet Stephen Spender, and, according to Goyen's report to Léger, "we clicked right away. . . . He is a rich, sensitive, shy and charming individual—has been lecturing at Sarah Lawrence College, will probably go to Reed College in Portland where Walt and I are planning to go in September or late August."[23] Spender and his wife, Natasha, were on a tour of the western United States, visiting writers and giving lectures. They stayed briefly at Taos during the midsummer, and then Spender himself, in the company of Leonard Bernstein and his brother, Bertie, came back to the Lawrence ranch to work on essays that would become part of *World Within World.* When Goyen and Berns moved to Portland in September, Spender relocated from Kiowa Ranch to their small adobe house across the highway from Frieda's.

According to Spender's biographer, David Leeming, the impressionable poet "developed one of his many 'crushes' on Goyen," and there is no doubt that the fascination was mutual.[24] Always on the lookout for that one person who could provide both personal and professional validation, Goyen was drawn as much to Spender's status as to his sensibility. "He is very much interested in my writing," he wrote to his parents, "and is trying to help me. He really is quite a famous man in the world and a wonderful human being."[25] To Hart, as always, he was more direct and emotional: "I thank God for him, as you do for Emmons—one waits and waits, trying to save up something, to gather up himself and hold, until finally there comes the Time. It seems here for both of us, and let us be grateful, and responsible."[26] In October Spender lectured at Reed and stayed with Goyen and Berns in the boarding house where they had rented a room so that Berns could take classes at the college. Spender had already invited his new protégé to come to London later in the new year to work on his book, and, according to Goyen, the two were working on a movie script together that they hoped to sell to a London studio.[27] Spender arranged to have "The White Rooster" published in its original form in *Horizon* to accompany an essay of his titled "The Situation of the American Writer," a monitory analysis of commercialism that featured Goyen's *Mademoiselle* experience as primary evidence. And perhaps most important of all, the always politic and well-connected poet wrote to Random House in January to recommend Goyen's novel in progress, already under consideration there; by February, the contract for *The House of Breath* had been signed. It included an advance of $500, half of which Goyen received immediately.

The money was important—crucial, in fact—since Goyen essentially had no regular income during the year in Portland. Though he had planned to teach at Reed—a few former Rice professors now worked there and had recommended him—the enrollment dropped and he was left on his own, a development he considered a blessing in disguise. "I am living by the seat of my pants," he wrote to Zoë Léger, "as always, but no grumbling. I love my work, I live within it like some womb, and in it exists the only reality, for me. Why complain, then, that I can't afford concerts or food I'd like or a new pair of pants, which I need badly, etc.? To regard the lack of these things as sacrifice would be a kind of dishonor to one's work, I believe."[28] Relief came first in the form of a grant from the *Southwest Review*. Its editor, Allen Maxwell, had taken two pieces of the work in progress, and in an effort to support this young Texas writer, he managed to scrape up enough cash to send Goyen a "fellowship" of $300, paid in four monthly installments of $75 each. "It means, probably, that I shall be able to finish my book," he wrote his parents, "and thank the Lord for that."[29]

At the end of the academic year, Spender was back in Portland for another visit, though by this point Goyen had added even more complexity to his personal life: he had begun to date a young woman and recent Reed student named Dorothy Robinson. The relationship may have been a response to the fact that Berns seemed to be getting serious about his girlfriend at the time, but whatever the motivation, Goyen moved quickly toward the idea of marriage. In early June he wrote to his parents that he "was very seriously in love," had discussed marriage with Dorothy, and they were making plans for her to visit Taos in the summer. To Dorothy Brett he described her as "ravishing": "I suppose I'm sunk, it's so crazy for me who never planned on this sort of thing lasting so long. . . . This gal has so much damned sense, you'd love her because she refuses to dress like the fluffy college girls . . . a wild-spirited, untamed nymph of a lovely dark creature. I wonder if she's too full of beans for me."[30] At the same time, Spender had repeated his invitation for Goyen to come to London in the fall, and plans were quickly made to travel to Europe with Dorothy Robinson and Berns, who had been accepted into the London School of Economics.[31] The nervous mix of willed poverty and an impossibly tangled romantic life activated Goyen's perennial migraines, for which he began taking "expensive injections."[32] Once again he understood his condition as a product of the tension between sense and spirit: "We free ourselves of certain fears and regrets," he wrote to Brett, "that have previously bound us to ourselves as we go along—in fact growth seems a perpetual kind of bondage and freedom; and I know that for me the only kind of liberation is through my work. . . . The great troublemaker is one's senses, with which [the artist] really works and through which he perceives, even has visions; yet those senses which can direct him into greater and deeper and more productive spirituality can, too, confuse him and torture him and even ruin him if he is not careful of what he is trying to do with himself."[33]

The five months in London and Europe were exhilarating, although in the end, the personal toll of Goyen's conflicting attachments would leave him in a fragile state—and more isolated than ever. Most important, he was able to finish *The House of Breath* by the middle of November. "The Spenders have given me a large cozy room in which to work," he wrote to his father in October, "and I have hundreds of books and a large desk."[34] But his need for absolute isolation and silence while writing caused problems for the family, who began to find him "outrageous" and demanding. (It was also likely that Natasha Spender understood all too well her husband's attraction to the young Texan she once described as "a man-eating orchid.")[35] So in early November he rented a work room on the third floor of a nearby house, where Spender himself also maintained an office, and was able to finish the manuscript there. When he wasn't working, there were people to meet—such as Edith Sitwell, whom he found "enchanting, terrifying, and exquisite; poisonous, absurd, and splendid"—and sites to see.[36] The Elgin Marbles drew him repeatedly, as he explained to Bill Hart, and became a sort of stylistic analog: "I have been often to look at the beautiful beautiful Elgin Marbles here in the British Museum; and I cannot tell you what an influence these ancient, worn and somehow sorrowful figures of stone have had on me. . . . These friezes and metopes have taught me so much about writing, about language. The kind of language I should like to find and use would be a frieze of words."[37]

But as the work went well, his personal attachments suffered proportionally. The relationship with Dorothy seems to have come apart fairly quickly. This failure may have been connected to a difficult trip to Paris at the start of October, during which she became seriously ill with a kidney infection. Despite a pleasant afternoon with Sylvia Beach at Shakespeare and Company, and an intoxicating drive past Versailles to Chartres, the ordeal soured Goyen on the city, which he found overly stimulating and emotionally frustrating. But there are also suggestions, hinted at by Goyen himself, that his interaction with the Spenders and their friends drove the couple apart: "At 4:00 tea-time in the winter it was dark, and they pulled Florentine-brocaded curtains and turned on lights; it was a time of austerity still, but people came to tea. Veronica Wedgewood would arrive. Dorothy wouldn't come up from the basement. She really hated this kind of thing. She vanished. She just wouldn't participate. So I was really quite alone with this. I guess I must have kept her under wraps. I must have been very bad to her" (*GAE* 84). What goes unsaid here, of course, is that Goyen and Spender were engaging in an only marginally disguised relationship and that Dorothy may well have been used, consciously or not, as cover for his proximity to Stephen. By mid-autumn, Dorothy had moved on to the Sorbonne and essentially dropped out of Goyen's immediate plans, which now included a trip to Italy over the Christmas holidays. According to the itinerary described to his mother, he would take a train to Geneva with Spender to attend "a European Cultural Conference as an observer from America." *Partisan Review*, for which he would write an article on the conference, was paying his costs as far as Geneva, and with his own money, he would travel on alone to Rome, Venice, and Florence.[38]

The trip to Italy, though short, had a significant impact. Rome, in particular, "got into [his] blood," as he explained to his Taos friend Spud Johnson: "[N]othing can match the sensuousness, the undercurrent of pure sensuality mixed with a haughtiness, a mysteriousness that exists in the worlds of Rome."[39] One goal of the trip was to meet Samuel Barber, who had written to express his interest in writing a "chorus for symphony orchestra" to a text by Goyen.[40] Goyen also stopped in at the American Academy to explore the possibility of a fellowship and, like many writers of the period, visited the gloomy palazzo of Princess Caetani, née Marguerite Chapin, the American expatriate who edited the little magazine *Botteghe Oscure* and who would later publish one of his stories. He loved the "haunting, serene, worn quality" of the city, even after he fell down the famed Spanish Steps and seriously injured his right knee. "I tore loose the cartilage," he told Johnson, "and now nothing but an operation will mend it—I can scarcely walk and then only by going stiff-legged."[41] Hobbled, he nevertheless made his way to Venice and Florence before returning to London, via Geneva, at the beginning of the new year.

The remainder of Goyen's time in England was absorbed by the surgery on his knee and the need for rehabilitation. With the Spenders now fed up with their demanding visitor, he depended on Berns and Dorothy, back from Paris, to get him to St. Albans Hospital, an hour outside of London, and then into a bedsit near St. Bartholomew Hospital, where he went daily for physical therapy. These emotionally complex and turbulent weeks during which three important relationships were coming apart became the basis for part of his second novel, *Half a Look of Cain*. Some of the tension is captured in the early scenes in which the two friends, a man and a woman, visit the patient, again named Chris, after his surgery:

> But when Chris came to, for those several minutes, the two were suddenly standing by his side as though the quarrel had meant nothing, and I saw Chris look at the young man and young woman with half a look of hatred and half a look of love and then pass on away into his death of sleep. There was something between these three. The friends had brought, this time, the few personal effects of Chris's and I took them for him. In a few minutes, they left. They did not ever appear again. They had delivered him here, to me, it seemed, and had vanished, leaving his few possessions with me. (*HLC* 21)

The decision to set this very personal investigation in the context of the crowded British hospital may have been a response to Goyen's heightened emotions as a patient in the ward. In considerable pain from the operation and sore from lying in the same position for long periods, he nevertheless got to know many of the other patients, including a teenage boy who had been hit by a car while selling newspapers. "He is 16 and a wonderful, long-suffering chap," he wrote to his parents; "never complains, was such a comfort to me."[42] But the noise of other patients frayed his nerves, and he began to feel he was suffering through other patients' operations as deeply as his own.

Once his rehabilitation was over, Goyen sailed to New York on March 2, with Dorothy. According to his *Paris Review* account, Robert Linscott, his editor at Random House, met them shortly after they landed and told her not to marry him: "'I feed him and Random House has kept him alive and probably will have to from now on. Don't marry him; don't even fall in love' . . . and he broke her heart. He really did. Poor Dorothy. He was right; I wasn't about to be saddled down" (*GAE* 86). This version of events may contain some truth, but it disguises the fact that the trouble between the couple included more than the threat of poverty, as Linscott must have known. As he had with Nell Schedler, Goyen approached the idea of marriage when he needed to or when circumstances pushed him in that direction, but he always seemed able to pull away when the reality came too close. Events in London and Paris had undermined whatever trust he had established with Dorothy, and his own behavior, both overt and covert, had contributed significantly, if not predominately, to the breakup. The adventure, if it was ever really serious, was over. Only weeks before, as Goyen was preparing to leave England, Spender, too, had parted with him. Though there are some signs of a rekindling in the years that followed, by the end of Goyen's time in England Spender had lost interest in the younger American. Years later, in a journal entry, Goyen recorded the awkward, painful ending: "On the tender ground, the scene between Stephen and me, 'My stop is coming. Please, Bill, please forgive me, please, Bill.' No. His stop came. St. John's Wood. He vanished. The train went on" (HRC 20.7).

CHAPTER SEVEN

The House of Breath

1950

I know, I am sure that my whole life is bound up with the legends of Icarus and Glaucus, and I find myself telling about them in everything I write.

LETTER TO KATHERINE ANNE PORTER, AUGUST 4, 1951

As Reginald Gibbons has noted, *The House of Breath* is an unusual first novel. Typical, in a sense, in its subject matter, it is atypical in its technical sophistication and formal daring. Goyen was thirty-five when the book appeared in 1950. His long, frustratingly delayed apprenticeship had finally ended. The book he had in one way or another been obsessively writing and rewriting, the story he had tried to tell in short fiction and student plays, in fragments written during the war and after, had finally found its form. By turning his attention to Trinity, to the absent place of origin and the geography of his mother's sadness, he could at last say something substantive about his own losses and secrets.

The book begins with a voice emerging in midsentence, as though the reader has stumbled upon a story being told by an anguished, almost fevered narrator. His loneliness drives him to memory, and in his isolation he begins to reconstruct the family of his past. These aunts, uncles, and cousins emerge as fragmented voices, sounds in his head that lead him imaginatively to the house that once held them. Here he momentarily restores them as fragile tissues of memory and begins the labor of reconstructing both the geography and the spoken reality of his history. "And to find out what we are," he declares, "we must enter back into the ideas and the dreams of worlds that bore and dreamt us

and there find, waiting within worn mouths, the speech that is ours"
(*HOB* 10).

And speech is indeed what he finds, speech that he both makes and
grants to the place itself as well as to those who once lived there. After
a ritual passage through the town, we are taken first to the river, the
source of natural power, fertility, and sexuality, later ruined by the oil
boom and industrial greed. The roaming speaker loads the little "taffeta
ruffle" of remembered waters with story and symbol, and soon enough
the river is talking, *telling* with the same urgency with which all the
voices in the book repeat their memories:

> Once, when you were swimming, naked, it happened for the first time
> to you in me. Christy stood on the bank and told you and Berryben to
> jump in and touch my bottom and see who could come up to the top
> first; and you were struggling to come up first, rising rising rising, faster,
> faster, when some marvelous thing that can happen to all of us hap-
> pened to you, wound up and burst and hurt you, hurt you and you came
> up, changed, last to the top trembling and exhausted and sat down by
> my banks in a spell; and had lost. (Christy knew, and tried to make you
> jump into me again.) (*HOB* 29)

This initiatory moment, retold by the river, is drawn directly from
Goyen's experience. As he explained to Rolande Ballorain in 1979, when
he was eleven years old in a school swimming class he experienced his
first orgasm: "It was the greatest mystery that haunted me for some
long time—a year or so—several years, and I didn't know what that was,
so that water—I was afraid."[1] That the river shares this secret reinforces
the combination of fear, guilt, and sexual mystery that emanates from
the story of his mother's near drowning. It also clearly demonstrates
Goyen's method of carefully weaving his own primary psychological
events into his complicated reconstruction of others' voices. The river is
here speaking to Boy Ganchion, a character connected to the narrator—
perhaps his earlier self—but also one of Goyen's several interconnected
and partial alter egos in the book. Perhaps in response to his mother's
intensely negative reaction to the pieces published in *Accent*, he had
significantly complicated the autobiographical presence by the time
he finished *The House of Breath*. The narrator, Boy, and Berryben Ganchion are all at least partial versions of his sensibility and share ele-

ments of his experience. And the fluidity of their interconnections, the sense that they are all versions of one another, allows, as David Cowart has argued, a "virtual anonymity" for the narrator who "paradoxically reveals himself to the reader without ever coming fully into focus."[2] As a consequence, the primary voice and remembering consciousness is both everywhere and nowhere, both distinct from the various voices in the book and the focal point, the ventriloquist whose mood colors all the book's revelations.

What elicits these voices is the recovery of the house itself, "fallen," abandoned by the younger generation and now a kind of shadowy stage where the narrator both speaks and hears the absent. Aunty is first, Lauralee Starnes, defined by the struggle with her wild and wandering daughter, Sue Emma or Swimma, whose story quickly follows, "told" or echoed by the empty well that returns the narrator's summoning cry. Swimma's story is essentially tragic, the familiar tale of a young woman predisposed to discontent, hungry for money and fame, disdainful of small-town parochialism. She leaves, becomes a stage star, has a series of failed marriages and malformed offspring, and ends up "sick and broke" in Houston. Like many of the characters, she seems cursed by her own unquenchable desires; she, Berryben, Folner, and, for a time at least, Christy, are the driven and restless children of mothers who mourn their leaving and wait for them to return. And it is the competing emotions of these two groups—one longing for the past and the return of their children, the other determined to escape the dying town at all costs—that structure the narrator's internal struggle.

Berryben in particular, as Goyen admitted in interviews, carries the weight of much of his own need, in adolescence and beyond, to define himself in opposition to the world of his parents. Berryben's mother, Malley, begins this section, conjured by the sound of the wind and capturing the fearful mourning of Emma Goyen and her emotional dependence on her son: "'Everthing that used to be in East Texas is ruined, there's a terrible change in the world; and I set here left behind in this old house by all my kin and by my dead husband Walter Warren Starnes and my dead daughter Jessy, and my wanderin son Berryben who's gone away through the world and will never come back to me'" (*HOB* 79). Described as her "salvation," Berryben is pitted dramatically against a hardened father, whom she blames for driving her son away. At particular moments her voice seems the direct product of Goyen's desire to speak to his own mother—particularly in the wake of her condemning letter—of things that were difficult or impossible to say. First, he gives her the questions he wishes to answer:

> "What was there that made you different from us all? A mother's got a right to understand her own son even though the whole rest of the world don't or cain't. . . . What was it made you different? Was it your father that wouldn't let you play the piano or be anything that hounded and scaired you? . . . You seemed like a little scaired animal of some kind. Somethin somewhere had shaken you up, scaired you so that nobody could ever hold you still. You trembled. . . . I knew you wanted somethin that we all didn't know about; and you kept it secret from me and would never let me know. That you wanted to go out after somethin in the world—somethin that your father never found but maybe grieved for." (*HOB* 97)

And then she provides the justification, first from the wind-fed voice of Berryben's dead sister, Jessy, who tells her mother to let Berryben "'go around or if he's hiding, let him hide. He's trying to dive deep down for something to bring up for us all to see and to save us by. I hope we can bear to face it when he brings it up. . . . But he'll redeem us all, in the end. I know he will. He only wants us all to wait and we will finally understand'" (*HOB* 92, 94). And then from Berryben himself, who provides the closest thing to a confession that Goyen had yet put into print:

> "I tricked you all to get away, but I couldn't tell the truth about the things that claimed me. Because you always said these things were sins. I always had that terrible guilt before you, had to tell lies and lies—*you really made me evil*, you made me be just what you were afraid I'd be. I served you all and let you all use me any way you wanted; anything you wanted me to be I was." (*HOB* 102)

The "things that claimed" him, as the book's larger concerns make clear, were sexual, though not exclusively so. Sexuality is a palpable presence in *The House of Breath*, but the claim it makes on its characters, particularly on Boy and Berryben, involves more than just a willful libertinism at odds with local mores. It is imagined and understood as a kind of identifying mark—sometimes a curse, sometimes a blessing—

that sets the self apart, creating a sense of burden and the need for ful-fillment, if at all possible, *elsewhere*. The condition of exile is in this respect a function of sexuality, but once created, this isolation can-not be limited to the specific calculus of sexual identity; the disloca-tion outstrips the cause, attaining a spiritual dimension far more per-vasive than any physicality. For Goyen, the emotional state produced by exile found an analog in the myth of Glaucus, the fisherman who eats the magic grass and is turned into a sea creature. Glaucus is doomed to be apart from those he loves, to be fundamentally separated as a being of another nature. His fulfillment as a person is possible only in water, the medium that Goyen always associated with the body's deep-est demands. The world Glaucus craves, however, is landed, and the unbridgeable gap becomes the source of a resentment that leads, in Goyen's version of the myth, to the glorification of self-sacrifice. Glau-cus, in other words, becomes Icarus, as Goyen understood these figures; the isolated lover takes on the role of self-destroying idealist, able to help others only through his own destruction. *Christopher Icarus*—not to mention several works that conflate Christ figures with nurses or caretakers—relies heavily on this thematic framework. In *The House of Breath*, its symbolic language is vital to those characters, like Berryben, who are closest to Goyen himself.

For the Ganchions in general, however, sexuality is more curse than path to liberation, and the older generations of uncles and grandpar-ents stand as a kind of warning, though often fraught with temptation, of the destructive power of lust. The taproot for this darkly sketched family tree is Granny Ganchion, the goitered fairy-tale crone who con-fers in her damp cellar with a spectral worm called Ole Fuzz. Based in part on Goyen's paternal grandmother, whose father was a Swedish sea captain, and overlayered with traces of Frieda Lawrence, Granny is both victim and agent of the family's sinful bent.[3] The worm, inspired by a legend Frieda told Goyen about the mythical German *Tatzelwurm*, speaks through the narrator's imagination with a cynical, darkly tinged voice, revealing secrets that Granny prefers to hide and urging her to tell her own story. Like Molly Bloom and Addie Bundren, Granny tells her sexual history, from her first experience with Vester Langley in Hare's orchard to her marriages to Jeff Cranberry ("shot in the buggy with me settin by him") and Gentry Ganchion: "Then nothin but sawmills forever after, I married sawdust" (*HOB* 141). Gentry, like the crooked-footed old man in "Old Wildwood," is satyr-like, a wanderer who leaves his wife's bed to seek out prostitutes and local black women and who is eventually driven off to die alone in a convalescent home in St. Louis. The old sawmill man seems destroyed by his desires just as his two sons, Christy and Follie, are variously consumed by needs and drives they can hardly understand, much less control. The entire family is defined by the sinister presence of Ole Fuzz, the traditional sign of fleshly decay and sin: "Ole Fuzz, you and I have loved this souring fruit—your scales are Follie's spangles, your warts are my goiter, wens, chancres and shale cover your body. Sometimes I believe you breathed out this house from your dragon nostrils. Sometimes I think *you* are the worm in that fruit, that *you* are the caterpillar in the leaf" (*HOB* 144).

Next to Boy and Berryben, the characters closest to and most important to Goyen in *The House of Breath* are Folner and Christy, the uncles who each in separate ways define the dangers and the possibilities of excessive desire in a ruined world. As he was in the "Four American Portraits as Elegy," Folner is mourned as a tragic figure, an openly gay man consumed by his attraction to the "beautiful evil world." He is both "Beast and Prince," or, perhaps more directly, both an inspiring example of self-declaration and a cautionary figure. On the one hand, he serves as a warning that the world won't allow such flamboyance to go unpunished: "He went all the way. He knew what he was and endured it all the way, to the bitter bitter end, burned down to ash by it, charred down to clinker"; on the other, the narrator praises this authenticity, imagining Folner as a lover: "I embrace him now, against this wall in the rain" (*HOB* 113). There is little doubt that Folner is the embodiment of Goyen's own attraction to the theatre, to the idea of a dramatic display of the self's kept secrets. His trunks, "filled with rhinestones and spangles and boa feathers and holding the wicked smell of greasepaint," recall Goyen's account in "Margo" of his own teenage rebellion with alcohol and stage makeup and lend support to Don Gerrard's memory that Goyen had said "all he wanted to do when he was young was dress in women's clothes."[4] But Folner is also a sign of the limit of Goyen's ability to speak of his own inner life, of the need to declare sympathy, and of the fear of full identification with the "doll-in-the-rain face" of Follie. At the funeral that frames his survey of Folner's life, the narrator secretly drops a "little purple spangle stolen from a gypsy costume" into

Folner's coffin, a gesture of solidarity but still a hidden, shared secret. And Folner, too, like Christopher Icarus and the Daedalus of *Section Two*, is a sacrifice, a redemptive loss, even if the meaning of that redemption is clear only to those who can see or feel it: "There seemed to be some misery over in the world. Some atonement, some ransom was paid for all of us, for all our Sins. Now, in due time and in right season, what resurrection of what spirit would assure us of the meaning of this death, Folner?" (*HOB* 122).

Folner, of course, is also called Follie, and he is both the town's and his own theatrical fool. Christy, on the other hand, combines sexuality and violence, desire and loss in a way that makes him the more complete and ambiguous model for the narrator/Boy. Instead of his brother's florid self-destruction, Christy embodies the loneliness and mystery of a larger desire that takes in sexuality but exceeds it. It is his experience of being lost and isolated that melds with the narrator's to form the opening of the novel, the detached figure wandering in the rain, searching the hellish park for signs of human contact. In a sense, Christy is desire itself, dark and unreadable, an unnamable want that broods silently on the map of the world:

> Christy often sat at night (and I sometimes with him) and looked and looked at the map, almost as if he were talking to the world and adoring the world and taking each part of it into himself as he looked. . . . Here, tacked on this wall in the kitchen of the house you held, Charity, was the world's body showing all the life in it; and all the life was in Christy and me—and our skulls became lighted globes of the world, that the map had stamped there, which each of us held in his hands, turning it round to find the worlds that each of us had given to the other. (*HOB* 18, 20)

This melding of identities—a blending that is also a warning and threat to Boy—is particularly crucial in the book's most significant episode, a long sequence in which Christy takes Boy hunting. The narrator prefaces this initiatory, deep-woods journey with two mythological moments, each an indicator of Boy's gradual fall into knowledge. In the first, he is accidentally wounded by Christy's axe: "Because I came too close to him once he came down on my thigh with his axe—so gently that he only cut a purple line under the skin and no blood came" (*HOB* 152). The wound leaves a "secret scar," a sign that suggests both a sexual stain and a circumcision-like mark of identity. In the second, Boy observes from a hidden place the bodily and sexual reality of Christy, his archetypal masculinity, and understands what he sees as a license for his own future as a fully realized, fully sexualized individual:

> There, in the garden, I, like an Eve, found him leaf-shadowed (and, like Eve, leaf would forever after make me stop to remember). There he lay, among vines now, so beautiful in his naked sleep, and so stilled (I thought)—a hot liquid summer night filling the world with the odor of greengrowing and moonlight—greengolden under the light he had fallen asleep with still on, little cupids of gnats wafting round him. . . . Shells open at their tide and moon on shores where only moon sees and tide knows: I am something old and mysterious and wise as moon and tide; for I have seen; and I will never tell but *be* what I see here, in my time. (*HOB* 154–155)

The homoeroticism of the watcher is less a function of desire than of identification: Boy sees *himself* in Christy, the mature version of what he will become, defined by his desire and determined to reanimate the world by the release of his natural sensuality.

Seeing a fully flowered sexual self is an experience not without its note of foreboding, however. For Boy, Christy is a dark and dangerous figure, the embodiment of isolated desire, need turned to violence. He is a killer as well as the bringer of life, and in an episode clearly inspired by Flaubert's "St. Julien," Christy moves through the woods destroying whatever comes within sight. Boy follows, hypnotized, sure that his strange and violent uncle will tell him "some terrible secret." In the heart of the woods that look across the fabled river, Christy then gives him the dead birds: "He said to me fly away from here—I give you these bird's wings to fly away with from here where we are all just the sawed-off ends of old tubafours rottin on a sawdust heap; fly up and away, across the river past Riverside and on away. And what brings you down will be what gave you wings to fly up and away, will be what needs to use you to speak with; be bird, be word" (*HOB* 160). Having established the fallenness of a broken world, Goyen gives us the heart of his redemptive mission. Christy's initiation, the ritual slaughter, becomes a kind of double-edged blessing, naming and charging the poet-exile with the paradoxical duty of escape and salvation. Granted wings, Boy must leave in order to become himself, and that becoming—or so the logic of *Christopher Icarus* and *Section Two* would have it—will save the fallen world through speech and memory. The river is the site of crossing, leaving; and language is born through death and violence and the power of unfulfilled desire.

The profoundly personal nature of this christening becomes clearer once we realize that Christy's blessing is followed by his recitation of Goyen's primal family story—the recasting of his mother's near drowning as the death of Christy's wife, Otey. Christy is called to dive for her missing body, and when he finds her "sittin bent over with her head on her knees in some sorrow" (*HOB* 169) he carries her upward, a long surfacing that recalls Boy's wounding orgasm:

> "As we rose up together all our life that we never had together happened within me—Otey cookin and singin in our warm winter kitchen and me choppin wood in the mornins. As we floated up through watery vines and ferns and slippery roots through scales and petals of sunlit water, layers breakin open over us as we broke through them like thin leaves of silver, I remembered that a hand does let down to you if you get lonesome, that a big broken birdbloodied hand does reach down to you, wet and alone and so lonesome; and that you are washed clean by the touch of this hand." (*HOB* 170)

The saving of the dead becomes a kind of self-saving or, at the very least, a way to give value to the losses that define us. Christy becomes the symbolic agent of Boy's salvation or rebirth. The blood of the birds is given back to the river ("They went down, a flotilla of feathers, like a floating garden, like a wreath to the river drowned, for Otey, for Christy, for all of us" [*HOB* 176]), and Boy is given both the freedom and the burden to speak from the place of exile: "Who am I, separated from all of them and from home, yet with the idea of them and the idea of home in my mind, claimed and cursed by these, blessed and marked, sent somewhere?" (*HOB* 180).

"A frieze of words"

The achievement of *The House of Breath* rests on its fusing of narrative and lyric poetics with the heightened speech of contemporary drama. Each voice is more than just a character talking; it is the manifestation of a formalized interior singing, a turning outward of an innermost self through an occasion and a mode of expression that is entirely and intentionally unrealistic. This lyricism is not unprecedented in the modernist novel, but Goyen's way of staging it and fusing it with narrative urgency created a unique fictional form, a static tableau that both acknowledges and resists the passage of time. His comment to Bill Hart about the Elgin Marbles bears repeating: "The kind of language I should like to find and use would be a frieze of words."

In part, this preference seems to have been a response to his own limitations elevated to the status of method. As he told Robert Phillips, *The House of Breath* came to him "in pieces"; "So, I thought of it as fragments . . . that was what established its form" (*GAE* 96). The pieces are written individually, at times ecstatically, and only later is the "design," as Goyen phrased it, worked out. "I generally make the parts the way you make those individual medallions that go into quilts. All separate and as perfect as I can make them, but knowing that my quilt becomes a whole when I have finished the parts. . . . The problem, then, is to graft the living pieces to one another so that they finally become a living whole" (*GAE* 97–98). Though this response to fragmentation came in part from his interest in modernist works like Ezra Pound's *Cantos* ("He made, above all, songs, and he told his stories lyrically, as I have felt driven to tell mine"), it is the combination of song and its spatial arrangement—the blending of "aria" into "quilt"—that distinguishes *The House of Breath* from other twentieth-century experiments. Goyen's voices are *set*, frozen in a sense, telling stories but not actually advancing a narrative. The point is not to move forward in time but to stand listening before a porch-like stage, to replicate a child's captive hearing of his elders' tales, plaints, and worries.

Style reinforces this sense of stopped motion, and Goyen's time in London seems to have opened him to possibilities with language that his earlier work had but dimly sensed. Unlike many other modernists, he had no interest in the reduction of language to hard surfaces. He seems instead to have intuited in the Elgin Marbles a kind of elaborate stillness, a quality he translated into sentences designed to hold his extravagant emotions in place. Repetitive, incantatory, his language risked obscurity in order to capture filigrees of feeling:

> Led by this hand you go to the well, made of stone and minaretted by a slender windlass where the rusty and battered bucket hangs like a ruined bell on a rotted and raveled rope in its tower. If I should cry down some name in this well, you think, what voice would rouse and speak out of the well to me? You cry down the name of Sue Emma Starnes, calling "Swimma-a-a! Swimma-a-a!" (come in 'fore dark) and you hear the round wavering answer, like a voice heard under water, "And all the daughters of musick shall be brought low. . . ." (*HOB* 57)

Alliterative pairings bind this linguistic world together ("battered bucket," "rotted and raveled"), aided by the ritualistic habit of repetition: "in this well" and "out of the well"; "If I should cry down" and "you cry down this name." There are off and near rhymes: "slender windlass"; "cry down" caught up by "you hear the round." And there are layerings of time: Swimma is called in both the present and the past, her life measured locally and in the distant vision of Ecclesiastes. And all of this is in one brief, though not unusual, paragraph. The texture throughout the book is similarly dense, thickened by a desire to charge each page as fully as possible with meaning. This "novel," then, often feels like a long poem, pushing oral narrative toward stillness, historical time toward song.

As a consequence, there is nothing else quite like *The House of Breath* in the history of the American novel. In fact, it may make more sense to look for its generic counterparts not in the midcentury fiction but in long modernist poems like William Carlos Williams's *Paterson* or Charles Olson's *Maximus Poems*. The grounding in a specific American geography, the layering of time in a language of density, the intertwining of narrative and lyric modes—*The House of Breath* relies upon these essential elements as fully as any other twentieth-century, experimental epic. Only its emotional rawness, its willingness to lay bare feelings and push language in pursuit of the most delicate tremors of emotion, set it apart from the modernist tendency in fiction toward stylistic and emotional "hardness." Goyen's novel asked of the reader in 1950 not only the slow attention to language normally expected of poetry but also a willingness to face emotions directly, without irony or shield. In retrospect, it may have been too much to expect from the literary establishment of the time, particularly when the book was offered by a mainstream publisher like Random House.

And yet there is no doubt that *The House of Breath* was a success, artistically if not commercially. Some of the initial responses to the novel complained of its unrelenting intensity and singularity of tone. The reviewer for the *Atlantic Monthly* deemed it "an ambitiously experimental book" but one "deficient in coherence and cohesion," too dependent on "linguistic pyrotechnics." A brief notice in the *Times Literary Supplement* found it "impossible not to admire the delicacy of observation, the sharpness of language, and the freshness of vision" but concluded that "the consistently poetic use of language finally defeats its own purpose." And the "Briefly Noted" section of *The New Yorker* complained dryly that all the characters speak "in the same minor key, so that the effect, while undeniably melancholy, is monotonous and also suspicious, as it is bound to be when one note is held too long."[5] But for those readers willing to accept the book's complex structure, charged language, and allergy to conventional plot development, the compensations more than repaid the energies required. As Ruth Chapin noted in *The Christian Science Monitor*, "*The House of Breath* is not an easy book to read," yet "to the careful reader" the "dense allusiveness" of the "poetry" and the "revelation of character" are "cumulative and overwhelming." In a similar vein, though with even more openness to Goyen's way of reimagining his form, Roger Shattuck claimed that Goyen had created "a new sense of *homesickness*" and a new protogenre: "I suppose that in the looseness of our speech, *The House of Breath* is a novel. However it comes closer to being an elaborate preparation for a novel, a *genre* this side of fiction in which reside qualities the novel can claim only tenuously. Action is dislocated by the constant burst of memory; event occurs, hovers in the mind, is fondled, and never fully disappears into a stream of narrative." He concluded by arguing that, along with Peter Taylor, whose *A Woman of Means* was published the same year, Goyen had placed himself "among the most accomplished young fiction writers in the country today."[6] A similar conclusion came from Edwin Muir in the *Observer*: "This is a book which everyone interested in what is new in literature should read."[7]

In some general periodicals and newspapers, reviewers found cause to complain of the book's subject matter. In a manifestly homopho-bic article in *The Saturday Review*, Oliver La Farge designated Goyen as a member of a "morbid" school of homosexual fiction, in which "mandarin and gothic writing" blends with horror and "repulsive-ness." Though La Farge offered an arguable objection to what he sees as Goyen's "false reaching for poetic effects," he seems mostly put out that "bi-sexual matings are recorded merely as historical fact."[8] In gen-eral, critics outside New York tended to find the book either baffling or disturbing, the exceptions coming, perhaps not unexpectedly, from those in Texas. In the *Houston Chronicle*, Charles E. White deemed *The House of Breath* "an important book . . . the most important, perhaps, to come from the pen of a Texan." Though he recognized that readers might disagree over whether it is a "good book," White argued strongly that it contained "some of the finest writing seen anywhere."[9] And from Lon Tinkle, a friend of Margo Jones's whom Goyen had met a few years before, came this ecstatic praise: "The sort of 'reality' in this book is a deeper reality than we are usually served. With it, one may salute the presence, though not of course for the first time, in Texas letters of the artist, the poet, as such. . . . William Goyen, who wrote his novel with the help of a fellowship from the *Southwest Review*, is a new stripe in this type of excellence: the pure artist."[10]

But the most significant review—and in one respect the most genuinely sympathetic reading—of *The House of Breath* came from Katherine Anne Porter in the August 20 edition of the *New York Times*. Considering the book as a postwar product along with Francois Boyer's *The Secret Game*, Porter called it "not a novel at all but a sustained evo-cation of the past, a long search for place and identity." From her own perspective as a writer-exile from Texas, she understood Goyen's depic-tion of the "jealous exclusiveness in family love" and the combination of ambition and guilt that haunts those who seek to escape it: "Now and again up from the mould one child will rise and go, and seek to become, feeling himself a Judas and a deserter, never to be forgiven, never to es-cape from the bitter love and reproach of those he left." And though she recognized the risks involved in Goyen's "extravagant" style, she considered it a fitting representation of childhood's "exorbitant experi-ence." Her final paragraph sets aside her objections: "To balance this fault [the risk of "over-saying"], the writing as a whole is disciplined on a high plane, and there are long passages of the best writing, the fullest and richest and most expressive, that I have read in a very long time—complex in form, and beautifully organized, shapely as a good tree, as alive and as substantial."[11]

With the largely positive reception of his first major work, Goyen had at last found the kind of recognition he had so long and desperately craved. Though the reaction of his family in Houston remained muted with disapproval and embarrassment, he had achieved a degree of fame, both local and national. Rewards quickly followed: the Texas Institute of Letters named *The House of Breath* the best first novel by a Texas writer for 1950. Within the next few years he would win a Guggenheim Fellowship and an invitation to Yaddo, the artist's retreat in upstate New York. Distinguished translators—Maurice Edgar Coindreau and Ernst Robert Curtius, whom Goyen had met in Taos in 1949—soon began work on French and German versions of the novel, and, for a time at least, it seemed that all of New York was at his feet.[12] As he wrote to Bill Hart, clearly both bragging and taken aback, he felt like Lucien Chardon in Balzac's *Lost Illusions*:

> Last week one night I walked down Park Avenue toward the apartment of one Alice Astor, where I was invited to dinner, with the voices of Granny and Malley and of Christy, of my room and my lonely haunted youth in it, calling in my brain; and I thought Oh New York City, you are my oyster, they are wineing [sic] and dining me because they hear I have written down a book that might be something. And with my hair perfectly combed, and untouchable, I went shyly in to meet Miz Astor and shook her hand of diamonds and rubies.

It was an opulence and a success hungrily sought and yet distrusted with near hostility, at odds with the tragic cast of the book that still haunted his steps: "Yet that life on those pages is my truth and my doom and it is after me, I can hear it following me down the streets of New York City—and one day it's going to catch me and take me back again, and then I'll be sick and sallow and gray, abusing myself, passed by, like Christy, on the streets, face lined like a dead man's; and I shall have my reality again, such a hard, suffering reality."[13]

The family home in Trinity, Texas. Goyen's birthplace. Source: *The Doris Roberts and Charles William Goyen Literary Trust.*

Goyen, his mother, Emma, and sister, Kathryn, Trinity, Texas, 1918.
Source: *the Doris Roberts and Charles William Goyen Literary Trust.*

Sixth birthday party, Trinity, 1921. Goyen is to the right of the cake with knife in hand. Source: The Doris Roberts and Charles William Goyen Literary Trust.

Goyen and his sister, Kathryn. Source: Harry Ransom Center, the University of Texas at Austin.

Goyen, sporting a cane, with his sister, Kathryn, in Houston. Dressed for the "May Fete" or May Day celebration as described in the story "A People of Grass." Source: The Doris Roberts and Charles William Goyen Literary Trust.

Seventh-grade class picture, James S. Hogg Jr. High School, Houston. Goyen is in the front row, fourth from the left. Source: *The Doris Roberts and Charles William Goyen Literary Trust.*

High school graduation picture, Sam Houston High School, Houston. Source: *The Doris Roberts and Charles William Goyen Literary Trust.*

Home on leave in Houston after graduation from Mid-Shipman's School at Columbia University, 1942. Left to right: Charlie Goyen, Emma, Kathryn, and younger brother, Jim. Source: The Doris Roberts and Charles William Goyen Literary Trust.

Ensign William Goyen. Source: *The Doris Roberts and Charles William Goyen Literary Trust.*

Dorothy Brett, Frieda Lawrence, and Goyen in Taos. Source: Harry Ransom Center, the University of Texas at Austin.

Goyen's house in Taos. Source: Harry Ransom Center, the University of Texas at Austin.

Walter Berns, Taos, 1947. Source: Harry Ransom Center, the University of Texas at Austin.

Goyen and Katherine Anne Porter, 1951; Arthur Long, photographer; Katherine Anne Porter Collection; Special Collections, University of Maryland Libraries.

Goyen in Capri, 1954. Source: Harry Ransom Center, the University of Texas at Austin.

Joseph Glasco, 1952, Kay Bell Reynal, photographer. Archives of American Art, Smithsonian Institution.

Goyen in the mid-1950s. Source: Harry Ransom Center, the University of Texas at Austin.

Margo Jones. From the collections of the Texas/Dallas History and Archives Division, Dallas Public Library.

Goyen on family visit to Houston, late 1950s. Left to right: Goyen, Charlie Goyen, Jim Goyen. Source: The Doris Roberts and Charles William Goyen Literary Trust.

Goyen with Doris Roberts, early 1980s. Source: *The Doris Roberts and Charles William Goyen Literary Trust.*

CHAPTER EIGHT

Marvello

1950–1953

For what can the artist belong to except what he must, despite himself, abandon (as ghost or flesh), destroy, turn away from so as to build it again.

GOYEN TO ROBERT LINSCOTT, MARCH 14, 1951

Porter's review of *The House of Breath* was decisive in making Goyen's first book a significant event in the literary world of New York. Though in later years he sometimes remembered otherwise, the two had met well before the review appeared, in California in 1947.[1] On their way to Napa, Goyen and Berns stopped in Los Angeles to visit their old shipmate Emmet Riordan and his wife, Anne. Equipped with introductions from Frieda Lawrence and such well-connected Taos visitors as James Laughlin, they paid court to a number of artists and writers in California, including Porter, Knud Merrild, William Everson, and Robert Duncan. Goyen was obviously impressed with Porter's directness and strength. "She spoke quickly and straight out of a wisdom," he wrote to Spud Johnson. "I found her powerful and full of integrity—one feels the *cleanliness* of her writing."[2] To Bill Hart he was more expansive: "She sat very beautiful and intense and spoke clearly and simply but always with fire and a stinging castigation of what she calls 'the muddlers': those who 'scum everything up' with their half-values, with their glib comments, and who will not give up much but want life and art to be somewhat easy and glamorous and quick. When she spoke of her *craft* it was like listening to a deft mechanic. She is a little like Frieda; in some way they have that same rare *hold* on visions and common sense."[3]

Several respectful and friendly letters passed between them over the next few years, and in the fall of 1949, when Porter moved to New York, Goyen had a chance to visit her more regularly. As with Frieda and Spender, he found in the established figure not merely a role model but a confirmation of his own talent and sense of uniqueness. It can be difficult to underestimate his almost desperate need for validation, and when someone notable appeared who might support and help him, be "with him" (as he often put it) against all else, his excitement could surpass mere gratitude. In the letter to her that accompanied the proofs of *The House of Breath*, he speaks of Porter with fear and reverence as a standard bearer: "Anyway, it would be such an honor to have you lay eyes on the book—although I'm running a risk of getting pounced on by you—because, as I've told you, you've been for a long time a guiding principle to me in my work, and it seems right to return a thing home once it is finished."[4] Though the respect was genuine, the flattery seems more a species of wishful thinking than a faithful history of influence. Goyen and Porter did share similar backgrounds, and there is little doubt that as a Texas writer of national reputation her career and work were inspiring. But she was less an aesthetic model for his work than an indication of what could be done with local materials. In his later memorial, published in 1980 when Porter died, he admitted an early desire to imitate her, but the very terms of his description suggest a writing temperamentally unlike his own: "When I first read the stories and novellas of Katherine Anne Porter, sitting in a frame house on a graveled street in Houston, my first feelings were of soundness in clean fresh writing. I wanted to do that! It was unadorned, serene, complete, what I read."[5] The extravagance of style and form in *The House of Breath* emerged from models almost antithetical to Porter's Jamesian restraint, and Porter's own disapproval of what she considered uncontrolled emotion is evident in her review. Nevertheless, despite or possibly because of their temperamental differences, each seemed willing to rationalize shortcomings in the other—Goyen for the chance to secure an ally, Porter for the possibility of a new acolyte whose attentions were clearly welcome.

In a general sense Darlene Harbor Unrue is correct to say that soon after the review appeared, Goyen and Porter began playing elaborate romantic games with one another, but it is also true that they were equally eager to deceive themselves about their own motives and the practical possibilities of their desires.[6] As their love affair began in earnest in February 1951 during Goyen's residency at Yaddo (for which Porter had recommended him), each was hiding significant personal details from the other. On Goyen's part it was his continued attraction to Walter Berns and a lingering connection to Spender.[7] In July of 1950, with a bottle of bourbon in one hand and a fresh copy of *The House of Breath* in the other, Goyen had met Berns's ship from England as it landed in Hoboken. They then traveled to Houston and Taos to see family and friends before driving to Chicago, where Berns planned to enroll at the University of Chicago. It was not a happy journey. The two lives had already significantly diverged, and though Goyen stayed in Chicago for a few months, he and Berns could never recapture that early happiness they found in El Prado: "We stayed [in Taos] only three days, then drove to Chicago through the strangest, most haunted kind of beautiful landscape: the aspens turning in the Colorado mountains, our tires blowing out on the roads, the old car huffing and Walter and I silent. It was almost too much. The last day we drove 15 hours and arrived in Chicago ill, both of us, and rather strangers."[8] In addition to a proximity to Berns, Chicago meant an escape from New York, a chance to work in isolation on the stories for his first collection without the distracting rounds of a social life he was both drawn to and repelled by.[9]

Porter, as she often did with new attachments, harbored deep suspicions even as she seemed to fall headlong into a romantic fever. (It is worth noting that even in her strong review of *The House of Breath*, she nevertheless imagines Goyen as a Texas Judas.) As Janis Stout observes, Porter's friends "had seen on multiple occasions the intensity of her infatuations and the equal intensity of her misery when hopeless involvements proved to be, indeed, hopeless. They knew that the extremes of her infatuation with a man portended extremes of recrimination against that same man later."[10] Even worse, Porter had a history of falling for bisexual men even though she maintained an intense hatred and disdain for homosexuals. With Goyen she was constantly on the lookout for signs of betrayal, particularly with other men, and she was not shy about confronting him when she doubted his loyalty. According to his journal at the time, this "theme" emerged very early. In an entry dated "Feb. 17, 1951 (notebook Yaddo)," he wrote,

> I feel so strongly the devil-woman in her—I will not be afraid of it—I am not.

But, too—she attracts, I believe, betrayal, because it is her one enemy in the world, in her life. "It is my theme," she said. Yet, so strange, how it seems to me that she calls to her those who are most capable of betraying her, because they are highly capable, highly complex men—devil-men, sometimes. Already she seems to define me traitor—and this hangs over us, over me, haunts me.

So—it is a tragic relationship—and in what manifold and complex and curious ways. Can either of us bear a tragic relationship, who has had so many?

But her tenderness! Her fragility. She *is* grass. (HRC 20.7)

As this entry makes clear, despite a considerable romantic attraction, Goyen was already reacting to the distrust Porter projected, and after his residency at Yaddo, other than a few weeks with her in New York, he was actively keeping his distance, putting off meetings and finding faraway places to continue the work on *Ghost and Flesh*.[11] Over the next several months, from May through September, he lived at various locations in Texas, in a house in San Marcos loaned to him by Dr. Rauch-Barraco and later an apartment he rented in Houston on Pickwick Lane.[12] The avoidance hurt and angered Porter, who alternately attacked him and begged for forgiveness until she could take it no longer. In the end, as Stout explains, she "turned on him the full blast of her abomination of homosexuality," and, according to Goyen, called him a "no-good, black-livered sonofabitch" in a drunken, early morning phone call.[13]

In a piece later included in the unpublished novel *Half a Look of Cain*, Goyen sketched the atmosphere of that time and particularly of his relationship to Porter, sexuality, and the literary culture of the early 1950s.[14] "At Lady A's" is a brilliant and surprisingly candid snapshot of a party at which the Porter surrogate "Lady A" presides, dominating the guests and the conversation with her strong opinions about writing and sex. "She was a nervous and beautiful little trailblazer and wilderness-breaker of a woman whose conversation—or monologue—was a physical exercise which gave her a good workout, taking such control of her at times that it would throw her into fits of coughing and collision with objects in the room" (*GAE* 32). Much of the piece is taken up with a dramatic rendering of Porter's speech, its willful, almost badgering tone and queenly presumption, often aimed at Goyen himself:

Don't you be another basket case, do you hear me, you stay good and true, you're strong honey though when I first knew you I thought the world would kill you if you just walked down its streets; but you're tough, darling. If you'd just *listen* to me, I don't know why you don't listen to me . . . and get this idea out of your head and grow into the man you were meant to be, what did your mother and father do to you when you were young that you haven't grown into the man you were meant to be? (*GAE* 34)

A conversation at the party turns to contemporary artists and homosexuality, and Lady A rushes from across the room at the sound of "that word." "They have never done anything lasting," she says, to which the narrator responds by arguing that "there are many ways of love and that it might seem true that any way of love, however outside the pattern of the majority, might be less destructive than the perversities of lovelessness." Lady A then challenges him to "go on over to their side," complaining, "[Y]ou're always defending them" (*GAE* 35). The narrator later leaves with a young woman, Lucy, and they end up at another party where the discussion is again about the sexuality of various writers and the use of contraceptives. Self-conscious and apparently uncomfortable for Lucy, he takes her home, but as they walk to her apartment, she explains how New York has toughened her. At her door, though he wishes to "stay the rest of the night," he holds back and they part "dishonestly."

As a portrait of Porter, the sketch is consistent with Goyen's notes at the time and with other accounts of their relationship. It vividly captures the peculiar energy of her homophobia even as it, more remarkably, gives us a glimpse of Goyen's ideas about his own sexuality, particularly his sense that "love" is a more significant determination than sexuality in combating "the perversities of lovelessness." His choice to end the sketch with a near heterosexual encounter may have been meant to confirm this bisexual vision, but as a concluding gesture— at least within this draft of the manuscript—it also has a slight air of falseness, as though the narrator's obvious interest in the question of sexual identity can be disguised by a typical gesture of masculine desire. Whether the reaffirmation of masculinity is meant to reassure the reader or is an indication of the narrator's own uncertainty—his response to Lady A's demand that he "grow into the man you were meant to be"—remains an open question.

Ghost and Flesh

The stories in Goyen's second book, *Ghost and Flesh* (1952), grew in part from the emotional turbulence of the Porter relationship and what he called "that deeply troubled time" in the summer of 1951 in San Marcos and Houston (HRC 20.7). On the run, in a sense, from New York and Porter but unable to return to Berns, who was getting married, or to El Prado, where the newlyweds were to spend their honeymoon, he felt more displaced than perhaps ever before. His plan to live in Margo Jones's Dallas apartment fell through, and he was left to choose between Dr. Rauch-Barraco's house in San Marcos and Merrill Street. The apartment he rented in Houston may have been a kind of compromise, allowing him the space to write but not preventing him from retreating to his parents when he felt the need for family support.

This physical dislocation, as it frequently did for Goyen, fed and reflected an urgent instability of self. His elaborate attempt in *The House of Breath* to understand and free himself from the past had done its work to a degree, but the partial exorcism of a long cherished subject had also made it much more difficult to have a clear and reliable sense of his role going forward. *Ghost and Flesh* was meant to provide the space to examine his current transitional state and build a vision that would move him forward both personally and artistically. As he explained to Robert Linscott, the collection was planned as a unified book, an "integrated whole, a *single* gesture although complex and varied in its meaning and meanings." As *The House of Breath* had been "a turning inwards towards a whole, within one's self," *Ghost and Flesh* would extend the "outgoing" gesture of the earlier book's ending, filled with people who are "driven by the need to communicate *beyond* themselves to something greater, more permanent than the everyday gestures of life, more stable, to be members of a whole: a 'household,' a lost family, a community of pilgrims, a cause, that physical world of first things." These "people of unrest" are "joiners, connectors, agents, instruments" in a broken world, and the artist, whose portrait is also included, is the shaper and carrier of these others' burdens, "laboring to make the epitaphs for all things dead and so keep them alive."[15]

Aside from "The White Rooster," the stories in *Ghost and Flesh* are by and large the product of this search for connection, and taken as a whole, they demonstrate a mature determination and a technical confidence gained from the successful experimentation in Goyen's first novel. Two of the stories are masterful: "Pore Perrie" and "Ghost and Flesh, Water and Dirt" create a new, highly distinctive form of story-telling that makes maximum use of Goyen's preference for dramatic, musical speech and staged narration. If *The House of Breath* allowed him to sustain a ventriloquism through which heightened speech could infuse a landscape, "Pore Perrie," for instance, more explicitly employs what Goyen was later to name the "teller-listener situation" (*CS* x). The story begins with a demand, almost childlike, from a returned orphan, now a man, named Son: "'Tell me the story of pore Perrie. Tell how she lived all her life till she died.'" As in *The House of Breath*, a prodigal child has made his way home not so much for information as to hear the ritual repetition of history, to *"get something straight"* about the ghost of memory that continues to haunt him. *Telling* therefore has the force of pronouncement, of taking responsibility for the past and for the shaping of remembrance. To listen, as Son does, carefully, critically, is to monitor the rightness of the words, to find security in their correct repetition, and to consent to his connection or kinship to the history so recounted. And yet the form is more complicated than this basic de-scription suggests: the teller-listener relationship between Aunt Linsie and Son is moderated by a third presence, a narrator who has likewise been a listener ("this is the story as it was told to me") and who, like Son, wants to "get it all straight," to understand "this Son's pain" and find the "tongue to tell it with." With a second teller comes a second lis-tener, and the narrator's intimacy and directness make it clear that we the readers of "Pore Perrie" nest strangely inside Son's listening, learn-ing the role of the returned orphan in search of a troubling past.

This ventriloquistic technique is a compressed version of the over-layered voices of *The House of Breath*, and it again provides Goyen with a complex set of filters through which to explore his own spiritual auto-biography. Son is yet another of his haunted escapees from small-town family life, present in his work at least since "The Seadowns' Bible." Here the character is literally an orphan, adopted by Perrie Polk and her husband Ace Wanger through the Methodist Church Orphanage. In a configuration that roughly approximates Goyen's childhood, the mother is gentle and mildly sad, the father a traveling lumber sales-man, and the son "very very nervous" (*CS* 41). So nervous, in fact, that Perrie takes him to the local doctor, who considers him "the most nervous child" he has ever seen in his practice (*CS* 41) and prescribes the removal of Son's tonsils and adenoids. (As Boy in *The House of Breath* had been a receptacle for Goyen's formative memories, Son is here given the role of reenacting a traumatic incident from the Trinity years, what Goyen often called the "botched" operation on his tonsils carried out in the local doctor's office.) By seventeen, Son is "dark and lean and beginning to be very different," still brooding and now potentially violent.

Goyen repeatedly described the dominant feeling of his childhood as "orphanage," and Son suggests a kind of thought experiment designed to clarify some of those feelings. On the night of the Fourth of July picnic, Son learns from local gossip that Perrie is not his mother, and on the way home he climbs over a barbed wire fence and falls, wounding himself. Like the scar on Boy's thigh made with Christy's axe, this is a sexual wound, hidden from all but the summoned doctor, and it suggests that Son's difference will have its physical manifestation, that he will in effect be exiled in body, by his body, while he longs to be present in spirit. Thus, later in the story (after he leaves to live with Ace, who has taken a job in Memphis), Son becomes the object of Perrie's mourning, a ghost who haunts her as memory and, later, as a shadowy absence visiting his childhood home in secret. In this near-spectral form, he finally appears to Perrie, now old and withered from her sadness at the loss of her child. Linsie is the witness: "I stood in the doorway and saw this in the lightning: Perrie was standing before her window, beautiful and white as a Saint, naked, the white voile curtains waving and falling and rising round her like the garments of an angel. She seemed young, like a vision of herself, frail and fleshly, and this vision was burned upon my sight, and upon the sight of Son, whose face was there at the window like a lantern; and it will be there till we both of us die, Son and me, I know to God" (*CS* 47).

The encounter kills Perrie, who, if not literally a portrait of Goyen's mother, is at least a reflection of how he perceived her sadness at his absence from Houston. As he admitted many years later in an interview with Jean-Michel Quiblier, his break from Merrill Street after the war was crucial to his development, but it came at a great cost to his sense of responsibility: "I didn't leave until the war began. I knew I needed to leave but I felt incapable of doing it. I needed to be forced to leave. . . . I felt responsible for them. I thought that if I left, they would die" (*GAE* 107). "Pore Perrie" imagines this death, asserting an inseparable mixture of anger, love, guilt, and mourning that constitutes Goyen's response to his family's continued pleas for his return. In particular, the story's cherishing of the mother's anguished voice—Goyen's way of turning Emma's cadences into a musical speech—suggests a strong desire not only to feel her grieving but also to be present at the effect of his own absence:

> [*Child a mine, child a mine, something touched you and changed you all over. I know some hand touched that good boy Son and left him never the same again. Some hand led him away from poor Perrie (Lord help me forget his face, his head of hair, let me forget him all over, the way he was all over, bless his hide, he was the only thing I ever had. I remember him in the garden counting the tomatoes for arithmetic, I remember him in the clothesyard bumping like a ghost through the wet sheets, I remember him in the pinegrove; child a mine.)*] (CS 45)

In his study of Goyen's short fiction, Reginald Gibbons has argued that the use of the teller-listener situation is Goyen's artistic signature. Noting his early experiences in the theater, Gibbons opposes Goyen's work to that of writers who attempt to control their readers' reactions, suggesting that Goyen's stories are invitations "into a social, dramatic situation that requires not [his readers'] obedience but [their] sympathy, [their] emotional responsiveness."[16] This respect for the reader—a figure imagined and transformed by a careful technical illusion into a *presence*—creates a relationship, making a claim that, if accepted, changes the emotional register of the reading experience. In terms of Goyen's biography, this strong and irrepressible demand was a function of his desire not merely for an audience but for a particular person, that one imagined companion, the intimacy with whom would pervade all aspects of his life and work. In this sense the listener in his stories is always a potential friend or ally, and the bond imagined between the storyteller and his singular audience is one of "kinship," whether blood relation or some other form of spiritual or emotional identification. The teller-listener structure, in other words, is a relationship of desire that underlies and energizes the traditional function of bearing witness.

In "Ghost and Flesh, Water and Dirt" this intensified telling takes place in a bar, the Pass Time Club, and the listener seems little more than an implied drinking companion, but the quality of the language and the sudden claim made by the speaker on our attention narrows the setting into a highlighted theatrical space. "I'm in my time a tellin," the voice tells the listener, "and you better run fast if you don wanna hear what I tell, cause I'm goin ta tell" (CS 50). The speaker is Margy, an older woman who was once married to Raymon Emmons, a handsome "rayroad man" who apparently killed himself out of grief over the death of their daughter. Now Raymon's ghost haunts Margy, riding onto the sleeping porch each night on a purple horse—the horse the daughter fell from—to talk through the night. Not even time spent away, living in California during the war and working in an aircraft factory, can rid Margy of the ghost of Raymon Emmons. When she returns to the small Texas town after the death of her second lover, the ghost is there, waiting in the old house now covered with dust, "the breath a ghosts" (CS 57).

There is no conclusion, properly speaking, to Margy's unprompted telling. She is simply haunted and driven to speak of her ghosts in whatever way she can, and it is the need to tell—the compulsion of psychological or spiritual desire—that is the story's true subject. Goyen tended to define "spirit" as that portion of experience not reduceable to the physical, particularly to the life of the body. Margy tells the story of her physical life—her movements, the passage of tangible events—but the remnants of memory and feeling, the ghosts, make that telling necessary, unavoidable: "Us humans are part ghost and part flesh—part fire and part ash—but I think maybe the ghost part is the longest lastin, the fire blazes but the ashes last forever. . . . And I think that ghosts, if you set still with em long enough, can give you over the flesh 'n bones; and that flesh 'n bones, if you go roun when it's time, can send you back to a faithful ghost. One provides the other" (CS 58–59). This statement, repeated in various forms throughout the volume, is not only the book's essential argument; it became an important formula for Goyen's intuitive but complex sense of the relationship between sexuality and identity. As he was to repeat to Reginald Gibbons in 1982, "'Ghost and Flesh,' I wrote—one's expressed right through the other, for me" (GAE 120). The thought seems to echo Whitman's project to equate body and soul: "I have said that the soul is not more than the body, / And I have said that the body is not more than the soul."[17] And yet Goyen's mapping of the overlapping territories of flesh and spirit is more complex and conflicted than Whitman's optimistic declaration. The shuttling back and forth from ghost to flesh suggests a kind of protective process, a way of understanding his sometimes feared, transgressive physical desires as moderated, contained (and possibly ennobled) by their translation into spirit. Flaubert's St. Julien hovers over this conception: the transformation into spirit through the embrace of the leper makes possible a vision of salvation through, rather than despite, the body. For someone who was repeatedly convinced of the dangers of the erotic even as he was ineluctably drawn to them, this hopeful vision provides a kind of reconciliation: erotic life saved as a conduit to spirit, spiritual life made real by its return to flesh.

As with many of the stories in *Ghost and Flesh*, the summarized "content" of "Ghost and Flesh, Water and Dirt," though important, fails to capture the experience of reading the story, which is as much musical as it is rhetorical. As he had begun to do in the extended "arias" within *The House of Breath*, Goyen here shaped the natural speech rhythms of East Texas into a concentrated form of lyric, structured by repetition and refrain and a particular attention to sound values. Margy's voice is a kind of chant at times, turning back on itself, rolling over the talismanic phrases of evocation and loss: *"Oh go way ole ghost of Raymon Emmons, whisperin in my ear on the pilla at night; go way ole ghost and lemme be!"* (*CS* 51). And the story's structure moves through a series of circles like the verses of a song, always returning to the chorus of set phrases that act as both a comfort and a defense against loss and madness. In fact, for as much "telling" as there is in the stories of *Ghost and Flesh*, there is an equal and opposing force of lyric stasis, as though the movement forward in time must always be balanced by a desire to hold time still, to repeat or hear once again the sounds of a world passing away.

This tension between music and narrative in the work as a whole is not always fully balanced, however. In some cases the stories move almost completely into a mode of meditative stillness, proceeding more by felt connections between images than through temporal sequence. "Nests in a Stone Image," for instance, presents a sleepless Easter eve as it occurs in the mind of a single character in a hotel room in San Francisco. Here the actual passage of time or sequencing of incident is not the main concern; the story is not an example of telling so much as it is a portrait of the storyteller trying to locate himself between the various demands of inner and outer existence. In keeping with Goyen's past explorations of what might be called the Christ position—the artist perceiving himself as both sacrificed to others and a source of special knowledge—the story gives us a kind of Gethsemane or dark night of the self awaiting resurrection. The "listener," as he is called, lies sprawled on the bed "like a five-point star" in a hotel figured as a "stone skull" that holds him "tenant in it like a captured and entombed idea" (*CS* 87). If this is Golgotha, then the figure is a modern, almost existential self in search of wholeness: "His tenancy had been a search through all the rooms for himself, to liberate an image of it, a constant self-regarding. For he thought how he would contain all his own life and have it clear and as it existed, regardless of the consequences. What matter what else he had gained, if he did not possess, as it existed, the shape of his own life, finding it out again and again, what human use had done to it?" (*CS* 87).

A part of this search is the reconsideration of his rootlessness. Cut off from his past and exiled from "the very dirt . . . which holds the bones of [his] blood-kin," he reconsiders the various relationships that might have provided that sense of connection he lacks. These past partnerships are understood as failures, both sexual and emotional, rendered as a series of memories of other rooms, places in his past where the hoped-for intimacy that would mend his exile fell apart. Outside voices—those of other tenants talking at a party, passing on the street below, making love in the room above—interrupt this interrogation of memory, but the reminder that there are other lives, other claims on his life offers only a temporary distraction, and he soon shifts back to another painful memory. The scene pictures the principle character sitting on a moonlit beach with a young woman. An unnamed tension exists between them which she tries to relieve through sexual intimacy. But the silent, almost catatonic young man cannot respond and runs sobbing toward the water. She quiets him, and the two walk down the beach, apparently waiting for another couple, "Wallace and the girl" who are alone in "the dark house on the cliff" (*CS* 96). After another shift of attention back to the other hotel guests, the isolated figure begins to find a kind of relief for the painful memories he had both evoked and suffered. "He had had, again, his pain; and now something had lifted out of him and risen up out of stone to where it would have its long long meaning" (*CS* 98). With the rising of the Easter sun, the idea of loss becoming sacrifice lifts the burden from him, and he essentially lets go of his past love, pronouncing a kind of benediction that makes an end to his past and prepares him for "another long beginning" (*CS* 99).

Of all the stories in *Ghost and Flesh*, "Nests in a Stone Image" is perhaps the furthest from traditional storytelling but the most significant as disguised autobiography. Though the ritual release of past loves seems meant to cover several relationships, the motivating hurt here is the loss of Walter Berns and the knowledge that during Goyen's troubled summer of 1951, Berns had married and was spending his honeymoon in Taos, in the house he and Goyen had built together. In a letter to Dorothy Brett, Berns himself suggested that "Nests in a Stone Image" was a summation of the emotional complexities surrounding the "terribly complex affair" of Goyen's engagement to Dorothy Robinson, and the relationship between the main character and the young woman may be an attempt to clarify Goyen's feelings about the breakup.[18] The scene on the beach can be somewhat misleading, however. Its purpose is not to indicate the young man's emotional sterility or his inability or unwillingness to engage in sex with a woman. It is to dramatize the narrator's anguish when he realizes that "Wallace and the girl" are alone together in the house on the hill. This jealousy and loss are the source of his despair, and the pain from what seems his abandonment leads directly to the story's final blessing and release: *"Because you were youth and bright-eyedness and I could never be young with you, because I was ancient and full of too many days, what I knew I did not want to teach you because it was of darkness and shadow and I did not want to corrupt your mirth, your glee, your brightness, no gloom, no tempests, no witchcraft, no sorrow, no doubt, no confusion, all clear all clear all clear"* (*CS* 99; emphasis in the original). This is an attempt, in effect, to say goodbye to Berns, to release him or exorcise him from Goyen's range of needs. That it isn't entirely successful can be gauged in part by the resurgence of Berns as a factor in Goyen's late story "In the Icebound Hothouse" where an almost identical *cri de coeur* concludes another disturbed narrator's confessions.[19]

Some of this combination of repression and revelation—couched in a musical or dream language—recurs in the final story of *Ghost and Flesh*, "A Shape of Light." Based on a folklore pamphlet that Goyen read in the offices of *The Southwest Review*, the story primarily concerns the obsession of a man named Boney Benson, who is driven to pursue a ghostly light said to move mysteriously over the countryside. The legend was familiar to Goyen, who had heard it repeated when he was a child; he told Margaret Hartley and Allen Maxwell that he had been shown what he called "Baily's Light," also known regionally as the Saratoga Light, by his parents.[20] This complex and almost symphonic tale consists of two main sections: "The Record," which gives a fairly straightforward account of Benson as a kind of artistic or philosophical obsessive, "along after the light and tormented by it" (*CS* 102); and "The Message," in which the narrator, a storyteller in a large city who remembers a childhood encounter with Benson, meditates on and expands the legend as a way of understanding his origin and role in the world.

The earlier section is clearly another of Goyen's briefs on behalf of his own artistic and personal project, a declaration of principles: "So this man made covenant with himself not to ally himself with any pattern of life or form of human activity that would keep him from his suffering after the lighted shape in which he sought the truth he was after" (*CS* 102). Benson becomes a general figure for the searcher, imparting his intensity and desire to a young boy he finds standing in "a meadow of bluebonnets and paintbrush" holding a string: "This was my lost child and I told him what he did not know, left my words with him, our covenant, and laid this charge upon him: *speak of this little species that cannot speak for itself; be gesture; and use the light and follow it wherever it may lead you*" (*CS* 105). In "The Message" we come to realize that this child is the narrator, who gives us the incident from his perspective as a boy flying a kite in a field near his house. Here Boney Benson is a strange, skeletal railroad worker in charge of seeing coffins on and off the local train. He approaches the boy and asks him if he has sent a message up the kite string. Benson sends up his own message on a "piece of barkish Indian Chief tablet paper written on in pencil" (*CS* 111), but once the slip of paper reaches the wood and tissue construction, the kite begins to fall, leaving the message to float away on the wind. When the boy wonders aloud where the message is going, Boney Benson "bent in a gesture that would haunt you forever and uttered a deep, stifled cry, as though something had hit him in the pit of the stomach and mashed his breath out" (*CS* 112).

For Goyen, this episode, which has the air of autobiography, again evoked the myth of Icarus. He explained to Porter that "A Shape of Light" "really tells the story of Icarus, for the message itself, cut adrift from the kite made of good stuff 'off the place,' soars and hovers and falls, and all search seems to be for it or to find a meaning for it."[21] For the narrator, this search involves reimagining Boney Benson, conjuring a meaningful narrative for the unfulfilled wanderer, a way of shaping and placing him that will settle the narrator's own pain and confusion. In this final telling, Benson is tortured by the loss of his wife and un-born child. Blaming himself, he mutilates his body and, according to one legend, buries his severed genitals in the grave: "The tale is told that a child was born in the grave, delivered itself of its tomb within tomb and, mole-like, began a life of its own underground, rising at nights . . . to wander phantom over the countryside" (CS 119–120). The "lighted shape" that rises from the grave becomes the light that Benson follows, eventually to his death in another country that is, in a larger sense, the "territory where there are no words . . . where there is only a kind of music, a wail, or a sigh, or a stifled cry: the gesture of the inex-pressible" (CS 122).

"A Shape of Light" seems to have been constructed not merely as a conclusion to *Ghost and Flesh* but as a grand recapitulation of its themes and materials. It not only gathers the thematic strands of this collection conceived as a single book but also, as though to point to the central maker and teller of the volume, explicitly echoes details from the earlier stories. Boney Benson's horse, for example, is the same purple stallion named King ridden by Raymond Emmons. The wan-dering, dusty figure at the center of "Children of Old Somebody" re-turns, metaphorically, as a version of King Lear layered atop the image of Benson: "They plucked out sweet old Gloucester's eye balls and his poor houseless poverty came wild out of the hill, and in his skins led the blind old turned-out Somebody down the road to the cliff" (CS 104). And like Son in "Pore Perrie," the young man who goes to meet Benson falls on a barbed-wire fence and cuts himself in the groin. The effect of these references, combined with the sometimes heavy reliance on the volume's key terms, not only provides the coherence Goyen was seek-ing but also suggests a writer grappling with material not fully worked out or expressible. The tension evident in *The House of Breath* between technical control and repressed subject matter emerges even more in-sistently in the stories of *Ghost and Flesh*; complex narrative structures seem built in order to get a handle on material too deeply buried or too emotionally charged to find exact expression. And yet this collision between word and spirit is precisely what Goyen was hoping to achieve and was willing to risk. The volume's studied vagueness made it remarkably original for its time, while clearly challenging readers' preconceptions of what short fiction should and should not attempt.

As a result, the reviews of *Ghost and Flesh* bore out readers' puzzlement—and sometimes outrage—at the way its stories resisted categorization and blended lyrical and narrative modes. In many reviews, only "The White Rooster," which leads off the volume, received direct praise for its vein of dark comedy and conventional dramatic conflict. Though the writing was often noted for its poetic effects, most critics found the characters too slight or misty to gain their sympathy. The anonymous reviewer for *Time* suggested that the stories "create a mood rather than people," and Robert Lowry, writing in the *New York Times*, considered the characters "more ghost than flesh," drifting "through a smog of loneliness."[22] A sharply critical review by Vernon Young in *The New Mexico Quarterly* had succinct praise for "Ghost and Flesh, Water and Dirt," but summed up the rest of the volume as "too damned sensitive for words . . . regressive, sexually evasive, and necrophilic, not necromantic."[23] Unlike, for instance, Roger Shattuck in his sensitive reaction to *The House of Breath*, most readers of *Ghost and Flesh* saw little reason to stretch their critical categories to account for the admittedly subtle, hybrid nature of the work. William Peden in the *Saturday Review* did recognize that the stories had "a magical quality rare in contemporary fiction," but even he found many of them overly complex in form and too heavily rhetorical. Castigating Goyen for too much "'fine' writing," he preferred "The Grasshopper's Burden," "one of the simplest stories" that "disturbs the imagination and haunts the memory."[24] The most sympathetic reading came from Margaret Hartley in the *Dallas Morning News*. The co-editor of *The Southwest Review* found a mythic gravity in the work and had no trouble with what other critics deemed unfocused: "The richness of the writing by which this [magical reality] is achieved and the acuteness of the seeing it sets down are little short of miraculous."[25]

These reactions established a range and character of critical response that was to prove frustrating to Goyen over the course of his career. Readers often began by categorizing him as yet another post-Faulkner Southern gothicist, a label he angrily rejected. Faulkner, Goyen claimed, was not an influence; he was "too *Southern*": "Thank

God for my southwesternness," he later told Robert Phillips, "that Texas thing . . . [S]omething kept me away from those sicknesses and terrors that come from that Deep South" (*GAE* 95). Despite the presence of ex-aggerated characters and decayed families in this work, he felt no con-nection to Southern history and the particular burdens of post–Civil War psychology. Instead his work was highly personal and predomi-nantly spiritual, a fiction that pushed the boundaries—and ignored the rules—of traditional narrative in order to explore the interior conflicts of a single self. And it was precisely this type of confessional writing in which the imperatives of the essay or spiritual autobiography broke down the distance typically required for fiction-making that proved most difficult for critics to recognize or accept. It was clear, of course, that Goyen was not a realist, but what many readers failed to under-stand was that he eschewed not only the stylistic trappings of realism but also its fundamental mimetic theories. He consciously rejected the tenet that the modern, self-aware writer should hide all trace of himself to let the characters and represented world live independently. Instead he sought what he called the "living voice," the immediate, at times des-perate, *presence* of an emotionally charged self. And if presenting that immediacy of speech meant the creation of less tangible settings or characters, it was a price he was willing to pay. His declaration to Regi-nald Gibbons in 1983 bears repeating: "Since I am *not* writing Zola-istic realism, then everyday reality, the detail of it, is obviously not going to sustain itself for me, forever. I'm not Dreiser; I'm not interested in that at all. I'm aware that there is no everyday trivia in itself, that beneath it, or going on within it, there's always some slight deformity of thought or action. It's the hidden life I'm talking about" (*GAE* 125).

Magnificent Joe

In retrospect, Goyen claimed that the writing of *Ghost and Flesh* had taken a heavy toll on his sanity. "I think the book made me quite mad; writing it, the obsession of that book. . . . It comes with a loss of reality. . . . It has to do with identity. I go through phases of not know-ing my own history. It's amnesiac almost. I've known this all my life; as a child I've known that" (*GAE* 99). The turmoil of the Porter affair com-bined with the irrevocable separation from Berns had left him feeling homeless and without that particular ally whose presence, no matter how turbulent, served to anchor his life and work. In a letter to Dorothy Brett, Berns himself explained that early in 1952 Goyen had suffered "a nervous breakdown. . . . For a time he lost the use of one arm and was generally in a state of complete collapse, although at no time was he without the use of his mental faculties." The cause, according to Berns, was "loneliness, a loneliness which can never be relieved."[26]

After a brief hospital stay in New York, Goyen returned to the small apartment on Morton Street he had recently rented. It was two blocks from the Hudson, close enough to hear the ships' whistles night and day. Working on a new novel and a dramatic adaptation of *The House of Breath*, he took time out only for a brief tour of Texas in May to promote *Ghost and Flesh*. A Guggenheim Fellowship was now paying some of the bills, and he contemplated a trip to visit Ernst Robert Curtius, his German translator, in Switzerland. But by the summer, he had reconsidered the expense and instead took advantage of friends' offers to escape the heat on Long Island. His new agent, Jim Brown, who had succeeded Toni Strassman, invited him for a weekend in July, and soon after, Lynn Riggs, the author of *Oklahoma!*, suggested that Goyen take the small extra house on his farm on Shelter Island.[27] "So far it is just perfect," Goyen wrote his parents, "and I hope I can stay on for a month or so. I am working well, I have been given a little cottage back in the trees, and I work all day out there, then lie in the sun and go swimming. Just what I had been hoping for."[28]

Despite his sometimes romantic notions of artistic isolation, Goyen seldom lived alone for very long. The search for that always elusive, ideal domestic arrangement where art and love could somehow reinforce one another never really ceased, and by the end of the summer he had found a new partner, a painter from Dallas named Joseph Glasco. From Riggs's farm, Goyen had moved to the estate of Alfonso Ossorio, the abstract expressionist painter who acquired the East Hampton property known as The Creeks in 1951. Born to a wealthy family, Ossorio played the generous host to a variety of fellow artists, including major figures such as Clyfford Still and Jackson Pollock. Goyen and Glasco began to share one of the estate's cottages in early August. "He paints in the large front room and I write in the little back room," Goyen explained to his parents. "This makes it very nice, for we can make our meals together, and you know what I am when I have to make my own meals—I just don't, usually. Everybody calls this the Texas House, and it surely is that."[29] A few months later Goyen offered, as usual, a fuller and more emotional account of the relationship to Bill Hart:

> We have joined, then, having rescued each other from a kind of death which you know well, and I write here only to bless the rescue and to honor it and to say that I pray God to keep us both forever grateful for it. You will one day meet magnificent Joe, green-eyed and fair, gentle and supreme artist. Wish our life well, for we have embarked upon it with every belief held back for life together, with every trust and faith the choice was made for, and honoring the Walters in the world who made such union possible and who gave it such meaning.[30]

Goyen and Glasco would stay together for a decade, living off and on in New York, New Mexico, and Pennsylvania. Ten years Goyen's junior, Glasco was born in Oklahoma but grew up in Tyler, Texas, a town larger than Trinity but part of the same East Texas environment so important to Goyen. Unlike the Goyens, however, the Glascos were wealthy. Lowell Glasco, Joe's father, was a prominent Dallas oil man who in 1952 received government backing to build the first pipeline to carry Texas crude to California. As a consequence, Joe was able to study art from the time he was eight and at thirteen was sent to a boarding school in St. Louis. He came back to attend the University of Texas but was soon drafted and served as an infantryman in Patton's Third Army in Europe. By the time he met Goyen in New York, Glasco had studied art in California and Mexico, had a one-man show at the Perls Gallery, and traveled to Europe and Morocco where he had met, among others, Jean Dubuffet and Paul Bowles. At twenty-five, he became the youngest artist to have work added to the permanent collection of the Museum of Modern Art when his drawing "Big Sitting Cat" was presented in a *Recent Acquisitions* exhibition.

In addition to experiencing a mutual sexual attraction, Goyen and Glasco shared a similar provincial idiosyncrasy when it came to the art they produced. Though Glasco was often grouped with the New York School of abstract expressionists, his work in the 1950s was largely figural, surreal, and, according to Julian Schnabel, uniquely outside the prevailing aesthetic: "At a time when the climate of painting was leaning toward abstraction, Joe was making figurative paintings. The figures weren't bound by the gravity of naturalistic space. They were suspended in an atmosphere of black lines, dashes and dots. . . . Joe's figures have a sculptural quality; in fact, they were paintings of sculptures rather than people. They were paintings of monuments or idols; they were mythological."[31] The affinity to Goyen's fiction is clear. The preference for the mythic over the naturalistic, the impulse toward the sacred or the totemic—both gestures underpinned by a stubbornly individualist vision—hint at a relative like-mindedness between the two East Texans. The connection may be clearest in a small text Goyen wrote for Glasco's 1956 show at the Catherine Viviano Gallery in New York. "The People of Joseph Glasco" articulates a vision of art as a record of "interior landscapes" constructed "out of a destruction, the way art works: they [Glasco's landscape heads] seem at once about to disintegrate and yet to order themselves out of their fragments with utter simplicity and through the means of one simple shape or form" (WRC 11.2). The desire for an unmediated, humanistic connection between art and audience as well as the avoidance of deliberate sophistication in favor of atavistic immediacy—these are the shared values; or, at the very least, Goyen's attempt to frame his friend's work in this way was attractive enough to Glasco to permit this kind of imagined unity of purpose. What the little pamphlet concludes about the "people" in the paintings and sculptures could easily stand as a description of Goyen's hopes for his sometimes less-than-independent characters: "they are not a breed of intellectualized, psychoanalyzed, self-conscious, guilty and precious sufferers; they do not represent phobias or modern manias, they show no self-pity or self-persecution either of themselves or their creator. They are an animal-God race, a strong, human, unhaunted race of the pure and enduring, undefeated soul" (WRC 11.2).

The household Goyen and Glasco formed together quickly became another of Goyen's imaginative retreats from a threatening world. In the loft they rented on West 23rd that autumn, he continued work on *Half a Look of Cain* and wrote to Curtius about this new partnership against isolation and loneliness: "There is a point where an artist must, it seems to me, relate his work and his vision to another human being, to a *beloved*; and I had come to that. . . . Already I see my work so much more clearly, I see it *through* the beloved."[32] The apartment, a loft at the top of a factory building, would eventually become the setting for Goyen's third novel, *In a Farther Country*. At night when the workers on the lower floors went home, the building (and according to Goyen, the entire block) was empty except for the writer and painter working at separate ends of their isolated floor. "We are in a fortress in the midst of this hellish, tearing city," Goyen wrote to Hart, "that seems to have been built for all the wrong things and purposes; we are in a fortress; at night, when the three floors below us are empty . . . we pull an iron gate across the stairway and snap the padlock on it—we are locked away up here."[33] There was a feeling of security in the shared space that Goyen had lacked since his time in New Mexico with Berns, and it's no surprise that he soon began to think of returning to El Prado to live and work with Glasco. In November they passed through Houston to pick up some furniture and then drove to Dallas to see Glasco's family. A few days later, they pulled in to Taos in time to see an older, more frail Frieda before she left to winter on the Texas coast. The little adobe house was still in good shape, though they worried about heating it for the winter. And Brett, "fine as ever," was happy to see them. But most important of all, Glasco clearly approved: "Joe loves it," Goyen wrote to his parents, "and is very happy here, already says he never wants to leave."

Half a Look of Cain

But more: an artist is a disturbed, distressed, obsessed human being. Joe and I are haunted and obcessed [sic] with our work. One spends half one's youth trying to escape his obsession and his torment, the rest of his life he spends struggling to find some way to live with it, as he has now learned that this is the very condition of his life— remove it and his life is violated and betrayed.

GOYEN TO DOROTHY BRETT, JANUARY 20, 1954

Writing to his friend the San Antonio writer John Igo in 1952, Goyen explained that his "great aim" as an artist was to "return literature to what is called 'sensibility' (but I would do that anyway, being made as I am, good or bad)—to combat sophistication, dishonesty, misrepresentation, etc.—to help us return ourselves to a way of *feeling*, a way of looking and responding to our own human experience."[34] The statement is important not merely for how it positions him against much of mainstream twentieth-century fiction but for its accurate self-diagnosis and determination. It may seem strange that a writer as willing to innovate and experiment as Goyen was would pit himself so dramatically against "sophistication," but for all his devotion to the techniques of modernism, his goals in deploying and developing them were sometimes deliberately—even triumphantly—naive. To work against the limitations of traditional narrative was not a way to display his own mastery of modernist method but a necessary response to the need to break through, emotionally, to another person. So plain and dramatic a goal required a kind of willful denial of authorial distance. It was as though a story was never merely a story for Goyen but a demand for an unfiltered intimacy with a potential "beloved."

This paradox of a complex, highly aestheticized fiction that nevertheless aims for emotional nakedness is perhaps nowhere as clear as in Goyen's second novel, *Half a Look of Cain*. If all of his work can be understood as experimental spiritual autobiography, *Cain* may be the most forceful, strange, and fully realized of Goyen's attempts to bend or reshape narration in the service of intimate personal connection. Not easily described, the book is a complex inter-nesting of fables told by a series of narrators whose identities are not clearly distinguished. In the basic frame story, a man arrives at a lighthouse near Port Angeles, Washington, and discovers the written log of the previous keeper, a weaver and former therapeutic nurse named Curran.[35] The bulk of the novel that follows is comprised of this final record of the dying keeper, an account that reaches back to the postwar years in London when Curran, a young American, was completing his training as a physiotherapist at St. Bartholomew's Hospital. Among his patients is another young American named Chris, who has injured his right leg in a fall in Rome. While Chris is unconscious from surgery, Curran discovers a notebook among Chris's things and begins to read its initial entry, the story "The Figure Over the Town." Later, Curran writes his own stories (or are they memories?) into Chris's notebook, first in his own voice and later "collaborating" with Chris, using materials from earlier stories in the notebook and blending them with elements of his own invention. Characters introduced by Curran begin to appear in sections supposedly written previously by Chris, and in a final revelation, the new lighthouse keeper of the frame story is revealed as—or has assumed the identity of—one of Curran's and Chris's characters, a "fallen aerialist" named Marvello.

This brief sketch of the structure fails to account for the complexity and depth of the narrative interweaving in this novel's fairly compact space, but it does suggest one of Goyen's major goals: to emphasize the necessity of a collaborative intimacy in his life and work. As he had written to Curtius, to see one's work "*through* the beloved" had become a necessary idea for him at this point, and *Half a Look of Cain* attempts a complete embodiment of what it means to communicate fully with another human being. Curran is both nurse and therapeutic "weaver," shifting and shaping Chris's body back to wholeness, and this contact—significantly physical as well as imaginative—produces a bond of full exchange: "I am speaking of a connection," Curran explains, "woven, as of threads and veins and vessels, through which human beings may communicate and tell each other everything. . . . And this connection was between his dreaming mind breeding the images, on one side, on the other side mine, the shaping mind, conscious, controlled—or struggling to be—and the traffic beyond the wall, below the river, beneath the sidewalk" (*HLC* 24–25).

In the notes for what were probably later revisions of the book, Goyen describes Curran as "an old fantastic healer or saviour *deliverer* . . . ; the maker, or remaker, artificer, fabricateur" (*HLC* 130). He is an older version of Chris, an avatar of Charon, the ferryman, preparing his younger self for maturity and death. Marvello, according to Goyen's notes, is "the purified idea of both—their collaborative product" (*HLC* 131). In biographical terms, this dialectical synthesis seems designed to come to terms, retrospectively, with the scattering of Goyen's identity after the immediate postwar years in El Prado. Chris is still Christopher Icarus, fallen into Curran's healing loom, as though Goyen's tumble down the Spanish Steps marked the apex of his early flight, the end of who he had hoped to become. And now he had turned to his other role, the nurse, the giver of wings—Daedalus from *Section Two*—to recover and build a new, synthesized vision for himself. "The Figure Over the Town," with its central image of the flagpole sitter, Shipwreck Kelley, provides an initial point of meditation for Goyen's body-soul obsession, for considering "how the sensual grows into or out of the spiritual Idea, hangs on the back of the spiritual Idea, dragging it to its knees; and the struggle, eternally, seems to be between these two" (*HLC* 26). Kelley is an artist, a performer, in the center of the small town yet isolated above it, and therefore a heroic image of purity and ascetic devotion to principle. And yet no matter how attractive or admirable, his idealism could also be dangerous, a miscalculated repression. Goyen's notes reflect the concern: "The danger of *the idea*. Symbol of man on flagpole as the idea *above* humanity: does this involvement with a 'lofty' idea isolate, cut off one from the living world of the ground?" (HLC 130).

The flagpole sitter has sublimated his sensuality to what is literally a higher calling, but this willful rejection of ordinary, sensual life inevitably evokes the possibility of its opposite, the sexualized "Act" of Marvello. Though similarly elevated, Marvello's is a contrasting art of the body; he has adapted his extraordinary "sensual properties," what amounts to an almost self-destructive eroticism, into a performance that evokes "the shape and instrument of love" (*HLC* 44), becoming in the process a willing object of desire to all who see him. As Curtius intuited, Marvello's story has its roots in the portrait of Folner from *The House of Breath*, but it is also clearly related to the theater-crazed Billy Goyen of "Margo."[36] Marvello is the paradigmatic Goyen youth, haunted by sexuality, an exile in a moribund hometown: "I had a fire in my brains. Alone around the place, my home, that seemed to be dying, I went about in my hot secrecy and my goading loneliness with my desire that made me speechless when it possessed me as though it burned my tongue out of my mouth, and seared my words away. I fell into fits of speechless trembling, and I did not know how to use it, my desire" (*HLC* 40–41). He runs away, chasing a circus in hopes of joining a family of aerialists, the Ishbels. With his particular gift for the sensual, Marvello quickly becomes the star of the family show and, like Shipwreck Kelley, an object of desire to all who see him. But unlike the flagpole sitter, who turns away from the overtures of the desiring crowd, Marvello both desires and depends upon sexual contact with members of his audience: "I gave it willingly to whomever [sic] wished it and if they were beautiful and if I wanted them. . . . I found and knew all the ways of love, and my lovers flocked after me and followed the show sometimes, from city to city. My body's hungers were insatiable" (*HLC* 43).

Like Kelley, Marvello soon provokes a social disturbance, a "revolution among the young," and as a result the public begins to turn against him. "They accused me of witchcraft," he explains. "But I had thought I was only searching for my own reality, regardless of the consequences, in a time when men could not find theirs" (*HLC* 45). Here the parallels between Marvello's sudden fame and Goyen's self-justifying reaction to his recent success become clearer. Marvello is offered prizes by the arbiters of his art but only if he compromises to assure its popularity. He is imitated by lesser aerialists and betrayed by those who, in his view, lacked his artistic courage: "For these saw that I was acting out their own secret desires, and delivered to me the punishment which they felt would come to them if they made real, as I had, their own hidden reality" (*HLC* 46). After being attacked by his brother artist, Pietro, Marvello falls and injures his right leg. Exiled, marked as a spiritual fratricide, he descends into debauchery, becoming little more than a sense-driven animal until he begins to seek regeneration through some higher connection to a loved one: "I knew I had to be brought to life, to my reality again through love, if I could find the one who would die with me and bring a resurrection, a rising to life: one who would admit and face the Cain in me and in all others and with me seek our common brotherhood" (*HLC* 50).

Like Folner, Marvello is a warning against too great an investment in the flesh, just as Shipwreck Kelley demonstrates the potential emptiness of pure intellect. These two performers of physical balance each suggest Goyen's abiding interest in an image that would allow him to justify, demonstrate, and control his unruly struggle between flesh and spirit. The idea of the acrobat had come to him very early in his development. A first and liberating influence was William Saroyan's *The Daring Young Man on the Flying Trapeze*, which Goyen checked out of the public library when he was sixteen and (as he put it) "voiceless" (*GAE* 58). If the cardboard piano was the emblem of his urgent, stifled youth, writing such as Saroyan's offered a way to smuggle a different kind of music from its paper keys. In Saroyan's initial pages, Goyen likely recognized the possibility of himself and seized its image:

"From a hill he saw a city standing majestically in the east, great towers, dense with his kind, and there he was suddenly outside of it all, almost definitely certain that he should never gain admittance, almost positive that somehow he had ventured upon the wrong earth, or perhaps into the wrong age, and now a young man of twenty-two was to be permanently ejected from it. This thought was not saddening. He said to himself, sometime soon I must write *An Application for Permission to Live*. . . . *Through the air on the flying trapeze*, his mind hummed. Amusing it was, astoundingly funny. A trapeze to God, or to nothing, a flying trapeze to some sort of eternity; he prayed objectively for strength to make the flight with grace."[37]

Saroyan's young man dares to write without a safety net, "to be honest and fearless in my own way."[38] His performance, in other words, combines display with revelation in a physical gesture that seeks the higher plane of spirit. This potential method for integrating personal and artistic tensions may have been reinforced a few years later when Goyen read J. B. Leishman and Stephen Spender's 1939 translation of Rilke's *Duino Elegies*. In the fifth elegy, the poet contemplates the traveling acrobats of Picasso's *Les Saltimbanques*:

> But tell me, who *are* they, these acrobats, even a little
> more fleeting than we ourselves,—so urgently, ever since childhood,
> wrung by an (oh, for the sake of whom?)
> never-contented will? (1–4)[39]

In a letter to Hart from 1942, Goyen evoked the wandering *saltimbanque* as his surrogate for coping with the demands of officer training. "The engineers, the mathematicians and the reasoners," he argued, have seized control of the times, forcing artists to vie for attention: "[We have to] walk on our head[s] with our feet in the air. But we must do this like genuine acrobats (like Rilke's acrobat) and make them marvel so at our gymnastic feat that they would paint us as Picasso did."[40] Though he may have conjured this image initially as a countervision to wartime "rational" or technological requirements, Goyen also understood the acrobats' essentially sacrificial function as representatives of a love unachievable by their "spectators":

> Angel: suppose there's a place we know nothing about, and there,
> on some indescribable carpet, lovers showed all that here
> they're for ever unable to manage—their daring
> lofty figures of heart-flight,
> their towers of pleasure, their ladders,
> long since, where ground never was, just quiveringly
> propped by each other,—suppose they could manage it there,
> before the spectators ringed round, the countless unmurmuring dead:

would not the dead then fling their last, their for ever reserved,
ever-concealed, unknown to us, ever-valid
coins of happiness down before the at last
truthfully smiling pair on the quietened carpet? (96–108)

This "supreme moment of genuine being," as Kathleen L. Komar points out, is also "one of nonbeing and seems possible only as such."[41] Thus the example or exemplar of the artist-lovers can only be registered through the sacrificial logic so attractive to Goyen, particularly in his early years. The exile will, once again, perfectly perform the balancing act of an art that assumes the shape of love, in the process assuming the burden of "saving" those who have alienated him. The performance will require, however, his own death, in a sense the renewal of his absence as he vanishes like Shipwreck Kelley, leaving behind only his "place" for others to inhabit.

In the third section of *Half a Look of Cain*, Goyen more directly confronts the darker implications of the final stanza of Rilke's fifth elegy. The story entitled "The House on the River, or: The Construction East of Town" gives us a compressed, mythic near-allegory of love between Chris and a young woman named Stella. Having met on the stairs of the boarding house where they both live, the couple soon fall into an almost wordless but savage passion. Convinced that the "suspicions of men" are always hostile to love, they find a "large, unreal house" (*HLC* 72) on a knoll beside a wide river. The "magnificent" structure is apparently slated for demolition, and like two exiles—"the world was made for two people only and it reveals itself fully only to two people, no more" (*HLC* 72)—they take possession. Like almost all of Goyen's fictional houses, this strange and almost spectral dwelling is a version of the archetypal "place" in *The House of Breath*, only this time with additional fantastic details: "Its color was a delicate raspberry and its many windows were deep blue and carmine glass. There were four gables, each with little tentlike roofs, and over these rose a grand tented gable whose precious windows shone like jewels" (*HLC* 72). Because of the encroaching destruction of the neighborhood for an unspecified construction project, the site is eventually encircled by a moat of river water, isolating the "enchanted country of this house" (*HLC* 72) from the rest of the world.

The turret in which Chris and Stella take residence instantly becomes an idealized space of "work" and love. In a description that mirrors Goyen's sketch of the loft he was sharing with Glasco on West Twenty-Third Street, the room is both cut off from the building below and divided into complementary work spaces. The two almost imaginary lovers live only for one another, and when they venture across the space that separates them from society, they are viewed with suspicion, as representatives of "a magnificent animal heritage," something "beautiful and dangerous" (*HLC* 76). Eventually the destruction begins to threaten their sanctuary. Stella becomes pregnant, they quarrel, and at the very moment that they recognize this shift in their connection to one another, a flagpole sitter appears over the city. The small and distant figure, whom they name Marvello, seems mysteriously tied to the unborn child; he crouches on the flagpole, folding "himself into a natal shape" (*HLC* 79). The destruction increases. Large explosions cause Marvello to fall from his perch, and the lovers, now with the newborn baby, lock themselves in their room as the house is destroyed around them. In the end, a ferryman waits to carry one figure across the river. Curran, the story's teller, offers this crossing to Chris as a way toward "healing and deliverance" (*HLC* 81).

The ideal relationship, the almost maddening binding with another person, succumbs equally to the hostile energies of progress and the demonic energies of sexuality and love. "Why should the act of love," Curran asks, "of the creation of beauty, provoke violence and fear and this half-Cain in men? We speak of how love purifies and chastens and spiritualizes, but we must be reminded that it demonizes, as well" (*HLC* 76). *Half a Look of Cain* turns to this problem again and again, obsessively threading its fragments into images that question but never unbind this dualism. Only the "weaving" of Curran the healer, manipulating the body of Chris—and the corresponding fictional braiding that makes up the book's dizzying structure—suggest a possible response, a way of holding in place the straining energies of this question. The goal, as it so often was for Goyen, is "healing": "All the world heals in one healing injured man: regenerate him and you regenerate the world. I think it is the worthiest task in this human world; and I would do it all again, had I to do it or were I called to it" (*HLC* 115).

The manuscript of *Half a Look of Cain* was completed in February of 1953. By May it had been rejected twice, first by Random House, which had published *The House of Breath* and *Ghost and Flesh*, and then by Harcourt Brace. The rejections puzzled and outraged Goyen. "I have quit Random House, in a great battle," he proclaimed to Margaret Hartley. "I told them, as I had a year ago, that I was in the wrong country, that they are deserters, traitors, and scoundrels; they will see, or I will."[42] The sense of betrayal only increased when Goyen learned that the manuscript had been sent for approval to a critic for *Time*. According to Anaïs Nin, who met Goyen around this time, "They paid [the critic] 175 dollars for reading it, and as he said 'No,' Random House turned it down. A new kind of rigged game in publishing. Since *Time* has the power to make or break a writer, the publisher might as well know in advance. These critics make as much as 2000 dollars a week in this way."[43] To Maurice Edgar Coindreau, who was busy translating *The House of Breath* into French, Goyen sounded a more plaintive and perplexed note: "The two American publishers who have seen parts of it have for some curious reason beyond me been 'shocked' by it! This has me bewildered. They all praise the writing, the form, etc., but they profess not to understand what I am talking about!"[44] As Gibbons suggests, part of the reaction was likely due to the book's transgressive handling of sexuality (*HLC* 133). Not only is Marvello a kind of multisexual being desired by all, both men and women, but his vaguely described "Act" takes eroticism beyond typical channels of desire into a near madness or mania that threatens even progressive notions of sexual behavior. "The Dangerous Archipelago," a section of Chris's journal that records his reaction to the aerialists' performance in Rome, begins with a description that dares to suggest a high-wire ménage à trois:

> The muscles of the two men, and particularly those of Marvello, who was powerful yet lithe, and the gentle liquid quiver of their buttocks, swelled and sank and tightened with the erotic grace of male passion. Their thighs and loins and bellies surrounded, as if to insulate it, that dangerous engine whose language The Act seemed to be, the hub and the shaft which turned the wheel of this marvelous machinery. . . . The two men drew near each other upon the wire in a gradually increasing ferocity of pressing, their torsos hunching and relaxing and hunching again as they balanced themselves aloft; and then the girl, a crystal and stellar creature, would slide down between them, delicately fitting as the blade of the sword; and together, in an overwhelmingly exciting climax, the two young men would fit against her almost as they were

molding themselves around her voluptuous form—it was marvelous the way their bodies fitted into one magnificent white body of flesh— and moved, like a machine, to lift her up as they had ejected her from the cleaving opening between their one body which their two bodies had made. (*HLC* 85)

The idea that the sexual tensions between two men and a woman could be resolved—or at least captured, held in a sublimating form—must have seemed both vitally useful to Goyen at this point in his life and compulsively necessary. Though there are echoes of other relationships in *Half a Look of Cain* (including those with Glasco and Porter), the book never strays far from its initial motivation: to provide a fictional space for Goyen to review and reimagine the emotional turmoil of his complex connection to Dorothy Robinson and Walter Berns. It is not necessarily a surprise, then, that editors at mainstream publishing houses would find such material shocking, but neither is it strange that Goyen would fail to understand their reaction. For him, this exploration of his own torn sexuality, here presented in its most daring form to date, could no longer be avoided. "It is, above all," he wrote to Coindreau, "a very urgent and necessary statement, for me."[45]

What is a bit more puzzling, as Gibbons rightly notes, is the reaction of Goyen's translators. Both Curtius and Coindreau ultimately suggested that he put the book away, that its subject matter was "ahead of its time," a judgment Goyen ultimately accepted, though not without considerable disappointment.[46] Sexual politics of the 1950s may have been at play, of course, but it is also possible that Curtius and Coindreau thought that the book's very personal material had not fully risen out of its private system of references. Goyen's sense that the book's material "lies in such a buried world" reinforces this possibility: that his highly developed method of psychological excavation, of exposing a still repressed personal symbolism, had taken him so far in this case that he had difficulty drawing in his readers.[47] As Curtius suggested in his response to the book, "But what will surprise him [the reader] is the absence of everything belonging to the outer world. It is an amazing phenomenon of a purely introverted attitude towards life . . . The reader has the feeling of being slowly involved in a dream, in which all the problems of your present life appear and center around Marvello."[48]

There is no doubt that *Half a Look of Cain* was the most daring—

and arguably, the most brilliant—work Goyen had attempted thus far. Not until his final novel, *Arcadio*, would he risk so complete and un-shielded an investigation of his own secrecies. He had, in effect, dared everything in this book and in the process made himself more vulner-able than ever to the consequences of his artistic idealism. "For me," he explained to Curtius, "I know that the work of the artist is a salvaging and a purification. Knowing this, what else can I do but what I do, how else can I be but what I am?"[49] Confirmed by the success of *The House of Breath*, Goyen had pushed himself through the trauma of *Ghost and Flesh* and toward a personal revelation even he could not fully contain or understand. The writing of *Cain* seemed to mark a breakthrough, even a shattering of something long protected, but it wasn't clear what its rejection meant to his search for balance. And where should he go from here, when this "necessary statement" remained unheard, appar-ently unwanted and misunderstood?

CHAPTER NINE 〜

A Farther Country
1954–1956

I am an exile, but at home, where every exile should be; and I do my work, there is so much to be done, I have not enough time nor peace; but I will not change.

GOYEN TO ROBERT LINSCOTT, AUGUST 16, 1954

Though a serious setback, Goyen's inability to find a publisher for *Half a Look of Cain* didn't slow his pace of work. He continued to move forward on the dramatization of *The House of Breath* and started a collection of stories tentatively titled *Crossings*. There were also collaborations and signs of interest from other writers. The French and German translations of *The House of Breath* were almost complete; a playwright, Greer Johnson, was working on an adaptation of one of the stories from *Ghost and Flesh*; and a group of filmmakers at Princeton was shooting a thirty-minute film version of "The White Rooster."

On a personal level, the return to El Prado was good for Goyen's physical and mental health. Despite arriving in bitterly cold weather and struggling to heat the small adobe house, Goyen and Glasco went to work, rising at six each morning and stopping only to shovel the snow from the adobe's flat roof or to make a simple dinner. Money, as always, was an issue. Fuel cost more than food, and Goyen continued to rely on his parents to make the occasional car payment or send extra furniture, and sometimes cash, from Houston. Even so, a short trip to New York in April only confirmed his choice to live in quiet and relative isolation. "Whatever happens," he wrote to Houston, "I'm going back to Taos, if I have to starve. That's where I want to be."[1] Glasco, too, seems to have adapted quickly and happily to the new atmosphere.

With the proceeds from the sale of some of his paintings, he purchased half of the El Prado property from Walter Berns and used the rest of the money to buy the materials to build a large studio onto one end of the house. The idea of a partnership was important to Goyen, and it brought a measure of financial relief to have someone who was committed to sharing ownership and the responsibilities that came with it.

Tiny El Prado hadn't changed much since Goyen's last extended residency in 1949, before the trip to England and the publication of *The House of Breath*. The remnants of the Lawrence circle were aging, of course, but still present enough to provide support and friendship. Brett in particular was a nightly dinner guest, walking over from her house with food to share and staying after to play Chinese checkers or anagrams. With the arrival of spring, Frieda returned from Port Isabel, happy to find young neighbors across the road again. It wasn't long before she was hatching a plan to give the Kiowa Ranch to Goyen and Glasco. "It would mean that we would live up there in the summers," Goyen wrote his parents, "with her in her little house, and the agreement would be that we would look after her while she lives, every summer up there, and gradually get the place into shape."[2] The idea excited and intrigued both Goyen and Glasco at first. "It's 165 acres, heavily wooded (the timber should be cut at once), two houses, four dwellings, swimming-pool, corrals, barns, etc." But the thought of so great a responsibility, particularly given their precarious finances, eventually put an end to the fantasy.

Despite Goyen's periodic yearnings for stability of place, he continued to resist anything that might compromise his freedom of movement or expression. And this ultimately included being tied down even to El Prado. A shortage of money restricted his travels during most of the year, and when he did receive $1,000 for a theatrical option on "The Letter in the Cedarchest," he was forced to spend most of it putting a new roof on the house. However, in February of 1954, word came that he'd received a second Guggenheim Fellowship, and by April he and Glasco were unpacking in a studio apartment on the Via Margutta in Rome. "Such a dazzlement and dash," Goyen wrote to Brett, "so much new and old, so much vivacity and beauty here, I have not been able, quite yet, to collect my mind."[3] In fact, Rome threw him almost immediately into emotional turmoil: "The sensuality, the spirituality, all wound together—the bitterness of these—and so much to feel, to question, to ponder: I went away, for a while, and I thought I couldn't bear it; too much was brought to bear on me; I lost my equilibrium."[4]

The plan had been to stay for six months or so, seeing the sights but, more important, settling in for serious work. Glasco would haunt the galleries and paint. Goyen would get back to the *Crossings* stories, now coalescing into a novel to be called *Spain*, and continue the play adaptation. In spite of, or perhaps due to, his reaction to the city, Goyen's writing intensified and accelerated at first: "Nowhere have I ever felt the sensual and the spiritual so warring with each other, and within myself. . . . It is a very good time from the point of view of my work."[5] The familiar tension between home and exile reasserted itself as well; the stories "Old Wildwood" and "A People of Grass," for instance, each begin in Rome, only to make their way back, once more, to East Texas. But if the war between flesh and spirit animated Goyen's work initially, Rome's expenses soon overwhelmed its inspirations. The apartment cost $100 a month, and though the food at the local markets was good—"artichokes, spaghettis, a bunch of anemones, a few eggs, slices of meat"—it, too, was beyond their slim means. Soon Goyen was scrambling to gather money from disparate sources. His publisher in France, Gallimard, owed him $100, but exchange problems made it impossible to transfer. Curtius sent a small sum out of his own pocket but not enough to allay the constant worry that the city would consume too much time and energy before any meaningful work could be accomplished. After only two months—the second of which Goyen called one of the unhappiest of his life—the decision was made to retreat to Ischia, the rocky island near Naples, to look for cheaper housing. "Rome was too much of a muchness," he wrote to Bill Hart, "a haunting place not knowing much what to do about itself, at this point in its history—the Romans, from my point of view, don't know whether they are Julius Caesar, Pope Pius or Ava Gardner, but they are damned well going to be a little of each, and profit by it."[6]

The little town of Forio proved just what the situation demanded: inexpensive, vivid, romantic. Not only was the "charming little house" only $40 a month, but the surroundings were both beautiful and simple, not unlike El Prado. "Now—this lovely place," Goyen wrote to Bill Hart, "with the melancholy sea all around, Naples two hours away, native filth and odors, one solid vineyard and grove of lemons, oranges, olives, pomegranates, cherries, figs. A noisy people who shout rather than speak, poverty-ridden, processions at dusk in the little streets with children throwing roses—petals to Maria, cheap, removed. . . ."[7] Now there was quiet and reduced anxiety for "long uninterrupted work-days," an ideal condition that lasted until the latter weeks of June when the possibility of publishing *Half a Look of Cain* in German accelerated Goyen's plans to visit Curtius in Switzerland. The aging translator and legendary man of letters had recently experienced a serious stroke, and Goyen was anxious to spend time with him before his health deteriorated further. As an added inducement, the Swiss-German publisher Peter Schifferli had recently offered to take on the controversial manuscript and wanted to discuss publication plans in Zurich.

Curtius had become an important and influential figure for Goyen. They had met at Frieda Lawrence's ranch in 1949, possibly at the urging of Spender, who had been close to Curtius for several years, and Goyen and Curtius had almost immediately formed an intense advisor-student relationship. Goyen recalled their conversation on that occasion as "one of the most impressive experiences of [his] life."[8] Curtius had arrived during one of Goyen's frequent emotional crises, and his advice and insight steadied the aspiring artist to such an extent that they became regular correspondents until the older man's death in 1956. The friendship was bolstered by Curtius's translation in 1952 of *The House of Breath*, a publication that put Goyen in the company of Faulkner, T. S. Eliot, and other important American writers rendered into German by that country's most eminent translator.[9] In a luminous preface, Curtius cast his idealistic friend as the archetypal isolated artist: "The loneliness of the young American who indentures his life to literature, let alone to poetry, is absolutely distinct from that of his European colleague, and infinitely more cruel."[10] He also praised the novel in terms that could only have been head-spinning to a young writer: "In William Goyen's book we shall find very different elements: substantive poetry (as I have already said); harmony with the deepest simplicities of existence; reunion of sexuality with love; but also an artistic discipline that is more reminiscent of Flaubert, Proust, Joyce, than of Melville, Wolfe, Faulkner."[11]

Like Frieda, Curtius had become one of Goyen's few trusted advisors, a man of deep sympathy and acute understanding of art and artists, and

Goyen's chance to see and speak to him again, particularly after the difficulties with *Half a Look of Cain*, held the promise of needed clarity in his life and work. So it was a visceral shock to get to Flimsdorf in the Oberland and find the mentor he so valued literally speechless. The stroke Curtius had suffered some months before had left him silent and unable to move on his own. Communication was almost impossible, and the difficulty of talking to an unresponsive listener left Goyen both puzzled and exhausted. Some years later, he sketched out the plot of a novel in which a young American travels to London to meet "an idol: a German Architect, a great mind of European culture." When he arrives, hoping to "find enlightenment and understanding in his own search," he encounters instead "silence and an invalided mind" (HRC 24.7). Unable to establish the connection he craves, the American moves in with the couple and becomes, simultaneously, the older man's nurse and the younger wife's lover. The story was apparently never developed beyond this sketch, but it gives a suggestive sense of how shocked Goyen was by this strange, one-sided encounter.

Goyen and Glasco stayed in Switzerland for only a few weeks, leaving in late July for New York before passing through Houston on the way to El Prado. The negotiations with the Swiss publishing house *Die Arche* did not go as smoothly as Goyen had hoped. "They are trying to swindle me," he wrote to Brett from Zurich, "to be as cunning as all publishers, and I am holding out. . . . I am tired to death of the wiles and tricks of publishers, and, alas, I have not found them any different here from those in America."[12] This distrust carried over into a subsequent meeting, a few weeks later, with Robert Linscott in New York, who, as Goyen wrote to Curtius, had "such a pall of death over him, he had no life; that city was dreadful, it paralyzed me."[13] The problems with *Half a Look of Cain* had soured the relationship with Linscott to such an extent that in a few months Goyen was writing secretly to David McDowell, another Random House editor, to ask for help.[14] McDowell was ultimately able to take over as Goyen's editor, and by the end of the fall offered him a contract for the newly completed novel, *Artifices of Spain*. Retitled *In a Farther Country*, it was published in August of 1955. "A little Romance" is how Goyen described it to his friends: "It is both merry and sad," he wrote to the ailing Curtius, "and I do hope you take to it."[15]

The Dream of Telling: *In a Farther Country*

"It is beyond all other places of telling," Marietta went on, thrilled to further elaboration, "beyond the bar, beyond the parked car, beyond the fireside, beyond the bed of lovers. I think, when we come to it, we might find it is a place of silence where only the riffle of a falling leaf, the bend of a blowing blade of grass, the dropping of one tear or the sounding of one measure of laughter, tells the last thing."

IN A FARTHER COUNTRY

At night all the buildings are dark and empty and we are the only residents in the strange block. But our loft is very nice and Joe works in one end, I in the other. A small, very old and croupy bird, a canary we bought in Kresses for a dollar and half, lives with us, and that is all.

LETTER TO MARGARET L. HARTLEY AND ALLEN MAXWELL,
SEPTEMBER 24, 1952

In the preface to his 1852 novel, *The Blithedale Romance*, Nathaniel Hawthorne attempted to define a particular kind of nonrealist space for the characters in his fictionalized utopian community. Perhaps disingenuously, he claimed immunity from political reflection and instead presented Blithedale as a "theatre, a little removed from the highway of ordinary travel, where the creatures of [the author's] brain may play their phantasmagorical antics, without exposing them to too close a comparison with the actual events of real lives." This world would be "like the real world" but imbued "with an atmosphere of strange enchantment, beheld through which the inhabitants would have a propriety of their own."[16] Hawthorne adapted the generic term "romance" to stand for this particular blend of realism and fantasy, a designation thought by many twentieth-century critics to have inaugurated the first genuinely American variation on the novel. Hawthorne seemed to be seeking a degree of freedom from the collective vision of the real, a way to tell stories that could express or shadow forth an inner landscape unique to the singular mind of the writer.

Though the term may sound anachronistic, Goyen had arguably been a type of romancer for most of his writing life.[17] His tendency to associate the occasion of telling with a particular location suggests a claim similar to Hawthorne's. In Goyen's case, however, it is the momentary magic of the scene of self-exposure that grants imaginative license to the storyteller; the freedom from the disabling touch of the real makes possible the "atmosphere of enchantment" and the peculiar viability of the fantastic. The "splendid, fallen house" of *The House of Breath* is the most obvious example of this kind of "removed" world, but particularly in the early 1950s, the adobe house in Taos came to stand in Goyen's mind for the possibilities of imagination in a hostile world. In many respects, the El Prado house was his first, and perhaps truest, attempt to realize an ideal personal and artistic space, and *In a Further Country* is his hymn to New Mexico and its promise of unrestricted revelation.

To emphasize his conviction that El Prado, for all its beauty and particularity, was significant as an *idea*, Goyen set the novel not in New Mexico but in a one-dimensional, hyper-urban Manhattan. The shop and apartment that bear the name "Artifices of Spain" was based on the large loft above a used piano store on West Twenty-Third that Goyen and Glasco shared in late 1952 before moving to Taos. The neighborhood of small factories bustled with people during the day, but at night the pair found themselves surrounded by the silence of empty buildings. The sense of isolation and elevated enclosure intensified the contrast between inner and outer worlds, an opposition central to the novel's almost magical claims: "At night when all the workers were gone away and the iron barriers drawn across the entrances to drab wholesale shops and small factories, the buildings might house a dream to which their daytime circumstances gave no room or harbor" (*IFC* 3–4). This is Goyen's nod to the Hawthornian romance; the small space is almost real but not quite, almost a dream but uncertain in its commitment to the ideal.

Into this world enters Marietta McGee-Chavéz. Like all half-magical characters, her appearance is sudden, unexplained, and transformative. She walks into a factory storefront owned by Thomas Harold MacDougal, purveyor of cheap plaster copies of Roman art, and almost instantly becomes its new creative source. Marietta is an artist, perhaps the last living "carrier" of the ancient art of Colcha embroidery. As her name suggests, she is divided between cultures, a conduit of old-world ideals in a corrupt, soulless city. A Mexican American father and a mother from East Texas have produced in her a "born conflict of blood": "For if she did have Spanish hips and the Spanish flash of face about the cheekbone and nose, these were compromised by the tow-headedness laid on her like a comic wig by inheritance from all her kinfolks on her mother's side in Trinity Country, Texas" (*IFC* 7). With her East Texas roots, Marrietta draws in part on Goyen's mother, whose middle name (Inez) may have suggested the idea of a Spanish mixture, and from Mary Ganchion of *Christopher Icarus*, who channels her deep sadness through her sewing and singing. She is also another stand-in for Goyen himself, who often translated his sense of inner division into a racial or cultural metaphor and who clearly identified with the idea of the pure artist at odds with a materialistic culture.[18] "I was that woman Marietta McGee-Chavéz," Goyen admitted in a late interview. "I had gone to live for a year in New York on West Twenty-Third Street, which is the ugliest place, really a hell street. I lived in a loft there, right smack in the middle of it. The feeling of hovering between the New York reality and the unreal enchantment of the mud life in the desert in that strange part of the world, that feeling led me to write a really quite autobiographical book."[19]

Given his recent conflicts with publishers in Europe and the United States, it's understandable that Goyen would want to construct a fable about the isolation of the artist in a commercial environment. Mr. Mac-Dougal's factory suggests a satire of contemporary publishing (his name may echo David McDowell's), producing cheap copies of genuine art, reliant upon the deep soul-work of the almost imprisoned artist: "From this island kingdom above, where Marietta McGee-Chavéz was Queen, as she said, and kept her old country, there depended this dependency of 'Artifices of Spain,' a solid lower peninsula where Thomas Harold MacDougal was outlaw King and substantially pirated the dream above" (*IFC* 5). Via her imagination, Marietta must maintain an inviolable space, a self-constructed "country" of individual vision that saves her from "the base of forgeries" (*IFC* 5) in the factory below. Her art, like Goyen's, is an act of self-healing, of making a "full and beautiful and recognizable design" that can hold together her inner divisions. MacDougal merely exploits the product of her pain, keeping her locked in a cage from which she continually and mysteriously escapes.

Marietta's wanderings are a form of homesickness, a search for connection to the lost sources of her conflict and art. She begins to pay daily visits to Woolworth's department store in part because it reminds her of an S. H. Kress dime store from her youth in Texas:

> In that hot, sultry wonderplace in the summer, there would be the boys loitering around the counters, the pretty sales-girls just graduated from high school and whom she wished she looked like, with long curls and sweetheart faces; or the mean flapper with the little pink hairelip, not caring about anything in her blood-red lipstick and hoop earings, and singing some torchsong as she arranged the boxes and bottles and tubes on her counter; someone calling, "Number six please! number six!" and holding in the air a five-dollar bill to be changed if ever number six would come with the money bag; and over it all, in the sky of Kresses, was the busy trolley clicking and carrying the money tubes up to the cloudy balcony where three pep-girls sat aloft emptying and filling them and knocking and rolling them around while they seemed to be confiding things in each other that might be about the whole dream of Kresses they were causing to happen below. (*IFC* 21–22)

Woolworth's has some of this same world-making magic, though with the added pleasures of nylons and plastics and a pet department, where Marietta finds a "faded-out Macaw" that she insists is actually a roadrunner from New Mexico. This "roadrunner" becomes her symbol and emblem, an exile like her, noticeably losing its life force because of its urban captivity. It also suggests her will—and Goyen's—to transform New York into Taos, to hold onto a vision of the self as isolated, natural, unsophisticated, and able to sing only through its connection to an unspoiled landscape.

Goyen eventually came to think of the roadrunner as his personal totem, reproducing its image on his stationery. As it does for Marietta, the idea of the common bird—"a strange combination of wildness and awkwardness, beauty and plainness" (*IFC* 22–23)—served as a reminder of what mattered most to him as an artist: that sense of honesty and rootedness that outweighs (but does not preclude) the impulse to refinement or polish. As Marietta explains to the sales clerk in Woolworth's, the Spanish knew the bird both as a messenger to his countrymen and as a *mestizo*, like Marietta herself, "a mixture of absurdity and dignity, orneriness and beauty" (*IFC* 40). Equally, however, the macaw is a kind of phoenix. Brought mysteriously back to life after its death in the department store, the bird becomes the reborn symbol of Marietta's imaginary "Spanish" world, its cry set against the noise of the passing trucks: "It is a call that could join two opponents, two warring halves, she thought, with her sadness again and yet with that old thrilling hope rousing in her breast" (*IFC* 52). The "roadrunner's" presence thus establishes the possibility of reconciliation through the telling of stories. Marietta's room becomes more than a workshop for her self-expression; it now offers a shelter for those lost in the city, "a speaking place and a joining place" (*IFC* 127).

Accordingly, visitors begin to appear as though drawn by an irresistible force. Their stories make up the bulk of the novel as it accretes examples of human loss and loneliness made bearable by the chance to speak to a sympathetic audience. The cast is both bizarre and oddly primitive, and the imagination that produces them almost childlike. There is an "egg-shaped" visitor named Mr. Cumberly; a fat, constantly laughing man carrying a mandolin with strings made from the hair of a dead woman; an English woman called Oris, who wears half-Wellington boots and a "cavalry-man's marching coat" and is accompanied by a white wolfhound; a wandering young man with seeds in his beard; an ex-bullfighter; a nun and priest; and a brusque, "earthy woman dressed in multiple Navajo skirts and a black velvet bolero" (*IFC* 156). Some of these obviously southwestern figures are fabulous versions of Taos personalities. Oris is built upon the "faintly uncouth" image of Dorothy Brett, who had a large hound named Palomar and wore what Goyen called "slapstick" clothes (*GAE* 18). The nosy neighbor Lois Fuchs expands upon the disruptive Taos presence of Mabel Dodge Luhan, whom Goyen once labeled a "malicious meddler" and a "woman practically nobody liked" (*GAE* 22, 23). But whatever the biographical sources of the characters, their importance lies in their commonality: they are all figures of artistic potential as the drive to expression emerges from trauma. Egg and seed images proliferate. Mr. Cumberly's shape finds its echo in Chalmers *Eg*strom and in the seeded hair of Oris and "seminal" beard of Jack Flanders. The characters carry the possibility of rebirth with them, in other words, in their shape or their gathered experience. To "tell a thing never told before," as Lois Fuchs puts it, is to "find a past" for yourself, and each of these characters is attempting to locate him- or herself in a history that is at last accurate and unreserved.

Of these staged stories, two in particular stand out. The sudden outburst of biographical confession by the young Jack Flanders had particularly deep roots for Goyen, growing in part from the biography of his old friend Bill Hart. Flanders is a scarred wanderer, separated from his missing mother and imprisoned father. Like Hart, he works in a library and learns to drink: "I met a very bad young man and we became close friends. We drank together. I told him about the best books in the library, for I read as many as I could" (*IFC* 132). Eventually he reunites with his mother and is able to visit the now-freed father he has never met. But the father has had a stroke and cannot speak, and Flanders can only write short notes on slips of paper to attempt to communicate with him. Compelled by a need to express himself, he thinks to become an actor, but the deadening silence of his family drives him to a self-lacerating madness. In the fields outside town, he slashes his own face and is pitched into a hallucinatory vision. Fishermen emerge from a shimmering sea, and one—"shy of eye and of dripping fair face"—pulls a strand of "green sea grass" from the nets, drapes it on his hair, kisses it, and casts it back into the water. The grass disappears, but the fisherman soon dives in after it, "smitten" by the magic of the sea. The dreaming Flanders imagines himself following him, searching him out in the depths: "I reached for the grass and plucked from his girdle a handful of little green seeds and tasted of them; and I rose like a shaft coming to the surface, all changed in myself. I had something marvelous and miraculous to tell, now . . ." (*IFC* 138).

Onto the basic outline of Bill Hart's early life, Goyen had grafted the myth of Glaucus. The story had haunted him for years. To Katherine Anne Porter he admitted that his life was "bound up" with the legends of Icarus and Glaucus, the one attempting to escape by flight, the other longing for a missing person or world. Robert Phillips, in his notes to Goyen's letters, correctly intuits that the primary value of the story for Goyen was its ability to capture the essence of his relationship with Walter Berns. Explaining his plans to Curtius, Goyen gave a sense of how the legend captures the sense of isolation and loss he felt after Berns's marriage: "Then I plan to leap immediately into a third book, this one about a subject that haunts me and one which I must try— it is about Glaucus, the Greek boy who ate of the strange weed of the sea and changed his life. He left a friend on the shore who, until this day, continues to watch the sea and the shore for his friend who might one day return; and he thinks himself to find, perhaps, the weed, the thought, the magic, the mystery which took his beloved friend from him and into a world which he cannot enter."[20] Jack Flanders's version may have been Goyen's attempt to rework the story into a more hopeful expression of artistic and personal development. Flanders rises from the water in an echo of the sexual, apotheosic surfacings of Boy and Christy in *The House of Breath*. He emerges in order to tell his story and recover the truth that restoration lies in the recovery of the knotted complex of sex and death, love and loss. And though his faith in that process begins to fail when he returns to the silences of his parents, other characters recognize the value of his vision. Oris, in particular, perhaps channeling the kind of advice Brett could give to her Taos neighbors, assumes the book's prophetic voice: "Give it up, let it go. Having cast it all upon the waters, watch it all go out to sea, endless sea; and wait on the shore. Wait, wait, wait; and believe. And, my dear Jack Flanders, slowly slowly it will begin to come back, your priceless present, and this time towfold, to give" (*IFC* 144).

Flanders's story anchors the book, gathering together in a more substantial narrative the themes of the other tellers. But the final tale is given to the interruptive presence of Lois Fuchs, who asserts her right to join the company and "tell a thing never told before" (*IFC* 157). Her chapter is entitled "Jaime," the name of her young lover but also a cross-linguistic pun on the French for "I love," *j'aime*. And it is indeed a tale of passion or erotic madness between the young Lois, who is a schoolteacher, and one of her students, a seventeen-year-old "Spanish boy." Lois's history is dominated by the death of her twin sister, Clovis, who reaches puberty only to die of blood poisoning associated with her first menstrual period. Clovis's death haunts Lois, who believes that the emergence of her own sexuality will kill her as well. She ignores and avoids her desires: "Every day I felt my prettiness going out of me. It seemed that Clovis had taken all our beauty with her into death. I did not think of love, fearing it and hating it. Clovis had taken all that part of us with her into her grave. When the other girls spoke of it I ran out of the room. What no one knew was that Clovis' Death was happening to me constantly, day after day, and I was dying with it" (*IFC* 160–161).

Lois is thirty-five when she begins the affair with Jaime. He is Catholic, and his parents are forcing him to enter the seminary in San Francisco to become a priest. As with most of Goyen's depictions of erotic relationships, the sudden, unpredicted passion verges on insanity as the two isolated and repressed figures burn out their frustration and anger on each other's bodies. The erotic once again struggles with the spiritual and religious, at times asserting its validity as a path toward salvation: "Lying in the brown grass, his brown body stretched out on the grass, I put pollen and seeds in the thick glistening black hair on his underbelly where they shone in sunshine like little sparkling lights. He did the same to me; was that a sin? He nailed me to the cross with the hammering; he lay over me lightly as the cross, arms stretched out, legs stretched out, and he nailed me to earth with the terrible spike of love; and he ground the seed upon my body" (*IFC* 162–163). The struggle between flesh and spirit is too much for Jaime, however, and he dies in the seminary hospital, brought like Clovis to an early death through the violent emergence of sexual knowledge. Lois survives in a half-state but comes to understand these two deaths as a process of finding the body of Christ through the desperate embrace of love and death: "I had Christ's death in me to give to Jaime, and he had Clovis' Death in him to bring back to me. The body of Christ was given to me, the bitter body of Christ. To ears that had heard my cries of love I confessed my sins; I received the Body of God from hands that had lusted my own body" (*IFC* 169).

The novel concludes with this wounded optimism and Christian emphasis on the resurrection of the spirit through the recovery of the body. Chalmers Egstrom, thought to be dead for the latter half of the book and stretched out in the bedroom awaiting his funeral, recovers suddenly, rising up like the roadrunner. The party reaches a kind of ecstasy of spiritual repair, even as the ever-present rumbling of the city's endless trucks gradually begins to overwhelm their joyful and prophetic exclamations. The dream of the apartment, the imaginative construction of "Spain" (and Goyen's willful recreation of Taos) can no longer keep away the reality of the commercial world: "They all seemed to be in the room, Mr. Cumberly, Oris, Lois Fuchs, Jack Flanders and all the rest; but they were on the point of leaving, whispering one by one at the door, with fingers at their lips, 'A Diós, A Diós, A Diós.' And now they were all gone, up the fire-escape ladder and away, into the thundering wind-roar of trucks in the early city morning, under the burning sign, and away" (*IFC* 181). In a brief coda that imitates Flaubert's similar gesture at the conclusion of "St. Julien," the direct description of a southwestern wall hanging tells us that the entire world of the book has emerged from the scene embroidered there, "entangled and half-vanished figures of men and women under a raveling sky, and standing before them the haunting shape of a bird" (*IFC* 181–182). The "romance," in other words, has been a fragile attempt to preserve a space of imaginative freedom in a world of brutal interests. Its prime artificer has been the weaver, the holder of the ancient secret of her art, now fading like her creation back toward the condition of grass.[21]

In a Farther Country can be both a delightful and a puzzling book, feeling more often like a play than a novel and making substantial demands on some readers' tolerance for fantasy. Reviewers were divided on its merits. For those unable to accept its basic premise of an imaginary world inside a New York loft, the use of nonrealistic story forms produced annoyance and confusion. The critic for *Time*, as might be expected, treated it as a piece of artsy contrivance without any attempt to come to terms with its themes, much less its methods. Donald Barr in the *New York Times* made a more concerted effort, declaring in the spirit of the New Criticism that the book was an "invalid" allegory that failed to create a system of believable and functional symbols. More perceptively, Barr argues that rather than embedding a message in his story, "Goyen has decided that the story is to be embedded in the message," and though he credits the author with considerable gifts—"his strength of imagery, his rhythmic sense, his glyptic phrasemaking"—he cannot accept the book's claim to importance or profundity.[22] An anonymous reviewer for *The Nation*, on the other hand, recognized the book's generic idiosyncrasy and the tendency of such works to "irritate or confuse readers" but accepted its ambition to create "a volume at once romance, poem, and myth": "Within this deceptively simply structure, Mr. Goyen has created an entrancing book. . . . The book certainly is artifice; Twenty-third Street was never like this. Mr. Goyen, however, is craftsman enough and poet enough to control his artifice and render it as art."[23]

Given the literary climate of the mid-1950s, this mixed and tentative reaction was not surprising. While the best-seller lists were dominated by biblical epics such as Lloyd C. Douglas's *The Robe* and such potboilers as *Marjorie Morningstar*, mainstream literary fiction looked very different from Goyen's. As justifiably celebrated as they are, books such as Bernard Malamud's *The Natural* (1952), J. D. Salinger's *Catcher in the Rye* (1951), and Hemingway's *Old Man and the Sea* (1952) offered

readily accessible narratives and often consciously restrained or colloquial styles. None could be described as difficult or challenging reads.
In those notable novels that did push the boundaries of content or
language—Ralph Ellison's *Invisible Man* (1952), Saul Bellow's *The Ad-
ventures of Augie March* (1953), or William Gaddis's *The Recognitions*
(1955)—the ambition was consciously intellectual, the scope of the text
encyclopedic, and the subject matter urban, modern, and ironic. Although set in an imaginary New York, *In a Farther Country* is decidedly
anti-urban, a plea for the spiritual rewards of a rural exile. Goyen combines the technical sophistication of modernist (some might say post-
modernist) narrative with a willful naïveté, a deliberate assertion of
the handmade. As a consequence, he could strike readers as both too
difficult and too simple at the same time, a writer who demanded a
high level of attention while undercutting his own sophistication with
a rhetoric of unrefined simplicity.[24]

It is here where Goyen's initial readers, unable to recognize this
combination of the modern and the homegrown primitive, arguably
failed him. Although they were generally able to accept the grotesque-
ries and exaggerations of definably "Southern" literature—particularly
in the marketable versions offered by Capote and McCullers—Goyen's
more assertive wrestling with the tenets of modernism caused confusion. Throughout his first three novels, he had effectively used the techniques of modernist fragmentation against themselves, supplanting
Eliot's extinction of personality with a concerted effort to expose the
writer's emotional core. As a consequence, the books, though grounded
in fiction, often feel more like anguished confessions or emblem-rich
sermons. They attempt to produce and represent an intimacy of exchange, both erotic and spiritual, that the ironies of the modern text
had disallowed. This is not to say that *The House of Breath* or *Half a
Look of Cain* are completely transparent or that *In a Farther Country*
lacks its moments of concealment. But despite—and sometimes because of—his repressions, Goyen's primary objective was to produce a
kind of emotional nakedness, to confront, in the deeper sense of *facing*,
his reader with the pure force of feeling. That such a daring and necessary drive to exposure was unwelcome to the market for fiction in the
1950s is hardly a surprise, but given Goyen's need to survive on the proceeds of his work, these reviewers' relative lack of interest in his work
could only have been disheartening.

"Not I, not I but the wind that blows through me"

Despite the comic and somewhat hopeful tone of *In a Farther Country*, its essential note is mournful. The world Goyen had known in Taos, particularly the close-knit community held together by Frieda Lawrence, was quickly fading away. He had drawn the ancient southwestern blanket described at the end of the book from an actual wall-hanging in Frieda's El Prado house; the crumbling tapestry Goyen saw there became a visual elegy for the little world he had found in Taos after the war. The mid-1950s, particularly the years 1955 and 1956, confirmed these intimations of loss, first with the unexpected death of Margo Jones in the summer of the novel's release and then with Frieda's death the following year.

The theater director Margo Jones had been a significant figure in Goyen's life since his late teens. A native of Livingston, Texas, not far from Trinity, she had encouraged the young playwright while he was still at Rice and worked with him as part of the group of artists and friends who helped start the Houston Community Players in 1936. Through Dr. Rauch-Barraco, who was Jones's dentist at the time, Goyen was introduced to a circle that included Zoë Léger and Nione Carlson, among other artists and actors, a loose collection of the like-minded who called themselves the "Left Bank" of Buffalo Bayou.[25] The short, curly-haired, explosively energetic Jones (her nickname was the Texas Tornado) was just the sort of promoter and collaborator Goyen needed: someone who understood what it meant to come from small-town East Texas and yet who had a wide smile and enthusiasm that could help him overcome his bouts of shyness. In his later remembrance of her, the piece from the *Six Women* manuscript entitled "Margo," Goyen caught the cadence of her insistent optimism and high drive: "You stood up before the City Council of Houston and said to them, 'Honey, I don't care *what* it costs, you got the money. Houston's got the money. Give me the Grand Ballroom in the Lamar Hotel. What the hell's a *ballroom* when you haven't got a damn *ball*? When you can have *theatah*, when you can have *plays*. Wonderful, magical *plays*. Honey we got to have some magic, some *wonder*. Give me that *ballroom*.' And you got it" (*GAE* 25).

After the war, the two had kept in touch by letter and through Goyen's occasional visits to Dallas, where Jones was building the Dallas Civic Theater, the first theater-in-the-round in the country. In 1944 she had jumped at the chance to serve as codirector with the actor-producer Eddie Dowling for the first production of her close friend Tennessee Williams's play *The Glass Menagerie*. The success of that production led her to Maxine Wood's *On Whitman Avenue*, produced on Broadway in 1946, and Williams's *Summer and Smoke* in 1947. By the early 1950s, Jones was well known for her innovative productions and her willingness to take on new plays and playwrights, particularly with her company in Dallas. It was almost inevitable that she and Goyen would work together on an adaptation of one of his stories or novels, and in fact she had been urging him to finish the stage version of *The House of Breath* so that she could direct it.

Their first opportunity came in 1955, when Goyen sent Jones a dramatization by the playwright Greer Johnson of Goyen's short story "The Letter in the Cedarchest." The dreamlike tale, included in *Ghost and Flesh*, was loosely based on Goyen's experience sharing a rooming house with Walter Berns in Portland. The principal character is Lucille Purdy, a fat woman whose husband has left her in a large and mostly empty house. She takes in three young men as boarders, and their youthful presence helps create a homey, communal feeling that boosts Lucille's spirits. Across the backyard lives a strange and apparently helpless neighbor named Little Pigeon, whose sister Sammye sometimes visits from the city. Little Pigeon begins to rely on Lucille to take care of her, and the close and girlish relationship between the two begins to upset the household, not to mention the neighborhood. The boarders eventually leave because of Lucille's hyperattentiveness, and Lucille moves into Little Pigeon's house. Sammye, both suspicious and jealous of the bond between her sister and Lucille, tries to break up the pair, but ultimately she can't "disturb the dream" of what Goyen calls "this playhouse" (CS 29). The three women ultimately decide to form a household together, their lives part dream and part reality but imaginatively free of restrictions or outside pressures. "All we want, I guess," Sammye summarizes, "is a household that will let us be the way we are" (CS 33).

The play, retitled *Whisper to Me*, attempted to reproduce this delicate magic, but the production in Dallas was not a success. Mounted as part of the theater's crowded summer season, it suffered from a two-week rehearsal period and last-minute changes in the cast. On opening night, the lead had to be played by Mary Dolan, Jones's business manager, who hadn't had time to learn all the lines. Though the local press was kind, the experience was exhausting for everyone involved and put a strain on Goyen's relationship with Jones.

To help with the final preparations for the production, Goyen and Glasco had come in from New York, where they were living on East 96th Street. (They had left El Prado in November 1954 so that Goyen could purse a contract with Random House for *In a Farther Country* and Glasco could check on his business affairs at the Catherine Viviano Gallery. They planned to stay only a few weeks but didn't return to New Mexico until June of 1956.) Though grateful for the effort and energy Margo devoted to the play, Goyen soon became concerned that she was exhausting herself and drinking too much. To help relieve her stress, Glasco began giving her painting lessons, hoping the concentration on a new creative activity might provide an outlet for her legendary energy. But in a wild night of drinking, painting, and listening to ecstatic music, Jones went perhaps a step too far, splashing and splattering pigments all over her apartment at the Stoneleigh Hotel. Goyen was in her room that night and in "Margo" describes the scene from the later perspective of his own alcoholism: "You just would not hold back that wild night, naked and crazy in the Stoneleigh Hotel in Dallas, raging with hurt and failure and disappointment and booze and pills, with the Ravel playing and the Stravinsky. You were gaudy and wild-looking and puffed up, painted and strutting with late chaos. . . . And as I turned to look back at you in your bed, insane with hangover and still half-blind with black-out, shaking and crazy and dying (*you* knew it), I did not know that I would never see you again" (*GAE* 26).

According to Jones's biographer, Helen Sheehy, at some point during this bacchic evening, Jones had "expressed her need" for Goyen romantically and sexually, and he had rejected her. This may be true, but it seems surprising that Jones would have considered him a romantic possibility. There is little in Goyen's letters or written comments to suggest that he thought of her in those terms, and the true nature of Goyen's relationship with Glasco could hardly have been a secret from her, who had visited their New York apartment and was as close to being a true confidant as anyone Goyen knew.[26] When Goyen was back in New York a few days later, Jones called him from the hospital. She had been found partially conscious in her apartment and was suspected of having kidney problems, but it soon became clear that the situation was much more serious. The hotel staff had cleaned the paint from her carpet using carbon tetrachloride, and Jones had been exposed to the chemical to such an extent that her kidneys and liver, already stressed by heavy drinking, began to fail. She died ten days later. At the time of that final phone call, Goyen knew only that she had pushed herself too hard and relied too heavily on alcohol. Possibly still reacting to her romantic overtures, he was angry and brusque: "We talked once more, on the phone, long-distance, and I yelled at you while you called back Oh Baby, Baby, please please listen to me, don't hang up, don't go away, don't leave. And I hung up, Margo. I cut you off. I never heard your voice again" (*GAE* 26).

Jones's death hit Goyen hard, his grief mixed with guilt and helplessness. He explained to Brett that "poor dear Margo was so bent on self-destruction that her doom hung over everything while we were there. Joe and I did try to help her, but one always wonders if he had helped enough when there might have been time. Still, it was too late. Joe had long talks with her about drinking and she was very grateful to him; yet it was too late."[27] He was unable to return to Texas for the funeral, though he felt he should have; money was, as always, a pressing concern and a primary subject of his letters to his parents. He had begged Jones to find a way for him to work for the funds to travel to Texas in the first place, and now the opportunities for income back in New York seemed increasingly limited. In August he signed a new contract with Random House that would pay him $150 a month with a $200 signing bonus, just enough to scrimp by on for the year. But he was increasingly aware that he would have to find some sort of supplemental income. "I don't believe I can any longer make anything like a living at writing books," he wrote to his parents, "so must think of something else to do to keep me going. The past few years have been too much of a struggle, I cannot go on like that."[28] To Curtius he was more despondent, given the muted reaction to *In a Farther Country*: "Nothing happens to my work in America. How could it, where there is nothing but television and millionaire best-selling authors who write quickly and stupidly?"[29] There was the possibility that *Whisper to Me* could be produced on Broadway, or at least optioned for a few hundred dollars, and television and Hollywood held out the vague promise of future projects. Teaching, however, was the most readily available source of steady money, and despite worries that it would once again draw down his creative energy, Goyen agreed in October to offer a writing class once a week at the New School for Social Research. "The class is large but the students are intelligent and adult," he explained to his parents. The contact with apprentice writers was good for him psychologically, pulling him out of his own self-concern for a while, and the $100 a month was a welcome addition to his meager cash flow.

Though the contract with Random House stipulated that he would deliver a new novel by August of the following year, it remains unclear what major project Goyen was working on during this time. The manuscript of *Half a Look of Cain* was frequently on his mind, and efforts continued in Europe to see the work published, whether by Arche Verlag or someone else. Various stories—some new, some reworked from *Cain*—were appearing in magazines, but he was mostly engaged in editing and journalism that he thought might bring more immediate payment. He had proposed an edition of Texas stories for which he hoped to receive $1,000 and had begun collecting texts from the New York Public Library and elsewhere. And he was asked to write a color piece on "small town Texas" for *Holiday*. It was during this period, and largely out of a need for money, that he began steadily reviewing books for the *New York Times* and other publications.

The summer of 1955 had been particularly hot in New York, and by the following spring both Goyen and Glasco had decided not to spend another sweltering season in the city. After a quick trip through Houston and Dallas to visit their respective families, they arrived in Taos to find the old house in need of significant repairs and Frieda Lawrence in declining health. In April she had been rushed to the hospital in Santa Fe with a virus complicated by diabetes. For the next two months, things seemed much as they always had: Goyen and Glasco enlarged one room of the house and replastered the walls in hopes of renting it out when they returned to New York in the fall. Work continued, aided by the cool nights and the welcome peace and quiet. Then in August, after a party for Glasco's mother the night before, Frieda complained of chest pains and was advised by doctors to stay in bed. A few days later, Goyen and Glasco received a late-night call from Frieda's doctor saying that Frieda had suffered a stroke. The two rushed across the road and found her in bed, paralyzed on her right side. They helped arrange for a nurse to spend nights with her and took care to see that Brett as well as Angelino Ravalo, Frieda's husband, both aging and long dependent on

Frieda, were okay. They took turns sitting with Frieda, at times giving her oxygen to ease her breathing, and both were present when she died on August 11:

> You died on your birthday, August 11, 1956, in the house across the road from mine, in El Prado, New Mexico, in a rented hospital bed sent out to you by Mabel Luhan, under "The Bocaccio Story," Lawrence's paint- ing of some nuns coming unexpectedly upon a naked peasant sleeping under a haystack (many said the naked peasant was Angelino.) It was a bad death, or so it seemed to me; God knows it could have been worse the way you smoked, though it was the gasped-out end of a whole huge life of a man and woman. You died sort of—courteously. . . . And I stood by [Angelino] as you drew your last deep hoarse breath, letting it go from you with a profound sigh. I stood with Angelino as he saw you die and he fell upon your body and wept in your yellow hair, "Frieda! Frieda! Don't go! Don't leave me, Frieda, Frieda! What will I do now? Where will I go, now?" (*GAE* 13, 14)

The burial took place at the Kiowa Ranch. Goyen read Lawrence's poem "Song of a Man Who Has Come Through" and the twenty-first psalm over her grave: "The weather was quiet and cool and a faint wind soughed in the great thick trees. As we walked away, down the hill, the huge Western sun was setting, blazing orange, away across the lonely landscape of purple ridges and red humps and golden desert lake-like stretches all vast and eternal-looking, your prospect, now, along with Lawrence's, as you lay in your velvet shoes, ready in your velvet hat, beautiful with rings and bracelets and fans and combs and necklaces" (*GAE* 18).

Though not fully evident at the time, Frieda's death marked the be- ginning of the end of Goyen's connection to Taos. He would never live or spend any significant amount of time there again. A month after the funeral, Goyen and Glasco returned to New York to a new apart- ment at 645 West End Avenue. In May of 1957, on a trip down to see his family, Glasco managed to rent out the house for $100 a month. A year later, Goyen was hoping that the place would sell and seemed to have very little attachment to it except as a possible source of income.[30] The little remote "Himalayan village" that Goyen and Berns had come upon after the war had grown and gotten richer, and with Frieda gone it no longer felt like the restorative retreat it once had been. During his troubled times in the mid-1970s, Goyen would regret having sold the little adobe house nestled against the Taos mountain, but for now he seemed almost eager to put it behind him. More than anything, after years of hand-to-mouth living and dependence on his parents, he needed steady money and a chance to prove to himself and everyone else that he could be a commercial as well as artistic success.

CHAPTER TEN 〜

Blood Kindred
1957–1962

I did not describe William Goyen's visit one evening. A man in
pain—gray-haired but with a youthfulness of gestures and face,
a young man upon whose body age could only imprint a few lines
and would never weigh down. A softness of voice, a gentleness of
manner. He had gestures of disturbance, his hands made efforts to
erase the lines of anxiety. What came to the surface was the injuries
received, the disappointments, the injustices, the brutalities of the
press. A wounded man. The ones who expected great love and are
wounded at the beginning later cannot register the love they receive
in the present, only the one denied them. The groove is made to
receive only the insults and betrayals.

ANAÏS NIN, *DIARY*, 1956

Goyen turned forty in 1955, an unhappy milestone for someone so intent on proving himself. As they did each year, his
family in Houston sent him gifts: new shirts, pajamas, socks,
a winter coat from his sister Kat, some Texas pralines, and money. "The
check was so generous," he wrote in thanks, "and I do worry about your
spending so much when I ought to be sending it to you. I thank you
with all my heart, and I know I'll be able to do something for you one
day not far off."[1] The family's willingness to send support and their
son's guilty gratitude are persistent notes in Goyen's correspondence
during the 1950s. Perhaps if the money came only on his birthday, it
wouldn't have bothered him. But prompted by one crisis or another, he
was driven to ask for help two or three times a year, sometimes in the
form of brief loans that he hurried to pay back whenever his income
improved. The idea that he would someday be able to send his parents

something, to buy them a house or new car or help pay their medical expenses, was a consistently wishful thought, as much a palliative to his own sense of absence as the boyish fantasy of a self-exiled son.[2]

Despite the *succès d'estime* of his early books, Goyen's lack of a sustaining income from his writing only deepened his long-nursed psychological wounds. The always perceptive Anaïs Nin saw this immediately when he visited her in New York: "A man in pain," she guessed, "a wounded man," unable to move beyond his original, fundamental sense of loss or betrayal. It was a problem noted early on by the more cagey literary presences in whose company Goyen sometimes found himself. Christopher Isherwood, who had frequently registered suspicion of Goyen's emotional needs, told the young, suddenly celebrated author that he would never survive unless he put on some psychological armor (*GAE* 85). The writing, despite its elaborate style and effects, was essentially too raw, too open, and what it offered in intimacy Goyen would pay for in misunderstanding and rejection. The remarkable vulnerability on display in his fiction may also have suggested that he would react in the way that Nin intuited, as someone who has been rejected in love. Money inevitably played its role in the accounting of such failures, and whenever Goyen found himself compelled to write to Houston for a small loan or other favor, new salts touched these old, familiar wounds.

Consequently, during the latter half of the 1950s he devoted himself increasingly to activity that had a higher probability of producing new income. He took on more teaching, offering two classes a term at The New School, and significantly stepped up the frequency of his book reviewing. He had begun placing reviews in the *New York Times* shortly after the publication of *The House of Breath*, beginning with John Collier's *Fancies and Goodnights* and following up a few months later with a prescient response to Flannery O'Connor's first novel, *Wise Blood*. Four more *Times* reviews followed in 1955, one in 1956, four in 1957, and six in 1958, with additional but less frequent appearances in *The Nation* over the same period. Goyen was a careful and sympathetic reader with a talent for penetrating description. Of O'Connor's not-yet-famous bluntness, he wrote: "There is in Flannery O'Connor a fierceness of literary gesture, an angriness of observation, a facility for catching, as an animal eye in a wilderness, cunningly and at one sharp glance, the shape and detail and animal intentions of enemy and foe. . . . The stark dramatic power of the scenes is percussive and stabbing, but Miss O'Connor seems to tell her story through clenched teeth in a kind of Tomboy, Mean-Moll glee."[3] He noted different strengths in Bernard Malamud's *The Assistant*, singling out the "marvelously true" speech of the characters and the book's slow accretion of "values and destinies and large truths."[4] Goyen's negative comments tended more often than not to be technical rather than thematic, as when he doubted the fullness of Peter Matthiessen's characterizations in *Partisans* or, in an otherwise favorable review, when he questioned the regional realism of William Humphrey's *Home from the Hill*. What may have been surprising to readers of Goyen's fiction is the quiet clarity of his critical eye. For someone whose imaginative writing could so insistently push the boundaries of expression, Goyen's approach to others' work was more often than not quietly professional.

The one notable exception to this exercise of critical distance proved to be the most controversial and assertive of Goyen's reviews in the *Times*. It isn't clear whether he specifically requested or was asked to review Truman Capote's *Breakfast at Tiffany's*, but from the first sentence it was clear that he had something to say about the writer to whom he was often compared and whom he had come to envy and resent. Calling Capote the "last of the old-fashioned Valentine makers," Goyen praised the "funny portrait of an ex-child wife" in Holly Golightly but bluntly called out Capote's "almost vaudevillian devices" and "tendency to overglaze situations, to overdress characters—not stylistically so much as conceptionally [*sic*]—a tendency to fool with characters on the author's terms of whimsy, not on the characters.'"[5] Capote's "cuteness . . . often supplants truth," and his stories can seem to be "more make-up than art." Most of all the stories in the volume seem childishly feminine, unserious, and unreal: "There is in this work the quality of doll-like glee, of creating a dwelling in a doily story-world entirely of the author's own tatting, of staying in it with his characters, come high water or low, until he has to get out of it—if he does. Then he might take the way out of chic, or of marshmallow romance; of spoof or cracker barrel."[6]

Though pointed and perceptive, the review is not a straightforward piece of critical judgment, and the motives behind it are sufficiently tangled to warrant a careful unraveling. Goyen had known Capote since the late 1940s when they were both working with Bob Linscott at Random House. *Other Voices, Other Rooms* had made its author fashionably famous overnight, and for a time Capote played the part of boy king in the publisher's Italianate offices on Madison Avenue. To Gerald Clarke, Capote's biographer, Goyen later described Capote's impish but solicitous personality: "I have a vivid memory of coming in those great doors one time and finding him sitting on a bench by the reception desk, a baseball cap on his head and his feet not touching the floor. It was as if he were saying, 'This is my place. It's a wonderful place, and I'm going to take you all through it and introduce you to everybody.' And he did take me to people, give me hints about what to do, and made me feel more at home there."[7] The two became warm friends and through the early 1950s regularly exchanged gossipy letters and mutual admiration. Capote offered ecstatic praise for *The House of Breath* and greedily sought information on Goyen's love affairs, though Goyen was intent on keeping his more serious affections a secret. "So: you are up to your naughty tricks again," Capote wheedled in a typical letter from Italy, "—why don't you tell me what goes on in your life? All you do is tease. And here I am thousands of miles away."[8]

Despite the apparent friendliness of these exchanges, Goyen very quickly became envious of the younger writer's commercial success while questioning the depth and commitment of his work. The attitude may have come in part from Katherine Anne Porter. Though Goyen disagreed at times with her violent attacks on the newly fashionable, more openly gay writing, he respected Porter's literary opinions in general and clung to the idea that his own work proved less commercial because of its uncompromising integrity. She encouraged him as a foil to what she thought of as thin, unsubstantial writing, and he responded, at least in his letters to her, with the defensiveness and artistic self-righteousness always at the ready when he felt threatened: "But I firmly believe, my darling, and you have helped teach me this, that a beginner must be free and unentangled. Whatever work he does, then, will be his *own* and it will come from *him*, not from contracts (which write a lot of books) or promises or liens. Let the Capotes and all the others take their fat advances, and live in foreign villas; I want my work to stay free."[9] Anything negative about Capote was red meat for Porter, and Goyen could vent his frustrations more fully to her than to anyone else: "*Why* do they keep measuring me against him or even thinking of me and him in the same breath? It is Mr. Cerf's doing, I know that and have known it. Never mind, I'll destroy that. I can see easily that *The Grass Harp* (Capote's new novel) is obviously influenced by *The House of Breath*, and Truman has written me to as much as tell me so: the poison is reaching for the antidote!"[10] But Goyen's habits of deception made him more than capable of playing multiple sides in some of his friendships. In October of the same year, he was giving *The Grass Harp* a substantial and laudatory review in *The Houston Post*: "And though so much is drawn through the mind of the careful reader by such a frail thread as this slender, matter-of-fact little tale, this gifted writer has seemed to this reviewer to control and harness this drawn mass so as to do little damage to or cause little effect upon the surrounding areas of his objective, as though a large wind blown through a tree caused two glass prisms to chime in the tree and scarcely disturbed the leaves and branches surrounding it."[11]

The wish to be considered separately from Capote was also very likely a part of Goyen's desire to be disassociated from the movement of gay writing that emerged in the late forties and early 1950s. His repeated assertions that he wasn't "Southern" clearly acted as a way of stating his independence from fashion and reaffirming his specific identity as a Texan. He did not, in other words, participate in the Southern Gothic and the post–Civil War psychodrama of the defeated. However, there are times when this denial of Southernness can seem like a shorthand for signaling his masculinity, a refusal to be feminized or defined as "decadent" by the literary codes of the day. Attacking *Breakfast at Tiffany's* may have been a way of dividing himself once and for all from what he considered a clichéd and cloying vision of sexuality, a chance to push himself toward something he considered deeper and more serious than Capote's campiness.[12] Whatever the motives, the review essentially ended his friendship with Capote, whose fury later came out in a nasty caricature of the Goyen-Porter relationship in *Answered Prayers*.[13]

Indirect statements of artistic purity, no matter how satisfying or necessary, rarely pay the bills, however, and Goyen still needed a way to make steady money. Undiscouraged by the minor fiasco of *Whisper to Me*, he continued to nurture fantasies of success in the theater. His adaptation of *The House of Breath*, on low heat since the early 1950s, now offered the best chance for a debut. The novel had clearly grown from theatrical roots in the first place, and its structure made possible a version that stressed the braided, almost fugal counterpoint of voices.

To establish theme and place, Goyen added a singer, who operates as a kind of chorus, and wrote five songs to be interspersed into the four acts of the play, set on the breezeway and in the cellar of the epony-mous house. Directed by Michael Murray and with sets and costumes by Joe Glasco, this "ballad for the theater" opened on April 8, 1957, at the Circle in the Square Theatre. It was widely proclaimed a success de-spite the ungenerous *Times* critic who compared Goyen unfavorably to Tennessee Williams and complained about the play's wordiness. Even in this rather sour review of a matinee performance, however, there seems little doubt that the audience was rapt and attentive: "Although fidgeting would have been perfectly understandable at this point, the polite respect paid by the audience is a clear indication that the Circle in the Square has achieved a faithful following, willing to stick through ups and downs."[14] A considerably more perceptive and sympathetic re-sponse came from Nin, whom Goyen had personally invited to the pre-miere and who had been supportive during the emotional strain of the rehearsals:

> Last night in the rain and slush we went to see William Goyen's *House of Breath* at the Circle in the Square. At last a bit of magic, poetry and subtle levels of feeling. What a contrast to Tennessee Williams, now dedicated to violence and melodrama. This was so emotional and full of poetry, like *The Glass Menagerie*. It seeks a free form for the theatre, an impressionism. Goyen calls it a ballad. A very moving theme. Seeking escape from home, parents, and never quite making it, even though in this case the home is death and stagnation.
>
> It was a success. They dragged him onto the stage and he is so shy, he hung his head down and looked at the floor.[15]

Though the run didn't last long, just over a week, extra performances were added, and the experience overall was positive for Goyen, if not directly profitable. There were new contacts and requests for more dra-matic work; "a fine producer, no doubt the finest in New York theatre," possibly Elia Kazan, asked for an original play for the fall season, and Goyen's film and television opportunities quickly multiplied. *House of Breath* itself, on the other hand, netted him just $57 and a satisfying but bewildered exhaustion. "Oh well," he wrote to Brett in the aftermath, "this is New York, and it is a nightmare where nobody knows what is true and what isn't. I am *not* embittered, just tired and confused, and that will pass."[16]

It may be tempting to see Goyen's turn toward theater and film as nothing more than an attempt to increase his income in the wake of disappointing sales of his books. But he had been quietly and consistently devoted to the possibilities of the stage since his college years, and, as was most obvious with *The House of Breath*, had built his original approach to the novel on the technical possibilities of staged speech within a longer narrative. Consequently, each new opportunity to develop the material of his fiction into drama offered both a validation of his approach and a chance to make more productive, and potentially more profitable, use of his talents. Even before the staging of *House of Breath*, he had been in touch with the film producer Fred Coe and was working on an original screenplay at his request. Modeled roughly on the aftermath of Dylan Thomas's death, the story concerned a recently deceased novelist from a small town in East Texas whose widow must cope with unwanted fame due to her appearance in several of her husband's books.[17] A movie company arrives to shoot a version of one of the novels, and the locals resent the intrusion while cherishing secret desires to appear in the film. Goyen may have considered the situation both timely and personal; the potential for dramatizing his own feelings toward Trinity and its negative reaction to *The House of Breath* must have been a primary attraction, and his long friendship with Frieda Lawrence would have given him plenty to say about the literary widow forced to deal with her husband's posthumous fame.

Though this screenplay was never produced, the connection with Coe did yield one brief brush with Hollywood that suggested enticing possibilities for future projects and income.[18] A few months after the closing of *House of Breath*, Goyen received an unexpected request to fly to California to write song lyrics for the film *The Left-Handed Gun*, Gore Vidal's revisionist western about Billy the Kid, produced by Coe, directed by Arthur Penn, and starring Paul Newman. The songs Goyen had written for the production of *House of Breath* may have convinced Coe that the lyric concentration of the play was the right sort of inspiration for the film's musical opening, a traditional western ballad with music by Alexander Courage. Though certainly written to the specifications of the finished film, the lyrics do tap Goyen's always-ready reservoir of isolation and homelessness:

> His name is sorrow,
> His name is pain.
> Where does he come from?
> What is his name?
>
> He belongs to all wandering, astray and alone.
> He belongs to all lonesomeness,
> Shadowed by lonesomeness.
> Tone the bell. Tone.

The job brought a quick $1,000, "but it was fifty thousand in experience," Goyen wrote to his parents. "I met many film producers and made many contacts that will bring results, I know. My own producer was eager for me to work with him again and I am sure that I'll get some kind of picture assignment sooner or later."[19]

This optimism was essentially well-founded at the time. Thanks in part to a new agent, Priscilla Morgan, Goyen was busily at work on the new play for Broadway and on several television assignments. This sudden rush of labor—which included, at various times, projects for *Playhouse 90*, an unproduced television variety show with his own original songs, and a potential adaptation of "The White Rooster"—eventually resulted in the play *The Diamond Rattler*, produced at the Charles Playhouse in Boston in May of 1960, and "A Possibility of Oil," broadcast on General Electric Theater in 1961. Both were developments of characters and situations from his fiction, primarily from material introduced in "Pore Perrie" and "Rhody's Path."

The play was not a success in tryouts and never made it to Broadway. Its two acts focused on the return of the wayward and guilty character named Son (from the story "Pore Perrie"), an adoptee who has fled a sexual relationship with his "aunt" Linsie: "Nothing could stop me and Linsie. We were lost in it. We wouldn't let each other alone. She burnt me blistered with woman and I went just woman crazy. . . . My wildness was like a thousand tongues crawling all over my body night and day; and so I ran."[20] After a life of wandering, Son joins an evangelist named Brother Peters, a snake handler who eventually passes on his ministry to his protégé. When Son comes home to the scene of his guilt, he learns that Brother Peters has become an almost mythic figure named Oil King, a wildcatter and speculator who, rumors say, can smell crude in a handful of dirt. Oil King recognizes his former assistant and asks him to join him in his new petrochemical evangelism: "We got something in common—or had it. That means we both lookin for the same thing." He confesses that the snake he used in his tent show had never been poisonous, and the miracles that Son believed he himself had performed were harmless, though inspiring, fakes: "Everything I ever did, I believed in; and it wasn't to harm anybody—or to lie to em. I just wanted to make life *shine* for people. And when they believed, I believed." Son is destroyed by the revelation that the religious "show" and the oil frenzy are essentially the same, a snare to capture the lost and those longing for new lives. He catches a new, poisonous snake and while delivering a final sermon allows it to bite him. He dies just as Oil King announces that the family's property contains oil. "Out by the graves," Rhody shouts, "*oil in the ground, Salvation!*"

Despite the promising exploration of the disturbing links between spiritual and material wealth, the surviving versions of the play suggest that Goyen was trying to accomplish too much in a relatively compressed space. A reader's report from the Arena Theater found *The Diamond Rattler* too literary or novelistic with too heavy a reliance on spoken exposition and explanation, and the play does read more like the awkward combination of two or more short stories than a concentrated dramatic action. Though he had been riding his usual high hopes before the production, Goyen was philosophical to his parents about the tepid reception: "The play was not at all a failure and there was great interest in it; I just never got it right, that's all. But I gave everything I had to it, so that's all right."[21] The thematically related "A Possibility of Oil," on the other hand, brought in $2,000 and the momentary pleasures of mild stardom. The production starred Joan Fontaine and was well enough received that Goyen was quickly asked for another script.

But the big payday, the one that haunted almost every letter to his parents, never materialized. The screenplay deal fell apart fairly quickly over the issue of payment for revisions: after delivering the initial draft, for which he was paid roughly $5,000, Goyen refused to continue producing rewrites without further payment. After weeks of wrangling, he finally announced to his parents he had "won" the "screenplay fight": "That is, I got it back in my own possession and away from all the crooks who were behaving badly. Now I'll try to re-sell it as quickly as possible."[22] It isn't clear whether Coe was one of the "crooks," but the resale apparently never occurred, and despite several more optioned books and screenplays throughout his career, Goyen never got any closer to film production than writing the lyrics for *The Left-Handed Gun*. The development money and proceeds from play productions were just enough, added to his teaching income and the money saved by living with Glasco, to keep him solvent.

One positive development did result, for a time at least, from his and Glasco's attempts to live more cheaply. In the summer of 1957, after more than two years living in New York (with only a few months in New Mexico during the summer Frieda died), they began renting a house in Erwinna, Pennsylvania, in Bucks County, forty miles north of Philadelphia. Both wanted desperately to get out of New York, particularly in the sweltering summer months, and the quiet country setting not far from Manhattan gave them a chance to keep in touch with business—Goyen's agent lived just down the road—while still feeling isolated and undisturbed. The nights were cool, there was room for a garden, and Goyen was soon writing to Houston to try to convince his parents to visit: "Prettiest country I've seen anywhere outside of Texas. . . . The house is very comfortable and plenty of room, you all will love it and also have a good rest and change."[23] A combination of fantasy and practical deception, such repeated invitations at the very least signaled Goyen's ease and pleasure in his new surroundings. The pair stayed at Erwinna for more than a year, moving to Ottsville, just a mile away, the following summer. This larger house was farther from the road, even quieter, and surrounded by seventy-four acres of farmland planted with wheat, clover, and barley. "Can you imagine me living, at last, on a farm?" Goyen wrote to his parents. "A real old-timey place . . . beautiful trees, five cats, the garden and three brooks."[24] As they did in Taos, the slower rhythms of rural life seem to have both relaxed and stimulated him, and despite the constant ups and downs of his persistent literary labor, his mood during this period was positive and optimistic.

The idyll soured only when Goyen's relationship with Glasco began to unravel. The catalyst for what turned out to be a roughly three-year disintegration was the sudden death of Glasco's father in November of 1958. The loss and its fallout—his mother came close to a nervous breakdown—pushed Glasco toward exhaustion and an increasing dependence on alcohol.[25] By the fall of 1959, he and Goyen had left Bucks County and were living in separate hotels in New York. Goyen's letters to his parents suggest an amicable parting, forced by Glasco's drinking, but later reflections describe a sometimes dangerous domestic scene: "The violence in Ottsville house. Joe broke a chair. One night I fled terrified into the dark and hid in the car and slept there until dawn, when Joe found me" (HRC 29.6). For a little more than a year, from January 1960 to May 1961, the embattled friends tried once more to share an apartment, but again the relationship disintegrated into sordid quarrels and violence. In February, after a drunken Glasco interrupted Goyen and Michael Murray while they were having dinner at Sardi's, Goyen went back to their apartment to find a party under way. The situation escalated until one of Glasco's drinking friends, David Doyle, pushed Goyen down the stairs, breaking his left arm and leaving cuts and bruises on his forehead (HRC 34.2). "Things are changing between Joe and me," he wrote to his parents a few weeks later, though without mentioning his injuries, "and I am afraid I cannot live with him any longer. . . . He has changed so much and does not live as I do."[26]

The relationship had lasted ten years, the longest of Goyen's life, and its end would mark a profound shift in his sense of himself. Another period of essential rootlessness followed. Over the next two years he lived at five different addresses in New York, not including various hotels and apartments in Germany and Switzerland during a five-month trip sponsored by the State Department. The summer after the separation, he rented a cabin on Fire Island, near a village called Lonelyville, a name even he could find absurd, though not enough to prevent him from engaging in serious self-examination:

I'm too much of a sensualist. I simply cannot live alone too long—away from bodies, forces, affections, flesh. I *must* have touch, flirtation, caress, romance—or I become morbid, self-pitying, dead, unidentified, restless and melancholy. *Now* I know this. I had always thought of myself as needing, having to be alone—I do, indeed—but not without passion—my loneliness is not fear—it is the need, the absence of passion. The truth is: I cannot bear to be unloved or undesired. There is no lustre in life without these. (HRC 28.13, emphases in original)

Faces of the Blood Kindred

Goyen's second collection of short stories was published in 1960 by Random House. *Faces of the Blood Kindred* gathers fiction written from 1951 to 1960 around a slightly longer story, "A Tale of Inheritance," which may have originally been conceived as a novel. Several of the tales appeared first in large-market magazines such as *Mademoiselle* and *Harper's*, with the rest going to such prestigious journals as the *Kenyon Review*, the *Transatlantic Review*, and Princess Caetani's *Botteghe Oscure*. A general theme of kinship, particularly the burdens of inherited traits and the inescapable responsibilities of family, binds together the major pieces of the collection, though the organization overall seems less intentional and is less overt than in *Ghost and Flesh*. On a technical level, the stories are similarly more relaxed and more patient than his earlier efforts. Some of the urgency to demonstrate his gifts had mellowed into a quieter, more meditative development of his persistent concerns with loneliness and exile, kinship and otherness.

"A Tale of Inheritance"—later titled "Zamour, or A Tale of Inheritance"—is one of three major stories in the collection and one of Goyen's finest and most strangely evocative tales. Told in a directly fabulist manner, the story concerns the three Lester sisters, who live in Goyen's Trinity stand-in, Red River County. The older pair, Cheyney and Maroney, have from the age of fourteen been distinguished by their delicate black beards, a minor deformity that nevertheless has a strangely positive effect on their lives. Drawn together and separated from the world by their difference, they pledge loyalty to one another and form a happy, self-sufficient household. Their sister, Princis, on the other hand, seems to have emerged from different stock. Beautiful and "slender," "chestnut-haired where her sisters' hair was of the coldest black," she longs to leave Red River County for the attractions of the city (*CS* 183). One night after a self-conscious outburst of anxiety, she decides to run away but instead finds a large black cat and brings it home, naming it Zamour, "a lovely name she had seen on a poster nailed to a tree on the road and advertising a magician who would come to the commissary with a carnival that she never saw" (*CS* 185).[27] Zamour becomes her loyal familiar, and when Princis marries a "railroad man" named Mr. Simpson, she takes the cat with her to live in Houston.

On Hines Street, Princis and Mr. Simpson settle into a small neighborhood "inhabited by migrants from little towns" (*CS* 187), some from Red River County. This slightly magical version of Merrill Street is the setting for another of Goyen's considerations of his mother's sense of loss and exile. Princis finds herself unable to adapt to Houston ways. She holds fast to the habits of Red River County, and within a year has become a kind of anachronism:

> She turned, within the very first year, back toward her ancestry, and this in a world turning toward the other direction, so that such a new world could not support the change—it gave no ground to build upon, she might as well have made a house of mosquito netting; and against what weather could such a flimsy dwelling protect her? Princis became, in the Neighborhood, a curio left behind by a diminishing race, the last of the little country women, as if that race were finishing in her in a little house on a street in a city. (*CS* 188)

Soon her strange inability to adapt—and her refusal to have sex—drives Mr. Simpson to drink, and when he dies of cancer of the spleen, Princis is left alone with Zamour in the decaying house, waiting for the promised pension from the railroad company.

Rarely emerging from the crumbling house, Princis becomes more and more isolated. She sits and waits for the pension that never comes until one day a hurricane hits Houston and almost destroys her house, filling it with water and tearing the roof away. Amidst the chaos of the flood and her complicated attempts to build a shelter and calm the terrified Zamour, Princis gathers her keepsakes about her, including the "face mirror that was willed to her by her grandmother[;] it was bronze and had green mold in the crevices, but on the back were the figures of two shy lovers under a tree" (*CS* 197). The cat eventually attacks her in its panic, scratching her face, and when she looks in the mirror to check her wounds, Princis discovers that she has grown a beard like her sisters'. Zamour escapes, and, rescued from the storm, Princis is taken to a rest home in Red River County, where she lives happily, visited by her sisters and distinguished by a contentment and kindness envied by the other residents.

Though built on Goyen's familiar concerns, "A Tale of Inheritance" has a unique atmosphere. As he did in portions of *Half a Look of Cain*, Goyen was able to free himself partially from his source material and allow a measure of imaginative play not always open to him in his earlier work. Here it is evident not only in the Lester sisters' carnivalesque beards but in such odd and evocative details as their fondness for playing duets on the xylophone and their peculiar absence of anxiety. The extended sequence of the storm, with its ever-shrinking stage comprised of the disintegrating house and the futile tent that Princis erects in her living room, echoes the similar flood story in *Half a Look of Cain*, though without the more obvious mythological gestures. Thematic material, too, is more fully integrated into the narrative, though it should be noted that Goyen's exiles do not usually achieve so happy a reconciliation with the pasts they've left behind. If, as the story suggests, inherited oddity is a sign of familial welcome and the key to happiness, then Princis is fortunate to have survived a storm that stripped away her feeling of exile and relocated her to an ideal place within her family. For Goyen, such possibilities seem available only within the mildly wishful world of a tale such as this.

The muted personal presence in "A Tale of Inheritance" offers a change from Goyen's tendency toward thematic statement, but it also signals a possible avoidance of his deeper artistic drives. Though Princis is reconciled to her heredity, Goyen's more typical wanderers exist in the anxious space between the need to leave and the desire to return. Pushed away and pulled toward the "place" designated as home, they run out their lives in an excess of ill-directed desire. Like Princis— and her primary source, Swimma from *The House of Breath*—Rhody of "Rhody's Path" is defined by just this kind of restlessness. Drawn away from the small town of her origin by a combination of pure avarice and a hunger for excitement, she has burned through three husbands and enough experience to wear the beauty from her face and leave her with an arthritic limp. Her return to the small town where she grew up still conjures a kind of excitement in her family. Some hope that she has come home to repent her wild ways and settle down. Others, like her young cousin Son, consider her an avatar of a strange, late-summer mood, an uneasiness brought on by a plague of grasshoppers and the sudden appearance of a flagpole sitter advertising a revival.

With her natural appetite for excitement, Rhody is soon in pursuit of both the flagpole sitter and the young revivalist, Brother Peters, whose tent is set up across from the house in Baily's pasture. Peters is a snake handler and carries two diamond-back rattlesnakes to demonstrate God's power to heal him of snake bite through faith alone: "He had converted and saved thousands," Son explains to the family, "through this example of the healing power of the Lord, saying his famous prayer as he was struck by this rattling spear: 'Hand of God, reach down and help antidote the poison of the diamond rattler of Sin'" (*CS* 167). But the night before the revival is set to begin, while the preacher and his "lady pianist" are eating dinner with Rhody and the family, word comes that one of the snakes has escaped from its cage. The revivalists—helped by Rhody, who is incapable of resisting such adventure—search in the night for the missing rattler, crisscrossing the pasture with flashlights. It seems almost inevitable to the narrator that Rhody will not only be the one to find the snake but that she herself will be bitten—and on the wounded, arthritic leg, as though the sin represented by the snake would naturally seek out the marred limb of the prodigal. And so it does. Though unlike the remembered snake handler from Goyen's childhood who died in similar circumstances, Rhody is quickly saved by Aunt Idalou's more "practical ways of salvation—including leaves of Spanish dagger plant in the front yard which Son ran and got, and hog lard" (*CS* 172). The preacher and tent disappear overnight, taking the flagpole sitter with them, and Rhody stays until the summer comes to an end and she bustles off yet again to appease her restlessness. Unlike Princis Lester, Rhody can make contact with home only briefly, for solace or healing, before she moves on again. She is the "child of the path in the pasture between home and homelessness, redemption and error" (*CS* 173), and her attraction to and repulsion from the house in the bitterweeds inscribes her destiny on the land.

It is no remarkable insight to realize that Rhody is a vehicle for Goyen's own feelings about his distance from Texas. His visits to Merrill Street were both restorative and crippling, and his family, like Rhody's, persistently hoped that he would come back to Houston permanently and live a more conventional life. And though the moral touch is relatively light in "Rhody's Path," the sense that the wanderer is seeking out or otherwise encountering a sinful life away from a simple but reliable goodness is always an important baseline to Goyen's thinking about his own isolation. If one of the themes of *Faces of the Blood Kindred* is the inescapable bond of family, those binding qualities are made more evident and more painful by the loss of daily contact. Kinship is understood as a burden, an unappeasable responsibility, and the one in exile has a particular vantage on the contradictory necessities of connection and separation. From one point of view, sinfulness becomes freedom; from another, it becomes a kind of identity. And yet the pull to return, the fantasy of reuniting without conflict—an essentially preadolescent dream—remains and sometimes grows stronger with time.

The recognition of the unpayable price of family responsibility is the central concern of the beautifully brooding and emotionally charged title story, "Faces of the Blood Kindred." Once again, the family lives in Houston, and a relative from the father's side—a Ganchion—comes to visit. James, "blond and faintly hairlipped," is fourteen, the same age as his fearful, sensitive cousin. He's the product of a broken home (his father "had run away" to St. Louis), and his mother is in the hospital with arthritis. To the shy cousin, James is almost exotic, a fearless figure of adventure: "He was a wild country boy brought to live in the city of Houston when his parents moved there from a little town down the road south. He said he wanted to be a cowboy, but it was too late for that; still, he wore boots and spurs. He hated the city, the schools, played away almost daily. The cousin admired James, thought him a daring hero" (*CS* 133). To the boy's mother, James comes from her husband's disreputable family, another wanderer prodded by hidden energies to bring shame on himself and others.

One afternoon, James takes his cousin to the edge of town to look at some Cornish fighting cocks. Since his family would not approve of cockfighting, the cousin feels guilty and afraid, and the sight of the "rooster-like man sitting barefooted in a little shotgun house" (*CS* 133) only increases his looming sense of evil. James, however, examines the roosters with a knowledgeable eye and buys "a big blue cock with stars on its breast" (*CS* 134) to take back to the city. Worried they will be caught, the cousin frets over the presence of the bird, wondering how James is going to keep it concealed from his family. But James has a hiding place in mind: a big fig tree at their grandmother's house, the branches of which reach down to the ground and form a "damp and musky cove" (*CS* 135) near the trunk. The tree is heavy with ripe, sticky fruit, and before they can secure it, the rooster gets away and flutters up into the branches. Fearful that the bird will "ruin Granny's figs," the cousin impulsively picks up a rock and throws it at the rooster, killing it. The guilt of the visit to the rooster-like man amplifies into the shame of this sacrificial death: "'I didn't mean to, I didn't mean to!' the cousin gasped in horror, and he backed farther and farther away, beyond the deep shadows of the fig trees. Standing away, he saw in the dark luscious grove the figure of James fall to the ground and kneel over his Cornish cock and clasp the tousled mass like a lover's head. He heard him sob softly; and the cousin backed away in anguish" (*CS* 136). James disappears and later turns up at his father's house in St. Louis. The cousin feels his complicity and responsibility transform into a sacrificial desire. The encounter under the tree laden with figs—as symbolic as they can be of an almost too-ripe sexuality—has been his initiation into the mysteries of desire and loss, and he counters the guilty shock of sexual discovery with a pledge of salvation: "The cousin walked away from the grandmother's house and went the long way home under the fresh evening sky, his fingers sticky with fig musk. . . . If he could one day save all his kindred from pain or help them to some home! 'I will, I will,' he promised. But what were they paying penance for? What was their wrong? Later he knew it bore the ancient name of lust" (*CS* 137).

Goyen had covered this territory before but never so compactly or with so charged an atmosphere of weight and feeling. Once again, the differences between the Trows and the Goyens form the moral structure of the story, and the young cousin finds himself attracted both to the eroticism of the Ganchions and the fearfulness of his mother's disapproval. Without making its correspondences obvious, the story suggests a young boy's discovery of his own illicit desires and the equally instinctive response on his part to repress or control them. That this repression leads to an artistic avowal, a project of saving and renewing, should not be a surprise to Goyen's readers at this point in his career, but his ability to continue to mine this material, even to compress and reinvigorate it, is remarkable. Even as he moved into middle age, the central psychological problem of his writing had not lost its force, though age had pressed on him a kind of reckoning with the burdens he sought to shift. As the story ends, the now grown cousin sees James's face in a crowd and instantly recognizes the claim it invokes:

"But the look upon James's face that moment that night in a strange city where the cousin had come to passing recognition and had found a transient homage, bore the haunting question of ancestry; and though he thought he had at last found and cleared for himself something of identity, a particle of answer in the face of the world, had he set any-thing at peace, answered any speechless question, atoned for the blind failing, the outrage and the pain on the face of his blood kindred?" (*CS* 138–139).

The most significant of the remaining stories in *The Faces of the Blood Kindred* are "Old Wildwood," which offers a portrait of Goyen's paternal grandfather, and "A People of Grass," the painful retelling of Goyen's childhood failure in the May Day festival.[28] "Old Wildwood" effectively reinforces the thematic arrangement of "Faces" by suggest-ing that the Goyen patriarch, the alcoholic with a "crooked foot" and wayward desires, is the hereditary source for the cousin's contradictory reaction to his own sexuality. The old man's carnal demands lead him away from the family, into a kind of local exile, and make him equally the patriarch-as-orphan: "The grandson belonged to an old, illustrious bunch of people of timber . . . , and it was he [the grandfather] who had brought all the others home to him, his grandson. Yet the grand-father seemed an orphan. And now for the first time, the grandson felt the deep, free sadness of orphanage; and he knew he was orphaned, too. That was the cruel gift of the grandfather, he thought" (*CS* 147). Orphanage becomes a kind of psychic state that paradoxically does not free the narrator from the hereditary bonds of family; instead, it merely highlights a fundamental loneliness within kinship. Rejected or self-exiled, Goyen's orphan distrusts his apparent freedom and exists in an irreconcilable double state, both distanced from and therefore exces-sively aware of the responsibilities of family.

To feel the pull of home at a distance is a standard enough trope, and many of the stories in the volume rely on it, but Goyen's repetition of the interruptive power of distant memory suggests an almost ghostly inability to live in the present. Repeatedly his characters begin by wan-dering in a distant city—New York or Rome—only to be reminded by some sight or encounter of a Texas memory that then consumes the world of the story. In "The Moss Rose," the lone walker notices the flower from his childhood and regrets his rootlessness. He plants the cluster of orange and yellow "stars" in a pot on his fire escape and hopes that their presence will allow him to rebuild the lost world to which he cannot (or will not) return. Similarly, in "The Horse and the Day Moth," the sight of a suddenly dead carriage horse near Central Park shocks the central character into thinking of a recent visit to his seriously ill mother. There in her garden in Texas, the mood of impending loss is leavened by the presence of a fragile moth, the survival of whose species across the years surprises him. And though he is haunted by the memory of his mother calling to him at dusk from an empty house ("Come on in now, it's darkening"), the moth's survival stands improbably as a defense against the implacable fact of death and loss. And so hope is wrung in small ways against large obstacles, typically by characters who are almost paralyzed by their isolation.

The final story in the volume, "There Are Ravens to Feed Us," allows the conflict buried within Goyen's meditations on kinship to emerge more fully. The main character works in a large apartment building and is constantly disturbed by the sounds of argument coming from the apartment beneath. Eventually driven from his own rooms to wander the city, he returns to find a wedding celebration under way on the steps of his building. The sight of the wedding party and "like a white vision the blessed figure of the bride" in front of his "haunted stone building" (*CS* 215) brings into question his earlier fear of the disruptive family in the apartment below. When he discovers that the wedding has issued from this very apartment, he begins to doubt the existence of the quarrelling voices: "Had they gone away, if ever they had existed, the accursed family?" (*CS* 216). This "house of violence" has vanished in the hopeful prospect of a union, leaving the turbulent narrator free to shape his own dream of "an event of glad tidings, some fulfillment of wish, reward, a day or a night of beautiful sensation" (*CS* 216) that will counter the despair of his isolation. But this note of resolution differs considerably from that of the other stories. The central character's psychological state is less certain and the change in his mood less logically related to the events he relates. If indeed the quarrelsome family below is simply a hallucination, the story suggests a furtive wish for peace from the conflicts of kinship that haunt the isolated individual. In a very indirect sense, the muted argument in the apartment below recalls Goyen's early unpublished story "The Crimes of Mirensky," in which the artistic son is driven away by his family's accusations of selfishness. Here the artist is partially separated from the turbulence of family life, but not enough to insulate him from their emotional reach. Only the fantasy of a reconciling ritual can exorcise the desperate mood that has brought family strife into conflict with the work of his imagination.

Though not as risky or technically adventurous as *Ghost and Flesh*, Goyen's second collection was a substantial achievement and perhaps the least complicated of his publications when it came to his dealings with Random House. The somewhat more conventional approach to storytelling may also have made the volume easier for critics to understand and accept, and the reviews were generally favorable. William Peden, writing in the *New York Times*, praised the author's intimate knowledge of his subjects, particularly the people of East Texas, and considered the new volume a step up from *The House of Breath* and *Ghost and Flesh*: "*The Faces of the Blood Kindred* is Mr. Goyen's best book, unquestionably, to date. In it he has created a deeply felt, moving, and sincere group of variations upon significant, universal themes and experiences." It is revealing that the one story Peden singles out for criticism, "A Tale of Inheritance," he finds "marred by the emotional extravagance, fondness for the grotesque, and over-elaborate concern for language and technique of [Goyen's] earlier fiction."[29] In other words, from Peden's perspective Goyen has improved by reining in what could arguably be called the most distinctive aspects of his work and taming them to the specifications of a more conventional audience.

While respectfully citing Goyen's uniqueness, most reviewers felt it necessary to express a mild degree of discomfort with his methods or to note the limited nature of his work's appeal. Terry Southern in *The Nation* suggested that only Goyen "devotees" would enjoy the new volume: "This is unfortunate because the stories are often pervaded by a sense of mystery and terror that may well be unique to the work of this particular writer."[30] And in a follow-up review in the *Times*, Thomas Lask complained of the lack of action in the stories and the tendency of the narrators to deliver "a number of beautiful sermons" rather than let the reader discover themes for himself. Oddly, but perhaps not surprisingly, Lask considered "The Geranium," the slightest and most obviously commercial story in the book, the "most effective" in the collection.[31] One of the most sympathetic readings came from Granville Hicks in the *Saturday Review*. Stressing the "strong note of nostalgia in almost all of Goyen's work," Hicks argued that Goyen's interest in the past was not escapist but heuristic: "Goyen, however, is not escaping into the past for the sake of escape; he is ransacking it for experiences that can give meaning to the present. With his very considerable poetic powers he brings an incident to life so that we can feel its significance." Hicks concluded by summing up Goyen's career to this point: "He is a writer who has been going his own way for a decade, a delicate way as a rule though he can be robust when he wants to be. He has four books to his credit now, and they establish a place for him."[32]

This "place" was tenuous at best, however. If by 1960 Goyen had managed to build an identifiable reputation as an unusual and uncompromising writer of fiction and plays, he continued to suffer the uncertainty of a career that produced little in the way of financial security or personal contentment. At forty-five, he was still scrambling for basic subsistence even as the one long-term, substantial relationship of his adult life was slowly unraveling. Something was ending. *Faces* may have been a moderate success, but it also marked a kind of terminus to the material with which he had struggled since adolescence. The deep mine of feeling that Goyen had worked in order to understand and transform his childhood turbulence into art had begun to run out. If he were to continue doing more than just the occasional adaptation of earlier material, he would need to find not so much a new subject as a new approach to writing about the adult he had become. The early song of the young man who read Saroyan in that humid room in Houston had played out its last variation in these stories, and from now on he would have to find ways to explore what had been left out or cautiously muffled in this early writing. In a similar sense, he would have to face the question of how to live and what to do with a life that seemed, all too often, to be pulling itself apart. "Life is still young for me," he wrote to his parents in language that must have seemed hopelessly emptied by repetition; "a lot lies ahead, if I can only make the right move and find my true way."[33]

PART III ∼

The Rider at the Door

CHAPTER ELEVEN

"A New Life"
1962–1964

I was so eager to be a father.

DELTA INTERVIEW WITH ROLANDE BALLORAIN (1979)

After the stage adaptation of *The House of Breath* in 1957, Goyen had begun working closely with members of the Actors Studio, eventually serving on the invitation-only Playwrights and Directors Unit. In the early 1960s, the group included, among others, Edward Albee, James Baldwin, Norman Mailer, James Leo Herlihy, and Terrence McNally. Goyen described it as a "group of novelists and short story writers with theatrical ambitions," and he made use of his connections and relationships there to further his work on *The Diamond Rattler* and on a new play he'd been developing.[1] A version of the aborted screenplay written for Fred Coe a few years before, *Christy* concerns the aftermath of a young author's death and the impact of his now-famous novel on his widow and extended family. The model for the successful book is clearly *The House of Breath*, and the family presented here is a compact representation of the Goyens and Trows who appeared there originally and who variously felt betrayed by it. As though to answer and reimagine the response to his work, Goyen set the play in the family house (the "house of breath") in Charity, Texas, and gathered them all together for an imagined reckoning and revelation.

In keeping with his long-standing conception of himself as a sacrificial figure taking on others' burdens, Goyen essentially imagined his own death in the person of a young author, Walter, whose voice haunts his uncle Christy with passages drawn almost directly from *The House of Breath*. Walter's wife Ruth, also a native of Charity, has returned to the small town and serves as an advocate for his work, defending it from the family's complaints. At times, she assumes a wounded voice that tracks closely to Goyen's own, telling the family directly that their beloved son and nephew was only trying to live up to the burden placed on him: "trying to be the image of the man *you* wanted him to be. Trying not to *fail*. Failure, failure. That's all he heard around here: failure, failure. Loss, disappointment. Save us, save us. From a little boy, heard it from you. You all drove him to do what he did. You *trained* him for it. He wrote a prayer book for you, a funeral service for you. You made a kind of priest out of him, so he could pray for you."[2]

As the family gathers, Ruth must decide whether to accept a lucrative offer from a Hollywood studio to turn Walter's novel into a film. Some family members are eager for the payday and the attention; others, like Christy, are ashamed of what the book reveals and want to escape any scrutiny a film would bring. Since the family is clearly in decline (to generate a bit of income, Walter's mother, Lucy, has recently rented out the pasture near the grandmother's grave plot as a parking lot for a trucking company) the money represents a kind of renewal, a potential salvation. As in the early story "The Crimes of Mirensky," Goyen found a way to place his own sacrifice at the center of the family's emotional and economic needs. Mirensky exiles himself, promising to send money in his place; Walter's death has produced a book, now translatable into a financial rescue that will validate his suffering.

Christy is the focus of the attempt to persuade the family that Walter's writing was an act of love rather than betrayal. Walter has left a sealed letter for the family to read before they make a decision on the movie contract, and it states that Christy must give final approval before any deal is made: "He gave me the tenderest story in God's world and I made a book of it. It is therefore his book and came to me from him." Accordingly, Ruth seeks out Christy in the woodshed where he maintains a secretive retreat and tries to convince him of the need to start a new life. "We have to live, to go on, to find a life for ourselves," she pleads. "For the sake of the man who's given us a chance to do so, now. Don't go down like he did, Christy: tied, trapped in himself. Let him free you; let him free me. Break loose, Christy."

As part of her argument, she produces a set of letters written by Lucy, Walter's mother, and suggests that she was responsible for pushing her son toward suicide: "He was at his rope's end. Seemed like every time he was in despair, one of these would come. Almost as if she wanted to destroy him." Ruth attributes Walter's obsession with self-sacrifice to Lucy's constant pressure during his early life: "She treated him like the Messiah of the family. She wanted him to carry the burden of the failure of his father, his grandfather . . . you . . . and to 'redeem' it, as she said. That was her word: 'redeem,' 'redeem,' over and over she said it to him." Eventually convinced, Christy later turns on Lucy with this new evidence and continues the line of accusation. Charging her with a kind of rapacious affection and a desire to keep Walter close to her, "gelded," Christy then reads from the last of the letters Lucy sent to her son before his death. Perhaps not surprising, but astounding never-theless, the letter is a near duplicate of the one Emma Goyen sent to El Prado after the publication of "Four American Portraits" in *Accent*. The revelation of this bitter mother's complaint creates the dramatic turning point of the play, a fitting climax for Goyen's public condemna-tion of Emma's manipulations. In one fraught moment, he had found a way to plead his long-simmering case, to justify his personal choices, and to take a cathartic but painful revenge. Lucy is suddenly brushed aside. Christy accepts the movie offer on the condition that she deed the family house to him, and the renewal promised by Walter's death comes, momentarily, to the uncle who understands him rather than the mother who does not.

But *Christy* is more than just a personal fantasy of vengeance and redemption. It is, finally, an almost classical tragedy. Though Ruth ap-pears to be free now to make a new life, she falls into a violent em-brace with Christy, who kills her accidentally in a grim echo of his wife Willadean's death by drowning. Christy's father—the aging, dispos-sessed patriarch outraged by the strange trucks near his wife's grave—is hit and killed by the departing traffic. And Christy himself, long im-potent after Willadean's drowning—like Boney Benson, he embraced her fresh grave and, less literally, transferred his desire into the soil—wanders back to the pond where she died, unable to escape the gravity of its depths. This sudden sequence of deaths may be excessive, but the losses suggest more than final judgments rendered on an exile's family. The tragic mood of *Christy* feels larger than Walter's story and more expansive than Goyen's personal desire to settle nagging questions of his own. As though extending the thread of *Faces of the Blood Kindred*, *Christy* suggests that personal dramas of redemption are still circum-scribed by the templates of heredity and fate. Walter may dream of providing a rebirth to the family that has rejected him, but such fantasies are more indicative of his character and identity, of who he is or was, than of how reality responds to our wishes.

In terms of dramatic structure and the traditional virtues of modern theater, *Christy* is Goyen's best play. Though *House of Breath* is more formally adventurous, none of Goyen's other dramas, generally translations of fiction to the stage, approach its economy and force. It seems likely that working with the Actors Studio and American Place Theater helped him concentrate his material to the needs of the stage, to wed narrative development and dramatic action more effectively than had been possible in his earlier efforts. The more collaborative atmosphere may also have helped him see how to integrate the personal more fully into the timeless and tragic. Though with considerably less comic absurdity, *Christy* recalls the late plays of Chekhov, grafting to the listlessness of modern provincial life the still passionate need on Goyen's part to force personal and family secrecies into the light.

"My lonely Kiel"

Though *Christy* was not produced until 1964 (in an unreviewed, workshop production), initial casting began in early 1961.[3] For the role of Minnalou—the brash, alcoholic aunt interested only in the movie money—Goyen asked the play's director, Wynn Handman, to approach a young woman he had admired in several Actors Studio performances. Doris Roberts was a spirited character actress caught in a failing marriage and struggling to push her career forward while caring for her four-year-old son. Initially offended that Goyen had asked her to audition for the part, she was surprised and charmed when he showed up at her door one rainy evening, script in hand, and begged her to read the play. "More than his courtly manner," she later wrote, "what struck me was his face. His mesmerizing gray-blue eyes shot through with dashes of green regarded me in admiration and concern."[4] As work on *Christy* progressed—delayed more than once by the difficulty of casting the leading man—Goyen and Roberts had repeated occasions to get to know one another and soon discovered a mutual attraction. After learning of her plans to secure a divorce in Mexico, Goyen immediately asked her to marry him, but Roberts turned him down. "I wasn't ready," she later explained. "I was so disillusioned with marriage and still experiencing the deep pain of the divorce, I just couldn't commit."[5] She left for California to pursue a possible acting job, and Goyen spent the summer on Fire Island near the Handmans in yet another "little house" that reminded him of Frieda's cabin at the Lawrence ranch. Once again tangled in a complicated romantic net that had left him at least temporarily isolated, Goyen decided against another year of teaching and instead took a leave of absence from the New School for a State Department reading tour in Germany.

The unexpected request to serve as a cultural ambassador was a welcome reminder of Goyen's popularity in Europe, particularly in Germany. According to Coindreau, Goyen's work had begun to attract attention there in the early 1950s with Curtius's translation of *The House of Breath*. "Germany knew him well before France," he explained to Christian Guidicelli. "*The House of Breath* had been treated in a very beautiful essay by Ernst Robert Curtius and had become the bedside book of the German youth."[6] Coindreau's own rendering of the novel, which won the Halpérine Kaminsky Prize for the best translation into French in 1952, expanded this continental enthusiasm to the point that *The House of Breath* was regularly assigned in advanced literature courses in France for many years after. It also attracted the attention of cultural luminaries such as Gaston Bachelard, who later included a brief discussion of the novel in his influential work of phenomenology, *The Poetics of Space*. Coindreau relates how Bachelard was particularly taken with the resonance of Goyen's work with his own and asked the translator to let Goyen know that "an old French philosopher admires him."[7]

At the end of December 1961, Goyen flew to Switzerland to spend a few days with Elisabeth Schnack, his German translator after Curtius's death in 1956. At Corseaux sur Vevey, they took in the sights and rode the little funicular up Mount Pelerin, "into the deep forest," as Goyen recorded in his day book (HRC 29.1). From there he traveled to Berlin for the first of his readings, which to his surprise and pleasure drew an audience of more than 2,000. Subsequent performances in Nuremberg, Munich, Freiburg, Tubingen, Saarbrucken, Heidelberg, Frankfurt, Hanover, and Basel, all within the month of January, left him exhilarated but tired. Back in Zurich to recuperate from a case of flu, he settled into the picturesque Hotel Florhof and spent his days writing. The tonic of attention offered a pleasant contrast to the United States. "I don't want to go back to New York yet," he wrote his parents, "so will stay on a little while longer. . . . People are so kind to me, and New York was so hard the last year, what with poor Joe and all that trouble—I might as well stay here if I'm happy and can work."[8]

Goyen stayed in Zurich through most of April, with only a few trips to Hamburg to discuss the possibility of producing one of his plays at the theater there. This link to northern Germany may have helped him decide to try to extend his stay in Germany for a few more months. After sending a request to the foreign service at the American embassy in Bonn, he was offered a position as a guest lecturer in American Studies at the University of Kiel, from May through July. Initially the idea of limited teaching, free lodging, and a salary seemed a plausible way to continue his residence and possibly allow him to build on the goodwill he had already experienced. But the gray city on the Baltic, newly rebuilt after heavy Allied bombing during the war, tipped him quickly toward depression. After only a few weeks, he was in a near panic, convinced that committing himself to this "ugly and dark and cold" city with what seemed equally cold people was a mistake. Though he had a pleasant room on the channel leading to the sea, he was unable to write, and his relatively light pay soon left him in debt. Before the month was out, he had resigned and fled to Hamburg to catch a plane back to New York. "I left Kiel suddenly," he wrote his parents a week later,

> after doing all I could to endure it. It was a disappointment to me to have to do this, since I was working for my country and wanted to give all I could. But Kiel was terrible, as I wrote you, and the people not pleasant and the whole thing was a dreadful mistake. . . . I have about $25 to my name at the moment, and it's been a fight to get money at once out of people in my business here in New York. That's discouraging, because in Europe I was treated like a fine writer and respected and admired everywhere. Here, it's still hard."[9]

As with many of Goyen's sudden crises and dysphoric episodes, it's difficult to pin down an exact cause for his negative reaction to Kiel. It wasn't the first time, nor would it be the last, that he had taken a sudden, visceral dislike to a place, suffering from what sometimes appears to be a kind of panic attack. Kiel, with its connection to the sea and to the German Navy—it was the birthplace of the U-boat and a major base for submarine operations during World War II—may have reminded him too much of his own war experience; there is, in fact, a suggestive resemblance between the letters written during this crisis and those he sent home from officers' training school or the *Casablanca*. But there are also hints, in notes and later recollections, that his psychological state was somewhat tenuous throughout the trip and that he had shown similar symptoms of distress earlier in his stay. An entry in his daybook registers his need to send a note to the American embassy to explain his "Switzerland oddnesses" (HRC 29.1). Another manuscript entry, dated Freiburg, May 12, 1962, is more suggestive: "So I go back to my lonely Kiel—my cold, stark, plain Nordland—and I'll hide there from all my Zurich pain and I'll be unto my self . . . and I can hear it now, for I have suffered the agony, again of coming back *into* myself, and I can bear it now" (HRC 25.10, emphasis in original). What seems implied in these painful registrations is a lost love, but there is little evidence of a specific relationship, no matter how fleeting, having occurred in Zurich itself. On the other hand, his daybook does indicate that he was still thinking about Glasco, calling him in February, buying a birthday gift for him in Berlin, and recording the fact that he was in nearby Amsterdam in early May. At the same time, Goyen was in regular contact with Doris Roberts, who may at one point have suggested coming to Europe with her son, Michael. In an undated manuscript titled "Letter from Germanz," a man who has just had significant dental work is responding to a letter from a woman who wants to leave her husband and come to be with him in Germany (HRC 25.2). The man tries to stop her, telling her his teeth are bad and that they have no way to take care of the woman's baby. The piece itself has the air of a comedy sketch (with a particular emphasis on the dental patient's marred speech), but the situation matches that of Goyen and Roberts closely enough to suggest that it could have had an origin in fact.

The complication of passions and loyalties of attachment involving Glasco and Roberts suggests that there may have been more to Roberts's refusal of Goyen's proposal than disillusionment with marriage. Goyen's past relationships, predominately gay, can hardly have been a mystery to many members of the theater community associated with the Actors Studio, and it seems probable that one or more mutual friends would have warned Roberts about his sexual history. In a possible effort to counter such admonitions, Goyen prepared a list of arguments in favor of the marriage, including an attempt to mitigate concerns about the influence of an "ex-homosexual" on Roberts's young son. Of course, these planned-for discussions may never have taken place, but it seems highly likely that the very real romantic feelings between the couple developed in a more complex atmosphere than Roberts suggests in her memoir. The trip to Germany may thus have been a catalyst for Goyen's lifelong feeling of isolation now that he felt cut off from both his past with Glasco and his imagined future with Roberts. No matter what the source of this turmoil, however, it is clear that he returned to New York in May shaken and isolated and increasingly convinced that his survival depended on some sort of personal transformation. "I was just worn out," he later explained to an interviewer. "I was completely lost—I had to change my life."[10]

Another Man's Son

Back in New York, Goyen settled again into his apartment at 214 East 51st Street and began reviving the process of getting *Christy* to final production. "Most of my friends are away for the summer," he wrote to his parents. "I eat most of my meals in my apt. and don't do anything much more than work. The play is the thing now and I have good hopes for it."[11] Despite this partially contrived image of solitude, he was not as isolated as his letters home would suggest. He and Roberts had resumed their relationship shortly after his return, and by January he was writing to his parents for the first time about the "girl"—Roberts was ten years younger than Goyen (she was thirty-seven in 1962)—he had introduced to his brother Jim on a recent visit: "Yes, there is a girl and I'm in a quandary about her. I've known her for two years and we are very close and understand each other very very well, and have helped each other." Given the history of Merrill Street's reactions to previous hints of marriage, it is significant that he felt certain enough by this point to begin introducing Roberts to his family. Perhaps in response to these earlier losses—or to Roberts's initial refusal—he was intent on proceeding much more carefully: "All of this will take time, and I intend to be sure about what I do."[12]

If later journal entries and comments about his marriage are an accurate guide to his thinking during this time, what Goyen intended was to start a family. In addition to having found in Roberts a new partner who could provide the sort of intimacy and alliance he continuously sought in others, there is a strong indication that he simply wanted a fresh start, a way of living that was more conventional, stable, and in line with his family's long-delayed expectations. At forty-eight, he may have seen this as his last chance to settle down and take on the kind of responsibility that would demonstrate to all concerned that he could live a traditional, socially respectable life. Fatherhood in particular was a powerful draw, as he later explained to Robert Phillips: "Well, by that time, you see, I was in a tough phase. I talked very macho . . . something like a bridegroom. I mean, he's just got the balls of his generation going for him."[13] This willingness to see himself in a highly masculine role may have been related to his father's poor health. After a heart scare a few years before, Charlie Goyen was no longer the threatening, constraining figure of Goyen's youth, and his weakness seems to have provoked a strong, if mixed, reaction in his oldest son. In notes made on Fire Island about a recent visit to Texas, Goyen registered his shock and sadness mixed with a barely muted triumph at seeing his once-dominant father so diminished:

> The old man is tired; he is all used up. He is not interested any more. His force is gone.
>   When mother and I stood in his room and looked at him sitting on the side of his bed, he head bowed, his eyes staring at the floor—was so white headed and pale . . . and wasted looking; so sad and tired and old. (HRC 28.13)

The almost powerless father in *Christy* may have provided a focal point for these feelings and an occasion for imagining a father-son dialogue about Goyen's future. To his grown son Christy, impotent since the death of his wife, Papa Ganchion urges a new fertility and the burden of fatherhood: "I want you to have a son, to find you a wife and make you a home, bring forth a son, like you Mama and me did; and know what it is to have your name on a son. To carry us on. It's all we can do, son . . . carry ourselves on through our children. Don't matter how the world changes, how people change, how things go down. We have to keep going, no matter what with. If it's a broken world, and disappointment, and everything less, don't matter."[14] In his 1979 interview with Rolande Ballorain, Goyen admitted that at this time in his life he was drawn to the idea of fatherhood with a particular intensity: "I took over this fatherhood thing as though I had conquered a whole country. You couldn't stop me, I was so eager to be a father. . . . I wanted the family thing and I wanted to do that."[15]

Goyen and Roberts were married on November 10, 1963, on the stage of the American Place Theater. Wynn Handman, according to Roberts, "appointed himself the producer of the wedding. Elia Kazan's wife, Molly, arranged the music, and the legendary theater director Harold Clurman" gave away the bride.[16] The excitement and optimism of the occasion was tempered the next morning when the couple received a phone call at their room at the Plaza notifying them that Roberts's son, Michael, had been abducted by his father. Settling the custody situation took several months, but the event made it clear that the challenges of balancing two artistic careers and caring for a contested six-year-old child would place significant emotional strain on both newlyweds.

Considerable pleasure mixed with mild bewilderment filled Goyen's correspondence at the time. To Dorothy Brett he was enthusiastic about the "adventure" of marriage: "I *love* it and can't imagine living any other way, although there are and have been large problems. But Doris and I battle through them and keep coming through."[17] On the minor side of the challenges may have been Goyen's basic adjustment from living in a childless environment to coping with the daily chaos of pet turtles and tadpoles brought home from Central Park. Somewhat more serious was the need for a steadier income to pay for a nanny and manage the expenses of two busy but irregularly employed artists. Additional teaching at Columbia University partially filled the gap, but the more permanent solution appeared to be a job in publishing.

Because of his frequent and dispiriting battles with publishers, Goyen had developed a strong sense of what he preferred and demanded from those to whom he entrusted his work, and he felt strongly that he could turn his own hard experience to good use. Similarly, his off-and-on teaching had given him repeated experience working individually with talented writers, for some of whom he had already served as unofficial editor and agent. He approached several houses, including Atlantic Monthly Press, outlining to director Seymour Lawrence both his general qualifications and a rich roster of literary connections: "There are some talented writers with whom I have worked and whose work-in-progress I have discussed editorially with them, including Edward Albee, Jack Richardson, Jack Gelber, William Inge (all novels)

. . . I also want to help attract, may I say, from other houses writers who may be discontented and restless there for want of the kind of editor I might be for them."[18] Though the search ultimately took more than a year, Goyen finally found the chance he was looking for at McGraw-Hill, where he was hired as senior editor at the beginning of 1966.

New financial imperatives could be addressed with his typical energy and activity, but the psychological complications of marriage and stepfatherhood created a less tractable sort of turmoil. Beyond the minor frazzle of his suddenly hyperactive household, Goyen was challenged by the immediate complication of balancing his new romantic life with his sudden role, no matter how indirect, as a parent. Both Goyen and Roberts later described the early years of their marriage as at times desperately intense, "a wild and beautiful passionate love affair" as he put it in his journal (HRC 20.7). And for Goyen in particular, young Michael's presence was both an important indicator of his new life and a frustrating or confusing barrier in his new relationship with Roberts. "In that tumultuous thing we had together there was this little boy," he later reflected. "He was always with us, always between us. Together in our wild love that often reached tragic proportions . . . we brought up this little boy" (HRC 20.7). Some of the stresses of Goyen's new life can be felt in a brief manuscript entitled "The Birthday Gift," in which a stepfather buys his wife a "china pitcher" for her birthday and hides it, with the son's help, in a linen closet. Unable to keep the secret, the young boy blurts it out in front of both adults, and the stepfather reacts angrily, hitting him. The distraught stepson then goes to the closet to look at the pitcher, picks it up, and, crying, drops and breaks it. Both parents later comfort the boy, and the sketch ends with the three of them on the boy's bed, the parents separated, literally and figuratively, by the son (HRC 25.5).

The eagerness for fatherhood that Goyen described to Ballorain included a strong desire to have a child of his own, so strong in fact that it may have prevented its own fulfillment. While the couple were vacationing on Long Island in August of 1965, Roberts suffered a miscarriage. "Doris was between three and four months with it," Goyen explained to Dorothy Brett, "and suddenly she miscarried it. . . . The worst thing of it was that we were on holiday and had to put Doris in a small-town hospital where she almost died, came very near to it."[19] What Goyen, understandably, did not explain is that he may have been pressuring Roberts to conceive, and the tension and near violence of this demand may have resulted in desperate arguments that brought on the loss. In an undated sketch entitled "Edith story, The lost Child" a narrator describes a couple who are staying in a small house by the sea. The husband accuses the wife of trying to prevent conception, badgering her to such an extent that she eventually rushes out toward the ocean. He brings her back to the house, but soon after, she begins to bleed and has to be taken to the hospital (HRC 25.6). In his later notes, Goyen recognized that he had caused "the loss of what [he] most cried out for" (HRC 27.5), and there is no doubt that the trauma, guilt, and disappointment from this incident added a significant weight to his list of personal losses.[20]

Complication, confusion, and a contradictory mixture of desires emerge clearly in writing he was beginning to assemble during this period for a project eventually called *Another Man's Son*:

> The mother kept thinking: I want this child to take this man as his own father, since I hate the child's own father. The father thought: I am the father. I hate this woman for taking my son away from me and giving him to another man. This other man is not the father; he's a pretender, he's a step-father. The new man thought: *who* am I? A sudden father, an instant father. This is not *my* son: that is, I didn't *make* him. Making another human being defines a father. But it is out of my wife and from another man, and it is in my house, and it is very nearly mine; but not *mine*. I love it, I want to help it in this foul and beautiful world; I want to show it something that I know; I want it for my own, *almost*, but I cannot wholly have it for my own because I didn't *make* it. (HRC 29.7)

If this push and pull of desire and responsibility was the gist of his new life, then the novel would attempt to take on these problems directly, as a way of clarifying and settling an inner turbulence. As early as April of 1965, Goyen was writing to Sam Vaughan, his editor at Doubleday, about this project that concerned "a step-father's passionate and romantic marriage to a woman who brings a young son into the marriage, the problems between the step-father and the step-son who brings an unseen intruder (his own father) into the household and the desperate relationship of the man and the woman."[21] Goyen would work on the manuscript off and on for the next several years until it slowly transformed into his fourth published novel, *Come, the Restorer*. But these early plans reveal that its goal was not only to settle his mind about being a stepfather but to reopen one of the deeper scars of his childhood—his relationship to Charlie Goyen. With *Christy*, he had effectively released pent-up resentments at the family response to *The House of Breath*; now he could "speak" to his father directly as both a son and a stepfather. The reward would be a more thorough, and more mature, consideration of many of his typical early themes: the ties of kinship, the stresses of paternity, and the spiritual possibilities of orphanage and adoption.

The Fair Sister

During his time in Zurich in 1962, Goyen had completed a new version of *Half a Look of Cain*. As Gibbons has suggested in his afterword to the edition published in 1994, Goyen had been trying for several years to find a publisher for reworked versions of the novel since its initial rejection in 1953. Once he returned from Germany in June, he expected Doubleday to publish it, but the publisher refused to go forward until he produced a more marketable companion volume, an expansion of his short story "The Fair Sister." Sam Vaughan had suggested the project, thinking the brief, comic tale that began the collection *Faces of the Blood Kindred* would make an enjoyable small book that might give Goyen a wider audience.[22] Though deeply disappointed yet again, Goyen badly needed what money he could make from any book deal, and once again he set aside teaching for the fall term and worked steadily on the new manuscript. By December he had submitted it to Doubleday, and after a few more revisions to add length, it was published the following September. *Half a Look of Cain* did not appear that year or at any time during Goyen's life. What became of the promise to publish it, if there ever was one, is unclear, but it seems likely that once again publishers balked at supporting so strange and radically inventive a text.

The Fair Sister (published in England as *Savata, My Fair Sister*) is a comparatively faint echo from the final clamor of Goyen's early work. The story had come from his African American cleaning lady, who had talked (mostly to herself) about her wayward sister while she vacuumed his apartment. (He even used the sister's real name, Savata, though in his version, as he explained later to Patrick Bennet, the sister was much less troublesome than her real-life inspiration.)[23] The cleaning lady's voice became the preacherly cadence of Ruby Drew, an overweight diabetic who sees herself as the righteous counterpoint to her lighter-skinned, glamorous sister, Savata. Ruby Drew has dedicated herself to the service of a Philadelphia evangelist known as Prince o' Light, a handsome former sinner whose great theme is the need to "bridle desire" (*FS* 8). Determined to save her lost sister, she boards a train for St. Louis where Savata is working as a singer in a nightclub. Like Prince o' Light, Savata is both strikingly beautiful and overwhelmingly sexual: "God knows what *she* was when first I laid eyes on her," Ruby Drew exclaims—"all feathers and sparkles revealing a physique that took your breath away; 'twas infernal, lewd and magnificent" (*FS* 2). Savata seems helpless in her desire for beautiful things and admiration, and only Ruby Drew's aggressive preaching shames her enough to make her leave the nightclub and move to Philadelphia for spiritual rehabilitation. There Prince o' Light trains her to be a minister, to rein in her natural sensuality and direct it toward salvation rather than titillation.

But Savata's beauty attracts trouble, and her own character is too weak to resist the pull of material desire. She escapes again to a nearby club, only to be recovered and installed in a church in Brooklyn. There she begins a very successful ministry that depends upon her ability to attract crowds ("mostly male" [*FS* 41]) and to transform the religious service into a theatrical production: "Her theory was that the Church is a theatre and ought to give its worshippers a chance to spiritualize out their mental emotions—the Church Modern" (*FS* 42). This success seems to conjure the appearance of Canaan Johnson, a smooth-talking teacher who begins by offering Hebrew lessons to the congregation and ends by moving in with Savata and taking over Ruby Drew's job as church manager. The remainder of the novella follows Ruby Drew's attempts to recover her position, save Savata from Canaan Johnson and herself, and possibly establish herself as the true minister of the Light of the World Holiness Church. Ultimately, after an unsuccessful lawsuit to reclaim her job, Ruby Drew has the satisfaction of seeing Canaan Johnson decamp with the church funds, leaving for Savata the humbling task of taking over Ruby Drew's housecleaning.

The Fair Sister is an unusual work for Goyen in several respects.

He had written stories that depended upon a thin layer of comedy to counterpoint his typical sadness, but he had never attempted a fully comic world, with characters cut to exaggerated proportions for the sake of laughs. He had likewise never ventured to represent African American characters as anything other than peripheral to an East Texas landscape seen by the small-town, white characters who populate his fiction. It seems likely that the short story began as simply another attempt to reproduce and stylize a telling voice, in a situation remarkably like those in his earlier tales: a middle-aged woman rehearsing a family woe to a relative stranger. But its expansion seems to have drawn him closer to the work he had lately been doing for the theater, and the novel version reads, as Robert Phillips has suggested, more "like the book for a splendid, big budget Broadway musical" than a thoroughly conceived piece of fiction embedded in its medium.[24]

Despite these apparent anomalies, *The Fair Sister* is thematically consistent with Goyen's major interests. Savata is yet another of his prodigals, a sensualist attracted to bright lights and self-display, unable to resist the shimmer of the material world. The descendent of Folner, Swimma, and Rhody, she carries the burden of Goyen's own guilty taste for such pleasures and allows him to divide the demands of the body from the aspiration to spirit preached by Ruby Drew: "That's the way I tried to see Savata and to understand her problems: Body. For us others, it's the soul that causes the troubles: the body makes no clamour, vaunteth not; it has gone by the wayside" (*FS* 2). A mild predestination operates here, in which the unattractive and overweight Ruby Drew has necessarily repressed the demands of the flesh, while erotic Savata seems helpless to control her ability to attract, and be attracted to, men. This division is precisely that described by Goyen as the alternative possibilities he saw for his life: the dreams of "vaudeville fantasy" counterposed to the desire to be a Christian missionary or "gospel Evangelist" (HRC 7.8). The church is the setting for the impossible conjunction of these desires, and the ministerial figures in *The Fair Sister* hope to use the sensuality of performance to lead others to spiritual rebirth. The risks, however, are great: both Ruby Drew and Prince o' Light are occasionally subject to Savata's temptations and retain their commitment to spirit only after repeated failures to resist. Evangelism was always a "show" for Goyen, and the show, like the circus tent in Bailey's pasture, was always an avenue to the sorrowful inverse of salvation. Flipping suddenly from one to the other—or simply confusing these related ecstasies—was all too possible and a continuing source of personal turbulence even as he neared fifty.

Even so, by virtue of its comedy, *The Fair Sister* does suggest that Goyen was beginning to see this struggle within himself in a slightly more detached fashion. Ruby Drew may be annoyingly self-righteous, but she does outlast and overcome Savata, who seems to have less and less energy as the story develops. Savata's power is natural and instinctive, but she possesses little more than a bodily force that gradually dissipates as she ages. As Goyen's representative of sensuality, she seems tired and emptied out by the end of the book, perhaps even subsumed by the increasing power of Ruby Drew. Her final escape does imply that desire can never be fully contained, but the equally bleak situation of the two sisters undermines any final preference for eros over spirit. All the characters, including the pious Prince o' Light, have their weaknesses, and it may be that each refracts Goyen's ghost and flesh thematics into subtly different patterns of desire fulfilled or resisted. Some the flesh consumes; others sublimate body to soul, but no one escapes the burden of what seems a perpetual choice.

As had become fairly typical for his books, reviews of *The Fair Sister* were mixed, though in this case some critics objected less to Goyen's approach to storytelling than to his choice to write a novel with African American characters. Robert Gorham Davis in the *New York Times* conceded Goyen's skill with "strange characters whose talk still has idiomatic folk flavor" but found his portrait of Ruby Drew in particular "unfeeling" and without "a trace of genuine religious or social concern": "His amused, condescending treatment of Negroes," he argued, "is in a literary convention thoroughly outmoded by the spirit of the time."[25] Similarly, if more vociferously, the reviewer for *Library Journal* considered "[t]he whole witless exercise [of the novel] . . . appalling. What could possibly have possessed a writer of William Goyen's talents to pull from his bag all the stale old stereotypes of the Negro . . . and pass them off as a novel at the incredible price of $3.50?"[26] But not every reviewer found the novel's characterizations demeaning. Recognizing *The Fair Sister*'s essential foundation in fantasy, Granville Hicks in *Saturday Review* thought it a "triumph": "What is fresh in Goyen's treatment [of religious show business] is that he has shown the mixture of motives so adroitly and made so amusing and at the same time so thoughtful a drama out of it."[27] Similarly, Peter Owen in the *Times Literary Supplement* read the book as a satire on "modern 'popular' religion" and found it to be "a superbly comic book written in a vibrant and jaunty colloquial American Negro prose that . . . dazzles and provokes laughter without a lapse."[28] And in an annual review of best books from the year, the Faulkner scholar Joseph Blotner called it "a remarkable *tour de force*: the first-person narrative of a colored woman in early middle age written by a white man from Texas."[29]

As Gibbons has perceptively noted, it is important to keep always in mind that "Goyen was in no way a realist, in either his aesthetic or the practical sense" (*HLC* 123), and the complications associated with the reception of *The Fair Sister* confirm this insight. From one perspective, the book's detractors have a point. Given the civil rights struggles of the 1950s and 1960s, an exaggerated comedy about black preachers, no matter how well executed, was likely to be considered by some as out of step, even reactionary. And for a white man to show so vividly the flaws and self-flattery in a poor black woman's character was a risk no socially conscious writer, no matter how well intentioned, would lightly take. Though the characters now seem relatively nuanced (particularly when compared to the broad comedy types of twenty-first-century African American comedy), it isn't surprising that in 1963 they reminded some readers more of the minstrel tradition than of contemporary reality. Yet it's also worth noting that the characters in *The Fair Sister* often seem remarkably similar—in voice, manner, and outsized or grotesque traits—to many of Goyen's typical, white Texans. The snake-handler in "Rhody's Path," for instance, could fit comfortably into Ruby Drew's world just as Goyen's later depiction of the evangelist Aimee Semple McPherson can be seen as a plausible extension of his idea of Savata. This near interchangeability across racial lines may also account for the success in the late 1960s of a biracial production of the play *House of Breath*, retitled as *House of Breath, Black/White*.

Goyen's lack of practical realism would also suggest that he simply failed to understand how his portrait of spiritually conflicted black characters would be received. He was shocked and dismayed to learn that Doubleday had reacted to the negative *Times* review by stopping the press run at 5,000, a decision that haunted him for years.[30] Whether his surprise indicated a degree of political naïveté is uncertain, but he clearly failed to anticipate a conflict with the era's developing racial consciousness. As a writer, he could be remarkably attuned to racial violence and injustice as it related to his East Texas boyhood. *The House of Breath* and several short stories are laced with surrealistic imagery of Ku Klux Klan atrocities as seen through the eyes of a horrified and sensitive boy. But even so, African Americans in his early fiction generally recede into the background, and their presence is either distanced or sentimentalized through that same boy's vision (the town tour in *The House of Breath* includes "the little Negro shacks" with "some good old Negro sitting on his front gallery or calling to little Negro children playing in the mudpuddles" [*HOB* 12]). Goyen and Berns's unpublished war novel *Section Two* did mount a significant challenge to Navy segregation, as in this apostrophe to a messmate named Artis: "No, Artis, you are beaten, you will never be able to raise your eyes and answer them defiantly, never protest yourself from their wrath, they have taken from you everything but the Blues, the one true inviolable Blues! But Artis boy, kind gentle fearful bewildered mess-attendant from the dry whiteness of the southern fields, the Blues *are*; and you *are*; and they will never understand you" (HRC 25.9, original emphasis). Or in this contrast between the life among the "servants" and the sterility of the officer corps:

> They can house you in slums, let you whisk the dust from their clothes in the antiseptic rest rooms, hire you for all the dirty jobs in the foundries, factories, laundries, make you change their linen, wash their dishes, shine their shoes, and confine you aft with the throb, throb, throb of the screw (and all this is why *they* must have you), but we still see the pulsating life in you, the great boundless physical aliveness about you, though we search all a war, we could not find in the Wardroom among the Idiot Men or in their Merry Idiot Wives. (HRC 25.9, original emphasis)

But this kind of direct perception of a social condition is rare in Goyen's larger fictional output. If nothing else, his unwary entrance into racial politics with *The Fair Sister* serves to remind us just how *interior* his fictional worlds really are, no matter what their subject matter. Despite the detailed attention to place and the stranger-as-listener, there is very little larger outsideness to Goyen's imagination. His fiction obsessively maps, as he himself candidly claimed, "the world inside one person's head" (*CS* x), and its failure to take notice of social or political realities is both its peculiar strength and an accepted weakness: "I have never identified my work with any cause, nor sought causes, political or social, as sources, stimuli, material for my work," he once declared. "And, thankfully, have no aims or needs to instruct or change ways of political or social action in order to identify, justify, or liberate myself" (quoted in *SL* xiv).

Though it fits convincingly into Goyen's major interests, *The Fair Sister* is in many respects the least distinctive novel in his oeuvre. For a writer who had essentially told this kind of story since the beginning of his career, there is a sense that his material had ceased to develop, that he was approaching the end of a deep vein of resentment and hurt. "I believe *The Fair Sister* has freed me, at long last, of my old web," he wrote to his old friend Bill Hart.[31] Though almost fifty, Goyen had been writing since his teens out of an essentially adolescent wound, and after four novels and two collections of stories, his energies had diminished, along with his patience with the hand-to-mouth life of the artist. The awkward reception of *The Fair Sister* forced a difficult recognition that meaningful financial rewards would continue to elude him. And though he would continue to work on *Another Man's Son* and take on projects for the theater, for the next several years Goyen devoted himself—sometimes happily, sometimes despairingly—to his new life as a husband, stepfather, and editor. The "hard, suffering reality" that he foresaw for himself at the height of his success from *The House of Breath* was close at hand.

CHAPTER TWELVE

A Living Jesus
1966–1973

*"He's not even your family," somebody said to him. "He's adopted.
Another man's son." "Who knows what a family is? We're all
adopted," is what Wylie Prescott said in his peculiar last years—
a philosophy which no one truly understood. "All sons of another
man," he mystically announced.*

COME, THE RESTORER (1974)

McGraw-Hill publishers was founded in 1909 when James H. McGraw and John A. Hill merged the technical book departments of their small, rival companies. By 1966, when Goyen was hired, it had grown into a multinational media corporation known primarily for publishing textbooks and informational nonfiction. Though the company had at times taken on what might be described as scholarly ventures (paying $100,000 for the rights to the Boswell Papers, for instance, in 1949), literary fiction was by no means its specialty or primary interest. In many respects, the publisher's Adult Trade Division was a peculiar place for a writer like Goyen to find his first real office job, not the least because of his own dramatic and passionate battles with publishers since the beginning of his career. Financial pressures and family responsibilities clearly pushed him toward the position, but this revolution in his life may also have been a way to turn old disappointments toward more positive ends. The failure of *The Fair Sister*—and more particularly, his publisher's lack of courage and loyalty—had deepened the open wound of resentment and disappointment at the setbacks to his career. Nevertheless, he felt he could be of use to other writers who might be facing similar editorial antagonisms. The nurse or caretaker in Goyen always remained close at hand, and it was no overestimation of his talents to realize that mentoring and promoting the interests of others were among his personal strengths. Though he had his rivalries, he could be a remarkably charming and deeply caring friend and ally to writers young and established. From this point on in his life, he gradually amassed a very large contingent of fellow artists who felt indebted to his attention and generosity.

Despite sometimes unrealistic expectations for his own work, Goyen was careful, savvy, and professional in his work as an editor. With typical intensity, he set about contacting agents and writers and began to work closely with both new and familiar faces on manuscripts in development. One of the primary tasks in his first year was to launch McGraw-Hill's First Novel Program, a significant effort, particularly by a publisher devoted to textbooks, to bring new writing and new authors to the market. As Granville Hicks noted in his regular column in *Saturday Review*, what was unusual about the program was the publisher's willingness to spend money on publicity: "Very often first novels are published in what can only be called a clandestine manner. It was therefore a matter of importance that this spring McGraw-Hill not only brought out seven first novels . . . but actually advertised them."[1] Among the initial group of chosen texts were Chester Aaron's *About Us*; *Digging Out*, by Anne Richardson (Roiphe); and William Herrick's *The Itinerant*. Goyen appeared in publicity photos with the three younger writers and peppered reviewers and the press with announcements and thank-you notes for positive notices.

As an editor, Goyen proved that he had an eye for conventional storytelling and character development. He was by no means an experimentalist when it came to offering technical advice, and perhaps because of his own struggles with sales, he could be as sensitive to marketing as anyone. The fiction writer Elizabeth Spencer worked with him on her novel *No Place for an Angel* and remembers him being "avidly interested in good fiction" and "helpful in working on many elements of the plot and characters."[2] In his statement of job goals for 1968, prepared for what appears to be a salary review, he wrote that his primary concern was "the author-editor relationship," which he called "the life and strength of a publishing house." As far as sales were concerned, McGraw-Hill needed a "realistic, intelligent, and sensible" philosophy that above all showed loyalty to its authors: "There is a tendency to kill living—i.e., selling and saleable—books, a tendency to step on anything alive and crawling. . . . Why this withdrawal?" (HRC 37.1). His concern for slower-selling books no doubt reflected his experience with *The Fair Sister*, but it also indicated a desire to blend, as far as possible, the needs of the author with the economic requirements of the company.

This essential adaptability may have led to his assignment to Catherine Marshall, the well-known inspirational author of *A Man Called Peter*. Marshall was the widow of the former minister and chaplain to the United States Senate, Peter Marshall, who died of a heart attack in 1949. After publishing a successful biography of her husband (made into a popular film in 1955), she began a thinly disguised account of her mother's early life working as a teacher in the mountains of East Tennessee. Shortly before Goyen joined McGraw-Hill, Marshall's editor Edward Kuhn left the firm, and Frank Taylor, Goyen's boss, needed someone sensitive to religious feeling (preferably a southerner) to help Marshall develop her novel. The eventual result, oddly but coincidentally titled *Christy*, was an immediate and long-term bestseller, with more than three million copies sold by 1975.

The kind of slow, patient editorial work that Marshall required was the type of interaction Goyen valued most, but energy spent helping others inevitably slowed and disrupted his own writing. In part, his diminished productivity can be attributed to the daily demands of an office job, but what he defensively called a "change in *metabolism* in the body of [his] work" masked both diminished energies and rankling disappointments.[3] A few small, nonfiction projects occupied his attention from time to time. Two study guides he wrote for the American R.D.M. Corporation in 1966, one on Willa Cather's *My Ántonia* and the other on Ralph Ellison's *Invisible Man*, may have addressed an immediate need for money in the months before joining McGraw-Hill. Contracts show that he was advanced $400 for each, and though he likely enjoyed the respite from fiction that such tasks afforded, this low-level work-for-hire must have been mildly dispiriting. Even so, his prose is professional and his comments and summaries reveal notable affinities to these two important but very different exemplars. Cather, whose investment in environment Goyen clearly shared, emerges as an alternative to midcentury urban irony: "The old sentiments, the old virtues, the dear affections of the human being—which our contemporary literature has come to debauch, mock and witticize, neuroticize, burlesque, and travesty—pulsate through this novel like the mystic seasonal forces of springtime." And just as her gentle mythopoetics reasserts her characters' connection to the land, so do many of her characters suffer from Goyen's own maladies, especially exile and homesickness: "The grave of Mr. Shimerda, dug in the earth (i.e. nature) and protected by it, becomes a natural monument to the man who unwillingly emigrated from his home country and who died of homesickness after struggling to combat a world he was incapable of matching."[4] In a similar channeling of personal interests, the study of *Invisible Man* casts Ellison as a "romancer" who creates not a protest novel but a romantic configuration of "ritual, myth, and fantasy." In a passage that sounds very much like self-description, Goyen describes the "hero" of this type of "romance-novel" as a "lonely protagonist, smitten with a past, family or racial or social, rising out of an intolerable darkness of family or race or society, exiling himself, willfully taking the road, or forcefully turned out to make his fortune—at any rate or whatever the circumstances, *alienated*—and, struggling against a society that raises barriers against his progress, kindles through cold and lightlessness his own enlightenment and makes his own salvation."[5]

Criticism may have worked like translation for Goyen when it came to finding alternative means of recuperating his creative energies. Since 1947, when James Laughlin commissioned him to render Albert Cossery's *Maison de la mort certaine* into English, Goyen had occasionally used translation as a freshening change from the cloudier demands of storytelling.[6] Reporting to Laughlin on his progress with the project, he relished the restorative honing of the work: "It was often like doing mathematics: a clearheaded, concrete piece of work to be done. Then it sent me back to my own work with sharper claws."[7] Though he had done nothing of the same length since, memories like this may have reminded him of a way to preserve his verbal vitality. During the same year he was at work on the study guides, he translated some or all of Rousseau's *Reveries of a Solitary Walker* for the National Translation Center in Austin. Roger Shattuck, who had published a highly sympathetic review of *The House of Breath*, may have solicited Goyen for the project, but Shattuck was also sharply critical of the result, questioning its accuracy and stylistic choices. It isn't clear how Goyen reacted to this aggressive but precise critique, but the project apparently fell through soon after. Though Shattuck had offered his help in correcting the shortcomings of the translation, Goyen appears to have pulled away from the work, which was never published.[8]

Besides the slowly developing *Another Man's Son*, an additional preoccupation during the mid- to late 1960s was the autobiographical text originally titled *Six Women*. Often described as Goyen's "memoirs," this never-completed project was conceived as a series of epistolary addresses to and about important women in his life. Though the lineup varied over the years, the "six" included Frieda Lawrence, Margo Jones, Katherine Anne Porter, Dorothy Brett, the Taos heiress Millicent Rogers, and Mabel Dodge Luhan. In a prospectus for a later version of the text, Goyen suggested that these women were role models of a sort, "out of the mainstream," and provided counterexamples to "the conventional" image "of woman as Serving Wife, Listener Only, Mother" (*GAE* 8–9). In many respects it isn't surprising that he would turn to memoir at this point in his career, particularly given the apparent conclusion to his early work that *The Fair Sister* seemed to mark. However, it is puzzling why these portraits of strong, usually older women were his preferred vehicle for relating the noteworthy events of his life. His description of the "conventional woman" may offer a partial explanation, particularly the phrase "Serving Wife, Listener Only, Mother." If there is a role to which Emma Goyen could be ascribed, this is it; she was not, whatever desires or complaints she may have had, a rebellious or independent woman. And if, as seems probable, Goyen found in Frieda Lawrence a kind of maternal substitute, someone he could talk to candidly and without fear of judgment, then the other women on the list may have filled similar roles—as counterweights, in other words, to Emma's disapproval. Only a few years before, he had created in *Christy* an entire play designed to answer—and revenge—his mother's infamous letter denouncing the "Four Portraits." It would be consistent, at the very least, if he decided to tell his own life by emphasizing those "other" women who had encouraged his work rather than attack it.

Structurally, *Six Women* was based not only on the principle of telling but on the extended idea of confession, revelation, and the sharing of experiences across time:

I am the teller of the story. Sometimes the story is told to the reader forthright, sometimes the story of one of the characters is told to another character in the form of a letter: the letters are not always written to the addressee herself but to another about her; e.g., I tell Frieda (deceased) about Brett's old age and death. Sometimes where the characters had known each other and I (obviously) both, news of one is told to the other in sections addressed to that listener. . . . The letters also tell these women (and men, where they come up in the story) things never told when they were alive: "I did not tell you then, or could not. Neither was it the time nor did I have the words for it; or I just forgot or was afraid to—or I guess I figured that there would always be enough time. 'Later,' I thought." Speech found *now* (so much later) for what was not (or could not be) spoken *then*. (*GAE* 9)

It isn't surprising that a writer devoted to the "teller-listener situation" would prefer structuring his memoirs this way, but it is significant that Goyen hoped to reproduce the kind of conversation that comes after a long absence. The form suggests that what he most wanted was a sympathetic listener modeled on the receptive mother who welcomes home a wayward son. And yet the plan for *Six Women* reaches even further than that: to say the unsaid, speak what cannot be spoken, beyond the barriers of time, place, and personality. He may not have been able to talk candidly to his mother, in other words, but he could share secrets with the motherly dead.

Still, there is no candor in Goyen's work that is not built upon repression. For if *Six Women* proposes a structuring role for older women in his life, it thereby avoids a direct discussion of his ties to men. In some cases this avoidance meant simply eliding certain presences, particularly those of Walter Berns and Joe Glasco. In his autobiographical writing, Goyen usually appears alone, a strangely unaccompanied and somewhat fragile "I," all the more fictive when we consider his intense need for companionship. The heightened presence of older women and the erasure of men suggests that his fear of exposure led him to choose "safe" memories over passionate encounters. Maternal women could be subjects of memory; men were objects of desire. Women brought out speech, narrative; men evoked silence, eros. *Six Women* gave Goyen the chance to clarify and segregate specific episodes in his life even as it allowed him to reconfigure, on a public level, his own personal history. And though he never completed the fully imagined book, the short pieces he published toward the end of his career, particularly "Margo," suggest a dazzling release of volatile material within and through the continued retention of secrets.

Overall, the McGraw-Hill years produced far more plans than completed projects. The daily discipline that had pushed Goyen forward during his early career necessarily slackened, and personal challenges, including an increasing dependence on alcohol, began to cripple his creative energies. His writing habits had been fixed at least since his early days in Taos. Up at 4:00 or 4:30 each morning, he sat quietly at his desk, often waiting for the voices of his past to gather and speak to him. He scrawled first drafts on small squares of paper, their margins often burnished with anxious, grooved doodles. The manuscript pages that survive suggest intense concentration of both source and material, and as his mornings began to fill with phone calls instead of writing, his productivity clearly suffered. Initially, the new work routine came as a relief. As he later told Robert Phillips: "[I was] so concerned with the writing of my own authors that I considered their books my own and I treated them as such. I entered into their creative process. Nevertheless, I was caught in the competitive crush and thrust of commercial publishing. There was no question of my own writing. I was relieved not to have to worry about my own writing. I scarcely grieved it or mourned it" (*GAE* 90–91). After a few years, however, his sense that he had come to McGraw-Hill with a special warrant to publish "quality writing" diminished, and the old bitterness returned: "I had my way for a while but then pretty soon night must fall and I was back with the old budgets and best-selling books and a lot of crap" (*GAE* 91). The hunger for his own work came back slowly, but the ability to summon those early morning voices, at least initially, did not.

Though as much symptom as cause, increased drinking is the most prominent of the internal factors that disabled Goyen's writing in the 1960s, even after he began to move away from publishing. Looking back years later, he believed that his addiction had surfaced around 1960, presumably during the long breakup with Glasco. His later, AA-inspired self-analysis indicates that he identified his "alcoholic being" with his penchant for secrecy, a trait born in turn from isolation and exile: "living with a quality of madness; feeling doomed; a feeling of wildness, of lostness, of sadness; that yearning; that feeling blue; that hunger for oblivion; that unnameable hunger; need for 'magic,' for other-worldness, for complete abandon; bitterness, of illusion; of hiding; of deep secrecy;

need for transformation; for transcendence; *for transfiguration*. Hiding. Secrets" (HRC 29.6, original emphases). But he also recognized that these feelings were related to the source of his creativity and that his need to serve others, to act as "nurse, saint & savior," created an inescapable and destructive cycle. (HRC 29.6) Isolation and secrecy fed his desire for others (or, more properly, for the one who could share his vision and inspire devotion), and yet the need to serve bred resentment and fear that the hidden self—the boy under the blanket with the cardboard piano—would be lost, sacrificed.

Both marriage and his work for other authors seemed to activate these contradictory desires. The diminished success of his own writing, particularly following the failure of *The Fair Sister*, thus became more than a matter of career frustration. To be reminded of its weakening reception was to be alarmed yet again at the fading of identity, and his reaction, fueled by drink, could at times be cruel and violent.[9] In her memoir, Roberts describes their turbulent marriage with an air of humor and forgiveness, but it seems likely that the fights she recounts were more than merely theatrical. Others report a nasty side of Goyen that could lash out unexpectedly, particularly to those many friends who found him charming, funny, and warm. Roberts came slowly to the realization that depression was feeding his need to drink: "Our relationship began in a bar and grew during hours spent in fascinating conversation over cocktails, so it was hard for me to know when drinking moved from the way we amused ourselves to the solitary way Bill dealt with his pain."[10] Though functional during the day, Goyen began to get drunk by himself at night, and advice from a psychiatrist to continue drinking (while he worked on the sources of his depression) didn't help. The problem would only increase through the mid-1970s, reaching its most acute phase after his move to Los Angeles to join Roberts there in 1975.

What effect Goyen's mood and nightly search for oblivion may have had on his daily work at McGraw-Hill is difficult to gauge. His relationship with his employer did slowly deteriorate, in part for typical reasons like discontent with salary and hours. He had begun petitioning for a raise as early as 1967 and wasn't shy about drafting long memos of complaint when he was turned down. That year his salary was $19,000, and he was asking for $20,000. The extra money must have come through at some point, however, because by 1970 he was hoping to work out an agreement to reduce his hours, work three days a week, still retain his senior editor title, and be paid $22,500. His more frequent absences from the office were an indication that his own writing was starting to fill his time, but they also suggest a growing disenchantment with everything at McGraw-Hill—and very likely the publisher's loss of patience with him.

The strain became particularly evident in an incident that angered Goyen for years. One of the highlights of his editorial work had been his prescient championing of the German writer Heinrich Böll. The future Nobel Prize winner had been unable to secure a U.S. publisher since the early 1950s, but according to the literary historian Mark Rectanus, Goyen eventually agreed to take Böll on as a McGraw-Hill author: "And from that time on Goyen was extremely supportive, even though Böll's works were not, at least initially, financially successful. Because Goyen believed in Böll as an author he did not make the acceptance of a new work contingent on the financial success of previous works, and by doing so established a strong basis and a degree of continuity for Böll's works in the United States."[11] Having essentially discovered and cultivated the increasingly prestigious author for McGraw-Hill, Goyen was therefore shocked to realize that he had been excluded from a lunch in Böll's honor when the author visited New York in 1971. For reasons that remain unclear, Goyen's superiors apparently told the assembled guests that he was out of town. "I never saw Mr. Böll while he was in N.Y.," Goyen later recorded with particular bitterness in his notebook. "Yet I had fought single-handedly to get him published, keep his books in print and keep him at McGraw-Hill. I had struggled with the Salesmen to get them to see his work, had struggled with my boss ('See if you can't get him to write like Günter Grass. He sells.') I had helped them pronounce his name—'like Burl in Burl Ives.' I had finally coerced them to buy the last novel, saying that I felt that he would one day win the Nobel Prize" (HRC 20.7).

The full context of the slight remains murky, but in Goyen's mind it represented yet another humiliation at the hands of publishers too concerned about money to recognize his contributions. Perhaps the McGraw-Hill management had decided he was too unreliable or simply too absent to be included in an important press event. Before being fired in October of that same year, Goyen had spent increasing amounts of time away from the office as his own writing began to heat up. Important, ground-shifting personal experiences had rekindled his energies, and he had clearly begun to lose touch with his daily responsibilities. At the same time, his increased dependency on alcohol—and what Roberts describes as a tendency to lash out at enemies during social occasions—may have created the impression that he was too unpredictable to invite to such a gathering. Whatever the case, this painful insult marked the end of his years as an editor. Though mildly embarrassing, being fired at last came as a relief and liberation. The urge— indeed, the compulsion—to write had indeed returned, and this new intensity was all that mattered. "Can you believe that I have *written*?" Goyen wrote to Robert Phillips in December. "That I sat down every day and worked at writing some days for 12 to 14 hours, as in the old days? A miracle."[12]

The Belleek Swan

In July of 1968, Charlie Goyen died of heart complications. Goyen wrote to Dorothy Brett soon after, describing his father's last days:

> Sad news—my father died on July 1 and we buried him in Houston on July 2. He lies under a big live-oak tree in a beautiful garden-like place. He had been ill for some months with a bad heart. I spent two weeks with him and had a wonderful, sweet visit with him before he went on. All his children, grandchildren, nephews and nieces came to sit with him and he settled his accounts and made his peace with all of them. I loved my father, as you know, and his death was harder for me than I had ever thought it would be.[13]

The power of his grief may have been a surprise because Goyen had been meditating for some time on the decline of his father and the fundamental nature of father-son relationships. In part this line of thought was a natural development of earlier attempts to understand his own sense of orphanage and exile. But his interactions with Roberts's son, Michael—and his strong desire for a child of his own—added a new layer to his thinking about what it meant, beyond the ties of kinship, to "father" another human being. His play *Christy* had provided some space for these considerations, but much of his newer thinking was being developed in the pieces of *Another Man's Son* that he was slowly assembling during his years as an editor. An early outline of the project describes it as being written in the form of letters from the stepfather (Goyen) to his own father (Charlie) "so that two fathers and two sons are involved."[14]

One probable piece of this manuscript survives as the short prose meditation "The Beleek Swan." This brief, elegiac description of the "precious little swan made of painted china" (*GAE* 4) that Goyen took from his father's belongings traces a process of mourning, of passing from flesh to spirit. The speaker holds the swan in his hand and tries to understand how so delicate an object could have been associated with "a man of simple realities . . . a man of woods and earth." He doesn't really understand why he chose this one, fragile emblem "and nothing more" or how it came into his father's possession in the first place. He does remember it from his childhood, an attraction that was also very clearly a prohibition: "I remember her from my earliest days in that house, I played around her and gazed at her, but never touched her. She sat in a frozen gliding, tiny and precious in shining colors of pure white and burnt gold, breakable, but miraculously preserved through all the years of the boisterous life of children" (*GAE* 5). So untouchable and vulnerable an object comes to stand for the father against whom Goyen so clearly rebelled and by whom he felt misunderstood and constrained. "The Beleek Swan" thus suggests a continued attempt to get closer to a Charlie Goyen who seems always out of reach. The feminine swan marks a determined choice by the son to take away with him the one symbol of sensitivity associated with a man of hard work and blunted feelings: "In my memory of my father the swan glides before me as though it were conveying my true Father back to me—the winged ferry from the far side where I am now struggling to regain this man since his life on earth is finished . . ." (*GAE* 5).[15]

That the speaker of the "Beleek Swan" "never touched" this proscribed object when it belonged to his father is both sorrowful and suggestive. The lack of access (an inability to reach Charlie Goyen's self or soul?) converts the swan into "the winged ferry" for an intimacy possible only now, symbolically, through relinquishment of his father's body. Thus the latter half of the piece registers the disturbance created by the thought that his father's face is still intact beneath "the slope of grass-fleeced ground" (*GAE* 5). The speaker issues a sort of envoi made from his mother's words ("Go on now—you go on!") spoken over the casket and repeated as though to push the body away so that a spiritual recovery can occur: "And now I see that I am seeking to make of you pure spirit and I cannot, in my travail, make pure spirit of you with your body lying whole in the ground" (*GAE* 6). The transformation of matter into thought becomes the basis for lifting the burden of mourning and, remarkably, transferring the status of "father" from Charlie Goyen to God: "Now I free myself of you and return to my only Father. Your seed made my body, but He created my soul. Now I stand face to face with Him. I am another man's son!"

This idea—that we are all sons of another man, all orphans yet all children of God—underpinned much of what Goyen hoped to accomplish in the work that led eventually to *Come, the Restorer*. But as positive as it may seem, such a claim could only arise through a confrontation of the still powerful estrangements of his early life. "The Belleek Swan" reveals just how difficult it had always been—and still was—to find common ground with his earthly father.

The Seizing

In the spring of 1971, several months before his dismissal from McGraw-Hill, Goyen spent a week as the guest of Alice De Lamar at her artist colony in Weston, Connecticut. What occurred there, and in the days shortly after in the West End Avenue apartment where he and Roberts lived, would have a profound effect on the rest of his life. As he described it a year or so later, the experience was "quite directly, a violent 'conversion'—or, better, (since I have always been what-you-call a Christian and man of faith) it was a dramatic and wild re-discovery of Jesus Christ which swept me out of the blue (and I mean blues, emptiness, meaninglessness)."[16] The sequence of largely internal events is difficult to reconstruct, but it does seem clear that Goyen had gone to Weston to work on his novel but ran into difficulties with the writing. Though his increasing detachment from McGraw-Hill had allowed him the occasional burst of creative energy, he still suffered from crippling phases of writer's block that evoked his most destructive and desperate feelings. As he had before—during the writing of *Ghost and Flesh* and his time in Germany—he came apart emotionally. He was tormented by the moths that fluttered around his work space in Weston, and there were ravens outside that tapped ominously on his window.

The dark, unsettling, and desperate mood came with him back to New York, where on the night of April 17 it forced a reckoning. His sense of persecution and loss fixated on a line from Genesis. Noah is testing to see whether the waters have receded, and he sends out a raven that flies back and forth until it eventually finds land. In Goyen's recollection, the sense is slightly altered: "Genesis 8, verse 7 I found on that terrible on that extraordinary night of Ap. 17 here on West End Ave. 'A raven goes forth to and fro and can find nothing to feed on'" (HRC 10.3). The ravens from Weston seemed to be haunting him with his own hunger and emptiness, and now, only a few days after Easter (and a few days before his fifty-sixth birthday), this despair gave way to a violent confrontation with a newly conceived Jesus: "a week after his crucifixion, he moved in on me and locked me down. It was a fierce onrushing. There was no way out, no other way but to him. He literally had me cornered; he pinned me down. He took me" (HRC 10.3).

The pressure had been building toward this moment at least since early March, though there is a hint in his notes that it was writing "The Beleek Swan" that had lit the fire months before. It may be too facile to see a simple correlation between the death of Charlie Goyen and his son's intense embrace of that "other father" as a spiritual substitute, but it is plausible that this newly felt absence—of the one person whose disapproval dominated his childhood—would allow Goyen to reclaim, in his own way, the spiritual tradition in which he was raised. This, too, as he understood, was a way of going home, returning or reconciling, of healing the exile's wound. As he wrote in a manuscript fragment entitled "My Discovery" with the subtitle "The Homesickness,"

> My search always came to me as "homesickness"—what I most deeply felt above every other feeling was this of homesickness, of having nowhere to go; lost, alienated, unbelonging. I was claimed, even then, was always claimed. From my first memories as a little child, sitting alone, child of grief trying to be glad.
>
> That just plain lonesomeness was for Him! (You!) (HRC 10.3)

And yet the ability to return—no matter how symbolic—was not the primary source of his intense excitement in that spring of 1971; the division from home and family had produced—and was the product of—a deeper self-division. What his particular idea of Jesus gave him at this moment of personal crisis was the ability to unify himself through acceptance of his own unruly sexuality: "You! You made me (showed me how to) love my humanity, my mentality in my natural (appetites and) hungers. In my flesh you were there, you touched my flesh in my (sexual) heats [written above: "bestial convulsion"] and my cruel lusts. You were there—in my sensual wildness, in the sting of my sex, you were there!" (HRC 10.3). In other words, Jesus "was there" because he was human, physical, sexual. Unlike what Goyen called the "Old family-ragdoll Jesus" who never "itched and scratched," the figure who seized him was "a man that touched and poked, patted and held and embraced," a "very touchable person" (HRC 10.3). Jesus was present in past sexual encounters that were indications of lust, uncontrollable desires now taken in, forgiven, understood by a savior who had himself experienced such "sensual wildness." And finally, in a remarkable if extreme moment in his notes, Goyen takes this idea of presence to its logical conclusion, imagining Jesus as a lover:

> You were there because you are a part of my body, of my nature, my flesh; but also because I called to you, cried out to you (and didn't even know it, often) in my flesh torment, in my bitter ecstasy, my cruel joy.
> By the gamey Gulf, trashy and rutty and hot, something of brine and shrimp [inserted: "erotic and lewd"], we fucked.
> You hunched with me, O Lord, you came with me. You knew me utterly in my near-madness of desire. (HRC 10.3)

If Jesus could understand his sexuality, even share it, then Goyen could be accepted, embraced by a more encompassing forgiveness. At the same time, his own contentious and conflicted sexual identity could be validated, his humanity, even normality, made certain by its incarnation in this sexually charged Son of God.

Two Books of Jesus

What Goyen called the "seizing" of April 17, 22, and 23, 1971, generated a wild and intense energy in his creative life that pulled him further away from his office at McGraw-Hill and ultimately caused him to be fired. Nothing, not even money concerns, could distract him from the immediate need to write about what had happened to him in that post-Easter week. His literary response took two forms: a projected re-telling of the gospels for a general audience and a shorter pamphlet that revealed, in a very personal way, his understanding of Jesus's humanity. Whether the pamphlet preceded the book or, perhaps more likely, they were written at the same time, the shorter work, a sometimes explicit depiction of people troubled by lust, seems a primary attempt to account for the rush of new ideas and feelings. "Jesus in My Body, Jesus in My Flesh" presents a surprising and intense series of scenes narrated by those ashamed of their participation in different types of sexual activity. The voices are tormented by their desires, often unable to resist temptation. They speak directly to Jesus as an intimate who understands and sometimes inhabits their unruly flesh: "Jesus in my body, you've kept me awake all night long. I've lain on the hardness on my body, up against my stomach just about the whole night, it seems. . . . My body moves against that hardness, presses and thrusts and turns and the fact that it all feels good makes me want to keep going on. But you, in my body, beautiful Jesus hard on my body, seem to be telling me to stop moving, to lie still, to wait" (HRC 10.3).

No doubt one of the most unusual—and perhaps most personal—of Goyen's unpublished manuscripts, "Jesus in My Body" does give us a clearer sense of just what he meant when he spoke, as he did more frequently in his later years, of the problem of lust. To Reginald Gibbons, in one of his last interviews, he was direct: "I see lust as demonic. I have never known it to be anything else! Have you? Good Lord! The lust is the very devil working, a demon in me—*my* lust. I don't know about anybody else's. I've had a demon in me" (*GAE* 126). To ascribe this devil-ish energy to Jesus himself was to suggest that even the worst sexual transgression was not beyond salvation, and it was this realization that now drove Goyen's hopeful frenzy. Months later, working at a friend's cabin in stormy New Paltz, New York, he drank heavily for three days, disturbed by the wind and rain and a strange emergence of noisy frogs:

When I was writing about You—you made me suffer, pay a price—to show me (let me know) that I had to suffer to enter you, your life, your force, your reality. You were hard on me then, Sir. You let me go almost mad, there in the far away house, alone. Your storm lasted a day and a night. Your lightning drove against my eyes like spears. I was sick. Paul

was blind for 3 days after You. Struck him to the dust with your light.
So this lightning!

But I called help!

In the flashes I saw at midnight the black bullfrogs sitting in a
huddle on the grass, under my window, driven out of the water. They
were like demons. . . .

And in the hot depths of flesh and the madness of gin drunkenness.
You! (HRC 10.3)

It's tempting to ascribe this despair simply to alcoholism, but the gin
seems to have been at least as much catalyst as cause. The years of difficulty with his writing, the challenges of marriage, of conventional life
and stepfatherhood, the channeling and suppression of his sexuality
(particularly his desire for men), intensified by the grief over the loss
of his father and the fading of his early life—all these elements had co-
alesced into a crisis beyond containment. Saving his identity meant
finding a way to give it value again, and the idea of Jesus as a man *essentially like himself* allowed him, for the time being, to survive.

The level of sheer desperation, however, may have limited Goyen's
critical sense, particularly his ability to judge how others would see the
work he was producing. As it had sometimes in the past, the intensity
of his vision overrode—or more accurately, skewed—his sense of audience. So elated at his rebirth and so certain that the world would bene-
fit from his epiphany, he sent the manuscript of "Jesus in My Body" to a
prominent publisher of religious books—a puzzlingly myopic, though
perhaps defiant, decision for someone who had spent the last six years
working for a major publishing house. Perhaps it was a small declaration of independence and he never imagined the company accepting it.
Perhaps he believed so fervently in the material that he thought it irresistible. Whatever the case, it was soon clear that his approach would
have to be refined. The shocked editors not only rejected the manuscript but sent a long letter expressing their astonishment that anyone
would send them material they considered pornographic.

Goyen's more mainstream response to his conversion experience
started in July 1971 with a visit to Sam Vaughan at Doubleday. Vaughan
remembers him coming into the office, "literally quivering with passion," explaining that he had a unique vision for a project now called

A Book of Jesus: "And Bill stood there, talking, excited, until he was preaching at us, looking slightly deranged, but convinced he knew The Man and he could tell the young who the Christ really was and what He was like."[17] The book he now envisioned would be brief, pocket-sized, a portable guide marketed to youth in the grips of the Jesus movement. It would retell the life of Jesus from the Gospels but in a thoroughly modern voice, clear and simple, emphasizing Christ's reality and political power, and, above all, his physicality. "It's a swift, striking (as in a blow), physical little thing," Goyen wrote to Phillips, "quite gracefully rude, like some farm instrument to be used by hand, a sickle or a hoe; and my Jesus snorts and sighs and groans, curses, spits, sticks his fingers in the ears of deaf people; and he *handles* mortality, touches the flesh of hundreds, heals that way."[18] It was a message that young people needed, and—at last his marketing experience kicked in—it would sell: in churches, to youth organizations, colleges.

Published officially on Good Friday 1973, *A Book of Jesus* stays close to Goyen's intention, relating the events of the Passion in a deliberately contemporary idiom, while quietly highlighting those aspects of Jesus's life that spoke directly to his recent discoveries. The short book is divided into three sections: "A Brief Life of Jesus," "Other Thirsts, Other Hungers: Some People in Jesus' Life," and "Words of Jesus." As he indicates in his author's note, the narrative is based primarily on the Gospel of Mark, though specific information and incidents are drawn from all four Gospels. The incidents are familiar, but his interpretive preferences are not difficult to spot. After a brief description of Jesus's baptism by John and the subsequent temptation in the desert, we are given both a naturalistic and a Goyenesque reading of Christ's desires: "Could he do it? Self-doubt, sometimes called Satan, took hold of him in the wilderness. After all, he did have a body; he was a man; he did have desires, needs, hungers, vulnerabilities. He could groan and sigh and weep and anger and hurt" (*BOJ* 7). This tendency to read supernatural events psychologically—or to give plausible naturalistic accounts of miracles—is not consistent throughout the text, but it does point toward a general desire to make Jesus and his actions fit into a twentieth-century conception of reality. The emphasis on Christ's humanity, particularly the demands of the body, is of course Goyen's central interest: to argue that salvation and healing can come from the flesh as much as the spirit. As he explains more directly in the book's second section,

This man Jesus was a man on earth, a man of flesh as well as of spirit. He knew how flesh hurts. He touched, with his hands, *physical* humanity; he handled the flawed bodies of thousands. Jesus loved the physical world and the suffering creature in man. . . . The man of spirit honored the flesh which, though it die, must be straightened if it is bowed over, made sound if it is unsound, made clean if it is fouled with disease, by restoring and mending. He did it with his own hands and often with his own spittle. He loved the humanity of flesh that he touched, embraced, handled. He was a great gentle Nurse, soother of flesh as well as comforter of spirit. (*BOJ* 89–90)

That Christ is imagined as a nurse should not be a surprise coming from the creator of Curran, the healer and weaver. There is a sense in which this version of Jesus is the culmination of Goyen's thinking about himself over the last thirty years. He had begun by feeling sacrificed to the needs of others (family, lovers) and worked to transform himself into a distanced servant, the mender of others' wounds. Now he had located an idea of Jesus that could mend his own deeper rift between flesh and spirit. As the healer of others' bodies, this Jesus becomes the ideal of self-repair. The salvation he offers is less about His assumption of humanity's sins than a way to understand and accept the self's own divisions. Physical healing, in others words, *is* spiritual healing, and Christ's most important, most meaningful act was his embodiment as flesh.

This idea of repair readily evokes Goyen's long-standing desire to "save" his family through acts of memory but to do so within a fragmented modernist aesthetic. Goyen's Jesus emerges similarly as a kind of modern prophet of the body: "He wanted a unity of physical being as well as of the spiritual being, and he set great stock in mending fragments, putting together what was broken, and so bringing back physical dignity and fullness to the individual" (*BOJ* 15). The echo of Goyen's fictional method—the stitching together of quilt squares—is unambiguous. To meditate on the life of Jesus was thus to reconsider, and perhaps strengthen, his own autobiographical myth-making, a strategy that included highlighting Jesus's role as misunderstood son:

We are told that his brothers and sisters and their mother, Mary, believed that he was out of his mind and should be brought home or given help. But what Jesus was feeling was quite the normal reaction of a young person functioning at his best. To be reminded of family affiliations at such a time is to be restricted, is to be made self-conscious. Such a son is doing a larger thing, a grander thing that surpasses all "relations" and has to do with only one relationship—a kind of divine connection between him and the thing he is afire with. (*BOJ* 27–28)

Jesus echoes the artist's dilemma of "The Crimes of Mirensky." Ridiculed in his home town (*BOJ* 37), he becomes the exile or spiritual orphan that Goyen had been meditating over for most of his career—a savior and the "Son of God," or in other words, "a servant to every man, . . . every man's Son" (*BOJ* 54). Accepting this role is not easy, however, and Goyen's Jesus reflects a struggle to come to terms with the mark of exile, his prophetic identity. His entrance into Jerusalem was "cleverly dramatized" in order to announce "his identity" (*BOJ* 52). It was the result of a difficult process of understanding who he was: "He had confronted his true identity in the world, he had accepted the demands of his destiny beyond the world, although it had been bitter to accept the cup" (*BOJ* 55).

Despite its apparently simple aims, in other words, *A Book of Jesus* is much more than a brief life of Christ: it is a clarifying statement of Goyen's understanding of who he was and had become. The little book is much less a confession of belief than a way of rescuing himself from self-hatred by transforming the Jesus of his childhood into a contemporary artistic and personal model, the isolated prophet misread by the world he saves. In this respect *A Book of Jesus* is not a conventional or even straightforward retelling of the Gospels, and Goyen's Christianity in no way suggests a conventional form of the faith.[19] His unorthodox interpretation was hardly invisible to many of the book's reviewers, though the primary complaint seems to have been that he had done little more than copy the Gospels.[20] The reader for the *Catholic Star Herald* offered the typical response: "Goyen wrote his book to give a clear, readable story of Jesus Christ. I fail to see, however, what advantage it has over the original Gospel accounts. The author is to be praised for his intentions, but I feel he has fallen short of gaining insight into the person of Jesus which has been conveyed by his four first-century predecessors."[21] A short, begrudging notice in *The Christian Century* made a similar point, though it acknowledged that this retelling "was no worse than many of the others; it may serve a purpose for some who are sneaking up on the Gospels."[22] Reviewers not affiliated with religious publications responded more positively. Joni Bodart in *Library Journal* found the book "a realistic, moving picture of Christ," and Goyen's old friend the director Michael Murray called it "a very fresh book of Jesus [that] may have the bonus effect of directing new readers to Mr. Goyen's other work."[23]

The deepest and most thoughtful response came from Robert Phillips in the *New York Times Book Review*. Phillips had come to know Goyen during the McGraw-Hill years when one of Phillips's novels was accepted for publication there. Though Goyen left McGraw-Hill before the book could be produced, he and Phillips became close friends and regular correspondents, and the garrulous and well-connected younger writer began to play an important role in encouraging and promoting Goyen's writing. Phillips published one of the first pieces of academic criticism devoted to Goyen's work, an essay on "The White Rooster" that appeared in *Studies in Short Fiction* in 1969, and followed it with a discussion of *In a Farther Country* in *The Southwest Review* a few years later. He was therefore in a position to appreciate what *A Book of Jesus* meant to Goyen personally and in terms of his career. He began by identifying Goyen's book as an inspirational retelling, in the company of Francois Mauriac's *Life of Jesus* and Robert Graves's *King Jesus*, and went on to emphasize Goyen's particular strengths of sensibility that made him ideal for this task: "It is because of Goyen's gifts as an intuitive and at time mystical writer that we should read his account of Jesus from baptism to crucifixion." Phillips understood that Goyen was trying to making Jesus not just contemporary but also present, real: "Here Goyen employs his considerable sympathetic powers to make the Jesus of the Gospels a real and individual being (as opposed to that artificial and composite one encountered in so many studies). His is a physical Christ who strides across these pages with energy and power, touching and teaching."[24]

With the help of reviews like this and Goyen's own, often intense publicity efforts, *A Book of Jesus* sold reasonably well, apparently better than any of his previous work. Though he had argued vigorously with Sam Vaughan for an inexpensive paperback affordable to students, Doubleday printed 5,500 hardcovers, agreeing to a paperback version a year later. At least for a time, the book allowed Goyen himself to function as an eccentric evangelist, surprising people at readings and dinner parties with recitations from his book and from a New Testament that he carried with him at all times. Yet the enthusiasm of renewed faith does not appear to have significantly stabilized his life over the next few years. The experience at Weston had given him a new vocabulary and a clarified sense of his purpose and identity, but it didn't solve the nightly problem of drinking or relieve the ever-more-frequent bitterness over his career. Despite what seems like a life-saving effort to put himself back together, Goyen still had far to go before he found the recovery he was seeking.

CHAPTER THIRTEEN

The Restorer

1974

(And oh, big man, do not bring again to me my yokefellow my
accursedness. The accursed thing in me has been there all my days.
In all my memory, there, in me. What is it? Oh, how can I put it?
Just a heartbreak feeling. Suffering in my mind, sadness, like oh I
want to cry for all things: my yokefellow my accursedness my cross
my suffering. Out of this dark disturbance repair me, restore me.
Help me put back. *Can anything that is hurt, taken away, displaced,*
broken, be restored *ever?)*

COME, THE RESTORER (1974)

In the early 1970s, perhaps to relax and shift his focus, Goyen
began taking tap-dancing lessons in New York. In a class that
included Hal Holbrook and other theatre friends, he found a
connection to that once-secret self who had hidden his dancing shoes
in his boyhood closet, away from his father's notice. What had been
buried—at first by others but also by himself—could now be rediscovered, opened again, as though to release some deeper desire long since
left behind. The pleasure of the experience may have prompted him
to write a sketch for a television play called "Soft Shoe." In this brief
scenario, a man named Harry Bright discovers a dancing school and
soon learns that he has a natural gift for the soft-shoe style of tap dancing. The discovery reawakens a dormant early desire never fully realized: "Something keeps him unrealized, bound; a dream, a loveliness,
is buried in him, unreleased; he has always wanted to dance soft-shoe."
The new attention helps him rediscover this outlet, but when he begins to understand that the rest of the world needs him to dance—or

wants to make money or borrow luster from his dancing—he develops a psychological block. Disabled by this seemingly predatory attention, he disappears; yet when he returns after an unspecified amount of time, he realizes that everyone he knows, even his cold and unresponsive wife, has adopted his vision and is now dancing the soft shoe. And because of this general acceptance of *his* desire, he, too, can dance again. Goyen imagines a final, receding shot of this new man, recovering his wholeness: "And as we pull back from him, he is a small figure going up to his true reality." On the outside of the folder that contains this material, he also penciled this note: "Now takes on a new meaning—of right now—he'll be himself—what's his—his youth" (HRC 24.12).

"Soft Shoe" was never produced and likely never developed beyond this brief outline, but it points toward Goyen's continued efforts to allow himself a more open—and more explicitly personal—expression of long-buried needs. It was clearly a way back to the young man who became infatuated with the vaudevillians in Houston, but the sketch can also serve as a reminder of Goyen's deep and consistent connections to performance and theater. Since the workshop production of *Christy* in 1964, he had remained in regular contact with actors and directors, in part because of Roberts's successful career on stage, but he was less often involved in actual productions because of his job at McGraw-Hill. Plans to adapt *The Fair Sister* into a musical emerged periodically, though casting difficulties ultimately postponed its production.

One project that did make it to the stage came about courtesy of a fellow Texan. The director Adrian Hall, then artistic director of the Trinity Square Repertory Theater in Providence, Rhode Island, convinced Goyen to adapt the dramatic version of *The House of Breath* for performance by two full casts of actors, one white and one black. Thus in November of 1969, *House of Breath, Black/White* premiered to considerable critical praise. The staging was imaginative, experimental, and, to some, dazzling. In addition to a small, rusty sawmill, the bilevel platform was scattered with what seemed to be fragments from the book's world: a windmill with an abandoned cistern, a rain barrel, a merry-go-round horse, and rocking chairs. In various scenes, Ku Klux Klan torches lit up the darkened theater or colored lights bounced up and down to indicate a country fair. Most memorable was Hall's decision to spread a large canopy of white silk over the audience to create the feeling of being underwater during Christy's dive into the river to rescue Otey. Reviewers found the play richly lyrical but expressed minor quibbles about the confusion of the black and white casts. Elliot Norton in the Boston *Record American* described it as "rueful, wistful, sad, often solemn. . . . It is also pessimistic; yet quietly beautiful; lovely in the sound of its words and its occasional music, ultimately compassionate for men and women struggling for happiness in a 'broken world.'"[1] In a similar vein, the reviewer for the Worcester *Evening Gazette* considered it a "marvelously lyrical paean to the inner pain of a family," and Kevin Kelly in the *Boston Globe* thought the production "hypnotic," "an eloquent search for the answer of [two families'] true brotherhood."[2]

This small but distinguished success was encouraging to Goyen, but as a revival of earlier work it seems to have had little positive effect on his production of new material. A few years later, however, a more engrossing project emerged, again at the suggestion of Hall. As part of Trinity Rep's 1973–1974 season, Hall wanted to mount a world-premier musical and commissioned Goyen to write a rousing, spectacular show about the California evangelist Aimee Semple McPherson. Given his long-standing interest in the theatrical potential of tent preachers, the assignment made perfect sense for Goyen. And indeed, *Aimee!*, as the play came to be called, can be seen as a clear extension of his earlier work in "Rhody's Path," *The Diamond Rattler*, and *The Fair Sister*. This time, however, there was a well-known, and suitably peculiar, biography to structure his story. The historical Aimee became a celebrity evangelist in California during the twenties and thirties. She began as a traveling preacher, touring the United States in a Packard christened the "Gospel Car" with her second husband, Harold, and later with her mother. But her real fame developed when she settled in California, began to speak on the radio, and built the enormous Angelus Temple in the Echo Park area of Los Angeles. She regularly spoke to capacity crowds in the 5,000-seat circular church and sometimes conducted faith healings while dressed in the flowing white gown that was her trademark. Then, in 1926, she disappeared while swimming at Venice Beach and was thought to have drowned. A month or so later, after frenzied searches failed to find her body, she turned up in the desert near the Arizona border, claiming she'd been kidnapped and held for ransom in Mexico. Little evidence could be found to support her story, and witnesses began to emerge who said they had seen her in the company of Kenneth Ormiston, a radio engineer who worked at the temple. McPherson was eventually tried but acquitted on charges of perjury and returned to her ministry with all the additional celebrity that an unresolved, media-fed scandal could deliver. She died in 1944 from what was determined to be an accidental overdose of sleeping pills.

Fresh from his own dark night of the soul and rediscovery of a physical Jesus, Goyen saw Aimee as "an extraordinary woman caught in the battle of spirit and flesh." Her "thirsts were tremendous. . . . This made her understand and love thirst in others. No wonder they loved her, as they loved the man Jesus."[3] She was a vaudevillian, a show-woman—the extension of Folner and Savata—simultaneously drawn by the glamour of the Temple, her own emotional and sexual needs, and the spiritual love of her followers. For Goyen, McPherson was not a charlatan but a naïf. In what seems a self-revealing description, he told a reporter from the *Providence Sunday Journal* that Aimee "was the truly innocent woman—really didn't know what she'd done even when she lied. . . . She needed love. She needed to love and be loved. When she went down a line of people and told each one that she loved them, she meant it" (HRC 1.5).

The plot of the play builds toward the climactic temptation of Aimee's faked kidnapping and night in the desert during which she decides between her ministry and the love of Charlie Jamieson (Ormiston). After early scenes of tent evangelism with her mother, Aimee ultimately faces the lure of success and sensuality in a fantasy sequence built around the symbol of her little blue traveling trunk. In his production notes, Goyen explained that she "has packed her dream things in the little blue trunk, glittering and expensive things for a dream romantic life, run-away things for a romantic escape of love and glamour and splendor and sex with a handsome, romantic and exciting man. Everybody has his own little blue trunk, let's not forget." This is Folner's trunk of spangles that comes back to Charity after his suicide, the original of which may have been Goyen's boyhood closet that hid grease paint, tap shoes, and his cardboard piano in its recesses—in other words, a container of desire, understood in Aimee's case as "the Devil and Forces of Evil (Sin, Lust, Romance) who are trying to 'kidnap' her away from her duty, from her people, from her Temple, from her God." Her ability to resist the trunk's attractions allows her to leave Charlie and return to Los Angeles to be put on trial, though she is finally reborn, "resurrected," in Goyen's terms, by the acknowledgment of her own human weaknesses.

The reviews for *Aimee!* were largely positive, though not without specific criticism of the script and staging. Many were impressed once again by Hall's innovative set work, especially his decision to extend the runway into the seats so that the actress playing Aimee could drive the "Car of Love" around and through the audience. Others, like the reviewer for *Variety*, found the overall production an exciting spectacle "with a strong central character and plot, imaginative and fast-paced direction, good songs and a capable cast."[4] Many critics seemed unsure of the overall effectiveness of Goyen's interpretation. From the *Boston Herald-American*: "The playwright's fault is in his failure to get enough of this on stage to make Aimee what he apparently believes her to be, an entirely sympathetic character, a woman who inveighed against sin from her heart and at the same time yielded to what she considered sin because of the perfectly natural weaknesses of the flesh."[5] But for those who accepted the idea that such conflicts were possible without corrupting the character into cynicism, *Aimee!* seemed a fresh perspective on the familiar figure of the lapsed evangelist: "Instead of envisioning Aimee . . . as a pious fraud or a sermon-spouting Monster," the reviewer from the Worcester *Telegram* noted, [Goyen] has characterized her as a goddess of religious love and fervor, a Mary Pickford-type who built a temple with gaudy dramas of martyrdom and promised that mortals could retain their favorite vices much of the time."[6]

Though tied closely enough to the historical Aimee to satisfy the requirement of the genre, *Aimee!* the musical is nevertheless an important expression of Goyen's perennial struggle between ghost and flesh. He clearly saw aspects of himself in McPherson, both her ineluctable attraction to the spotlight and her guilt and distrust of that very impulse toward the sensual that made her successful. In his notes he emphasized the cost of this all-consuming need to "love":

The play is about a great Force, an extraordinary woman caught in the battle of spirit and flesh. Aimee fell to the same forces—material possessions, the flesh, worldly power and worldly beauty—as those she "saved." They must have loved her that much more. The Lord, too!

He who loves much is in need of much understanding and forgiveness. For, in doing more, in loving more, he "sins" more, makes more mistakes, *hurts* more. The man Jesus said that he forgives and under-stands these generous lovers more readily than the others. (HRC 1.5, original emphasis)

The shift to the male pronoun in the second paragraph may be inci-dental, but it gives the entire passage the air of self-analysis. In "loving more" Goyen had indeed "hurt more" and perhaps hurt others more than most, but he had found a way to understand himself and an idea of Jesus that offered forgiveness for the body as well as the soul of the "generous," error-prone lover.

The Wire-Walker: *Come, the Restorer*

Despite his departure from McGraw-Hill, despite the occasional successes with theatrical work and *A Book of Jesus*, writing—the daily practice of sitting in his early morning room and waiting for the voice to speak—had not gotten any easier for Goyen. While working on *Another Man's Son*, the novel he resumed in earnest after the sudden rush of the Jesus book, he resorted to dictating to Roberts's mother, Ann, who had owned a successful stenography business for many years. "Work is hard as ever for me," he wrote to Phillips during this period; "just won't flow and makes me hurt too much; I'm now, in desperation trying to dictate to Ann . . . directly to the typewriter. I've never tried this and, after the first trial I'm not sure it will work. I need to see the words and I lose the intimacy with words that come through my own hand and which I see on the page as I go. Fuck it, there's no avoiding the pain and travail of work for me."[7] Some of the general difficulty was related to his con-tinued drinking, but there were also problems with the project itself. The original idea of a novel about the early years of his marriage and the challenges of being a stepfather had begun to stall. As he later ex-plained to Rolande Ballorain, "I could never make it work, and the more I worked at it, the more I got away from it, because I was telling a lit-eral story which began to bore me. At least I didn't want to reproduce life, and I was doing that."[8] Never a realist, Goyen couldn't free him-self from his source material sufficiently to let his imagination take the reins; at the same time, the problems that had generated the idea in the first place had been resolved or altered into new shapes. In despair, he simply dropped *Another Man's Son* and began inventing an extravagant, folkloric tale set in East Texas. "I threw the truth away," as he later put it. "I took all the feeling—the experience I had gone through in trying to tell the story and put it back into a fabricated one."[9]

There may have been more than one catalyst for this retreat from realism to fabulism. His conversion experience at Weston and the subsequent work on *Aimee!* and *A Book of Jesus* had left him with an intense interest in charismatic or prophetic figures who could symbolize his own struggle with sexuality. It may have been an amalgam of these two stories—Aimee's ministry and strange disappearance built upon the gospel structure—that led to the creation of Mr. de Persia, the repairer of old photographs whose story comprises the first section of *Come, the Restorer*. Mr. de Persia, with his Levantine name and legendary restorative powers, is a savior of memory, bringing the dead back to life in the reborn image. But he's also a healer, fixer, the maker of complex inventions to restore the broken:

> Mechanically gifted, a genius at creating complicated constructions, he had constructed a delicate, efficient world of contrivances composed of levers and purchases, slings, tension springs, gears, trestles, trapezes, pulleys and braces for the crippled to survive in, for the limbless (arms, hands, legs, feet) to travel with (drive, walk, even dance). Therefore the afflicted loved him. He was, then, a healer—a creator, really—for he had made new people; they sort of rose from the dead, because where they had been halt before, now they could walk, even though mechanically, like crabs, like robots or puppets; and where they'd been flat on their backs paralyzed, he raised them up on trapezes and slings with ropes and pulleys. (*CR* 27)

Echoing the healer/weaver Curran from *Half a Look of Cain*, de Persia has all the characteristics of Goyen's idea of the artist. He reassembles the broken pieces of the world, even when the brokenness can't be completely healed. And in a fallen world—in this case an East Texas under threat from the oil industry—he offers himself as the savior of the pastoral, the "sweet gardener" (*CR* 10) whose power promises fertility "in an age of breakdown" (*CR* 11).

Perhaps because of this fallenness, de Persia himself is soon disabled, found in a coma, lying in a glass casket, though somewhat miraculously sporting a "full erection" (*CR* 17). The small town of Rose,

Texas, and the entire region of the Big Thicket are mesmerized and attracted to the mysterious body, seemingly both dead and alive. He becomes a kind of risen/unrisen god, filling the town with sexual energy, attracting those in need of healing or revival:

> Now that Mr. de Persia had space around him, hundreds and hundreds more began to come to him in search of his widely publicized powers. Now, not only the curious, the lecherous and the adoring came, but also the afflicted. People came shouting because they were deaf and could not hear themselves talk, staggering on crutches because they were crippled, and led by others because they were blind. Others were brought on cots and there were even humpbacks, harelips, grossly fat people, and an assortment of your usual run of deformities including, it was said, a morphodite from Grapeland. (*CR* 30)

De Persia is the analog, in comic form, of Goyen's Jesus, attracting those whose bodies cause them to suffer. But his ability to heal, if it exists at all, is ambiguous, a psychological influence more than a direct laying on of hands. Like Aimee, de Persia may be a sham or a genuine prophet, and when he is kidnapped by two young men and a woman in a blue balloon, he reenacts Aimee's controversial disappearance, here with a parodic "ascension" over East Texas. After an airborne copulation with the mysterious Gypsy Selina Rosheen—a union that produces the book's central figure, Addis Adair—de Persia's body is seen parachuting down into the impenetrable Thicket. A frenzied search follows, but no trace can be found. Instead he becomes another Big Thicket legend, alive in the regional faith in his future resurrection.

De Persia is thus both God the Father and John the Baptist. As John prepared the way for Jesus, de Persia makes possible his son, Addis, an orphan adopted by Jewel and Ace Adair. The couple's sexless marriage indicates their connection to Mary and Joseph: "The town spoke of [Addis] as one who had a virgin mother and was a son without a father (and spoke of his adopted father, Ace, as a man who had a virgin wife)" (*CR* 59). Addis grows up to be a dark, strange but beautiful youth whose isolation and hint of mixed blood evokes Christy from *The House of Breath*. His father Ace dies in a railroad accident, driven to this near suicide by sexual shame and lack of intimacy, and Addis disappears, leaving his mother to keen over the absence of the son she saw as her "redeemer" (*CR* 70). This self-exile wanders the countryside becoming over time both an artist (he teaches himself to walk a tight-rope made of an old clothesline) and a "saint" who never speaks: "Yet he never opened his mouth, this speechless wire dancer, this strangely appealing saint of the clothesline in the dry desertland, on the dusty mesas of the Panhandle" (*CR* 89).

In many respects, Addis is a typical Goyen alter ego, though here the "orphan" son has accrued new levels of detail from several differ-ent sources. First, he is not a new character at all but a development of Son from the early story "Pore Perrie." As part of his effort to create a fresh, fantastic exploration of the themes of *Another Man's Son*, Goyen apparently revisited both this story and the play *The Diamond Rattler* (as well as the screenplay, "A Possibility of Oil"), drawing the basic nar-ratives from each and grafting them into a larger frame of the Jesus and *Aimee!* material. Second, he was almost certainly inspired by an article in *The New Yorker* by Francis Steegmuller about the Texas-born, cross-dressing acrobat Barbette, born Vander Clyde, who became a sensation in Paris in the 1920s and 1930s.[10] Clyde grew up near Round Rock, Texas, at the turn of the century and learned to walk the tightrope by practic-ing on his mother's clothesline in his backyard. He joined the circus in San Antonio as part of a trapeze and ring group and was persuaded to perform in women's clothes as an added attraction. Soon he developed a solo act, taking the stage name Barbette, and in 1923 sailed to Europe under the auspices of the William Morris agency. His odd but fascinat-ing combination of androgyny, grace, and danger seduced the Parisians, particularly intellectuals and artists like Jean Cocteau, who wrote in his 1926 essay "The Barbette Act" that "the reason for Barbette's success lies in the fact that he appeals to the instinct of different audiences as if they were one while he reconciles conflicting opinion without being aware of it. Indeed, he appeals to those who see the woman in him, to those who sense the man in him, as well as to others whose souls are moved by the supernatural sex of beauty."[11] According to Steegmuller, Cocteau considered Barbette the embodiment of the poet, caught be-tween the indifference of the audience and the danger of his own cre-ation. The artist and filmmaker was so captivated by this "strange little devil, this Saint-Just in dreams" that he cast him in his first film, *The Blood of a Poet*, as a countess applauding a card game that ends in a suicide.[12]

If in fact Goyen had never heard of Barbette prior to Steegmuller's profile, the discovery must have been electric. After all, he had explored, deeply and personally, the idea of the acrobat in *Half a Look of Cain* and created in Marvello a character who seems eerily similar to the androgynous Texan who captivated Cocteau. It is possible that Goyen was aware of Cocteau's essay prior to 1969; in fact, it seems more than coincidental that Marvello begins his career as part of the family performance called "The Ishbel Act." But it was only in the transformation of Son into Addis Adair that Goyen apparently seized the idea of a Texas acrobat who could embody his own personal struggle for balance. In the remote pastoral of the "self-seeding, self-incubating, self-mothering" thicket (*CR* 126), Addis strings his clothesline in the limbs of a lyre-shaped tree and practices a peculiar sort of artistic discipline. Completely naked, he performs in this "bower" and "theater," a "seminal garden" in which Goyen's deepest fantasies of self-display and sexual expression reach their apex:

> In this wonderful tree on whose brotherly trunk he had hung the tobacco can with Ace's photo in it, Addis Adair, marvelous ornament, walked naked on the clothesline he had stolen from Jewel's house—oh so long ago, it seemed to him now. His erect penis, bowed like a Satyr's, guided him like a compass needle, balancing him, weighting him and buoying him aloft, leading his steps like a wand, like a life preserver. Often as he moved on the wire in his voluptuous bower, his seminal garden, he shot his seed into the air, silver-white and flashing in the moonlight. Shooting! The flashing pulses and charges of shining white and silver burst from him and flung through the moonlit air, some unearthly creature of wilderness that had lighted there, coming out of the mysterious drumming deeps of the forest where tree linked with tree, locked as if by handclasps. (*CR* 128–129)

The astonishing sequence titled "The Green Tree and the Dry" begins in solitary male and adolescent fantasy and ends as a testament to the destructive power of lust. In its first half, Goyen evokes the masturbatory poetics of Melville and Whitman, charging sperm (or as the book's title would have it, "come") with the symbolic freight of romantic self-expression. The tree is a lyre, a poet's instrument made from nature—not to mention an astonishing East Texas version of Coleridge's aeolian harp—and Addis plays upon it with his body, this child of nature join-ing Nature sexually: "and the tree dazzled and trembled through the body of this beautiful flirting and flickering and shooting figure, phan-tom and elusive and mystical, in its innocent heat, its virgin holiness, its wilderness glory" (*CR* 129). Barbette may have been the inspiration for the wire walker from Texas, but Goyen is less interested here in the androgynous idea than in the innocence of a sexuality devoted solely to the self's expression. In biographical terms, Addis's withdrawal to the thicket to practice his secret arts seems a fabulistic version of the young Goyen's escape to the "wild place" near his Houston home where he first began to write in secret. In this stage-like tree in the cloistered thicket, he can perform a kind of vaudevillian exposure of his sexual being, his exile a protection from the strictures of kinship.

What ultimately disturbs and destroys this willful idyll is the ap-pearance of a woman. But Addis's Eve is not merely the embodiment of time and forced maturity, she is his adoptive mother Jewel, now un-aware that the strange creature floating in the tree is the son whose absence she mourns. The sight of "this tree god, this treedevil" in the hyperfertile thicket elicits her long-dormant sexuality, and she is seized by desire to the point of madness: "She became quite crazed. In the dark, humid underbrush she hid, naked, and panted and throbbed, drenched with her heats. She lay spread and opened in the warm leaves and moaned voluptuously in her hot agony and yearning and hunger. She tore at herself" (*CR* 130). A destructive, animalistic sexual encounter follows, in which both are so consumed by lust that they lose their indi-viduality and humanity: "Thus they went, touch-and-go, one taking the other's thrust, seesaw, a human machine, a wheel-driven machine of some kind, a pump, a dynamo, in the deep Thicket, in the hidden bower, under the marvelous tree" (*CR* 133). When Jewel finally leaves the woods, Addis is destroyed by her absence. No longer self-sufficient, he feels castrated and begins to identify with his lost "father," Ace:

> And oh had Ace shared this with him, Ace who witnessed it from his photo on the tobacco can on the tree, Ace whose presence had been all around him, had Ace hunched with him and come, at last, at long last, with him in his near-madness of lust. Yes, he knew that Ace was there, with him in his sexual heat and his cruel lust and in his bestial convulsion. In the new mystery of his sex, Ace was there; in the revolu-

tion, the fire and the shattering and the newness of the world, Ace was there; and in the sadness of manhood, the sadness of come, the sorrows of woman-lust, the sorrows of comers, the frailty of coming manhood, in the old male-sorrow, father-sorrow . . . there was Ace; he was there!
(*CR* 135–136)

Several important, and very personal, strands of Goyen's recent thinking are woven into this passage. The idea of Ace as a secret sharer in moments of lust comes directly from Goyen's notes about his discovery of the physical Jesus and from the pamphlet "Jesus in My Body." Ace can understand and forgive because he, too, was subject to uncontainable desire and died because of it. But Ace also contains an echo of Charlie Goyen. The tin box in which Addis keeps Ace's picture contains "a small glass swan" (*CR* 83), his father's "Belleek swan" that Goyen claimed after Charlie's death. Ace is thus a gathering point: he is the new Jesus who understands the fallenness of the body; he is father and son, stepfather and childless husband, who dies—like Jesus and like Charlie Goyen?— so that his son can live, that is, find a way to understand his own relation to the world, find expression and selfhood, rise out of his boyhood dream into maturity.

Except that Ace, for all his symbolic value, cannot save Addis from the incestuous pull of kinship. Jewel's appearance is a reenactment not only of the fall of man but of the loss of childhood. This oedipal pattern was present in Goyen's writing almost from the beginning. The manuscript of *Christopher Icarus* is essentially built on a crude version of the idea, and *The House of Breath* retains the structure of the Freudian "family drama" in the relationship between Malley and Berryben. The device for signaling this substrate in *Christopher Icarus* was substitution: the central character falls into a sexual relationship with his aunt, his mother's sister. In a note to Patrice Repusseau sent during the 1970s, Goyen made clear that the aunt functioned as a surrogate for the mother, a situation repeated in *The Diamond Rattler*'s retelling of "Pore Perrie."[13] In the play, Son engages in a frenzied affair with his aunt Linsie, a lustful obsession that seems to anticipate the bestial rutting of Addis and Jewel. Now, apparently past the need for this kind of indirection, Goyen took the more daring path in *Come, the Restorer* of imagining an oedipal embrace between adoptive mother and son, bringing closer what had been only suggested in the short story.

The moment of encounter between mother and son that concludes "Pore Perrie" leads to Perrie Polk's death, leaving Son alive to wander in his exile. The incestuous coupling between Jewel and Addis kills them both; Addis hangs in the tree by his jaw, fallen from his tightrope, out of balance, deranged by a desire that is no longer self-contained or self-expressive but tangled with time and death.[14] For him, Jewel is not merely his adoptive mother—in fact, he never knows her identity in this section of the story—but a kind of ur-mother and ur-woman, the initiator of an unceasing desire that is ultimately possessive and de-structive. Before their meeting at the tree, Addis's sexuality had been limited to self-expression, the masturbatory act in the lyre; it became with Jewel a performance of birth and death, of procreation and the entrance into the temporality of fathers and sons. Put another way, the mother is here the secret purveyor of both desire and death; she brings with her the consuming interests of family and kinship, and her body is the very emblem of this need and threat. In still another remarkable, though bizarre, passage, Addis rages at the rapaciousness of the female body:

> He was blinded by such realistic images of her sex, the very fold and wink and cut of it, that he thought he could reach and touch it: her sex sucked and pouted before his eyes, hung hairy and swollen and wet and open; or it rose from under her big belly, wide and broad, a firm, split swelling as big as his hand, that could scarcely cover it, cupping it and grasping it like a warm grisly living thing, rolling it and molding it and piercing it and handling it, all of it, all split open like a big tight melon, as it quivered and sucked, oral and swallowing, or grabbed his fingers and seemed to struggle with his hand, this big, live hot meaty being that lay in there, humid and grainy and viscous and hairy, between her legs and slit up her soft shaggy belly. He was blinded by her devour-ing cunt. He would fall to the ground and cry out, beating the ground with his fists. Where was his lonesomeness, where was his sweet pure orphanage? (CR 134).

There is evidence among Goyen's papers to suggest that he may have shared, at least in part, Addis's contradictory and almost dys-phoric relationship to the female body. In a brief manuscript possibly related to drafts of Six Women, a voice—perhaps Goyen's own or that of an imagined narrator—makes notes on what he sees as the different attitudes of men and women toward their genitalia. Men are described as "totally narcissistic" during boyhood: "they adore their penis, are in awe of it, proud of it, driven by it." Women, on the other hand, are said to "hate their vaginas" and to enjoy sex less (HRC 20.4). Thus the married or "sexually committed" male—no longer free in his solitary and boyish sexuality—is trapped by what the narrator describes as women's typical attitude toward their bodies. The piece as a whole has the air of a grievance by a married man with a less than satisfying sexual relationship, but what seems both pertinent and unusual is the focus on the unattractive and unclean image of the female body. The opposition between a boyish eroticism of play and a female sexuality of pain and disgust matches Addis's strangely panicked cry at the loss of his "lonesomeness." Before Jewel's appearance at the tree, Addis is the apotheosis of boyish sexual isolation, but when she appears, he falls into a maddened and dependent desire for the "devouring" body that has taken his innocence.

Despite its often comic tone, *Come, the Restorer* presents Addis's loss as essentially tragic. Not only does the desire for Jewel kill him, but she hangs herself soon after discovering his body, seeing his birthmark, and recognizing him. She is discovered by the long-lost Mr. de Persia, Addis's biological father, who brings no restorative power, only a kind of aged bewilderment. He notices the grave where Jewel has buried Addis among the tree's roots and finds her swollen body hanging from the clothesline. Then as though to underscore his feebleness, he entangles himself in the branches while trying to free her. The great tree of the thicket, Goyen's harp-shaped symbol of nature's fecundity and power, finally holds the bodies of father, mother, and son, three deaths that signal an end to the mythical life of East Texas.

The new era that follows is destructive and dystopic. Its symbols are oil and a fire indicative of an obscene form of greed that supplants spirituality. Its principle figures are a snake-handling preacher who becomes an evangelist for the discovery of oil, and a "firedevil" named Wylie Prescott, who embodies the demonic spirit of the new age. Goyen brought the figure of Oil King, the former snake-handler, directly from *The Diamond Rattler*, adapting much of the action of the play to fit into his expanded mythology of the region. Wylie Prescott, on the other hand, is a new creation, the avatar of everything Goyen hated about the changes brought to East Texas by the oil boom. Inspired in part by the famed firefighter Red Adair, Prescott serves as a portmanteau figure for those who brought the petrochemical industry and its attendant forms of progress into the sleepy woods of Goyen's childhood. Wild-catters, speculators, drillers, builders of chemical plants, real estate developers—all find root in Prescott's biography. He begins as a battler of oil fires who wears an asbestos suit with a devil on the back, walking into flames to put them out. The destructive power of fire allows him to become a developer, clearing and building first on the "burnt-out timberland in the Thicket north of Rose" (*CR* 153). His affinity for fire gives him an almost mystical sensitivity to oil: "He clawed in seeps with his fingernails after smelling oil, and behold, he pulled out oily fingers. He bought some rigging and bored his own hole in the Thicket. Oil shot up, mixed with mud and rock, and devastated an acre" (*CR* 154). He becomes rich and powerful and cruel, destroying the thicket with an "ancient instinct for devastation" (*CR* 156):

> He was a walking Plague, a pestilence, locust, frog, grasshopper, tree moth, a devourer, worse than any chemical spray or poison, a devastator. He took away from Nature its pure self, its forces, and did not put back anything, but he added fake stuff—chemicals, preservatives, coloratives. His factories murdered rivers, spoiled freshness, soured and embittered sweetness, withered green. He was the first, the leader, the beginning of the generation that poisoned itself, that spoiled its own, that ate its own poison. (*CR* 156)

All of the animosity of Goyen's long-nurtured grievance at the loss of his own childhood in Trinity emerges here. But what had once been little more than a rural boy's instinctive recoil has grown into a more mature critique not only of Houston but of the ethical and environmental toll of its growth. Goyen's personal loss is perceived and understood as a regional destruction, and *Come, the Restorer*, as a result, contains one of the few pieces of directly political writing he was ever to do. Though not in any way an activist, Goyen saw his own life as structured by the twentieth century's thirst for oil, the cost of which was the pastoral landscape of his childhood. He presents this loss, here and elsewhere, less as a function of political and economic decisions than as a casualty in a spiritual war. Prescott is a devil; the land is Eden. And

Goyen's own fall from boyhood innocence to adolescent misery (country to city) provides the structure for East Texas's loss of soul. His environmental politics are therefore tragic and lead to a call not for action but acts of mourning.

So deep a sadness does not preclude the satisfactions of revenge, however. Prescott is made to pay the price for his devotion to fire. He becomes a sexless reptile with "a weblike growth of skin over many parts of him, scaled like a snake's" (*CR* 164). And though he builds a mansion and marries the biological mother of Addis Adair—the mysterious Gypsy woman Selina Rosheen—he is incapable of love or embrace. In his old age he takes in strays and adopts the wandering, including Oil King and his ancient rattlesnake. Prescott becomes another Ace, an adoptive father who can no longer act as a real father, who longs for family but can only assemble a kind of substitute menagerie. The ties of kinship return to haunt him, and he dies unconnected, his heart burned away by an old wound, a "small dagger of fire" swallowed years before (*CR* 169). Though the avatar of the new age of petrochemicals, Prescott has only been the catalyst for the transformation of Rose, Texas, into a "rich and conservative city not very friendly to folly or patient with fancy" (*CR* 180). His mansion and factory are absorbed by the city that is itself the symbol of regional avarice and modernity.

Come, the Restorer retains some of the difficulties of story combination that afflicted *The Diamond Rattler*. Goyen's tendency to produce narrative pieces that he then tried to sew together had always caused him difficulties, and here the loose-fitting joints between tales can seem both purposeful and tenuous.[15] Nevertheless the book contains some of the most extravagantly imaginative writing of his career, so flagrantly drawn, in fact, that critics were again divided over its effectiveness. Several found the comedy rich enough to account for all of its narrative looseness. The reviewer for *Publishers Weekly* thought the book "an enchanting tale . . . a kind of a song, both joyous and sad," an impression expanded upon by Peter G. Kramer in *Newsweek*. Even more positive accounts came from Goyen's longtime supporter at *The Dallas Morning News*, Lon Tinkle, and from the young Frenchman Patrice Repusseau, who was working on the thesis that would later become *William Goyen: de la maison vers le foyer*. Tinkle, not always easy to please, found the novel "an audacious and virtuosic verbal feast" that is "perhaps not a coherent whole" but is a "boldly conceived novel" that is a "genuinely exciting and mental workout." And Repusseau offered a more complete and perceptive reading of the text in terms of Goyen's development: "The pendulum keeps oscillating between love and death, ghost and flesh. Mr. de Persia . . . and Addis Adair . . . impersonate two aspects (father and son?) of a Christ endowed with a huge ungodly phallus. . . . All the major characters hold within themselves this swaying dialectic of the opposite (sacred and profane, good and evil, potent and impotent, etc.) which gives the book a back-and-forth motion culminating in a scene of primitive and frantic coition." He concludes by saying that "Goyen has exorcised his demons (his angels?) with verve and gusto in a complex fabric of magical and haunted visions." Such sympathetic readings were likely outweighed, however, by Shirley Ann Grau's unamused reaction in the *New York Times Book Review*. Though appreciative of Goyen's short fiction, she considered the new novel "a private dream" without "pattern, without plot (except in the crudest sense), without forward motion." She objected to a symbolism that she found inconsistent as well as to a "deliberate" fragmentation that relied too heavily on the "reader's emotions rather than his intelligence." The sequence "The Green Tree and the Dry" she deemed "embarrassingly silly," and she simply rejected the entire method of the fiction as "impossibly exaggerated."[16]

Grau's response underlines yet again the wildly opposed reactions Goyen's fiction could elicit. Critics averse to symbolism or uneasy with his untamed imagery tended to find the work too emotional and too elusive for their tastes. Those willing to accept a nonrealist intelligence that developed ideas lyrically rather than analytically seemed more open to its rewards. In this sense, Grau's harsher criticisms are not so much incorrect as based on a category mistake from which Goyen suffered all too often. Taken for what it is, *Come, the Restorer* is both a remarkable book—a kind of mad American fever-dream of sex and loss—and a vitally important development in Goyen's career.[17] In the most obvious sense, it represented a return to publishing fiction after a ten-year absence. But even more significant was the fact that despite its reliance on older material, the writing broke new ground. Not since *Half a Look of Cain* had he worked so deeply into the symbolic or oneiric spaces of his psychology. His typical themes of orphanage, the struggle between spirit and flesh, and the binding limits of kinship are all here but newly clothed in imagery as strange and daring as any he had yet produced. In part, this release of creativity seems due to the inspirational rediscovery of Jesus, as Goyen understood him. And yet there is a sense in which this personal experience failed to create a complete artistic transformation until Goyen's Jesus fused with the carnivalesque strangeness of Barbette. This combination in two resonant figures of sacrifice, performance, androgyny, and salvation both clarified and intensified Goyen's private mythos. Out of this still-raveled knot of personal and prophetic history he would extract the major work of his later career.

CHAPTER FOURTEEN ❧

Precious Door
1975–1981

from under the rubble heap
            m'elevasti
from the dulled edge beyond pain,
            m'elevasti

out of Erebus, the deep lying
    from the wind under the earth,
            m'elevasti
from the dulled air and the dust,
            m'elevasti
by the great flight,
            m'elevasti
                Isis Kuanon
from the cusp of the moon,
            m'elevasti

EZRA POUND, FROM "CANTO XC," COPIED INTO
GOYEN'S AA NOTEBOOK, CIRCA 1976

With two new books published in 1973 and 1974, on top of the production of *Aimee!*, Goyen seems to have emerged from his publishing work and writing problems with new energy and focus.[1] Many difficulties remained, however, most significantly the combination of depression and drinking that had given the crisis in Weston its intensity and desperation. He was approaching his sixtieth birthday, the kind of milestone he dreaded when it reminded him of goals not accomplished and work that others had ignored or forgotten. On top of this potentially destabilizing reminder, he soon found himself displaced yet again, spiritually lost in a landscape he disdained and despised.

For one so hypersensitive to the problem of belonging, moving was always fraught with potential trauma for Goyen. The apartment on West End Avenue in New York that he'd shared with Roberts since 1963 had become a kind of nest and shelter, and he was reluctant to leave the community of writers and theater friends that had grown up around him. But Roberts's career had been building steadily throughout the 1960s. On Broadway, she had appeared in a number of successful plays, including Neil Simon's *The Last of the Red Hot Lovers* in 1969. By the mid-1970s she was in demand for more television roles and began commuting to Los Angeles while Goyen took temporary teaching jobs at Brown and Princeton. Then in the summer of 1974, her mother Ann died. As a way to allay the sadness in their diminished family, the couple and now-teenaged Michael sailed to Europe on the cruise ship *The France*, a voyage notable for a strike by the crew that left the passengers stranded in Le Havre harbor.[2] After the trip, Roberts felt more determined than ever to pursue her opportunities in Hollywood and bought a house with the proceeds of her work in advertising. Goyen reluctantly joined her in the summer of 1975 and almost immediately felt lost. "Long silence denotes moving," he wrote to Phillips, "(a charming little house) and unhappiness. I've turned against this deadly place. Been very blue. Want my West End Ave. seclusion. Miss New York. Miss you and my friends and all the old ways. But Doris works and wants to stay. . . . So I'll do my best. But it's not for me. Suddenly I knew it. I find it very hard to work."[3]

In part, this reaction was simply a delayed despair that had already taken a serious toll and led to a suicide attempt. During a previous stay in California, while Roberts was busy working on a film, Goyen had been having small but dispiriting health problems. As it had during his nervous breakdown in the early 1950s, one of his arms had "gone dead," and he'd recently undergone surgery for a torn retina.[4] Three months without being able to use his eye had added to his depression, and unable to write, he drank more and more. He'd also been prescribed a variety of medications, including sleeping and pain pills. In this addled and depressed state, he got a call from Sam Vaughan urging him to drive to Newport Beach, where Doubleday was having a sales conference. Though Goyen had never driven in California, he managed the 100-mile trip without incident and found that Vaughan had organized a small dinner in his honor. Grateful and warmed by this unexpected reception from friends and editors, he decided to stay the night, but once alone in his hotel room, his mood instantly darkened: "I suddenly thought I don't want to live; I don't care." He took "hundreds of pills" but after lying still for a few minutes began to panic. Since he knew Roberts had a 5:00 a.m. wake-up call, he phoned a friend instead and asked her to come and get him. Already vomiting up the pills, he asked her not to call the police or a doctor but simply to drive him back to Los Angeles: "WELL, of course they called the police," he later told Phillips, "and they called the doctors and everybody and they came to the room and I said I'm fine, and I'm throwing up and everybody . . . no one knew about this." His friend arrived early the next morning, and Goyen insisted on sneaking out of the hotel disguised in her clothes: "I can't be seen in the lobby because I can't walk. I'm still asleep. And my publishers are down there all having breakfast." It's difficult to imagine the strangeness of this scene—and tempting to read more into this moment of traumatic cross-dressing—but Goyen's consistent desire to control his image, even in moments of great crisis, likely led him to take such extreme measures. In any case, the odd couple made it out of the lobby undetected and drove directly back to Los Angeles.

The account of this episode in the *Paris Review* transcripts has a comic and absurdist air that belies its danger. To his old friend Ellen Garwood, a writer and the wealthy wife of a Texas Supreme Court justice, Goyen confessed that he did not "have enough medicine" to end his life and that he was "still afraid . . . searching for hope."[5] Later, in the sketch for *Six Women* titled "Margo," he built from the memory of Margo Jones's alcohol-fueled death a fuller contemplation of his own self-destructive drinking. The piece concludes with the ominous suggestion of a kind of fated repetition:

> You'd been twenty years in the ground in Livingston Texas under the liveoak tree when I got to that Newport Beach hotel in California. In that hopeless night, there in that Newport Beach hotel, I saw before me many departed; and I saw your fantastic figure, crazy rainbow hair, face color slashed and strutted, beckoning to me.
>
> And I, too, fell to my own floor in that beach hotel in California, saw

in the haze of my sinking away, shining on my hands, my feet, my naked body, red, green, purple, yellow. (*GAE* 29)

If in some respect Goyen had always been afraid of becoming Folner (who "took sleeping pills at midnight in a hotel in San Antonio" [*HOB* 113]), he was equally unsettled by the thought of repeating Jones's fevered burnout. It was as though the family curse—most specifically the alcoholism of some of the Goyen men—could extend to all of East Texas, bringing Margo Jones into this wider and more dangerous realm of kinship: "Of all of them Margo is my sister—demonic, rapturous insane in booze and in reverie and golden dream."[6]

California evoked this nightmare. Goyen's first impulse was therefore to flee to a reliable haven. A letter from Brett put the idea of New Mexico in his head, and that fall he was on a plane to Albuquerque, hoping to find a way to buy back his little adobe house in El Prado. He kept a notebook during this trip and recorded not only his new impressions of these old haunts but memories of his first arrival in New Mexico with Berns: "The de Vargas Hotel. Walter and I arriving in a snow storm, I believe we got a room there. It was a cheap rate hotel. Now it looks first class, thrives—as everything in Sante Fe does."[7] The practical question was whether Brett could legally give back to Goyen a piece of the land he once owned. The house he had built with Berns had been sold, probably in 1958, and now was owned by John Manchester, Brett's art dealer and caretaker during her later years. Brett had willed her own property to Manchester as well, presumably in return for his services. Despite Brett's pleas, Manchester refused to hand over any property to Goyen unless he paid its full value. Since Goyen had very little money ("another reason for my despondency"), he couldn't afford what had become expensive Taos real estate, but he was reluctant to give up on what seemed for the moment like the key to his salvation.[8] "A *great* mysterious vitality came into me," he wrote to Ellen Garwood, "a *saving*, life-restoring power came, out of the great mountain near my house, out of the land, out of 'my' house, out of the mysterious force in . . . Brett."[9] This surge of welcome energy came to him after spending the night in his old house, and it convinced him, at least momentarily, that reconnecting to this place—regrounding himself in an ideal landscape—could restore what Los Angeles had taken away. He wrote in his notebook: "I am helpless, stranded. It is as though my books had never been written, did not exist. I feel, have felt, unknown, without identity. This is why El Prado, the place of my self-discovery, and of my early vision has touched me so deeply this time." Ultimately, the lack of money made this desperate move impossible. It was a last attempt to recover the lost world of Taos, and it was the last time Goyen would see Brett. She died two years later, at the age of 93.

The Collected Stories

This unsettled trip to New Mexico bears a resemblance, in manner and tone, to one of Goyen's finest stories, written a year or so earlier. The narrator of "Bridge of Music, River of Sand" doesn't return to Taos, but he does revisit the landscape of his upbringing (and the spot that corresponds to Emma Goyen's near drowning in the Trinity River). On a "sentimental trip through home regions," this speaker is clearly unstable, hallucinating a naked diver who leaps from an old railroad bridge into a dry riverbed (CS 283). In the end he wanders away from this suicidal vision, shaken by his attempt to recover a past that seems to haunt rather than reassure. Goyen left New Mexico in much the same state of mind. The need to reconnect to old places was strong, but the pain and loneliness of his distance from Roberts, combined with his intensified depression at what he considered the failure of his writing, left him unmoored. He had become both the naked diver and his troubled witness, desperately seeking a lost fertility but finding nothing to nourish his recovery.

His distress had not gone unnoticed, of course, even in the months and years leading up to his suicide attempt. A few years before the crisis in Newport Beach, Goyen's nephew Don Gerrard, who ran The Bookworks publishers in Berkeley, persuaded Random House to copublish a collection titled *Selected Writings of William Goyen: Eight Favorites by a Master American Storyteller*.[10] The 1974 volume included excerpts from *The House of Breath*, *In a Farther Country*, and *The Fair Sister*, along with stories from *Ghost and Flesh* ("The White Rooster," "Ghost and Flesh, Water and Dirt") and *The Faces of the Book Kindred* ("Old Wildwood," "A People of Grass"). The story "Figure over the Town" rounded out the volume, for which Goyen wrote a brief but revealing introduction. In very spare prose he set out a basic autobiographical narrative, describing his childhood psychology as "quick and scared; serving,

secretly unsettled; imaginative and nervous and sensual." His conception of his own writing, what shapes and drives it, was both resigned
and determined:

> It was clear to me now: I saw my life as a writing life, a life of giving
> shape to what happened, of searching for meanings, clarification, En-
> tirety. It was my Way: expression in words. From then on, I managed to
> write, with little or no money, with growing distinction—which, I have
> come to see, brings little usable reward—awards, honors, little money.
> What I wanted was to make splendor. What I saw, felt, knew was real,
> was more than what I could make of it. That made it a lifetime task, I
> saw that.[11]

Another opportunity to reflect and make a statement about the
goals and shape of his career came soon after, thanks to Robert Phillips.
After the publication of *Come, the Restorer*, Goyen was still under contract with Doubleday for a novel and his projected memoir. Because of
his inconsistent productivity, he was in near despair at having nothing ready to show his editors. He had originally planned to complete
Six Women but had produced only a few sketches. On his own initia-
tive, Phillips gathered all of Goyen's stories that had been published
in magazines and previous collections, made photocopies, and presented the manuscript as a surprise for his friend's birthday. A tearful
Goyen was stunned, grateful, and relieved to submit the text in February of 1975 to Doubleday, who forgave him the other contract.[12] Again
he wrote a brief but significant preface for the book, in which he out-
lined his basic conception of the short story: "I have felt the short-story
form as some vitality, some force that begins (and not necessarily at
the *beginning*), grows in force, reaches a point beyond which it cannot
go without losing force, loses force and declines; stops. For me, story
telling is a rhythm, a charged movement, a chain of pulses or beats. To
write out of life is to catch, in pace, this pulse that beats in the material
of life" (*CS* x). The reliance on metaphors from music stands out most
clearly in this clarifying account. A story is a rhythm, and its telling
embodies its pulse in a performative language that implies a listener:

> But for me, as I have written, I've been mainly interested in the teller-
> listener situation. Somebody is telling something to somebody: an

event! Who's listening to this telling? Where is the listener? I've not been interested in simply reproducing a big section of life off the streets or from the Stock Exchange or Congress. I've cared most about the world in one person's head. Most, then, I've cared about the buried song in somebody, sought it passionately; or the music in what happened. (CS x)

In part because his method was so intuitive, Goyen was not given to fully developed theoretical statements about his work. Consequently, this preface is a crucial record of the kind of thinking that led to some of the most arresting short fiction of the twentieth century. Again, the indirect evocation of the cardboard piano is crucial here: the story and its telling are moments of witness that emerge out of an enforced silence; the listener must be present to hear and recognize—to attest to and register—the self, the identity telling the story. In this sense, to care about "the world inside one person's head" is not a solipsism but an absolute claim on the value—and validity—of inwardness. That such a telling remains tangled in the processes of music merely suggests that all intimate revelations remain partially concealed or, to use a different Goyen metaphor, unthawed.

There are 26 stories in all in *The Collected Stories*, including the first two collections plus a few ungathered texts and sections of *Half a Look of Cain*. The response to the volume, though not without the occasional reservation, was warm, admiring, and respectful in a way Goyen had seldom experienced in his career. Two reviews stand out: Richard Rhodes's deeply sympathetic reading in the *Chicago Tribune* and Joyce Carol Oates's penetrating and reverential response in the *New York Times Book Review*. Rhodes emphasized the recurrence of the idea of "breath" throughout Goyen's work, a body of writing he considered "extraordinarily subtle," a successful blending of "the folk tale with the abbreviation of the modern short story." Unlike so many reviewers in the past, he accepted Goyen's symbolic method as essential to the nature of his writing: "Goyen's symbolism is uncanny, ghostly, breath-like too, displaced by his quality of vision from the ordinary. . . . He is not deliberately obscure, but he is writing about qualities of memory and feeling, shifts in loyalty and love, that ordinarily function or occur outside any frame of words." This tendency to reach beyond articulation Rhodes perceptively located in Goyen's combination of "mature experience with childhood memory, which may stand for the juncture in the life of every child where what was wordless begins to come into words. At that juncture Goyen does his work, there and at the juncture, which parallels the childhood one, between words as music and words as sense."[13] Oates offered a similar generosity of attention based on the acceptance of Goyen's distinctive gifts, "that curious blend of the surreal and the tender, the nightmarish and the visionary." Perhaps even more gratifying to Goyen, she recognized his consistent mastery of "the form of the short story" and placed him at the root of midcentury writing: "One can see, for instance, how Flannery O'Connor must have learned from 'The White Rooster,' and it is quite likely that many other writers have learned from Goyen to seek out what he calls 'the buried song' in their characters." She urged readers to be patient with these lyric evocations, to read them aloud if possible and repeatedly in order to let their meanings emerge, in order to appreciate "their musical, delicate authority, their evocation of transient, visionary moments that might otherwise be lost in that large 'disorder' of the world."[14]

Goyen was "overwhelmed" by Oates's "rich and full and tender" reading of his work. "I read it all in one gulp," he wrote to Phillips, "now I'll savor it piecemeal and slowly. I never expected such thorough, careful attention."[15] It must have been doubly a surprise since prior to this review he had tended to see Oates as part of the literary establishment that had excluded him. Along with John Updike, she symbolized a kind of success he still longed for, and in his darker, often alcoholic moments he wasn't above lashing out at anyone who seemed to have the recognition he felt he lacked.[16] But a touching reaction to his work, like that of Richard Rhodes, moved him to contact and, if possible, form a new relationship of allies: "I sent him a note," Goyen explained to Phillips, "and today he answered with an equally loving letter. . . . He's marvelous—a new discovery."[17]

Goyen could add the good feeling generated by *The Collected Stories* to another honor that occurred earlier in the year. It had been twenty-five years since the publication of *The House of Breath*, and Random House in conjunction with Don Gerrard's Bookworks had decided to issue a new "Silver Anniversary" edition of the novel with an event to honor its classic status. "People (critics, writers, editors) are writing from all over," Goyen wrote to Maurice Edgar Coindreau, "and a great ad will be published. This makes me feel proud, shy and older! . . . There will be a reception at the Gotham Book Mart, and pieces in the *New York Times Book Review* and *Publisher's Weekly*."[18] This kind of attention was obviously welcome, particularly for a book that represented Goyen's earliest artistic impulse, and it was a pleasure to hear from old friends like James Leo Herlihy who wrote in with love and support. But as sometimes occurs with anniversaries, the marking of time showed its double edge: pride at a past accomplishment was mixed with anxiety about subsequent failures and present ambitions. One sign of his emotional unsteadiness may have been Goyen's willingness to alter the original edition of the novel to remove a few overt sexual references. For example, in section XII of the original text, during the long monologue about his past, Christy describes wandering through Shreveport in a cold rain and coming upon a park:

> [The place] seemed like the very patch of Hell where there was couples whisperin, men to men and men to women, and I went into a city toilet and saw drawn pricks hangin long on the wall and messages of lovers left for lovers written there; and crap from the toilets erupted up onto the floor and I had trod in it. Then I came out and felt alone and lost in the world with no home to go home to and I felt robbed of everthing I never had but dreamt of and hoped I could have, I felt fouled by the filth of what men leave and had left behind them; and then I thought, "Oh I am young and have somethin to give and to be used and to write on a wall." (*HOB* 166)

In the revised version, Christy walks "upon a park that seemed like the very patch of Hell where there were couples whisperin, men to men and men to women. Then I felt alone and lost in the world with no home to go home to and I felt robbed of everthing I never had but dreamt of and hoped I could have; and then I thought, 'O I am young and have somethin to give and to be used.'"[19] As Reginald Gibbons explains in his afterword to the restored, fiftieth-anniversary edition of the novel, these "minor changes and deletions . . . seem unnecessary," and the thinking behind them may have been compromised by Goyen's lack of confidence in his work (*HOB* 189–190). It is difficult to believe that this particular cut was motivated by sexual squeamishness, particularly after the Rabelaisian frankness of *Come, the Restorer* released the year before, but there may have been something about the scene (the conjunction of sexual loneliness and human waste?) that Goyen found distasteful after so many years.

If the *Collected Stories* and the reissue of *The House of Breath* prompted greater retrospection in Goyen's sixtieth year, the interview by Phillips for the *Paris Review* could only have intensified it. Conducted that June at Phillips's house in Katonah, New York, the discussion ranged widely over Goyen's biography and ideas about writing. For the first time, under extensive questioning, he offered penetrating descriptions of his early experiences in Houston and Taos and crystallized some of his intuitions about form. In an inspired moment, while discussing his approach to the novel, he conjured up the image of a quilt: "But it seems to me that the unified novel, the organic entity that we call a novel, is a series of parts. How could it not be? I generally make the parts the way you make those individual medallions that go into quilts. All separate and as perfect as I can make them, but knowing that my quilt becomes a whole when I have finished the parts. It is the design that's the hardest. Sometimes it takes me a long time to see, or discover, what the parts are to form or make" (GAE 97). The textile metaphors from *Half a Look of Cain* and *In a Farther Country* emerge more clearly here to ground Goyen's sense of the spatial arrangement of narrative fragments. (The image also recalls his encounter with the Elgin Marbles and his notion of writing as a "frieze of words.") Combined with his cherished conception of writing as song—and his books as song cycles—this homespun analogue reveals a great deal about the lyric and narrative impulses he often sought to reconcile. Time (in the form of story) seems here contained in a pattern that is both fragmentary and meaningful—but that ultimately allows for a kind of keeping or saving, a blanket of memory to be stored in a chest, held onto, or passed on.

The interview also reveals Goyen's talent as a raconteur and sharp-edged gossip. The sequence recounting his friendship with Carson McCullers is both funny and malicious, a condescending portrait of a writer he often grouped with Capote as both a competitor and subject of envy. He was fond of stating the difference between his Texan or southwestern roots and "Southernness," what he here calls "those sicknesses and terrors that come from the Deep South" (*GAE* 95). As is clear from his review of *Breakfast at Tiffany's*, he worked consistently to separate himself from what he considered the glittering but insubstantial delicacy of Dixie kitsch.[20] In his more despairing moments, it never ceased to gall him that writing he thought inferior—less serious, with less at stake—could be seen as more important than his own.

Of course, good interviews can sometimes produce inadvertent self-description, and in his attempt to capture McCullers's weaknesses Goyen may have clarified one of his own. Asked by Phillips whether she could have written an autobiography, he replied: "She did not have 'a hold of herself,' as a person would say, enough to look back and see herself in situations. She never could have written an autobiography; it would be impossible for her . . . she had disguised herself so much . . . And what a past, you know? Her mother . . . the Mother of *all* these people . . . Thank God mine seems to be quite okay—I'd be raving mad at this point" (*GAE* 88–89). Though he did attempt an autobiography and would ultimately produce potent sketches such as "Margo," the echo of Goyen's own complications shadows this analysis. His very real difficulties with his mother are too easily discounted here, and he allows his own disguises—subtle and various as they were—to slip behind the vivid account of McCullers's eccentricities. Though everyone quietly edits his past, it is worth noting that Goyen makes no mention of Berns, even in the context of Taos, avoids his affair with Spender, and similarly elides Joe Glasco. Given his marriage and potential privacy concerns, these omissions are understandable, but they also underline a sometimes fierce desire to control his public reputation.[21] In this respect, his account of a weakened McCullers may have allowed him to strengthen his own self-esteem at a time when his confidence, despite mounting honors, remained low.

In retrospect, 1975 should have been one of the best years of Goyen's life, at least in terms of recognition offered for his life's work. But by its end, he considered it one of the worst. To Phillips, he described his sixtieth as "a just-about totally negative year. . . . What I thought was my most distinguished book and certainly one of the most distinguished books in American books in decades got not one distinction given it—Zero."[22] Neither *Come, the Restorer* nor the *Collected Stories* was issued in paperback; despite strong reviews overall for the latter, sales were apparently poor. Goyen was also despondent over how the books themselves were produced. He considered the bindings to be cheap and shabby and consistently felt that Doubleday had failed to publicize his work adequately. The year had been his bid for recognition and honors, and when the big prize or payoff failed to materialize, his mood turned darker.[23] His problems, of course, went much deeper than disappointment at his career, and it's hard to imagine a tangible reward that would have relieved his depression. His drinking, which had accelerated dangerously since the move to Los Angeles, made a clear reckoning of his pain impossible. In lucid moments, he did recognize the larger problem, though a solution seemed as far away as ever:

> In L.A., April 9, 1976
>
> My 60th year was one of my loneliest, my most displaced, my most orphaned and homeless. My fantasy was the same as that of my 16th, 17th, 18th year; my longing, my searchings, my pain, my lostness the same as in all my years. Age does not change these, in me. The same as on Merrill Street, long ago. (HRC 31.1)

"Runnin down those cold dark streets with God"

Roberts's account of Goyen's alcoholism in *Are You Hungry, Dear?*, while selectively detailed, makes clear the toll drinking had taken on him over the course of their marriage. Their relationship had begun "in a bar" and developed "over cocktails," and after a particularly sodden evening from which they both awoke "splayed around the floor [of their apartment] like victims of a car wreck," Roberts began to understand the situation. She gave up drinking, but Goyen did not: "Bill continued to drink, and, because I didn't, I saw his behavior much more clearly."[24] Admitting that Goyen "could be quite cruel" when he was drunk, she describes marital arguments with a resilient humor that belies what must have been deep pain and frustration. Goyen's work with a psychiatrist, who diagnosed depression, had little overall effect on these regular confrontations, and by the time the couple had settled in Los Angeles in the summer of 1975, Goyen's drinking had increased alarmingly. Not only did he feel isolated from his community of New York friends, but, as Roberts notes, Los Angeles reminded him of Houston: "He lived all the failures of his life anew, this time inflamed by the dry weather and palm trees of Los Angeles. The warm climate and vegetation are similar to that of his Texas home, a place that brought too many painful memories."[25] After spending his early life trying to escape from the repressive climate, both meteorological and psychological, of

East Texas, Goyen felt trapped in yet another sterile environment with nowhere to go and no way to live. He had graduated from martinis to straight vodka, and, according to Phillips, he basically "freaked out."[26]

The breaking point came later the next year. Roberts had begun attending Al-Anon meetings to better understand how to deal with the challenges of living with an alcoholic. After a particularly difficult evening during which Goyen had drunkenly accosted several guests at a party given by Norman Lear, she refused to argue about his behavior but let him give vent to his feelings:

> "I don't want to live," Bill said.
>
> "I know that, and there's nothing I can do to change that if that's how you feel," I said. "I wish I could. If there was something, I'd do it."
>
> "I write a book and what happens to it?" he said. "It gets taken off the press. I write another book and they don't even send it out for blurbs. It's like giving birth to these babies and they die. They're stillborn. You get up to the top of the mountain and you go sliding back down. And it takes everything in the world to come back up. You write the next one and nothing happens. Who knows when I will write another one? Who knows?"[27]

After a long night of frank discussion, Goyen called Alcoholics Anonymous the next day. Like all new attendees, he began going to meetings every day at first and kept track of his self-analysis in a notebook. In September he started a semester's teaching job at Princeton and began attending meetings in New York:

> Sept. 8. 6:15 Mustard Seed meeting, 122 E 3rd [St.]. Disappointing and cold; the leader, a woman bedecked with bracelets and chains of gold, presumed authority and gave an authoritative comment or dictum on following each person's story. She said our Higher Power could be anything—"an ashtray." The meeting seemed dark and lusterless, even spiritless, after, except for the face of Doris, a young black woman and the spirit of a beach man. Still, it was my fellowship, my family. (HRC 29.6)

"Fellowship" and "family" were clearly resonant and essential terms for Goyen, who had been writing about this kind of community of storytelling and self-repair for most of his career. The small groups of pained and displaced characters that fill *In a Farther Country* and "Tenant in the Garden," for instance, illustrate the idea that telling one's own story is fundamental to finding a place and creating a full and functioning identity. As Ernest Kurtz explains in his history of AA, this concept of personal narrative was central to the program's therapeutic strategy from the beginning: "The fellowship's faith in the efficacy of the telling by stories about personal experience was rooted in its memory of Bill Wilson's first call on Dr. Bob Smith. This faith in Word and Witness was also itself witnessed to by the 'story section' of its hallowed book, *Alcoholics Anonymous*." Storytelling, which was allied but not equated to confession, was a way of demonstrating acceptance (the acknowledgement of reality) and "limited control."[28] Combined with the somewhat secularized, structural elements of religious faith—the need for a "higher power," no matter how symbolic—this rigorous practice of telling and listening must have fit familiarly into Goyen's deep and recent memories of spiritual practice. There is no doubt that the experience at Weston and Goyen's subsequent engagement with the idea of Jesus had constituted an idiosyncratic return to his Methodist upbringing. However, these experiences, and the writing that followed, also reinforced his long-standing literary interest in the structures of salvation and rebirth. His approach to storytelling had always leaned on the concept of repair and restoration, the knitting together of broken fragments. Now this same impulse, to heal and save (in both senses), was realized in a much more mundane yet vital way.

The process of self-reflection encouraged by AA came naturally as well. In a large black notebook, Goyen recorded his attempts at a painful retrospection focused on his history of drinking. Those themes that had been obsessive in his work from the beginning—early exile, isolation, secrecy—now came to signify deeper causes of addiction: "Even then (back in Houston in the 1930s, fearful, terrified even, nervous, anxiety-ridden, yearning) I knew it was going to be too much to bear sooner or later and that I would seek oblivion somewhere, in some way. It was certain, to me, that I would not endure this pain always. I thought it would be early death. I, as I thought, finally reached for this oblivion, this self-effacement, in alcohol" (HRC 29.6). Certain elements recur in these accounts that echo significantly in Goyen's writing. His early work, particularly *Christopher Icarus*, had registered the burden of his perceived role as caretaker; the demands of relationships and family stood in opposition to independence and expression. Now he circled back to this central insight: "1. In childhood taught that my place was to take care of them. 2. Since childhood worry over others, anticipation, anxiety, fear, projection." He is drawn back to the phrase "nurse, saint & savior" several times in these accounts, and on an index card tucked into the notebook at some point sketched this pattern: "obcessive [*sic*] servitude and total surrender for years—to Joe, to marriage (*family pattern*). Led to *alcohol* to kill *feelings* (resentment, fear)—alcohol led me here" (HRC 29.6, original emphases). This demand for self-sacrifice, as Goyen felt it, then fed a penchant for secrecy and imaginative concealment: "1. Blanket over chairs—hidden world, exquisite aloneness. Self-pity, abasement, secretiveness. 2. What is 'reality'? I said. 'And *whose* reality? Who wants *that* reality. Let those others have that. I'll make my *own* reality" (HRC 29.6, original emphases). The image of the boy hiding under the blanket—whether to listen to music secretly because his father disapproved or later to write against that disapproval— remains powerful and important to these strained meditations. Goyen recognized the problematic connection between what he here calls his "alcoholic being" and his creative life. The secrecy had been a response that later developed into drinking, but it also created what was unique and sustaining about his art. The drive to make his own reality, to build another world that hides from and confronts his life, was both creative and destructive, a way to live and a way to die.

Precious Door: New Stories

Goyen attended AA faithfully for the rest of his life. On visits to far-flung campuses to give readings, he often asked those looking after him to drive him to local meetings, though he sometimes worried about what people would think when they found out he was an alcoholic.[29] Given his emotional fragility, maintaining sobriety was in no way easy; however, the benefits were soon evident in newly intense and inventive writing.[30] The first product of this rediscovered clarity was a story based on an image that had haunted him since *The Book of Jesus*. In the final section, "Words of Jesus," the first quotation he lists is from John 10:9: "I am the door: by me if any man enter in, he shall be saved, and shall go in and out, and find pasture." In his working notes on the experience at Weston, Goyen seems possessed by this familiar metaphor, as though seizing on it—truly seeing into it—for the first time:

> Here I am, standing before you, Like you said for me, I am a door for you. Open me! And walk through me! Free, unlocked, unbound. I, the door, need to be opened, too. Who understands a door? And if you walk through me, to your own, standing only one minute in me to see the openness before you, then I shall have come to my own too: open and unlocked and unbound, feeling you pass through me. Something of me will pass through, with you, and in you. We will both be open, and free. I am a door, I am a door, I am a door. (HRC 10.7)

The sense of discovered space—of liberation—is palpable here, as though the boy under the blanket had come to see a way out that no longer involved keeping secrets. Jesus-as-door is a near double to the constrained seeker, needing passage in order to share a new reality. The door is thus more than a figure for Jesus's instrumental function as sacrifice or "way" to salvation. The "I" and "the door" are companions, necessary to one another, bound in a relationship that allows one to transport the other.[31]

"Precious Door," the story that emerged from these meditations, is one of Goyen's deepest and most brooding. Grounded in his East Texas boyhood, the simple account records the memory of a hurricane that hit the narrator's hometown when he was twelve years old. In the yellow stillness preceding the storm, the narrator's younger brother finds a young man lying in a nearby field. The father realizes that this unconscious stranger is wounded, and with his son's help he takes in the body and begins to wash and treat the stranger's injuries. Soon the wind begins to blow, and for their protection all of the family except the father and son leave for the shelter at the local high school. The stranger's injury is grave, and despite attentive nursing, he soon dies:

> My father prayed over the young man, laying his carpenter's hand on the brow of the suffering man and clasping his hand in love and hope. And then I heard my father's words, "He's dead."
>
> We said the Lord's prayer together on our knees by the dead stranger's pallet. The rhythmic clanging of the wind against something of metal, our washtub maybe, tolled over our prayer. (*HHM* 43)

As the storm hits and the roads and fields begin to flood, a second wanderer appears at the window, "a figure of flying hair and tearing clothes with wild eyes and a face of terror" (*HHM* 44). This is the dead man's older brother. The two had been riding boxcars from Memphis to Houston, perhaps to find work on a ship and travel the world. But they had argued, and the older had stabbed the younger in a rage. Distraught with grief, the guilty brother insists on taking the body back out into the storm, and in the flooding aftermath days later the narrator hears strange tales of "a floating door bearing the bodies of two men . . . moving on the wide river through several towns." This odd vessel is last seen riding perilously into the Gulf of Mexico, topping "the crests of dangerous rapids so serenely that it was easy to see the two men, one, alive and fierce, holding the other, dead" (*HHM* 47).

On a basic level, "Precious Door" captures a heightened and intimate moment between a father and son. The storm and the wounded stranger bring the two together, creating a tight, dramatic space that allows the narrator to see his father's tenderness in a moment of true charity. Father and son "nurse" the wounded man, and the son notices his "father's face" filling "with softness" in the firelight (*HHM* 42–43). In effect, the narrator is able to observe—and later remember—a demonstrated warmth and love often absent from Goyen's fictional fathers. And yet despite this loving retrospect, an undercurrent of loneliness and desire pulls at the boy's feelings: he can see his father's gentleness toward the stranger, but he also intuits that the stranger foreshadows his own future, away from family, possibly estranged, searching for someone to love: "I felt for the first time the love that one person might have for another he did not know, for a stranger come suddenly close. . . . And I hoped then, with a longing that first touched me there on that wild and tender night in our faraway parlor in that hidden little town, that one day I would know the love of another, no matter how bitter the loss of them would be" (*HHM* 43). The two brothers are thus another kind of example, of how intimacy might be offered and shared, even if it ends in sorrow and violence. As Ben—the older, Cain-like murderer—gently rocks the body in his arms, the boy feels his father's arm around him and understands the contrast between his fragile but sheltered childhood and his uncertain and painful future: "I felt my everlasting love for him, my father, but in my head rang Ben's words, *we had a plan*. My blood rushed in exciting hope. And that hope was that one day I would have enough courage to be this tender as this man was now at this moment, if ever I was lucky enough to find someone who would take my tenderness. And to have, together with someone, a plan" (*HHM* 45–46).

The image of the two brothers leaving in the storm—and later caught together on the door floating toward the sea—registers the tragic loss in love as well as its power to recover or reconcile. The term "reconciliation" had become important for Goyen, and his reliance on it here indicates the shift in attitude that his AA experience had begun to produce. Though the general concept may have arisen out of program material, it is more likely that he found it in Paul Tillich's *The New Being*, which he began reading shortly after his first meetings. In the second chapter of this collection of sermons, Tillich describes the "New Being" as the product of a kind of "*re*-newal: The threefold '*re*,' namely, *re*-conciliation, *re*-union, *re*-surrection."[32] A reconciliation with God is necessary because we feel fundamentally inadequate to His demands and therefore "hostile" to our existence. In language that must have resonated with Goyen, Tillich describes a familiar pattern of modern alienation: "Everybody carries a hostility towards the existence into which he has been thrown, toward the hidden powers which determine his life and that of the universe, toward that which makes him guilty and that threatens him with destruction because he has become guilty." This hostility is directed both inward and outward, toward the self and others: "Be reconciled to God; that means at the same time, be reconciled to ourselves. But we are not; we try to appease ourselves. . . . And he who feels rejected by God and who rejects himself feels also rejected by others. . . . We tried hard to make ourselves acceptable to them, and we failed. And their and our hostility grew. Be reconciled to God—that means, at the same time, be reconciled with the others!"[33]

In the story the father becomes the voice for this kind of healing. After the brothers disappear into the storm, he tells his son that "the love of God works through reconciliation," which he describes as "coming back together in peace" (*HHM* 46, 47). The door on which the brothers move becomes the image for this tragic recovery of kinship, a togetherness possible, the image implies, only because of, or through, death itself. The implication for Goyen was powerful. On the one hand, the story implies a kind of recovery and rejoining with Charlie Goyen similar to the one he imaginatively constructed in "The Beleek Swan."

Here as there, the father often seen as callous or cold is instead warm, thoughtful, and caring. Father and son find a togetherness rarely possible in life, bound through the needs of a stranger. In this sense, "Precious Door" is part of the long mourning for his father that continued in the 1978 lecture "While You Were Away" and suggests a still-fresh need to revisit this relationship in the hope of belated repair. At the same time, the story of the two brothers closely reflects Goyen's separation from Walter Berns, a deep wound that began to resurface more clearly during his later years. The two young men with a plan to travel enact the close bond and eventual falling out between the veterans who built the house in El Prado, a story repeated by Goyen's relationship with Glasco.[34] Reconciliation thus implied finding an image that could hold, in charged tension, the continued grief of Goyen's deepest losses. In this way, the door serves as both an opening and closing, a chance to signal release from burdens, freedom from pain, while opening the self to a new life.

"Precious Door" accomplishes these deeply personal goals through a rigorous purification of story to the terms of myth. In this case, the pattern follows closely the structure of the divine visit, the narrative sequence common in biblical and classical literature that depicts the appearance to humble people of a god in disguise. Goyen may have been familiar with Ovid's rendition of the visit of Jove and Mercury to Philemon and Baucis, the poor, aged couple who give their best to these visitors and are rewarded for their piety. We can say with certainty that he knew Christian versions of the test of hospitality because his favorite Flaubert story, "La légende de St. Julien l'hospitalier," ends with the miraculous transformation of Julien via his embrace of Jesus, who is disguised as a leper. And no doubt his childhood Bible study would have made Matthew 25 reflexively familiar: "For I was ahungered, and ye gave me meat: I was thirsty, and ye gave me drink: I was a stranger, and ye took me in: Naked, and ye clothed me; I was sick, and ye visited me: I was in prison, and ye came unto me."[35] In "Precious Door," the father not only takes in the wounded stranger but also repeats the gesture of welcome so often underlined by these tales: "My father lifted up the stranger and carried him like a child inside the house to the parlor, where few people went. It was a cool shadowy room used only for special occasions. It looked like my father wanted to give the wounded man the best we had to give" (HHM 42). To give the stranger one's best, even though meager, indicates a humble piety, a recognition of the value of others and the fragility of human connection.

According to Patrice Repusseau, who saw early versions of the manuscript, the most revelatory and powerful moment of "Precious Door"—when the father looks at the dead stranger and says, "He looks like somebody"—originally read, "He looks like Jesus Christ."[36] The revision is significant not only for its technical virtue (the less definite "somebody" engages a larger mystery) but also because Goyen has imagined this visit as more than a Christian parable. The younger brother suggests both Christ and Abel, both divine guest and brother sacrificed in a struggle with his darker part. The recognition of the value of the stranger, the loving ability to welcome others beyond the bounds of kinship, has the power to reconcile not only brother to brother but father to son and past to present. The self-acceptance Goyen found and promoted in *The Book of Jesus*, in other words, could now extend outward to heal those deep breaches with others that had long troubled him. It could even offer the possibility of bridging the gap to his own childhood, addressing if not erasing the pain of his separation and the loss of home he had felt so keenly as a child because of the move from Trinity to Houston.

As Repusseau aptly puts it, "Precious Door" inaugurated what might be called Goyen's late style: "the more acute bareness . . . , the new driving urgency, and the intensity of feeling that are among [its] trademarks."[37] It was a significant opening tale that Goyen later envisaged as the title story of a collection of post-AA writing, but even more important, it indicated a new gravity, a kind of intensified stillness in his work that coincided with sobriety. "Bridge of Music, River of Sand" may have shown some of this mythic distillation, but its stress and anxiety seem unrelated to the slow dwelling and rich figuration that "Precious Door" gives us. There is a meditative patience here that feels unprecedented for Goyen. If his compositional method had long been dependent upon waiting for voices to speak, those voices had found a new calm, a clarified quiet unlike anything he'd heard before.

"Arthur Bond"

The set of new stories of which "Precious Door" was a part included early versions of the novel *Arcadio* and the related, masterful short story "In the Icebound Hothouse." This burst of productivity also brought forth a trio of tales loosely connected to Goyen's alcoholism and his perennial struggles with sexuality and self-healing. "Where's Esther," for instance, comments most directly on the transformative powers of alcohol in the form of the flamboyant Esther Haverton, an inveterate drinker who breathes boozy inspiration into every party she attends. Her personality is rude and uproarious, but when she goes on the wagon, she shrinks into dullness: "If I didn't know her so well," the still bibulous narrator complains, "I'd say she was a changeling—that somebody kidnapped Esther and replaced her with a blah stranger. . . . This calm person lying there is not Esther. As though she existed out of booze. Vodka made Esther!" (*HHM* 37). The story presents sobriety as necessary but puzzling and grim. When the narrator herself goes "on an alcohol-free diet," she starts "feeling crazy. Nerves jumping out of my skin; rattling the coffee cup. And who sleeps?" (*HHM* 38). Goyen's own lack of sleep was a persistent problem during this period, and he seems here to be meditating on the tragicomedy of a newly sober outlook, as though he recognized the need to learn an entirely new way of living: "Oh, I think I need some help. I don't know what to do. If I drink I'm like a bad Esther—and anyway, what's a drink without her? If I don't drink, I'm like Esther now, drab, dull, dead, plain. Will somebody please tell me what to do?" (*HHM* 39).

"Where's Esther" tries on a gossipy woman's voice similar to Goyen's mimicry of Katherine Anne Porter in "At Lady A's." The more substantial "The Texas Principessa" conjures a close counterpart: voluble, intimate, the distracted but almost nonstop tattle of a middle-aged woman in Texas high society. This narrator tells how she inherited a Venetian palazzo from an old friend, a Texas heiress who had married an Italian prince. But her unfiltered stream of anecdote and gossip often loops back on itself, forgetting its trajectory and losing its place. Her always-reliable home base is the refrain, "That ever happen to you?," a question not always logical in its placement but uttered as though to provide a resting point and take note of her listener.

The story she eventually tells, of Horty Solomon living grandly in Venice, hosting a variety of flamboyant guests after her husband's death, would be little more than a splash of garish Texas color were it not for Horty's unexpected death, a poisoning brought about by a spider that emerges from the heart of a "perfect" summer peach: "Guess where the spider was? In a peach. Living at the core of a great big beautiful Italian peach from the sea orchards of the Mediterranean. . . . When she broke the peach open out sprung the horrible black spider. I saw it in a flash. And before she knew it, it had stung her into the bloodstream of her thigh, right through pure silk Italian brocade" (*HHM* 26). Goyen pursues this classic image of death curled silently within the seed of beauty even further. For not only does the Texas Principessa receive a fatal bite—a sexual sting that suggests a delicate excess of eroticism turned against her—but the spider reproduces her extravagance in the design of its web "sparkling in the dew" with "diamonds and rubies and emeralds—like something Horty would have worn" (*HHM* 28). Though the narrator seems unaware of this warning, except as a vague feeling of unease, the web serves as an analogue of the palazzo and perhaps of Venice itself. Not quite a Goyenesque revision of Thomas Mann, "The Texas Principessa" records a death in Venice that feels naturalistic and self-induced, a darkly comic encounter with the terrible turning of pleasure.

The third of these brief, highly vocalized tellings, "Arthur Bond," gathers the themes of the first two and transforms them into one of Goyen's most compelling, if very short, short stories. Perhaps an adumbration of Blake's "The Sick Rose" or Hawthorne's "Egotism; or, The Bosom Serpent," this baleful legend condenses the idea of inner conflict to the disturbing image of a worm that lives inside a man's thigh. Picked up in the "swampland of Louisiana when he was a young man," the apparently willful parasite gradually begins to control its host: "Sometimes for quite a spell Arthur Bond said it stayed peaceful, other times twas angry in him and raised hell in him, twas mean then and on some kind of rampage Arthur Bond said, stung him and bit him and burnt him, Arthur Bond said, and itched and tickled and tormented him" (*HHM* 29). An updated version of Granny Ganchion's Old Fuzz, the talking worm of sin and sex that lurks in her basement, Bond's tormentor is similarly humanoid with a "pretty" face "like a little doll's" (*HHM* 30). It once emerged from Bond's knee, but when the doctors tried to pull it out the head broke off. They preserved it in a jar through which the face could be seen "lolling in its fluid" (*HHM* 30). The remaining "headless worm" burrows deeper into Bond's leg and groin, its "vile tail" possibly "curled around his balls" (*HHM* 31). No longer just a disturbing inhabitant, it becomes the motivating force of Bond's existence:

"Worm took over his life, commanded his life, he had a devil in him, a rank, vile headless devil in him, directing his life" (*HHM* 30). Eventually Bond drinks rat poison to try to kill himself and the worm, but the attempt only rouses his demon to vengeance, and in a fury of whipping and writhing Bond finally dies "rank green and foaming" (*HHM* 31). The headless worm survives, however, inside the dead body, now lashed into a casket that leaps and bumps with the crazed energy of its contents. In essence, the worm has consumed Bond, become Bond, and the man's body is nothing more than a "costume" for the powerful demon inside him (*HHM* 32).

As in all of Goyen's stories, "Arthur Bond" is told by a voice, in this case an urgent, prophetic speaker probing the meaning of the unsettling figure in his mind. Haunted by the image, the idea of invasion, the speaker tries to transform it, see into its sinful shape the possibility of Christian reversal, the *felix culpa*:

> . . . living power of Arthur Bond living on in my mind has begun to make me wonder something about him, something sweet about him, like he is a kind of Saint in my mind, kind of an angel; maybe twas hand of God put a struggle in Arthur Bond to pull him and throw him and lay him down, to show His mighty works like the Scriptures say, and finally let him go on, free, finally, to a new life hereafter and a better one; had to be better, couldn't be worse'n what he had, pore Arthur Bond, was kind of a Saint; was worm God's worm? (*HHM* 32)

Despite the sacrificial logic of the fortunate fall, this question remains unanswered. The resonance of Arthur Bond's story combined with the tenuous emotional state of the speaker provide little more than a desperate solace. Faith is held up as a final protective gesture against an all-too-real and present confusion: "Did God put a worm in a man's thigh to show me something, used a worm to show me something and to win eternal life for a man in the hereafter, to be a Saint, to be an Angel, my God the workings of Jehovah's ways, a worm to make an Angel, oh Lord why is there so much darkness in this life before we see the light of things your ways are strange your ways are dark before we see the light" (*HHM* 33).

Goyen's later understanding of lust as "demonic" is worth reemphasizing and repeating here: "The lust is the very devil working, a demon in me—*my* lust. I don't know about anybody else's. I've had a demon in me" (*GAE* 126). "Arthur Bond," in its simplest sense, might be considered a development of this idea, but its oddity of detail prevents it from falling into easy allegory. Bond's worm may be a figure of lust, as well as the range of destructive emotions that accompany it, but it rests on the tenuous psychology of its teller, a destabilized and hungry seeker who seems more than capable of ascetic hallucination. The strained "saintly figure"—again, evoking Julien in his visionary extremity—*sees* allegorically, dreams in images that mix the modern and medieval. And it is this urgency of the spiritual search, the unstable questioning of a dark dream, that gives "Arthur Bond" its weird power. Out of the deepest despairs and perplexities of his own life, Goyen had begun to infuse his storytelling gifts with a new but curiously premodern intensity. He had come closer than ever to one of his deepest, though sometimes unconscious, goals—telling, indeed embodying, the life of a tested "saint." In the manuscript materials surrounding *Arcadio*, he tried to capture this complex of strangeness and eros:

> In sex, no one is immune to the allure of *otherness*
> ecstatic memory // erotic saintly figures
> rhapsodic memory // eroticized saintly figures
> erotic heroic figure
> figure of grandeur (HRC 7.8)

CHAPTER FIFTEEN

The Nurseryman
1976–1982

Across the icebound bottomlands, over the sleeted slues,
With beak of horn and hornéd nails, chiming his terrible Midnight,
Grinds the bird of fire whose prey we are.
His image in the rime of the bog is rainbow . . .
We are Beast, we are Prince, we are Heartbreak,
We are destiny of fire, we are ashes and cinders,
O artifices of fire and breath, grinding in our own ruin's cinders
Under a moon of breath and smoke blown across a sky of ice.

"THE BIRD OF FIRE," 1949

Since the autumn of 1976, Goyen had been living part of the year in his New York apartment, which he and Roberts maintained even after the move to California, so that he could commute a few days a week to teach at Princeton.[1] As he had done since the mid-1950s, he relied on occasional visiting appointments to help bring in income, but by all accounts, teaching meant much more to him than just a paycheck. In the first place, it brought him into contact with other writers, something he missed acutely during his time in Los Angeles. It also provided opportunities to inspire and mentor young artists in a way that recalled his own relationships to important figures in his life such as Frieda Lawrence and Ernst Robert Curtius. Those who worked closely with Goyen at Brown or Princeton or Hollins College (and later at Stephens College and USC) describe him as an extraordinary teacher, a riveting presence in the classroom who gave time and attention to his students far in excess of what was required. This attention to others, always a feature of his personality but intensified by his sobriety, went well beyond teaching; it extended to a large number of friends and colleagues who were often astonished by Goyen's warmth and care.

One of Goyen's Princeton students, the novelist Madison Smartt Bell, remembers a kind, gentle-voiced presence who suffered from insomnia but seemed surprisingly open and vulnerable. What Bell took to be an almost shocking unguardedness emerged most clearly during a reading Goyen gave of a work in progress: "What he had in his hand at the time," Bell remembers, "were some pages of longhand manuscript, heavily written and rewritten, like a palimpsest. We could see through the paper when he held it to the light. His voice was a rich and delicately tuned instrument, but he was not performing with it very deliberately. Often he would interrupt himself and talk at some length about difficulties he was having with the work. When he did so he would look all around and try to meet our eyes and hold them. At times it seemed as though he would weep."[2] The display both shocked and impressed Bell, who confessed to difficulties reading his own work in public. In fact, it was his own avoidance of a public reading that provoked Goyen's anger at him "for the first and only time." To get out of presenting his fiction at a student reading, Bell asked a friend to read it for him, but the "stunt . . . truly and deeply disgusted" Goyen. "For once," Bell explains, "he did not hesitate about letting me know. I hadn't seen any problem with the scheme when I came up with it but when he talked to me I saw that it was craven and contemptible, something I ought to be ashamed of, and I was ashamed."[3] Goyen's vision of writing as not merely serious but desperately personal, necessary, and inescapably one's own made him a sometimes mesmerizing figure to many of his students over the years. As he had during his publishing days, he could provide the kind of help editors and teachers typically offer (technical advice, careful criticism), but it was his fierce commitment and high artistic faith that students and colleagues remembered.

Bell's reminiscence also provides a glimpse into Goyen's personal challenges during these AA years. The insomnia, which was related to his recent sobriety, may have been fueled by renewed anger at his publishers and the still-painful question of where to live. The handling of *Come, the Restorer* had bewildered and infuriated him, particularly after he was informed by Doubleday that it planned to shred several thousand copies. He angrily broke off relations with Sam Vaughan and

Stewart Richardson, the trade editor at Doubleday. "My disappointment has grown over the years," he stated with the fierce intensity of his customary self-defenses. "I have repeatedly made it known to you. The physical quality of my books—the tiny type face, the slim appearance, the flimsy binding, the cheap paper have embarrassed me. . . . The absence of advertisements, the failure to reprint my books, the pitiful handling of my last novel, *Come, the Restorer,* the lack of energy and interest invested in all of my books . . . should be sufficient evidence to embarrass you and bring you relief at being shed of me."[4] The site of a "mountain of the novel," as he explained to his agent Roberta Pryor, "heaped under a pert sign that said, 'Books for a Buck'" at the local Barnes and Noble had sent him further into a sorrowful panic. "[W]hat was so bad was that my photo covering the back was displaying leeringly."[5]

This reaction should be understood as more than just disappointment at poor sales. There was a sense in which the "lostness" of Goyen's books reinforced or restated his basic sense of rejection and isolation, present since childhood. To write, to tell was in one respect a way to exist in his stories and the books made from them; to see these products of his painful effort destroyed meant that he (his work) was no longer present; he did not belong, as he often suggested in his notes; he was not "welcome." A year or so after this incident, while teaching at Hollins College, he recorded a dream:

Hollins, March 14, 1979

A dream of inhospitality—even of rejection—of a spectacular feast to which I was not wholly welcomed—the hostess reluctantly admitted me. I came with a friend. The hostess must have been jealous of me; my feeling was that she did not want to share with me the voluptuous feast she was cooking; vast chunks of rosy chicken—taller than she—a wall of rosy chicken turning on a spit; and all kinds of colored foods, and piles of grain and dried fruits (raisins, etc.) that I scooped with my hands. There were very large deep bowl-like plates and people began to fill them and eat out of them; and although no one invited me to take a plate I finally did, and filled it and ate, quite timidly, ate it, feeling apart and slightly [illegible word] strangely—unwanted. The feast was rich and splendid and voluptuous and highly colored. (HRC 28.1)

It isn't necessary to have a precise identification of this "spectacular feast" to see in it Goyen's original sense of exile brought forward to the present. He often fell back to the phrase "turned away" in these notebooks: turned away from home, from welcome in the literary world, from the generation of writers to which he should belong but did not. No doubt the difficulty of living in Los Angeles sometimes seemed an additional rejection, another isolation pulling him away from the world whose approval he still sought.

In many respects, that world meant New York, and his time at Princeton, although positive overall, may have ultimately made his adjustment to Los Angeles that much more difficult. Though he had found moments of easiness or even pleasure in Southern California, its dullness and monotony continued to weigh on him. (At one point in his notebooks he recorded a radio weather forecast for California: "Mostly the same." [HRC 28.1]). Even so, the journal for 1978 and 1979 suggests a slow shift under way, the sense that something new had begun to develop in Los Angeles, while New York represented an old life that he needed to relinquish. By the end of 1979, after a somewhat troubled trip to Europe with Roberts, he appears to have found a greater clarity on this still-nagging problem: "That living in this apartment is an old idea. That the old life is gone. That the new life for me, beginning with my rebirth, is in California. There I have, after pain, found new life and new work. To try to fall back, recapture, relive the old patterns of life here, feel the old feelings, brings pain that is old, that I do not have to feel again, brings old disturbances, old attitudes that I do not have to have again" (*GAE* 181).

In part, this new attitude reflected a shift in feelings recorded a year earlier in a remarkable extended journal entry headed "Christ in the Palm." In a few pages of ecstatic prose, Goyen recorded another transformative, mysterious moment of redemptive vision:

> This morning I have suddenly seen the palm. I touched the coarse animal hair, the leathery strips that wrap around and crisscross and bind like bindings {on} the loins of the gross, beast-like trunk of the palm. . . . I saw suddenly the power of the palm {and its mystery} and I suddenly remembered that the palm is Jesus' tree and branch and that its fronds were strewn on his path and that he carried it in his hand into the city on that Sunday before his death and new life five days later. (*GAE* 177)[6]

Until this point, the palm trees of Los Angeles had been objects of loathing to Goyen. As Roberts suggests, the climate and vegetation of southern California had probably been too reminiscent of the similarly tropical Houston, where a shorter and thicker species of tree is common. The lines of palms hovering high in the distances of L.A. seemed to embody the vapid and superficial world in which Goyen felt trapped. But in this moment of emergence from "sickness" and "deepest despair" after a "week-long insanity" (*GAE* 176), he found himself taken over by a rush of newness. As in Weston, this spiritual upwelling depended upon the sensual apprehension of a physical Jesus, this time bound up with the erotic shape and bodily substance of the palm:

> Jesus' palm, strange tree of humility and triumph, of pain and death, of surrender and victory. Bitter tree. Blessed leaf! Beast of the Apocalypse. Hairy and rough-sided, its coarse hair, sexual and bestial, its rough sides, its daggerlike leaves, toothed blades and saw-like branches edged with teeth of thorns, its ugly stumpish trunk, its ragged hangings rattling from its sides. Something of John the Baptist about it, fierce and soft, shaggy and wild. Something of St. Francis about it, ragged and beggary and {fierce and} meek. The palm—truly a being of the spirit, coarse and rough, forbidding, mystical, terrifying, even; a presence of humility, awe, holiness, of sexual lust and sexual beauty. (*GAE* 177)

Again echoing Julien's embrace of the leprous Jesus, Goyen imagines a similar transformative contact with the palm as Christly body.[7] Such a coupling, if offered "naked in humility and as an act of forgiveness," would be both a redemption and a crucifixion: "Oh terrible embrace—of the scaly leper, of the scabbed beggar! . . . Had I embraced Christ's body on the cross, the spiked and thorned body of Christ would have torn me. It was a harsh body then in its suffering, in its dying." But the cross also holds "the utmost tenderness, the softest flesh of new life and love and ultimate forgiveness" (GAE 177–178).

Wonderful Plant

This ecstatic moment of willful transformation suggests how deeply Goyen needed to resolve his estrangement from Los Angeles. Though there was probably no single moment of insight or revolution that removed all his objections to southern California, he did finally reconcile himself to the idea of living and working in the place he had disdained for so long. One practical move that helped with his writing was the decision to rent an office at the corner of Hollywood and Vine. Roberts had grown tired, as she explains, of keeping "a quiet house" and asked Goyen to find somewhere outside the home to work.[8] He agreed and in June 1979 started spending his days in a little office on the twelfth story of an old bank building in sight of the Hollywood Pantages Theater and Capitol Records building. The office had a view of the local hills and the San Gabriel mountains, often covered with snow. Surrounded by what Goyen described as "porno movie offices," the room contained little more than a table, a desk, and a day bed. He put together a small bookshelf to get his scattered reading off the floor and taped a handwritten note above his standing desk that said, "You do this because this is what you do."[9] "It's right smack in seedy old Hollywood," he explained to interviewer Patrick Bennett. "It's just wonderful. I begin work at home, because I don't much want to go down there at that hour, up at four-thirty at Quebec Drive, working back in a sitting room in our house until about seven. Then I get ready and go down to the office."[10]

Roberts suggests that the faded high-rise reminded Goyen enough of New York to give him the illusion of a familiar urban world: "He'd open the windows to hear the traffic and buses on that busy intersection and feel as though he had the best of New York in the middle of the beautiful Mediterranean climate of Los Angeles."[11] Though resistant at first, he did begin to appreciate the warm weather, and the quiet space above the street provided the kind of isolation and sovereignty of place that he needed in order to write. When not at work, principally on the material related to the emerging *Arcadio*, he read: biographies of artists were important to him at this time, perhaps suggesting a persistent interest in how others had managed their own creative struggles. There were lives of Piranesi, Liszt, Delacroix, Rembrandt, and Kierkegaard. Models were crucial; the need to push forward and keep his spirits up was always pressing:

—The attitude I find so hard to change about writing again: What's the use? Fighting—gently, *not* desperately bitterly—the feeling of failure in my work, that, again, it has come to nothing—everywhere, Europe,

New York, Texas—old, I thought, strongholds of my identity as an artist—nothing, all, it seems to me, faded out, turned back.

And here, in my old room on Hollywood and Vine again, I do not want to have the old feelings of failure and lostness; I have come through that; it is all new, I am new. My work will be new. (*GAE* 180)

This somewhat delicate mixture of depression and determination can be found in the small book *Wonderful Plant*, a children's story that Goyen published in a limited edition with Palaemon Press in 1980. Here one Tony Sepulveda, a lonely and depressed inhabitant of Los Angeles, befriends "two little green people" (insects) named Mr. and Mrs. Purple, who live in a large potted plant that "a friend had brought [Tony] in consolation" (*WP* 1). Tony explains to the Purples that he dislikes Los Angeles, which he calls "The Western Southland," because it is not his home: "I'm lonesome and out of place and homesick" (*WP* 2). But the Purples offer a kind of friendship and community, and Tony soon becomes engrossed in the complicated life inside the little world of the plant. The Purples are expecting a child and will soon have to retire into the plant for the birth, but before they do, they introduce Tony to the Order of Benevolent Insects, a "sort of Police, to protect [the plant] from dangerous and hostile enemies" (*WP* 11). The Order includes the Commander—"a spright man wearing vivid colors: red, purple, green"—an assortment of other brightly colored bugs, and Earth Worm, "the drabbest of all," who tries to equal the others in display by "applying a little purple eye make-up and a bit of rouge and lipstick" (*WP* 13).

Earth Worm suggests a comic version of Old Fuzz as well as Arthur Bond's doll-headed parasite; he is also quite clearly a Folneresque cross-dresser, a female impersonator whose "natural movement was a wiggle" (*WP* 13). He craves "creative expression" (*WP* 15) and seems incapable of following orders or fitting in with the squadron of insects. After an attack by a cutworm is thwarted thanks to an enormous, ugly creature named Child of Earth ("the gentlest, sweetest-natured being in all the kingdom"), the bugs put on a show to try to cheer up Tony Sepulveda, who can't sleep at night and has "bad depressions" (*WP* 20). Though ridiculed by most, Earth Worm, made-up and dressed as a woman, is determined to attempt a few bird calls, but the cursing of the imprisoned Cut Worm causes him to produce instead "what sounded exactly like a Bronx cheer or the air escaping from an inner tube" (*WP* 23). Humiliated, Earth Worm refuses to accept the idea that, despite his natural shape, he can't sound like a bird, and when asked what he wants out of life, replies, "'Everything . . . . And I'm going to get it. I just started late, that's all'" (*WP* 24).

The story concludes with a wedding and a birth. Cut Worm, arrested to prevent him from damaging the plant, explains that he was merely smuggling his sweetheart Alice Aphid into Wonderful Plant "to steal some of its juices" (*WP* 33). A court gathered for his trial decrees that the two should marry, but after a comic ceremony in which Cut Worm excitedly and accidentally cuts a leaf, the couple flee from the other bugs, and attention turns to the Purples's new baby. As the baby grows, the seasons shift, and the plant prepares for hibernation. Before all the creatures disappear, however, Tony meets the Keeper of the Bulb, Dr. Emmanuel Mole, a blind mystic who spends all his time studying the plant's regenerative source: "Yet in the winter comes a rebirth," he explains to the still-depressed Tony, "a resurrection of the leaves. Buds begin and it all shifts up and above again. Fabulous Bulb is radiating its vital force upward into life and fullness in the light. . . . It is pure seminal nature . . . pure *making* stuff of growth, knowing when to hold back and restrain vitality and when to break open and shoot forth itself" (*WP* 45).

With its strange and not always childlike comedy, *Wonderful Plant* seems more serious than it pretends to be. On the positive side, it demonstrates a return to the playfulness of imagination that Goyen could easily activate in his early years but that had weakened while he was drinking. The story suggests that he had recovered sufficient energy to produce what often reads like a delicate *jeu d'espirit*. On the other hand, it can be difficult to ignore the personal echoes in this little world of humanized insects. If Tony Sepulveda, mired in the "City of Sameness" (*WP* 41), is an obvious stand-in for the author, it's also clear that Earth Worm and even Cut Worm, who can't control his instincts, reflect familiar Goyen preoccupations. To know your own nature, this peculiar tale asserts, is absolutely essential, but to understand how it will be received by society can be just as important. Community, as Goyen had consistently stated for years, requires a kind of openness and welcome even to the strange and lost, and the world of *Wonderful Plant* provides these stabilizing, natural bonds, even for a lonely exile.

The Dark Host at the Door

Tending plants and other forms of gardening were important to Goyen. When the writer Erika Duncan visited him in his New York apartment in the early 1980s, she noticed how difficult it was to see out the windows "because of all the plants" and how Goyen seemed to be nursing "five luminous purple bulbs" that were emblems to him of "Easter and the time of resurrection."[12] The garden had been a consistent, traditional, and yet deeply personal image in his writing for years, from the fertile bottomlands of *The House of Breath* to the suburban retreat of "Tenant in the Garden" and the extraordinary mythic thicket of *Come, the Restorer*. This sequence of meditations on the properties of renewal—as well as the sometimes overripe sexuality that can emerge from such spaces—culminated in a story worked on throughout the later 1970s and published eventually in the journal *TriQuarterly* in 1982.[13] "In the Icebound Hothouse" is much more, however, than just another rumination on Goyen's unique conception of the pastoral. In a relatively compressed space, this strange and hallucinatory narrative encapsulates much of his most profound and intimate lifetime experience, reaching back to the early 1950s and reassessing his struggles with alcoholism and writer's block. Of all his short stories, it comes the closest to being a complete spiritual autobiography condensed into the classic shape of one person's "telling."[14]

The action of the story is strange but fairly simple. The narrator, a "visiting poet" at a northern university, has witnessed a suicide. Unable to speak, he writes his version of events—almost a kind of confession— for the police. He explains that for several days he had been walking by a greenhouse on campus that was coated with a layer of freezing rain. Attracted to the tropical warmth and color visible through icy windows, he had knocked on the door, but the Nurseryman, who appeared to be drunk most of the time, refused to let him in. After several similar attempts to find entrance, the narrator was standing outside the door one morning when he heard "something like the rushing sound of wings" (*HHM* 53) and looked up in time to see someone fall through the top of the hothouse. The roof caved in; the door opened. The narrator stepped inside and saw the body of a young woman, naked, positioned "like an anatomy lesson figure" with "arms outstretched, legs spread" (*HHM* 53). The Nurseryman appeared to be confused and disabled by this catastrophe, but soon his hidden "passion" emerged, and he fell upon the dead woman, "clutching her to his body," dying himself as he joined with her "into one strange being, half-clothed, with one head of wild and furious hair" (*HHM* 57). And then for reasons he cannot explain, the narrator had picked up a "little spade" and tried to scoop out the heart of the Nurseryman. "I wanted the No-man's heart," he tells police, "now not so much in vengeance as in calm curiosity" (*HHM* 58).

This sequence of events, mythic and potent as it is, constitutes only the skeletal structure through which the storyteller probes his own shadowy psychology. As in "Bridge of Music, River of Sand," this teller is troubled and unreliable, a writer with "a hole in [his] breast," blocked from expression, "frozen," impotent (*HHM* 55). The hothouse seems to represent a kind of fertility and power denied him, a world of love and growth and sexuality he can no longer enter. The Nurseryman, the narrator's similarly disturbed double, refuses him hospitality, as though this earlier version of the narrator's self is warding off a dangerous, sterile future. The Nurseryman drinks; despite his proximity to the restorative powers of the garden, he is an alcoholic, and the narrator is obsessed with the apparent contradiction: "What ate at you, green man, that you drowned your sorrows? What blighted your joy, nurse, that you sought relief in the deadening of it. What is the canker worm that ate at your roots?" (*HHM* 49). The narrator gropes at the meaning of this strangely connected other self, at this dream that seems to be about his life but will not resolve itself into a simpler message. The garden seems to be a solution to his loneliness, but it ends up shattered, "fouled." The lack of welcome, the denial of entry, evokes both old failures in love and deeper, more fundamentally painful memories of family rejection. Ultimately he remembers the door to his childhood house, its glass pane etched with "the figure of a mysterious rider with a plumed hat astride a phantom horse the color of a cloud" (*HHM* 60). The figure on the door challenges him, prevents him from entering, as though someone in his family had put the rider there to stop him from coming home.

Though this basic summary may suggest obvious parallels to Goyen's life, "In the Icebound Hothouse" digs so deeply into the mysteries of his past and current struggles that it resists simplification. It is easy enough to recognize him in the narrator who moves from campus to campus with only temporary appointments and who struggles with the delicate psychology of the blocked writer. But the story goes further than ever in probing the sources of these disturbances with an angry insistence desperate for answers. In a basic sense, the Nurseryman may correspond to Goyen's "drinking self" who will not allow him to reenter a productive, loving world, but this shadow man also provides the opportunity to question, in a heightened form of AA journalizing, the causes of his alcoholism: "Why does the Nurseryman drink? I questioned. . . . Did the delicate death of things drive the gardener to bottle? But does he not know, has he not heard that all flowering things fade and die? That the grass withereth when the wind blows over? All things die? Does he not know?" (HHM 50). And after his death, the gardener has "the look of Cain" in his green eyes: "Or at least half that murdered brother's look—a look of horror and look of madness—the brute look of the ages: killer's brother" (*HHM* 54). Thus the gardener—Nurseryman, nurse, Curran the weaver and healer—is half killer and half savior, Goyen's favorite allusive metaphor since *Half a Look of Cain* for the conflicting impulses he saw in himself.

More intriguing still is the repetition of the triangular relationship from *Half a Look of Cain* in the three figures of the narrator, the gardener, and the fallen "girl" (*HHM* 57). Though potentially too schematic a reading, it is possible to see in the naked, diving college student the mythologized image of Dorothy Robinson, Goyen's former fiancée, here "sacrificed" so that the door to the nursery, to love and welcome and the warmth of sexuality, would open. Seen from this perspective, the Nurseryman suggests a version of Walter Berns, who is most likely addressed in the final pages of the story. Moving further into the almost imagistic investigation of his writer's block, the narrator understands his "frozen," icebound state as sexual and emotional impotence: "What has frozen the juices, stopped the flow in the Poet-in-Residence with the hole in his breast?" (*HHM* 55). His answer is "love unreturned," protesting, "But a poet is a person of love, whether he's producing, at the moment, or not; a person with love to give" (*HHM* 55). After declaring that the poet is also "somebody who needs to get love back," the narrator speaks directly—and with a remarkable and unguarded intensity—to a person from his past:

> You back there who the hell did you think I was, somebody giving all that passion and not getting anything back? How long did you think I could go on like that? I must admit it was my choice to go on like that. I kept hoping you'd change. That you'd come to me. Give me *something back*. And so I went on; giving, giving; went on too far, went into a territory where I couldn't turn back, where I was lost; a territory that was dark and where I felt dark feelings toward you, resentment and hate. My God, I who could love you so much. I, torn lover, who wanted to put you together with tender hands and wanted to tear you apart with the hands of a savage. Love not got back! You somewhere! Perverter! Spoiler! Perverting what was beautiful, fouling what was beautiful. Fouler! Fouler! Fouler! I don't know what kept me from striking you in those days. Because of your fear, your little lack of courage, your selfish little fear. (*HHM* 55–56)

This violent and unrestrained passage offers the most direct expression of Goyen's long-contained feelings about Berns and the failure of their early relationship. Though the language here is more direct, it matches his earlier journal entries about the impossibility of his attraction to Berns as well as his letter to Spud Johnson in 1951 that describes a mixture of generosity and dark anger at Berns's marriage: "His roots grow very very deep in me; and though I rejoice at his new happiness, there are times when something low and deep in me, removed by now so far far back in me that I scarcely know what it is or where, will not be still, but fights and grieves."[15] It took almost thirty years for this repressed resentment to emerge into a direct statement, and the intensity of emotion expressed here seems to have surprised even Goyen himself. After a reading at Harvard in 1981, he wrote to Repusseau that he was almost embarrassed by how the performance of this very new story had gone: "The story gets passionate (within a cold framework or shell) and personal and I remember reading it passionately toward the end. I may have overwhelmed the young people—who are, themselves, withdrawn and pushed-down-seeming. The story . . . is, I feel, a turning point for me: some large, long-carried feeling is disemburdened of me. . . ."[16]

As strong as it is, however, this feeling of personal betrayal and "fouled love" is still one step removed from the story's central recognition. The Nurseryman who denies entry may contain the images of both Goyen himself and Berns, but more significantly, the gardener is the emblem of that first rejection, the primary exile from nothing less than the house of breath itself:

> That house rises before me, built once more. Again on the pit floor of my life, it blows into shape before me. That house. It seemed perfect in its simplicity. Its quietness within itself. The humility of it, resting there shady under the trees; the dirt yard, the noble footworn steps. . . . Surely it led me to poetry, for it had given me early deep feeling, mornings of unnameable feelings in the silver air, nights of visions after stories told by the lamplight. (*HHM* 59)

This memory evokes the image of his mother's hand mirror with the "faint little cast" in the glass that never goes away; the idea of frosted glass—of the hothouse itself and its closed door—thus conjures that "frosted frontdoor pane" of the old house, guarded by the figure of a mysterious rider etched in the glass. And so arises the fundamental question of Goyen's life and work, reduced here to a few urgent questions: "Who put the rider there? Who of my ancestors put the rider there? . . . Who among the old dwellers of these rooms was dark? Who put the dark host at the door, rearing suspicious horse and suspicious plumed dark rider shying back from the homeless traveler, from the guest half-welcome?" (*HHM* 60). The forbidding door echoes the "precious door" on which the warring brothers of that story ride into the Gulf, but the saving passage is closed now, "frozen," its possibilities—of redemption and love offered by the Jesus who says, "I am the door"— cut off, leaving only darkness and unending questions.[17]

In his *New York Times* review of *Had I a Hundred Mouths*, the collection of stories published two years after Goyen's death, Vance Bourjaily called "In the Icebound Hothouse" one of the "great short stories of the century."[18] With its tight, confessional structure and hypnotic stream of related imagery, this urgent tale combines the best of the American symbolist tradition (echoing Poe and Melville in particular) with Goyen's own specific gift for stark emotional nudity. Whether or not we know the biographical elements that feed the telling, the story remains deeply mysterious, resonant as a dream but with a coherence under the surface that delivers a singular aesthetic force. "In the Icebound Hothouse" can be seen, then, as a culmination of Goyen's return to writing after joining AA, a way to clarify, if not analyze, the depths of his lifelong feeling of isolation and loss. As a revelation of old wounds in Goyen's new "late" style, it trails only his last major work, the novel that began as a short story titled "Nature's Quirk" about a hermaphrodite sometimes called Sideshow. These two pieces of fiction emerged from the same essential impulse and image set, a "world" Goyen had found and come to cherish as the one pure thing left to him: "I am enchanted by this world," he wrote to Patrice Repusseau in 1978, "and care only for it and wish I could sink into it away from any other. It is totally mine, has nothing to do with any other world, really my own secret and to Hell with editors and publishers and reviewers and critics and booksellers. Fuck them all, I must find a way to live without them and make my stories only for my self."[19]

CHAPTER SIXTEEN

Arcadio

1983

For me, literature documents lust.

JOURNALS

In the emotional rush that engendered and briefly followed *A Book of Jesus*, Goyen planned to assemble at least two more short biographies of spiritual figures. He was most interested in St. Francis and St. Paul, personalities he considered particularly attuned to the senses and their potential connection to spirit. Paul's sudden conversion, "abruptly turning his life around about-face under the power of faith and love" (HRC 27.2) and Francis's literal contact with nature provided useful analogues for the reconciliation of ghost and flesh. The miracles and incidents in their lives offered new chances to explore the idea of the saint's progress that had played so important a role in Goyen's work since his discovery of Flaubert's "St. Julien." "Erotic saintly figures," Goyen called them in notes from the early 1980s, heroic in their wounds and self-divisions, but ultimately transformative, miraculous, saving figures who were themselves brought back to wholeness.

In his obsessive return to this idea, he was building on a long list of similar characters from his earlier work: Folner, Marvello, Addis Adair, and Arthur Bond in particular. All had shown signs of division or difference; all had tried, with mostly tragic results, to still an inner turbulence through redemptive acts. But none had completely embodied, in a much more literal sense, the very idea of the schismatic self. While working on the set of late stories that came to him after his sobriety, Goyen saw such a character emerge. According to his notes from this period, it may have happened while he was developing "In the Icebound Hothouse." There the "girl's" body that falls from the nearby building through the frozen glass roof may have originally been a hermaphrodite. In a note headed "Last Vision of Arcadio," Goyen wrote that this "is the body [thrown through] that dropped through the glass roof of the greenhouse that fell among the vines and [blossoms] blooms gleaming and raw, spotted with bruises with clawings and scratchings and glazed with semen" (HRC 4.6, brackets in original). The mysterious body that contains both sexes (or all of sexuality), abused, broken, destroyed in what appears to be an excess of desire—this was the fallen figure that opened the forbidden door. At some point during the development of this work, Goyen saw that the fallen body had its own story to tell. What emerged over the next few years became the fullest expression of his interest in the erotic saintly tale, a novel that offers a complete, cumulative investigation of his emotional and spiritual life.

Like so many of Goyen's fictions, *Arcadio* begins with a frame that establishes the dramatic moment of storytelling.[1] A primary narrator, distant from home ("in an ancient holy city") tells us that he recently discovered a postcard in an old book: a reproduction of William Holman Hunt's "The Light of the World," a pre-Raphaelite depiction of Jesus (tapestry robe, Arthurian mien) carrying a lantern as he knocks on a weedy, wooden door. The postcard inspires a "vision—an 'apparition' [his] mother would have called it—made of true memory and outrageous fabrication" (*AR* 1). The memory emerges as another version of the stranger's visit familiar from the story "Precious Door." Through flashes of summer heat lightning, family members sitting on a country porch notice an otherworldly figure standing in a nearby field, "with hair streaming down to the ground and eyes as glowing as lanterns" (*AR* 2). The "shy visiting stranger" soon disappears, but the incident prompts longing in the boy narrator and a story from his uncle Ben, his older counterpart who "had gone away early in passion" and returned from his wanderings "made dumb" (*AR* 8). Now close to death from cancer, Ben tells of a time years before when he came upon someone bathing in the Trinity River. With the intensity of all hidden watchers, Ben crouches in the bushes, mesmerized by "the bending and gathering and tossing figure, glistening with water, washing itself as if twas making slow dancing movements and twas only washing itself; and then twas when I saw that it twas part a man and part a woman, the man part was sweetly washing the woman part and the woman sweetly the man, the woman part baptizing the man and the man baptizing the woman" (*AR* 6). He finds the bather's clothes and possessions under a nearby tree. From a small, white Bible, he takes a picture postcard, "The Light of the World," that had been tucked inside.

Out of this "song of farewell" (*AR* 8) from his Uncle Ben, the narrator begins to weave his own vision of the hermaphrodite named Arcadio. In this longer tale that comprises the rest of the novel, the narrator becomes the listener, discovering Arcadio under an abandoned railroad trestle that serves as the stage for his speaking.[2] What we learn fairly quickly is that Arcadio is not only doubly sexed, he is mestizo, half Mexican and half Anglo-Irish, that is, half "Texan." He speaks in an oddly musical, unreal voice that mixes Spanish and English to produce a childlike dream of cadenced language: "My name is Arcadio, and I will not do you no harm, come under the shade of this old rayroad trestle if you wan to. Train's gone. *Por favor: siéntase*, set down please, here by the blooming vines of morningglory and honeysuckle that smells so sweet in the morning sun, here in the bed of the river, white bed of shell, river's gone too" (*AR* 13). Goyen himself described the voice as "an amalgam of East Texas speech—rhythm and dialect . . . Mexican . . . Biblical rhetoric . . . all washed over and enriched by a narrative elegance ranging from Cocteauesque (near-Camp) and the comic-folk hero's absurd of the *Pícaro*."[3] As is so often the case in Goyen's work, this lyric voice (through rhythms and inflections) defines the character more precisely than any exterior trait. Arcadio, himself a sort of dream, speaks a dream language, a fabricated linguistic music that sings its story. This monologue (or more properly, aria) is punctuated by the refrain "You wan hear?"—a phrase that Goyen likened to "n'est-ce pas?" and that receives a variety of inflexions, from gentle question to earnest command. The phrase acts as a signature of sorts and a constant reminder that this telling, like so many in Goyen's oeuvre, requires and makes room for a listener.

Arcadio's physical appearance may be less important than his voice, but it does bear more than the usual significance among Goyen's storytellers. The "old war uniform" (*AR* 15) he wears came to him from a stranger, but it suggests that his life has been a battle both with others and himself. He is a veteran, in other words, and the litany of his abuse reads like the harrowing picaresque of an ultra-Candide. Raised in a whorehouse in Memphis by his sex-crazed father, Hombre, Arcadio becomes an underage prostitute until he runs away out of sickness at his own sexual desires. After living with a variety of rich men, he joins a traveling freak show and finds a home with the other "attractions" until his estranged mother, Chupa, shows up one day and convinces him to leave. The momentary connection to the mother he never knew is welcome, but when he reveals his body to her, she abandons him again. Told that he has a half-brother who was raised in a jail in Missouri, he sets out to find him, hoping to hear something of Chupa along the way, but Tomasso (the boy he finds singing in a church in Virginia) dies soon after from a mysterious and unexplained "hunger." Eventually, Arcadio comes upon Hombre as well, but his alcoholic father proves little more than a legless ruin eaten away by lust. Despite Arcadio's efforts to save him, Hombre dies in a hideous seizure brought on by DTs and general corruption. A survivor of so much loss and degradation, Arcadio finally makes peace with himself but has no family or companion except when a stranger consents to hear his story.

For someone who had identified himself as an exile for so long, the idea of reconciliation, "coming back together in peace" (*HHM* 47) had always been attractive to Goyen. It's a concept that began to appear in his work during the early 1960s, around the time of his marriage and particularly in the play *Christy*. His subsequent work with AA and his reading of such authors as Tillich and Hans Kung fortified his sense that he needed to repair his divisions (both internal and external) to achieve some degree of contentment. The perception that drove *The Book of Jesus*—that Jesus himself was physical and so understood the body's demands—led to further expression in such stories as "Precious Door," in which the warring brothers are simultaneously parts of a single self and family members at odds. In this sense, "reconciliation" came to mean finding peace with his own inner schism as a way to bridge—at least imaginatively—old, familial distances.

Arcadio caps this line of thinking, offering the fullest expression (both symbolic and narrative) of Goyen's dividedness and detachment from the kinship he sought. Arcadio's specific form of reconciliation begins with his body and the need to accept but transcend its solipsistic demands:

> I am equipped for lust, just sitting down or standing in one place, tantalized by my own very body, sometimes itching and burning, sometimes soft open and hard, lip and cod, one part hungering for the other, and

it available and welcoming and no hunt necessary, hunter and hunted I hunt myself, the hunt leads me no farther than the distance of a reach across my own body, what I seek in my maddened quest is at hand, a simple journey of my fingers, merely within grasp, yet I have gone almost *loco* in the game of it, the tricks and games, I became cunning, I became shifty and secret and coy and *macho* and *galán*. I was the battleground of myself I almost tore myself in two. (*AR* 58–59)

Over the course of his life, Goyen came to understand lust as a kind of self-consumption, a dehumanizing force that turned people into machines. Arcadio's body may seem to suggest the difficulty of choosing between genders, but this is not his true dilemma. An inward-turning desire threatens him most directly, the thought that his body could feed on itself and turn away from the outside world. In its darkest form, this temptation becomes a mode of incest, captured by his memory of Hombre and the "infernal *figura*" (*AR* 127):

Oh God, I said, Oh *Jesucristo* I said, take from me this infernal *figura* of the past. Twas in that house on the wharf over the river, you remember, growled that voice, there was the three of us. We both had it at the same time Johna and me. I heard my father's voice, *demonio*, growling like a dog *feroz*. You went crazy. Then we changed around and the woman part sat on me and leaned back to let Johna come at the man part, squattin. I was under, coming up from under, and Johna was squattin, straddlin. Then you just went crazy and took charge, like a bull. You had it all. We changed around so much, everbody going after everthing, we was all three just crazy people, couldn't finally tell who was who or who was where. (*AR* 129)

Though incest within fiction has long been a symbol of psychological involution, Goyen takes this idea perhaps as far as it can go. In what might be considered the darkest version ever of the Freudian family drama, he imagines a kind of family lust, the consumption of selves by an intimacy that excludes otherness. In lust, the necessary distance for ethical relationships fails. Others are reduced to the basest demands of the self, and in the process the self ceases to exist, now animalized or transformed into a machine. The *figura* is a form of madness, a self-feeding circle, like the odd image of Julius Hohensteckel, the "foul-mouthed individual" (*AR* 121) Hombre remembers whose lips gradually twisted until they rested just under his left ear. Profanity poured from the mouth directly into the ear until the tongue could reach inside and "feel iz brains, bunched like a cluster of grapes" (*AR* 123).[4]

To escape the infernal *figura* and all it implies, Arcadio turns to the little white Bible in Spanish that he carries with him at all times. After escaping the China Boy whorehouse, he at first thinks to free himself from his demanding body by cutting away a part of himself: "I tried to fix myself with a piece of glass but couldn't get the courage to do it— and to tell the honest truth I couldn't make up my mind which of myself to try and eliminate" (41). During this "terrible night of dying" in his "soul," he hears Jesus talking to him: "[Jesus told me] to accept myself just as I was, that He made me as He had made all things and would be my companion from then on . . . . Oh Jesus *Jesucristo*, I said, are you like me? Like you, said *Jesucristo*" (*AR* 41–42). In language that clearly echoes Goyen's experience at Weston, Arcadio finds a measure of peace in the idea of a spiritual or divine companion who shares his body's demands. Later, he sees this physical Jesus as the fundamental stranger, the knocker at the door who needs help, the simultaneously welcomed and welcoming figure of "The Light of the World." Jesus becomes the opening, the way out, offering escape from the bonds of a body that keeps Arcadio imprisoned. But Jesus is also the stranger who must be admitted, fed, and cared for, the anonymous or hidden god testing the faith and hospitality of sinful humanity.

Escape and welcome are major concerns of the novel, which gives us repeated stories of lonely, longing figures who must free themselves from real and symbolic bondage. Arcadio's "excape" from the Show is an echo of the liberation of his brother Tomasso from the Missouri jail, through the "beloved old hole" (*AR* 101) dug by the inmates who helped raise him. In a manuscript note, Goyen underscored the need for liberation from the self's own traps and attentions: "'Clearing the show' means 'coming out,' coming out of hiding. Not to be left back anymore, not to be turned out. Free in the meadows and prairies, among the live oaks and bluebonnets, self-delivering—Oh God, deliver me of myself. Free me of self-excitement. Looking for the *glory* of it—(can't help it) always the potential of self-seduction, self obsession, self-hustling, self-devouring" (HRC 4.7). Within this plea for autonomy rests a need for acceptance and welcome. The self must be steady enough to acknowledge *itself* for what it is, and it must be free enough to be welcomed by others. Arcadio in his telling welcomes the listener with whom he slowly develops a relationship, no matter how fleeting. He is also given the space and time to tell his story by someone respectful enough to grant him attention.

Goyen relied on a number of sources in *Arcadio*, but one of the most significant was a polemic by Father John J. McNeill titled *The Church and the Homosexual*.[5] First published in 1976, this early argument against Catholic teachings on homosexuality includes a reinterpretation of the story of Sodom and Gomorrah that caught Goyen's attention. (The torn-out pages that deal with this incident can be found among his *Arcadio* manuscripts.) According to Father McNeill, the traditional reading of the destruction of the cities of the plain as a divine punishment for homosexuality is incorrect. "It would seem fairly certain," he argues instead, "that the sin of Sodom as understood in biblical times was primarily one of inhospitality" (McNeill 46). As Goyen certainly knew, this interpretation relies upon the mythology of the divine visit. The angels sent to the city in disguise participate in the tradition that would later include the Greek and Roman gods as well as Jesus. The city is destroyed because most fail to welcome the strangers; only Lot's family provides shelter, and for this they are spared. Thus Sodom and Gomorrah, traditional symbols of homosexual corruption, instead become emblems of a failed hospitality, *"inhospitalidad,"* as Arcadio says. *Arcadio*, like "Precious Door," takes up this argument and extends its ethic to include all outcasts, no matter how constructed. Reconciliation cannot occur without hospitality (to the self as well as the stranger), while inhospitality creates the exile. After retelling the story of Sodom and Gomorrah from McNeill's perspective, Arcadio makes clear its ethical message as well as the proper response to a lack of welcome: "Be kind to strangers and take them in and do not turn away strangers who knock on your door and give them somethin to eat if they ask for it and give them shelter, they may be a very angel. . . . So *compadre, Oyente,* if anybody does not welcome you, turn and go away from them and shake the dust of their house and of their town and of them off your feet and go on your path to where you are agoin" (*AR* 34). Goyen's fundamental sense of exile here finds justification in the failure of those communities (town, family, region, literary world) to accept him for what he was. The story of the visiting stranger gave him the chance to reclaim the Christian ethical tradition and simultaneously justify his own difference. If Jesus was a figure of reconciliation and could enable self-acceptance, then He could also set the example of how to love and welcome, how to open the door.

Less fantastic or fabulistic than *Half a Look of Cain* or *Come, the Restorer, Arcadio* is arguably the most personal and revealing of Goyen's many spiritual autobiographies. The intimate connection to his own personal history emerges most clearly in the setting: Arcadio tells his story while standing under the railroad trestle near the town of his birth, Trinity, and the river that shares its name. This is the site of the story "Bridge of Music, River of Sand," near the old bridge his mother was afraid to cross and the spot in the river where she—and he—almost drowned. Again and again Goyen returns to this spot to ground investigations of his past. It is the ur-landscape, the sacred source, and Arcadio seems to be his most direct psychological and sexual self-portrait. But what exactly is the relationship between Arcadio and Goyen? It can be tempting to see the hermaphrodite as little more than a symbol of dividedness, particularly with respect to gender or sexuality. Goyen certainly lived a kind of bisexuality, and Arcadio is literally, physically bisexual, a conjunction that likely prompted Jean-Michel Quiblier's question in 1982:

> Interviewer: What do you think of bisexuality?
> Goyen: I think that the very nature of life is bisexual. It is a question of affection and tenderness. When tenderness exists between two human beings, love is neither masculine nor feminine. . . . I have loved men and women and I believe that the experiences I've had with others are based upon a profound affection that is absolutely, profoundly, sexual but not limited by the notion of heterosexuality, fidelity, etc. I believe that the saints knew all of this. Certain ones among them—St. Francis, for example—have a sense of sexuality. (*GAE* 109)

The contention here echoes the language of "At Lady A's," and the reference to St. Francis seems to warrant thinking of Arcadio as a figure of surplus tenderness, beyond the limits typically imposed by static conceptions of gender. In this sense, Arcadio is not so much torn between male and female as he is overburdened by his body, seeking a way to balance an excess of desire with a spiritual understanding of the body's weaknesses. Beginning with *A Book of Jesus*, this preoccupation with taming and justifying the range and persistence of his sexual desires dominated much of Goyen's autobiographical thinking. Even as late as his sixtieth birthday in 1975, he complained to Phillips that this "awful year" was "marked by a constant hard-on (one of the most tormenting heats of my sixty years)."[6] From the anguished pleas for self-control in "Jesus in My Body" to the unruly presence of a parasitic sexuality in "Arthur Bond," trouble arose consistently from an inability to constrain his body's demands. Marriage clearly helped to some degree, but if his imaginative life is any indication, the increased emotional stability that his bond with Roberts provided did not necessarily bring calm and contentment to his stormy sensuality—or to the range of his desires. Despite age and his triumph over addiction to alcohol, in other words, what he called lust was still a problem for Goyen, and *Arcadio* seeks a form of storytelling—of confession and justification—that will contain it without removing its power.[7]

However we understand the relationship between the dream-work of Arcadio and Goyen's own complex sexual identity, the novel itself is undoubtedly his most complete and successful self-investigation. The energy and revelatory power of *Half a Look of Cain* and *Come, the Restorer* here find a cleaner, more direct form of expression without any corresponding loss of extravagance or imagination. With his sequence of late stories, particularly if we include "Bridge of Music, River of Sand," Goyen had produced his most consistent and enduring work, a series of astonishing tales that resonate strangely and lastingly while defying categorization. Of the novel, Reginald Gibbons wrote in the *New York Times Book Review* in 1983 that Arcadio's "song may be Goyen's finest achievement. The work of a master fabulist, it was one more courageous foray into fiction unlike anyone else's, haunting the reader with its tenderness and ferocity."[8] And only a few years after his death, Joyce Carol Oates introduced his final collection of stories, *Had I a Hundred Mouths*, by calling Arcadio "Goyen's most powerful symbol of this inexplicable doubleness—the physical expression of a paradox that is primarily spiritual. All serious art celebrates mystery, perhaps, but Goyen's comes close to embodying it."[9]

CHAPTER SEVENTEEN

The Wound and the Bow
1982–1983

But pain and affliction do carry a blessing in them, I believe. Illness is a spiritual condition. It brings us to see something we had not seen before—seeing the meaning of our suffering.

"RECOVERING," 1983

In April of 1982 and a year later in 1983, Goyen lectured at New York University as part of its Writer at Work series. These two talks, which were to be among his last public statements, open a window onto the often retrospective thinking of his final years. The first, "Autobiography in Fiction," recapitulates many of his fundamental thoughts about writing: the importance of place to his imagination, the acquisition of his own stylized language made from East Texas speech, and his relationship to the "romance" tradition of Hawthorne. He also clarified, perhaps more directly than ever before, the sense of absence or longing that pervades his work. This "homesickness" he distinguished from nostalgia, describing it instead as a desire to grasp the present so as to relinquish the past, even while perceiving that the "very livid *now*" was always inadequate, "unacceptable," "not enough" (*GAE* 60).

The lecture also reveals an interest and project of his last years: the attempt to write about "the young Greek named Philoctetes," the lonely, wounded archer trapped on an island, too devoted to his own injury to take up his unfailing bow. Goyen had read about the story in Edmund Wilson's *The Wound and the Bow* and had subsequently sought out the "clean and classic little play" on the myth by André Gide (*GAE* 60). There is little doubt that he saw in Wilson's description of the play something of his own struggle between personal pain (the fundamental wound, the mark of exile) and the need to turn that pain to a creative purpose. As early as 1937, he had written to Bill Hart about the difference between those who "strive assiduously to heal their wounds, silently and alone in some dark secret place" and those who "keep their wounds open and raw."[1] For most of his life, those who knew him had identified him as, in Anaïs Nin's words, "a man in pain . . . a wounded man."[2] And now he read Wilson's account of Philoctetes as "a man obsessed by a grievance, which in his case he is to be kept from forgetting by an agonizing physical ailment."[3]

In the plot of Sophocles's play as recounted by Wilson, Philoctetes is at first deceived by Odysseus, who brings the young son of Achilles, Neoptolemus, to the island of Lemnos to trick the archer into joining the Trojan War. Ultimately, Neoptolemus refuses to deceive Philoctetes and in sympathy with his condition agrees to take him "back to his native land."[4] This act of faith and friendship moves Philoctetes, essentially freeing him from his loneliness and burden; he sails to Troy and defeats Paris to help end the war. As *Arcadio* had indicated, Goyen recognized the dangers of Philoctetes's solipsistic attention, even if at times he had difficulty resisting the lure of isolation. Philoctetes gave a clear example of the risks of this sort of involution: "A person who sees life and others exclusively in terms of his own affliction is out of a literature we all know. Exclusive self-nursing, tending the 'curse,' the 'difference' that separates, produces darkness, a sunless, festering creation" (*GAE* 61). Rescue, as the story suggests, comes in the form of the stranger, whose honesty and faith—friendship given under trying circumstance—proves strong enough to lift the self-imposed curse.

Though his sense of the interior, psychic wound reaches back to his earliest writings, Goyen's interest in the body's expression of inner states may have intensified in his later years, particularly after a series of health issues began to shape his life. Following problems from a detached retina in the mid-1970s, he underwent "unexpected surgery" in 1978, which kept him laid up for three months.[5] Not long after, early in 1980, he began to notice that some of the fingers of his left hand were beginning to curl inward. He was diagnosed with Dupuytren's contracture, an inherited condition in which tendons in the palm thicken, causing the fingers to curl.[6] (Though in a few instances during the course of his life Goyen spoke of losing the use of one of his arms when under extreme emotional stress, that psychological reaction appears unrelated to this disease, which is known to affect northern Europeans and heavy drinkers disproportionately.) The surgery may have been "ghastly," as he wrote to Elizabeth Spencer, but it caused only a minor interruption to his work.

In the fall of 1981, Goyen began teaching in the creative writing program at the University of Southern California (USC). The director, James White, had approached him the year before and offered to pay him $2,500 to teach a graduate-level workshop. (Goyen had looked into part-time teaching at the University of California, Los Angeles [UCLA] but had been offered only $550 per course.) "He was pleased to be wanted," White later wrote of his first encounter, impressed with Goyen's candor and natural eloquence. "There was no question that he would be a good teacher because he spoke of writing as naturally as he spoke of the weather. . . . He was his own subject and his feelings were deep, but the expression of them was moving, funny, personal."[7] Goyen enjoyed the work during that initial semester, but during the spring he began to run a fever that his doctors couldn't explain. He told White that his "lymph nodes were swollen" and "his blood work [was] confusing."[8] The following summer, he was diagnosed with lymphocytic leukemia, a type of cancer that begins in the white blood cells (lymphocytes) in the bone marrow and spreads to the blood, lymph nodes, and organs. By August he was in the hospital suffering from what Roberts describes as "fevers as high as 105 degrees that affected his epilepsy, sending him into grand mal seizures."[9] After an adjustment to his medication, Goyen responded positively, emerging from what he described as a near-death experience to a new energy and "more work, deeper work."[10]

Cancer treatments now structured his life, and despite the willed optimism of his letters, the challenges of the disease sometimes heightened his sensitivity to anger and despair. Always alert to real or perceived slights, he could explode at minor inconveniences that seemed denigrating. White relates an incident that occurred when Goyen arrived for lunch frustrated that his parking permit at USC wouldn't allow him a place in the faculty club garage. In an emotional scene, fueled in part by the early stages of his cancer, he stormed out of the dining room and quit his teaching job for the rest of the semester.[11] His long history of feeling exiled and unwelcome could flare up more quickly now, given the stress of shortened time and energy. As another friend from the period, Eve Caram, puts it, "Bill was a person with a great capacity for tenderness—one with so much love to give—to his family, his students, his friends—all were dear to him—but the other side of that was anger," particularly when he felt rejected.[12]

Along with the increased strain of illness, Goyen was experiencing new difficulties getting his work published. An effort to find a home for *Arcadio* and the other new stories had been under way since early 1980, and after rejections from Random House and William Morrow, he began to correspond with a young editor at Houghton Mifflin, Thomas Hart.[13] One question that remained unresolved for a time was whether to develop *Arcadio* further into a stand-alone novel or include it, as originally planned, in a single volume with the stories he had produced since the mid-1970s. The correspondence with Hart is filled with Goyen's gratitude and relief at finding someone interested in his work, but it also reveals a guarded nervousness over what he considered the editor's youth and inexperience. As he complained in a letter to Phillips, he didn't like being "critiqued": "I've written him [Hart] a strong letter letting him know how I feel about showing unfinished work and about premature criticism. I'm educating him. But he still seems attractive as an editor, and certainly devoted to my work; and once we see clearly what each other is like to work with, we might have a good relationship."[14] Part of the rocky start to the exchange had come from Hart's reaction to a draft of *Six Women*, the autobiographical work that Goyen still hoped to publish alongside the new fiction. Hart's "disappointment" had seemed premature and unfair to Goyen, who expressed his own uneasiness with showing work-in-progress to an editor he didn't fully trust. But he was willing to follow Hart's advice about *Arcadio*, opting for the time being for the more compact version.

By September, Goyen was writing hopefully to Caram to say that Houghton Mifflin would publish the "new book of stories" titled *Precious Door*, which would include "eight stories and tales," including the short version of "Arcadio." He was therefore shocked to learn just a few days later that the editorial board had turned down Hart's proposal, citing Goyen's long history of poor sales. The publishing world he had known in the 1950s and 1960s, where powerful editors routinely made publication decisions, had changed. "Editors seem paranoic," he wrote to Robin Moody, the owner of Daedalus Books, "and terrified that some great hand (of a marketing person, or even of an Editor-in-Chief) is going suddenly to appear and wipe out everything they've been doing. Some Houghton Mifflin hand seems to have done just this. I can't live or work in bitterness and that's gone, but *hurt* lasts longer (I can work with hurt, always have)."[15] It was this sort of disappointment, the kind of wound that seemed cumulative after so long a career, that fed Goyen's outbursts and sensitivity when his health began to deteriorate. An urgency to get his work into print, combined with a sometimes unconcealed resentment at his limitations, began to drive him forward.

Although the book of stories and *Six Women* were foremost on his mind, Goyen had been pursuing another project for a year or two that he hoped might bring in some extra money but that undoubtedly also had personal resonance. In a letter to his agent at the time, Phyllis Jackson, he laid out his plan to write a "full-fledged biography" of his old friend and fellow playwright William Inge. Goyen had known Bill Inge since the early 1950s, when he went to see *The Glass Menagerie* in Chicago and Tennessee Williams had introduced the two "small-town men."[16] Later they had encouraged one another in New York, and Goyen had helped Inge with his fiction when he began to write books in the early 1960s. There is no question that Goyen saw Inge's life as similar to his own, and he appears to have sought out this opportunity to meditate on the "tragic" life of an artist who faced challenges he himself understood. The description of the project he sent to Jackson sounds uncannily like a prospectus for his own autobiography:

> The life of Inge was undoubtedly a tragic one, but the Life is not going to be a downbeat one nor a bleak one. . . . There must be a frank discussion of Inge's homosexuality—without, of course, doing any harm to his family or personal integrity. He was an alcoholic. His work did not succeed as he had hoped it to—and yet he was an immensely successful playwright. But his work degenerated; he seemed to lose sight of its center (the horror of all artists); it lost its vitality, its fibre. He could never find home. His loneliness was unbearable. He was cut off from humanity. . . . Yet his work, which was about himself, his own preoccupations, his own intuitive sense of human relationships, his own work was his victory; and we are beginning to see the depths of meanings in it, its contemporary relatedness; his work is on its way toward refreshing itself.[17]

Though the project never left the planning stages, Goyen did attend a two-day seminar on biography in Austin as part of his preparations. Whether he was ever likely to complete such a task is difficult to know, but it does seem clear that thinking about Inge gave him the chance to reimagine the shape and meaning of his own life at a moment when its possible conclusion seemed all too near.

Following the Houghton Mifflin debacle, Goyen continued to pursue publishers for his fiction projects, and after an unsuccessful discussion with Farrar, Straus, and Giroux, he was relieved to find a sympathetic reader in Carol Southern at Clarkson Potter. By the time of his complicated and dangerous hospital stay in August of 1982, he was gratified to learn that the longer version of *Arcadio* would be published as a separate book with the collection of new stories—and possibly *Six Women*—to follow some time thereafter. During the next several months, he underwent chemotherapy that interfered periodically with his work but also seemed to urge him on when he had the energy available to write. "I haven't been this productive in some years," he wrote to Roberta Pryor in February. "*So*—my condition is chronic, *not* acute and terminal. It can be treated and *remissed*—a good word."[18] By early March, he had finished the treatments and was preparing for his second lecture at NYU to be given on April 13.

"Recovering," the talk Goyen gave that day in New York, is one of his calmest and most beautiful meditations on the life of the artist. Once again he spoke of wounds and the artist's struggle to reconcile himself to past and pain through a perilous, interior grappling. The biblical Jacob helped bring this metaphor into focus, first in his struggle with his brother Esau for blessing and birthright, later in his contest with the angel beside the "night river" (*GAE* 66). Jacob has wrestled with the angel or himself ("which is it?") and emerges wounded, limping away from this stalemate with the deepest secrets of his nature. As Goyen made clear, the image correlated directly to his working life: "I've limped out of every piece of work I've done" (*GAE* 66). In considering the idea of recovery, he thinks of Jacob as a figure who has restored his spirit through a deadly struggle with a primal adversary. This struggle is the "work" of art, "that going home, that reconciliation with old disharmony, grief, grudge" (GAE 66). This spiritual transformation arises, for Goyen, out of an engagement with his own experience; as he had said many times before, he is his subject:

Long ago I knew that another could not give me my life, only help to find it. I could only know life through myself, or recover it myself. I continue to be astonished by my own history. My own experience keeps justifying living. Others' experience in history has supported and inspirited me; but finally my own has got me through. The most I have been able to offer others and can now is this self-consciousness, ferocious protection of personal feeling. (GAE 67)

Before he will release the angel, Jacob demands a blessing and is renamed. This reward or gift—the renaming that is the sign of a rebirth of spirit—derives from the courage to confront the thing that wounds you, leaves you alive but marked.

It is this narrative of redemption that Goyen wished so fervently to claim. He rejected the idea that unhealed sickness (or madness) is the proper source of art. He himself had been one of the unhealed who chose "the hypnotism of illness" (*GAE* 68). Like Philoctetes, still on Goyen's mind, "so concerned with his wound that he forgot his bow," the unrecovered artist tends the curse, "produces darkness, a sunless, festering creation" (GAE 69). Only when he returns to the war and takes up his bow does Philoctetes return to life, a symbol of the kind of healing that Goyen had always sought but that now more than ever was made real by his illness: "But brother Philoctetes, your healer arrived, the wound was closed, the bow won the battle; and O brother of the cave and the pain, I too have once again shaken free, flipped like a fish from the hand that stretches toward me; I kick towards light, but the finger touch is on my heel. Lend me your bow! Come before me!" (GAE 69–70).

Leander

Arcadio may be the summation of Goyen's attempts to tell the story of his own wounding divisions, but it was not his final work of published fiction. While the story of the *mestizo* hermaphrodite was working its way through the publishing houses, he was intensely occupied with a set of linked tales that seemed to emerge with greater speed and more concentrated anger than ever before in his career. Two of these— "Had I a Hundred Mouths" and "Tongues of Men and Angels"—were published in *TriQuarterly* just before and after his death. Together they suggest the scope and unprecedented power of the longer work he had in mind, a multigenerational tale of East Texas racial and sexual violence to be called *Leander*.

Of these two completed pieces, "Had I a Hundred Mouths" stands more steadily on its own as a story, delivering a deeply visceral blow to the reader. Essentially a compressed saga of lust, the tale is told in a familiar Goyenesque situation: two cousins, the older now in puberty, listening to an uncle (the initiatory, Christy-like spokesman for sex and desire) describe a family horror. The older cousin takes on this knowledge as a kind of burden: "Later, in the wrestling with it, he figured that he had already come in lust long ago, born in it, that he had already inherited it in his flesh . . . , already had it in his blood, had been waiting only to be brought to it when the time came" (*HHM* 4–5). And because of this dark understanding, the boy seems charged with the responsibility to tell again, another weight for an already overburdened self:

> At home, more was expected of him than he could fulfill. But he would never let them know his inadequacy. He carried the world, boy Atlas. His father, his uncle's brother, could not make enough money from his job to give his family what they "deserved," whatever that was; but that was his father's cry, especially when he was drinking. . . . The older nephew's mother reminded him of his mission, charged him to be the one who would give them their deserving. (*HHM* 6)

In "Autobiography in Fiction," Goyen had briefly discussed the story of Atlas, relieved by Hercules of his burden, free to seek the golden apples of the Hesperides. "Why did Atlas come back?" he asked. "Why didn't he run for his life?" The question haunted him because he saw himself in the figure of the "bowed-over man walking forever as though he were still carrying the whole world on his shoulders" (GAE 61). People had told Goyen throughout his life that he seemed "held down by something." And indeed he had pictured himself, in the context of his family's needs, as a lonely boy who ultimately ran away from the "great stone" of his mother's expectations. Could he go back? Would he return like Atlas to take up the burden again? But the place, the garden that "slopes down to a river" no longer exists. And so Atlas becomes an image of the weight of knowledge, the carrying of known burdens even in the farthest reaches of exile.

The uncle's story emerges as part of that great weight of the past. Once again Goyen has returned to a small town in East Texas that resembles Trinity. Once again an extended family lives intimately in a large house.[19] And on a sleety November day they watch the weather, anxious about the safety of Louetta, the uncle's teenage cousin on her way back from town. As the day gets colder and darker and the ice falls thicker on the leaves, the uncle, then seventeen, sets out in search. Penetrating deep into the woods, he finds Louetta in a "cave" of brambles and tree roots where she had been raped moments before by a man the uncle describes as "a big red nigger" (*HHM* 8). Frightened and darkly aroused by the scene, the uncle repeats the actions of the black man (whose own story is told later in the "Ormsby" section of "Tongues of Men and Angels"), falling into a frenzy of lust that initiates a long sexual affair ("We did it in the cave, day and night, wild. We was lost" [*HHM* 9]).

Before long, Louetta has a child, and when he sees that the baby is black, the uncle takes the boy to be raised by the family's washer woman. Leander, as the mixed-race orphan is named, is "light-complected as a light Mescan boy" and "carried something unusual over him" (*HHM* 10, 11). He seems to resemble Louetta, but no one suspects that she's his mother. When he turns twelve, she gives him a "red ring" that he comes to cherish, but as he grows older, he begins to show signs of the lustful madness from which he was born. Then one night in a deep, moonless darkness when most of the family is away, Louetta is raped again by a stranger she identifies only as black, but in her fist the uncle finds Leander's red ring. In despair, Louetta throws herself into the well beside the family house, and when Leander cries out at her funeral, the Klansmen drag him into the woods, castrate him ("cut him clean as a woman and hung his young manhood on a tree branch" [*HHM* 13]), and burn his body with tar and feathers. The uncle finds the surviving but now bestial boy hiding in the same cave of brambles where he was conceived, but despite attempts to care for this surrogate son, he can't prevent Leander from disappearing into the thicket. "I knew," the uncle tells his nephews, "that he had seen himself in the pond" (*HHM* 17).

What first strikes the reader of "Had I a Hundred Mouths," particularly those familiar with Goyen's lifelong meditations on Trinity and East Texas, is its relentless violence. No distant longing for a lost time colors this baleful history. The narration is a steady march of horror, exposing the older, more sensitive cousin to the dark source of his nature. In his penetrating essay on Goyen's later work, Repusseau attributes this new directness in Goyen's final stories to his cancer diagnosis: "At the very end of his life, . . . Goyen thrashed about and screamed with his old pain and rage because he wanted the scales to fall from his eyes so as to see the light. He couldn't help assaulting himself, pushing himself over the parapet, face to face with the chasm, in a most uncomfortable position which made a radical change absolutely necessary. That is why there is so much violence in his last stories, violence to break and clean the old coatings and layers of dust."[20] And indeed he did feel pressed for time, urgent, which made the stories come quickly, directly, like thoughts clarified by lifelong meditation. Repressed (or at least glossed over) memories of early terror emerge into a harsher light. "But the town," Goyen told Gibbons in 1983, "which for me was the river and the fields, and the wonderful things that bloomed, that are so much in my stories, was still stalked by some horror all around it" (*GAE* 123). The primary image of this "medieval world of terror" was the lynching and the haunting figure of the tarred, burning black man from Goyen's childhood memories. "But the horror of the Klan, the blackness of that, the evil of them, just pervaded the whole land. And there always seemed to be henchmen in it, and it seemed to be a nightmare of mutiny and banditry. This is the world I was in" (*GAE* 122).

Mythic structures of incest and unspeakable knowledge helped frame these memories, which combine local racist lore—the image of the black man raping the white woman—with Greek tragedy. "Had I a Hundred Mouths" focuses on the uncle's complicity in this racial and sexual violence, the intermingling of black and white in the regional curse of lust and fallenness. The white uncle duplicates the actions of the nameless black man, and though he shows compassion to the orphaned Leander, he shares the Klansmen's frenzy for blood. Divided like the place itself between compassion and fear, he participates in the castration. His cursed and incestuous couplings with his cousin suggest that the world of the story—the mythic locus of his nephew's upbringing—has turned in upon itself, ruined by obsessive self-concern. The very country itself has failed to avoid the inturning that threatens Arcadio and is represented by the terrible *figura*. The well, the same cistern out of which the voices emerge in *The House of Breath*, is fouled.

This image of deep regional pollution becomes clearer in the second part of the projected novel that appeared a year after "Had I a Hundred Mouths." "Tongues of Men and Angels" expands and complicates several of the characters in the earlier story, providing short narrative sketches that deepen the family history. There is Joe Parrish, Louetta's father, who went crazy when his wife ran away "with a good young Mexican" (*HHM* 61). When he returns after a long wandering and learns that Louetta has drowned in the well, a demon tells him to jump into the mud-filled cistern. In an echo of the diver in "Bridge of Music," Joe Parrish ends up buried headfirst in the well with only his feet visible above the sediment. When the rescuers try to pull his body out by his ankles, the feet hideously break free. Eventually someone seals the well and writes in the fresh concrete of its cap the words, "THIS WELL ACCURST" (*HHM* 65). Joe Parrish's wife Blanch also returns to the family home, now with her Mexican daughter Inez Melendrez. The house seems to haunt Blanch (she hears footsteps on the roof), and she dies after falling from the ladder she uses to obsessively pursue the source of the sounds. The house burns, and Inez Melendrez runs away and marries a rich oil man; she has a child who dies when he is three years old, and she renounces her wealth and joins a Carmelite "nunnery."

Goyen's development of these regional legends also includes a backstory for the father of Leander, the black man whose name we now learn is Ormsby. This "wild person," who migrated from near Mobile, Alabama, to Moscow, Texas, to work in a sawmill, courts trouble: "he drank whiskey with the Cushata Indians and fucked them and cut them across their throats and faces with a nasty knife. He was wild with his red dick and mean with his knife and was locked up a lot and bound to posts and trees to keep him from tearing up half a town—or his own self" (*HHM* 69). But like many of Goyen's characters who follow their darker natures over the edge, Ormsby descends into madness. After raping Louetta, he finds his way back to Alabama and sinks himself, literally, into a swamp filled with alligators, hoping they will tear him apart. When he survives and emerges from the mud and insects, he's quiet and gentle, filled "with a peace he could not understand" (*HHM* 70). He returns to Moscow and confesses his past to the uncle, who overcomes his rage and invites Ormsby to live with him. Though harassed by the Klan for their interracial household, the two survive until Ormsby dies and the uncle leaves to search for his brother and sister.

The final section of "Tongues of Men and Angels" returns to the two cousins, now grown, who had first heard the uncle's story together but came to live distant, separate lives. The older cousin returns to his hometown to seek out the younger, whose signature is required to sell the family land. Unable to find him, he settles on the land and builds a new house until one day a strange figure approaches, the now-mute cousin whose tongue has been cut out by the Klan for revealing its secrets. The story told by the disfigured and abused cousin is one of Goyen's strangest: after the KKK cut out his tongue and "put a fish hook in it and hung it on the branch of a tree," the cousin goes mad, "tormented by the image of the lapping tongue and of the genitals of black men he had helped castrate" (*HHM* 75). He becomes a sort of sex slave to the Klansmen, who discover that his maimed throat "was so sexually maddening that . . . they fought each other over it out of self-loathing and unending whipping prurience" (*HHM* 76). A demon helps the cousin escape and make his way home, later offering to restore his tongue if "he would use it to show the poor Mexican people in the peafields of the Rio Grande Valley among whom he had worked how to spell words and how to add numbers" (*HHM* 76–77). The cousin, known as El Mudo to the people in the valley, becomes a kind of political evangelist, eventually fighting back the KKK's effort to bust a nascent farmworkers' union.

As Repusseau has argued, this moment in which sexual obsession, sexual violence, homosexuality, and abuse become a basis for speech and communal expression is extraordinary—not only for the outrageous imagination at work but for the willed transformation of silence into voice: "Losing speech is also going down too low, drowning oneself in a darkness of fear, self-loathing, and sexual obsession. And rising is recovering, speaking again freely, being able to utter clearly and lightly, in the light, what mustn't be hidden but, on the contrary, should be proclaimed at the top of one's voice for everybody to hear."[21] It is as though Goyen had found a story for his own strange emergence as an artist from East Texas—the birth of a speaker or singer out of violence and fear and repression, overcoming and expressing the sexual divisions that had marked him from the beginning.

Even considering this rebirth of the silenced tongue, however, "Had I a Hundred Mouths" and "Tongues of Men and Angels" offer less sanguine visions of redemption than many of Goyen's earlier stories. The harshness of this East Texas history is not entirely balanced—not canceled out or overcome—by the conversion experiences of characters like Ormsby and El Mudo. This is not to suggest that Goyen had lost faith in this kind of personal transformation, but his willingness to grant clemency to the sources of his youthful pain seems limited by a fierce desire to reveal regional evils. On a personal level, this liberation of his deepest angers produced a remarkable moment in his work— nothing less than the destruction of the house of breath itself. When the narrator hears of the burning of the family house, he makes his way to the site with a specific goal in mind:

> I later came to the place to see what was left of the door. I found in rubble on a jagged piece of glass the perfect head of the horse rearing passionate and proud in his curling delicate mane, and took it. I looked for the rider but never found him. He must have lain on the burnt ground in a thousand pieces of blackened glass. I would give anything to have found the rider of that precious horse, horseman lost forever. (*HHM* 66)

Along with the sealing of the well, this imaginative purgation of his own creation—the deepest emblem of his past and the origin of his life's work—seems a deliberate gesture on Goyen's part, a relinquishment of an image set (house, door, horse, rider) that had haunted and driven him for years. If the rider at the door had always been the dark figure of prohibition and exile, then he could at last, even if reluctantly, see it destroyed, broken, finally reabsorbed by the bitter land of his birth.

"No More My Own Body"

That spring of 1983 when he delivered "Recovering" at NYU was a hopeful time for Goyen. He had written quickly and forcefully during the past year, and the fruits of his work were starting to coalesce into *Leander*. His interview with Reginald Gibbons was to appear soon in *TriQuarterly*, and *Arcadio*, the proofs of which he saw later that summer, would be published in September. There were plans for a trip to France to visit Repusseau, who had become his preferred translator, and the Easter trip to New York couldn't help but raise his spirits. By June, however, it was clear that the months of chemotherapy had not worked. Throughout his illness, he had shown tremendous determination to get better, almost willing his own recovery, but this time he couldn't hide his disappointment. Though more treatment would follow, his ability to fight the cancer steadily weakened. About a year after his first, traumatic hospital stay, he was again admitted to Cedars Sinai, where Roberts and a steady stream of friends did what they could to encourage him and make him comfortable. On the day he died, as Roberts recounts it, "friends started drifting into his room. He had a very large room in the hospital, and they would sit on the floor, and they would sit on couches or chairs or windowsills, or they would just stand and lean. They wanted to be around him. They wanted to be near him. They wanted to let him know how much they loved him."[22] Cards and letters had been pouring in for weeks, a tribute to just how intimate and tender Goyen's relationships could be. His correspondence over these final years is remarkable for its attention to the lives of others, not just their literary aspirations or the ups and downs of their careers, but to their motivating hurts, the feelings (of pain or wonder or loss) that drove them forward or prevented them from making their way. He understood this kind of struggle perhaps more acutely and more completely than most, and, by all accounts, he had an extraordinary gift for making others feel his concern.

On August 29, 1983, William Goyen died, surrounded by friends, in Roberts's arms.[23] He was sixty-eight years old. Memorial services were held in both Los Angeles and New York, and his body was interred at Pinelawn Cemetery in Farmingdale, New York. He had once told an interviewer that despite his connections to Texas, he would not be buried there; the lack of welcome he had felt most of his life precluded any final reconciliation with the soil of his birth. Instead, he found a place next to his mother-in-law, Ann, a gesture that seems to respect the possibilities of new families over old. For Goyen was, if nothing else, a writer who sought a new kind of kinship, an intimate and receptive gathering of wanderers with stories to tell. He had committed his life to this principle: that one must speak, not in order to relieve the burden or to cure it. He was insistent that writing was not therapy. It was, however, a way to be, to exist through the rescue of all that was lost in a life. It was a blessing and a holding on, a naming and a relinquishment—a gesture of saving that stayed with him to the end.

Even in his final days, he had continued to write, his hand moving unsteadily across small notepads or scraps of paper. One of these surviving fragments can still be found among the trove of manuscripts and materials in his archive in Austin. In very shaky handwriting that somehow seems as intent as ever, he continued to wrestle with the angel: "But it is no more my own own body. Does not not belong to me to me. But it is your body? Is it not in God's hands? Can you let your it it go?"[24]

Acknowledgments

Without Reginald Gibbons's help and encouragement, this book would never have been written. Since becoming literary executor of Goyen's estate in the early 1980s, he has done more than anyone to keep William Goyen's writing before the public. Gibbons's study of the short fiction is essential to anyone who approaches this subject, and his work as an interviewer and editor of Goyen's manuscripts has been crucial to the development of this study. When I first contacted him in the late 1990s about my desire to write a Goyen biography, he was generous enough to take me seriously and give me his time and attention repeatedly as I worked on the project over many years. I can only hope that this book is adequate recompense for his helpful advice, kindness, and inspiration.

Any study of Goyen's writing owes an immense debt to the work of Robert Phillips and Patrice Repusseau. Phillips was the first and most important of Goyen's scholarly readers and played an invaluable role in promoting Goyen's career at a time when it was desperately needed. His critical articles, introductory study, *Paris Review* interview, and edition of Goyen's letters are the pillars upon which any reading of Goyen is inevitably built, and this book would not have been possible without the information and insight available in his criticism. Repusseau has not only served as Goyen's major French translator for many years (after taking over from his mentor, Maurice Edgar Coindreau) but also is arguably the most perceptive and deepest reader of Goyen's complete oeuvre. His research into Goyen's childhood and early writings as well as his extraordinary essays on the late stories have been essential to this project, well beyond what is indicated in the text. In addition to his published criticism, he has also shown remarkable generosity in sharing his research and materials, including texts, letters, and photographs not available in Goyen's archives.

I would like to thank a number of Goyen's friends and family members who were willing to relate memories and impressions of him: Doris Roberts, Robert Phillips, Reginald Gibbons, Patrice Repusseau, Don Gerrard, James White, Joyce Carol Oates, Eve La Salle Caram, John Igo, and Elizabeth Spencer.

I am particularly indebted to the librarians and staffs at the Harry Ransom Humanities Research Center at the University of Texas, the Woodson Research Center at Rice University, the Katherine Anne Porter Collection at the University of Maryland, the Beinecke Rare Book and Manuscript Library at Yale University, the Special Collections department at the University of Delaware, the Special Collections Research Center at Syracuse University, the Archives of American Art at the Smithsonian Institution, the Houston Public Library, the Dallas Public Library, and the staff at the Taos Public Library and Millicent Rogers Museum in Taos, New Mexico. I am especially grateful to the interlibrary loan staff at the University of Denver's Anderson Academic Commons and to humanities specialist Peggy Keeran for help in tracking down hard-to-find documents. Jean Cannon, Bill Fagelson, Ronald Donn, and Anders Jeffries provided useful assistance in locating and copying documents.

Jan Gorak read portions of the manuscript and suggested several important improvements. The two anonymous readers for the University of Texas Press likewise gave careful consideration to the text, and I am grateful for their suggestions and corrections.

Initial research for this project was funded by an endowed professorship from the University of Louisiana at Monroe. Additional support for travel and research came from the University of Denver's Faculty Research Fund. I am thankful for sabbatical and research leave that made the completion of this text possible.

Portions of this book have been previously published in different form. I would like to thank the editors of *The Southern Review, Raritan,* and *Southwest Review* for permission to reprint work that originally appeared in their pages.

My wife, Hillary, and son, Ethan, have never failed to be supportive of what turned out to be a long and challenging obsession, even when the three of us were losing our way on the back roads of New Mexico or poking around rainy graveyards in East Texas. Needless to say, I couldn't have completed this project so happily or so memorably without them.

Finally, this book is dedicated to the memory of Martin Pops. Marty taught at the State University of New York at Buffalo for more than forty years and during that time led his many students, of which I was one, in a sensitive and passionately intelligent reading of the great books of American literature. He was one of the most cultured, friendly, and funny people I have ever known, and while writing my dissertation under his direction I learned more than I can say about what it means to respond—wholeheartedly—to a lasting work of art. Much of what I am as a reader and scholar I owe to him.

Notes

Introduction

1. Richard Rhodes, "William Goyen's world is enormous and enormously minute," *Chicago Tribune*, November 9, 1975, F3.

2. David Foster Wallace, "E Unibus Pluram: Television and U.S. Fiction," *Review of Contemporary Fiction* 13, no. 2 (Summer: 1993): 151–194.

3. Stuart Wright's 1986 bibliography lists published translations in Argentina, Denmark, France, Germany, Italy, Portugal, and Spain. See *William Goyen: A Descriptive Bibliography, 1938–1985* (Westport, Conn.: Meckler Publishing, 1986), 159–165.

4. Ernst Robert Curtius, "William Goyen," in *Essays on European Literature* (Princeton, N.J.: Princeton University Press, 1973), 463–464.

5. Gaston Bachelard, *The Poetics of Space* (Boston: Beacon, 1994), 58.

6. The more recent addition of material from Goyen's journals and other autobiographical writings, published in Reginald Gibbons's *Goyen: Autobiographical Essays, Notebooks, Evocations, Interviews* (Austin: University of Texas Press, 2007), has provided new access to Goyen's archive.

7. Author interview with Don Gerrard. Kathryn Goyen became an evangelical minister later in her life.

8. Goyen to Clyde Grimm, July 17, 1970 (*SL* 330).

9. Goyen to Robert Linscott, March 14, 1951 (*SL* 179).

Prologue: The Drowning

1. Rolande Ballorain, "Interview with William Goyen," *Delta* 9 (1979): 7–45, 25. "Others drowned in you, too—three Charity girls almost did while wading and squealing and one of them did and this was Otey Bell, rescued by Christy Ganchion, but too late. They rolled her over a log but she was drowned" (*HOB* 22–23). In a letter to Robert Phillips, Goyen explained that "Bridge of Music" was based on a memory: "This seems to be a sudden vision of my life, out of memory (it's a real place—in Riverside, Texas, just outside Trinity; the bridge was real, the trestle was real, those were my parents and sister, the incident was real)." Quoted in Robert Phillips, *William Goyen* (Boston: G. K. Hall, 1979), 109.

2. Ballorain, "Interview," 25.

3. Ibid., 42.

Chapter 1: Trinity: 1915–1922

1. Thad Sitton and James H. Conrad, *Nameless Towns: Texas Sawmill Communities, 1880–1942* (Austin: University of Texas Press, 1998), 5.

2. Both Goyen and his family used the spelling "Billie" until his teenage years, when it became "Billy." See HRC 54.4.

3. Unpublished manuscript sent to Patrice Repusseau by Goyen.

4. Quoted in Patrice Repusseau, "Lunar Plexus: On William Goyen's 'In the Icebound Hothouse,'" *Mid-American Review* 13, no. 1 (1992): 3–38, 17–18.

5. Author interview with Don Gerrard. Rolande Ballorain, "Interview with William Goyen," *Delta* 9 (1979): 7–45, 42.

6. The incident is likely a memory from Goyen's childhood. It appears in *The House of Breath* in almost the same form: ". . . like the time of the hunting trip that I was forced to go on and was almost shot because I had cracked a pecan off to myself in the woods, standing in the lemongreen light of trees, and the hunters had crept upon me and aimed at the cracking noise I made, like a squirrel they hunted, and would have shot if I had not emerged just at the moment from the thicket and looked, pitiful and pitifully, at them. Then they cursed and turned upon me and turned upon each other because they were tired and a bit drunk and the sun was hot and there was a boy who did not want to hunt, not even to shoot his nigger-shooter, but only crack his nuts, alone, and foil them" (*HOB* 23–24).

7. WRC, boxes 5 and 6.

8. Genealogical information, including copies of letters written by William Walter Goyen during the Civil War, are in HRC 43.10.

9. William Goyen, "Right Here at Christmas," *Redbook* 150, December 1977, 77–78, 77.

10. Goyen, "Right Here at Christmas," 78.

11. Ibid., 78. May could correspond to Goyen's aunt Gay, born 1905. His father's other sisters were Hazel (1896) and Bessie (1898).

12. "When my first novel was published, my father's fears and accusations were justified—despite the success of the book—and he was outraged to the point of not speaking to me for a year. This could, of course, have been because the book was mostly about his own family—the sawmill family I spoke of earlier" (*GAE* 74).

13. In the 1964 play *Christy*, a similar grandfather explains that his crippled foot came from his "Irish mother's own foot that stomped me in a black-eyed Irish tantrum when I was at the age of four" (HRC 18.2).

14. Ballorain, "Interview," 16. Later in the same interview, when asked if Follie, or the person he is based on, was homosexual, Goyen replied: "Yes, Follie was the pure, the modern—we would recognize him, he's just the transvestite that is so popular among—God, people pay money to go see them in night-clubs" (20).

15. This is not to say that the novel is without connection to Goyen's family or to the Trinity locals. Katherine Lederer's reminiscence of growing up in Trinity and reading the novel when it appeared confirms that the town's population eagerly bought the novel looking for—and finding—correspondences to people and places they knew. See "Of Time, William Goyen, and His River," Katherine Lederer, *Mid-American Review* 13, no. 1 (1992): 42–44.

16. Sitton and Conrad, *Nameless Towns*, 110. In a 1979 interview, Goyen was asked whether there were KKK members in his family, and he replied, "It was true in my family. I saw that" (Ballorain, "Interview," 16).

17. The 1998 dragging death of James Byrd in Jasper, 95 miles from Trinity, recalls precisely this sort of horror and suggests the scattered resilience of the region's historical racism.

18. Interview with Patrick Bennet in *Talking with Texas Writers: Twelve Interviews* (College Station: Texas A&M University Press, 1980), 246.

19. Wanda A. Landry, *Outlaws in the Big Thicket* (Austin: Eakin, 1976), 50.

20. There is no doubt that the Trinity River of Goyen's childhood changed dramatically after his family left the area. The damming of the river at Livingston and the redirection of some of its tributaries forever altered its flood cycles and changed the landscape around it. Katherine Lederer, a literary scholar who also grew up near the river, shared Goyen's "almost physical shock at the devastation that had replaced the river" as seen from Riverside years later. See Lederer, "Of Time," 42.

Chapter 2: Merrill Street: 1923–1931

1. Thad Sitton and James H. Conrad, *Nameless Towns: Texas Sawmill Communities, 1880–1942* (Austin: University of Texas Press, 1998), 199–200.

2. The unedited transcript reads: "(the result was quite a sprinkling of homosexuals and alcoholics among his own brothers and sisters)" (HRC 35.14).

3. Stephen Barnhill, "Portrait of the Artist as Young Texan," *Sallyport* 32, June 1977, 6–8. In a 1977 interview with Rice's alumni magazine, Goyen didn't explain his father's reaction, but there is little evidence that the dance lessons continued.

4. Ibid., 7.

5. Interview with Patrick Bennett in *Talking with Texas Writers: Twelve Interviews* (College Station: Texas A&M University Press, 1980), 239.

Chapter 3: Rice Institute: 1932–1941

1. Rolande Ballorain, "Interview with William Goyen," *Delta* 9 (1979): 36.

2. This is the only mention in Goyen's correspondence or notes of his treatment by a mental health professional during his youth. Given his obvious emotional difficulties and occasional conflicts with his family, it isn't surprising, however, that he or his parents would seek out such help in his high school or early college years.

3. Stephen Barnhill, "Portrait of the Artist as Young Texan," *Sallyport* 32, June 1977, 8.

4. Shelby Hodge, "The Heights now . . . and then," *Houston Post*, May 7, 1978, BB 1,2.

5. Barnhill, "Portrait of the Artist," 6.

6. Patrice Repusseau, *William Goyen: De la Maison Vers la Foyer* (Pantin, France: Le Castor Astral, 1991), 70.

7. Ibid., 72.

8. Goyen to William Hart, March 3, 1937.

9. George Williams to Patrice Repusseau, August 1, 1975. Courtesy of Patrice Repusseau.

10. William Goyen, "The Seadowns' Bible," *Delta* 9 (November 1979): 113–119, 115.

11. Ibid., 115.

12. Ibid., 113.

13. Many of Goyen's Houston friends, including Zoë Léger and Nione Carlson, came from this group, who sometimes called themselves the "Left Bank" of Buffalo Bayou. According to Jones's biographer Helen Sheehy, "the group christened shy Bill Goyen the 'Houston messiah,'

because he hailed from the town of Trinity in East Texas and because he refused to get out of his car when he first met them because he thought they were so wild." See *Margo: The Life and Theatre of Margo Jones* (Dallas: Southern Methodist University Press, 1989), 29–30.

14. Nan Hoos to Goyen, April 25, 1975 (HRC 43.10).

15. Repusseau, *William Goyen*, 71.

16. Goyen to William Hart, September 1938 (WRC).

17. Goyen to William Hart, June 1937 (WRC).

18. William Goyen, "Playwright and Audience in Elizabethan Drama," 1939 Thesis, Rice Institute, HRC 27.7.

19. Goyen, "Playwright and Audience."

20. Goyen to Emma Goyen, September 18, 1940.

21. Goyen to William Hart, September 1939 (WRC).

22. Goyen to Reginald Francis Arragon, January 16, 1946 (*SL* 39).

23. Goyen to Archibald MacLeish, June 1940 (*SL* 9).

24. Goyen to Archibald MacLeish, June 1940 (*SL* 11).

Chapter 4: Ulysses: 1942–1945

1. Stephen Barnhill, "Portrait of the Artist as Young Texan," *Sallyport* 32, June 1977, 8.

2. Despite his frequent claims to have been in the Navy for up to five years, Goyen's record shows that from February 1940 to early 1942, he "taught world literature in translation" and "courses in Freshman writing" at the University of Houston. Goyen's Navy record is in HRC 33.8.

3. George Williams describes meeting Goyen on the street in Houston a year after the United States had entered the war: "He was dressed in the uniform of a 'common sailor' of the U.S. Navy—and immediately broke out into a kind of apology for being seen in that kind of outfit. He knew he was too good for it." George Williams to Patrice Repusseau, August 1, 1975. Courtesy of Patrice Repusseau.

4. Goyen to Charles Provine Goyen, July 14, 1942 (WRC).

5. Goyen to William Hart, August 2, 1942. Emphases in original (WRC).

6. Goyen to Charles Goyen, July 14, 1942 (WRC).

7. Goyen to William Hart, August 2, 1942 (WRC).

8. Goyen to Emma Goyen, October 8, 1942 (WRC).

9. Goyen to William Hart, October 7, 1942 (WRC).

10. Goyen to William Hart, October 7, 1942. Emphases in original (WRC).

11. Goyen to William Hart, November 30, 1942 (WRC).

12. Goyen to William Hart, February 7, 1943 (WRC).

13. Goyen to William Hart, January 11, 1943 (WRC).

14. Of course, whether the Navy was a choice depends upon the accuracy of the story Goyen told about his draft reprieve. If he did promise to join the Navy when he was sent home from San Antonio, there may have been little he could have done to avoid it. But it's also possible that the story of that promise was a retroactive attempt to explain why he ended up joining the Navy as a seaman.

15. "Air: The Navy's Babies," *Time*, September 4, 1944.

16. Goyen to William Hart, February 11, 1943 (WRC).

17. Goyen to William Hart, March 27, 1943 (WRC).

18. Goyen to William Hart, March 27, 1943 (WRC).

19. Untitled manuscript enclosed with letter to William Hart, March 27, 1943 (WRC).

20. Goyen to William Hart, March 7, 1943 (WRC).

21. Goyen to William Hart, March 27, 1943 (WRC).

22. Goyen to William Hart, May 14, 1943 (WRC).

23. Goyen to William Hart, June 1, 1943 (WRC).

24. Goyen to Emma Goyen, June 7, 1943 (WRC).

25. Goyen to Emma Goyen, October 22, 1944 (WRC).

26. Goyen to Emma Goyen, December 18, 1944 (WRC).

27. Goyen to Emma Goyen, January 3, 1945 (WRC).

28. In fact, problems with the *Casablanca*'s propeller and stern tube were responsible for keeping it out of combat areas and turning it into a training ship. As Barbara G. Jones explains, the drive shaft developed a "whining sound" that "was significant enough that a Japanese submarine could have detected it miles away." The problem may have helped keep the *Casablanca* out of danger long enough to avoid the fate of its early counterparts such as the *Liscome Bay*, which was struck by a torpedo in November of 1943. See *The Role the USS Casablanca (CVE-55) Played in World War II in the Pacific* (Lewiston, N.Y.: Edwin Mellen, 2010), 76.

29. Jones, *Role*, 122.

30. See Jones, *Role*, 146–147. On another occasion, the *Casablanca* had to slow down to pick up a sailor who had attempted suicide by jumping from the deck of a nearby transport ship (Jones 244–245).

31. Goyen to Charles and Emma Goyen, May 21, 1945 (WRC).

32. Goyen to Charles and Emma Goyen, May 21, 1945 (WRC).

33. Goyen to Charles and Emma Goyen, August 8, 1945 (WRC).

34. HRC, 28.12.

35. George Williams to Patrice Repusseau, August 1, 1975. Courtesy of Patrice Repusseau.

36. Goyen to William Hart, October 19, 1945 (WRC).

37. Goyen to Charles and Emma Goyen, August 8, 1945 (WRC).

38. Goyen to William Hart, September 29, 1945 (WRC).

Chapter 5: El Prado: 1945–1948

1. Notebook entries from the mid-1970s describing this trip are in HRC 31.1.

2. Goyen to William Hart, March 4, 1946 (WRC).

3. Goyen to Emmet Riordan, September 26, 1946 (*SL* 62).

4. Rolande Ballorain, "Interview with William Goyen," *Delta* 9 (1979): 24.

5. Goyen to William Hart, September 29, 1945 (WRC).

6. Goyen to William Hart, April 29 and May 4, 1946 (WRC).

7. Goyen to William Hart, July 15, 1946 (WRC).

8. Goyen to William Hart, July 15, 1946 (WRC).

9. William Goyen, *Nine Poems* (New York: Albondocani Press, 1976). Of this small set of early poems, the only poetry Goyen published, some appeared in *Voices* and in *Poetry* in 1949. They were later gathered and published in a limited-edition volume in 1976.

10. Goyen to Emmet and Anne Riordan, June 6, 1947 (*SL* 71).

11. Goyen to Dorothy Brett, September 5, 1947 (HRC 49.1).

12. Goyen to William Hart, November 10, 1947 (WRC).

13. Though some of his own experience does seem included in the portrait, Goyen based the description and some of the details of the character on Spud Johnson, who ran a small but influential printing press in Taos and came to Napa at Goyen's suggestion to teach a print shop class.

14. The manuscript of *Section Two* is in HRC 25.9.

15. See Barbara G. Jones, *The Role the USS* Casablanca *(CVE-55) Played in World War II in the Pacific* (Lewiston, N.Y.: Edwin Mellen, 2010), 248.

16. Goyen to Toni Strassman, August 18, 1946 (*SL* 57).

Chapter 6: Christopher Icarus: 1948–1950

1. "The Crimes of Mirensky," manuscript courtesy of Patrice Repusseau.

2. "Reprise de 'The Crimes of Mirensky,'" manuscript courtesy of Patrice Repusseau.

3. He once told Katherine Anne Porter that his first attempt at fiction, written when he was eighteen, was titled "Fly High, Icarus." See Goyen to Porter, August 14, 1951 (*SL* 224).

4. Both are obvious allusions to Joyce's *Portrait*: "Let us not, as Stephen Daedalus would not, serve any cause in which we do not believe, whether it be 'family, country or church.'" Goyen to William Hart, March 14, 1947 (WRC).

5. A pencil note on the manuscript in Goyen's hand, perhaps added years later when he sent these early works to Repusseau, reads: "Fucking his mother's sister who he's so fond of and who comes from Oregon (the place his mother misses so much) is fucking his own mother."

6. Despite later statements to the contrary, letters and notebook entries show that Goyen read Lawrence during this period, both the novels in manuscript that were still in Frieda Lawrence's possession and the poetry. See *SL* 37, 44, and 55.

7. Joyce Carol Oates suggests this connection in her introduction to *Had I a Hundred Mouths, New and Selected Stories 1947–1983* (New York: Clarkson N. Potter, 1985).

8. D. H. Lawrence, "The Escaped Cock," in *The Virgin and the Gypsy and Other Stories*, ed. Michael Herbert, Bethan Jones, and Lindeth Vasey (Cambridge: Cambridge University Press, 2005), 130.

9. Ibid., 137.

10. See Goyen to Margarita G. Smith, October 25, 1946 (*SL* 64) and Goyen to Zoë Léger, February 4, 1949 (*SL* 130).

11. He also worked very briefly for the *Dallas Morning News* as a reporter-reviewer.

12. Goyen to James Laughlin, April 17, 1948 (*SL* 99).

13. Quoted in Goyen to William Hart, June 3, 1948 (WRC).

14. William Goyen, "Four American Portraits as Elegy," *Accent* 8, no. 3 (Spring, 1948): 131–141, 138.

15. Goyen to Zoë Léger, April 17, 1948 (HRC).

16. Goyen to William Hart, June 3, 1948 (*SL* 107).

17. Goyen to Emma Goyen, June 2, 1948 (*SL* 104–106).

18. Patrice Repusseau quotes from a note to an early draft of *The House of Breath* that blames Emma Goyen's disapproval for his sense of exile: "The deadly paralyzing sense of guilt, sense of Sin she (my kin) gave me—made me son of grief. . . . Put such a burden on the back of every experience of the sense, of the flesh—and put terror and sense of shame and guilt in experience of show and music—turned them secret and finally destroyed them. Wretched

relationships, marred love—(even now I have the sense of shame concerning my relationship with Walt)—this explains my 'exile,' my feeling alien, not being able to return 'home' or to my kin." "Lunar Plexus: On William Goyen's 'In the Icebound Hothouse,'" *Mid-American Review* 13, no. 1 (1992): 9–38, 32.

19. Goyen to Emma Goyen, June 2, 1948 (*SL* 106).

20. Goyen to William Hart, October 16, 1945 (WRC).

21. This sexual incompatibility is also referenced in Thomas E. Wright's *Growing up with Legends: A Literary Memoir* (Westport, CT: Praeger, 1998), in which Wright describes his own brief affair with Goyen in 1951; see pp. 34–37.

22. Goyen to Zoë Léger, June 9, 1948 (*SL* 109).

23. Goyen to Zoë Léger, July 3, 1948 (HRC).

24. David Leeming, *Stephen Spender: A Life in Modernism* (New York: Henry Holt, 1999), 170.

25. Goyen to Emma and Charles Goyen, September 9, 1948 (WRC).

26. Goyen to William Hart, August 24, 1948 (WRC).

27. Goyen to Emma and Charles Goyen, January 3, 1949 (WRC).

28. Goyen to Zoë Léger, December 5, 1948 (*SL* 123).

29. Goyen to Emma and Charles Goyen, November 12, 1948 (WRC).

30. Goyen to Dorothy Brett, May 13, 1949 (HRC).

31. According to John Sutherland, Spender also "put himself out to get Goyen's patrons (Mabel Dodge, notably) to come through with the cash that would enable Bill to travel"; see Sutherland, *Stephen Spender: A Literary Life* (Oxford: Oxford University Press, 2005), 340.

32. Goyen to Dorothy Brett, March 8, 1949 (*SL* 133).

33. Goyen to Dorothy Brett, January 18, 1949 (*SL* 126).

34. Goyen to Charles Goyen, October 20, 1949 (WRC).

35. See Sutherland, *Stephen Spender*, 340; and Christopher Isherwood, *Diaries, Volume One: 1939–1960* (New York: Harper Perennial, 1998), 676.

36. Goyen later remembered one of Sitwell's strange performances: "We went to her house and she read one night; she sat behind a screen because she wouldn't read facing anyone or a group . . . behind a marvelous Chinese screen and you would hear this voice coming through the screen . . . all those people. . . . That was a world Spender gave me and was a great influence on my life and on my work" (*GAE* 84–85).

37. Goyen to William Hart, November 21, 1949 (WRC).

38. Goyen to Emma Goyen, December 5, 1949. There is no evidence in Goyen's letters to suggest that Spender accompanied him or that Goyen ever wrote such an article for *Partisan Review*.

39. Goyen to Spud Johnson, January 5, 1950 (*SL* 151).

40. Truman Capote's biographer, Gerald Clarke, describes Goyen as "Barber's lover for a while," presumably during late 1950 or early 1951 before Goyen went to Yaddo in February. Goyen did visit Capricorn, Barber's house with Giancarlo Menotti in upstate New York, during this period, but if a relationship developed, it was very short-lived and left no trace in Goyen's letters or papers. See Clarke, *Capote: A Biography* (New York: Simon and Schuster, 1988), 138. The planned vocal symphony never materialized.

41. Goyen to Spud Johnson, January 5, 1950 (*SL* 152).

42. Goyen to Charles and Emma Goyen, February 20, 1950 (WRC).

Chapter 7: *The House of Breath*: 1950

1. Rolande Ballorain, "Interview with William Goyen," *Delta* 9 (1979): 25.

2. David Cowart, "Family as Text in *The House of Breath*," in *A Goyen Companion: Appreciations of a Writer's Writer* (Austin: University of Texas Press, 1997), 1.

3. Katherine Wilson Goyen, Katie, was born in 1867 in Alabama and died in Houston in 1939. Her father, George Wilson, immigrated from Sweden and met her mother in Alabama. "Possible malignancy of goiter" is listed on her death certificate under cause of death. In *The House of Breath*: "'You was born and raised in Alabama, ran with a flock of children through the pastures like geese; and your papa was a sea captain besides ownin about a dozen Negroes that worked his cottonfields . . .'" (139).

4. Author interview with Don Gerrard.

5. "Remembrance of Things Past," *Atlantic Monthly* 186, Sept. 1950, 81. "A Private World," *Times Literary Supplement*, December 7, 1951, 761. "Briefly Noted, Fiction," *New Yorker* 26, Sept. 2, 1950, 73.

6. Ruth Chapin, "Poetic Evocation of a World," *Christian Science Monitor*, Sept. 16, 1950. Roger Shattuck, "Six First Assignments of Guilt," *Western Review* 16 (1951): 85–90. In the *Hudson Review*, Northrop Frye found the novel "remarkable" and "outstandingly clever." "Novels on Several Occasions," *Hudson Review* 3, no. 4 (Winter 1951): 611–619.

7. Edwin Muir, "A New Writer," *The Observer*, December 2, 1951, 7.

8. Oliver La Farge, "Degeneracy in East Texas," *Saturday Review* 33, Sept. 9, 1950, 19.

9. Charles E. White, *Houston Chronicle*, August 20, 1950.

10. Lon Tinkle, *Dallas Morning News*, August 20, 1950.

11. Katherine Anne Porter, "This Strange, Old World," *New York Times*, Aug. 20, 1950, 5, 17.

12. Coindreau later explained that he was attracted to the book by reading some of the less favorable reviews from critics he tended to disagree with. But he gave full credit to Curtius for discovering *The House of Breath* and popularizing it in Germany. See Maurice Edgar Coindreau, *Mémoires d'un traducteur: Entretiens avec Christian Guidicelli* (Paris: Gallimard, 1992), 79.

13. Goyen to William Hart, July 10, 1950 (*SL* 161).

Chapter 8: Marvello: 1950–1953

1. Goyen was not above changing facts to boost his chances of success. He candidly told his parents that he had lied to his publishers about his age, telling Random House that he was 33 when *The House of Breath* was published rather than 35. "I suppose I'll never get over resenting the years the war took away from me, so I feel like cheating." Goyen to Charles and Emma Goyen, April 18, 1950 (WRC).

2. Goyen to Spud Johnson, August 12, 1947 (*SL* 83).

3. Goyen to William Hart, November 10, 1947 (WRC).

4. Goyen to Katherine Anne Porter, May 3, 1950 (*SL* 159).

5. Goyen, "Katherine Anne Porter: An Appreciation," in *Katherine Anne Porter Remembered*, ed. Darlene Harbour Unrue (Tuscaloosa: University of Alabama Press, 2010), 120.

6. Darlene Harbor Unrue, *Katherine Anne Porter: The Life of an Artist* (Jackson: University of Mississippi Press, 2005), 218–219.

7. In September, Goyen wrote to Hart, perhaps not with complete candor: "My relation-

ship with Stephen is very difficult at this point, for abscense [sic] always does some damage—I don't mean that either of us has changed, only that coming back to him, leaving Walter, seemed suddenly so terrifying a thing." Goyen to William Hart, September 20, 1950 (WRC).

8. Goyen to William Hart, September 20, 1950 (WRC).

9. One unexpected result of his time in Chicago was the chance to meet T. S. Eliot, who had read *The House of Breath* at the urging of Elizabeth Bowen: "Mr. Eliot was at the University of Chicago, and I happened to be there for one winter. So we came together, and I went and sat and had tea with him one afternoon. It was terrifying. I think I still had on orange shoes; you remember we used to wear those old shoes in Texas, and orange is the only color I can think of to describe them. I felt very hicky and country, even though I had been in London that time. He just scared the hell out of me." Patrick Bennett, *Talking with Texas Writers: Twelve Interviews* (College Station: Texas A&M University Press, 1980), 235.

10. Janis Stout, *Katherine Anne Porter: A Sense of the Times* (Charlottesville: University of Virginia Press, 1995), 177–178.

11. In 1980, Goyen offered the following memories of his Yaddo experience to Robert Phillips: "I lived in the cottage on the corner with a good workroom and a big long bedroom. . . . I remember that I was emotionally quite badly disturbed then, during that Yaddo time (2 months?) and that once Elizabeth thought I might have to leave—for help." Goyen to Robert Phillips, August 19, 1980 (*SL* 372).

12. This street no longer exists in Houston. It was removed during the construction of Interstate 10.

13. Stout, *Katherine Anne Porter*, 182 (HRC 20.7).

14. "At Lady A's" was most likely written as part of Goyen's autobiographical work *Six Women*, which would place its composition somewhere in the 1960s or 1970s. He may have decided to incorporate it into a later version of *Half a Look of Cain*, which remained unpublished until after his death.

15. Goyen to Robert Linscott, March 14, 1951 (*SL* 178, 179).

16. Reginald Gibbons, *William Goyen: A Study of the Short Fiction* (Boston: G. K. Hall, 1991), 24.

17. Walt Whitman, "Song of Myself" in *Leaves of Grass* (New York: Vintage/Library of America, 1992), 244. For an indication of how Whitman influenced Goyen early in his career, see *GAE* 58.

18. Walter Berns to Dorothy Brett, February 29, 1952 (HRC 49.2).

19. In a letter to Spud Johnson, Goyen described his feelings over Berns's marriage as "bitter" but resigned: "But the truth of it is that it is beautiful, it is Walt's fulfillment, also the fulfillment of Walt's and my long and marvelous relationship. We *do* go on, and can; and shall. His roots grow very very deep in me; and though I rejoice at his new happiness, there are times when something low and deep in me, removed by now so far far back in me that I scarcely know what it is or where, will not be still, but fights and grieves." Goyen to Spud Johnson, June 1, 1951 (HRC 49.3).

20. Goyen to Margaret L. Hartley and Allen Maxwell, October 8, 1951 (*SL* 229).

21. Goyen to Katherine Anne Porter, August 14, 1951 (*SL* 224).

22. *Time* 59, February, 25, 1952, 104; Robert Lowry, "A Smog of Loneliness," *New York Times*, February 10, 1952, 5.

23. Vernon Young, "Ghost and Flesh, Vinegar and Wine: Ten Recent Novels," *New Mexico Quarterly* 22 (1952): 322–330.

24. William Peden, "The Lower Depths," *Saturday Review* 35, March 22, 1952, 17.

25. Margaret L. Hartley, "William Goyen's Texas in Luminous New Tales," *Dallas Morning News*, February 10, 1952.

26. Walter Berns to Dorothy Brett, February 29, 1952 (HRC 49.2).

27. If his correspondence is an accurate guide, Goyen moved through agents relatively quickly during the early part of his career. Throughout his writing life, he appears to have been more comfortable dealing directly with editors and was quick to discard agents who made what he considered to be inappropriate suggestions about his writing.

28. Goyen to Charles and Emma Goyen, July 23, 1952 (WRC).

29. Goyen to Charles and Emma Goyen, August 31, 1952 (WRC).

30. Goyen to William Hart, October 19, 1952 (*SL* 252).

31. Julian Schnabel, "Joe Glasco," in *Joseph Glasco: 1948–1986: A Sesquicentennial Exhibition* (Houston: Contemporary Arts Museum, 1986), 26–28.

32. Goyen to Ernst Robert Curtius, September 26, 1952 (*SL* 249).

33. Goyen to William Hart, October 19, 1952 (*SL* 252–253).

34. Goyen to John Igo, July 27, 1952 (emphasis in original) (*SL* 246).

35. The lighthouse is likely based on the Dungeness Lighthouse, which Goyen would have come to know very well during his training missions aboard the *Casablanca* in the Strait of Juan de Fuca.

36. Quoted in a letter from Goyen to Maurice Edgar Coindreau, February 3, 1954 (*SL* 266).

37. William Saroyan, *The Daring Young Man on the Flying Trapeze* (New York: Modern Library, 1941), 20–21.

38. Ibid., 58.

39. Rilke, *Duino Elegies*, trans. J. B. Leishman and Stephen Spender (New York: Norton, 1939), 47.

40. Goyen to William Hart, August 2, 1942 (WRC).

41. Kathleen L. Komar, *Transcending Angels: Rainer Maria Rilke's Duino Elegies* (Lincoln: University of Nebraska Press, 1987), 107.

42. Goyen to Margaret Hartley, April 27, 1953 (*SL* 255).

43. Anaïs Nin, *The Diary of Anaïs Nin, 1955–1966* (New York: Harcourt, 1976), 63.

44. Goyen to Maurice Edgar Coindreau, May 10, 1953 (*SL* 257).

45. Goyen to Maurice Edgar Coindreau, May 19, 1953 (*SL* 258).

46. See *HLC* 133 (*SL* 266).

47. Goyen to Ernst Robert Curtius, December 13, 1953 (*SL* 261).

48. Quoted in Goyen letter to Maurice Edgar Coindreau, February 3, 1954.

49. Goyen to Ernst Robert Curtius, December 13, 1953.

Chapter 9: *A Farther Country*: 1954–1956

1. Goyen to Charles and Emma Goyen, March 29, 1953 (WRC).

2. Goyen to Charles and Emma Goyen, October 7, 1953 (WRC).

3. Goyen to Dorothy Brett, April 14, 1954 (*SL* 267).

4. Goyen to Maurice Edgar Coindreau, May 5, 1954 (*SL* 269).

5. Goyen to Maurice Edgar Coindreau, May 5, 1954 (*SL* 269).

6. Goyen to William Hart, June 5, 1954 (WRC).

7. Goyen to William Hart, June 5, 1954 (WRC).

8. Goyen to Ernst Robert Curtius, August 22, 1949 (*SL* 137).

9. T. S. Eliot called Curtius "one of the most illustrious" critics of his time and expressed a deep personal gratitude to the man who brought his own work, among that of many others, to the attention of the German public. See Hans Reiss, "Ernst Robert Curtius (1886–1956): Some Reflections on the Occasion of the Fortieth Anniversary of his Death," *Modern Language Review* 91, no. 3 (July, 1996): 647–654.

10. Ernst Robert Curtius, "Goyen," in *Essays on European Literature*, trans. Michael Kowal (Princeton, N.J.: Princeton University Press, 1973), 464.

11. Curtius, "Goyen," 464.

12. Goyen to Dorothy Brett, June 30, 1954 (*SL* 273). Though Goyen believed at the time that *Half a Look of Cain* was to be published in German, it never appeared under the imprint of *Die Arche*.

13. Goyen to Ernst Robert Curtius, September 22, 1954 (*SL* 278).

14. McDowell is best known for the role he played editing and publishing James Agee's posthumous novel *A Death in the Family* in 1957.

15. Goyen to Ernst Robert Curtius, March 10, 1955 (*SL* 285).

16. Nathaniel Hawthorne, "Preface," *The Blithedale Romance*, vol. 3 of the *Centenary Edition of the Works of Nathaniel Hawthorne*, ed. William Charvat (Columbus: Ohio State University Press, 1962).

17. In a 1966 study guide, Goyen used the term to describe Ralph Ellison: "Judging from the quality of his only novel to date, we might justifiably speak of Ralph Ellison as a 'romancer'; that is, a poet who creates a novel concerning itself with social themes but treats them romantically as opposed to naturalistically or strictly realistically." *Ralph Ellison's Invisible Man: A Critical Commentary* (New York: American R.D.M. Corporation, 1966), 9. A similar point is made by Steven G. Kellman in "'You Wan Hear': Dialogic Imagination in *Arcadio*," in *A Goyen Companion: Appreciations of a Writer's Writer*, ed. Brooke Horvath, Irving Malin, and Paul Ruffin (Austin: University of Texas Press, 1997), 72.

18. Marietta is also a transformation of Curran, the weaver/healer, from *Half a Look of Cain*.

19. Patrick Bennett, *Talking with Texas Writers: Twelve Interviews* (College Station: Texas A&M University Press, 1980), 243.

20. Goyen to Ernst Robert Curtius, April 9, 1951 (*SL* 189).

21. The blanket was based on a wall hanging in Frieda Lawrence's Taos house: "[O]nce I saw in Frieda's house—she lived on a ranch and I lived with her—there was a beautiful tapestry that just tormented me it was so beautiful—it was all hanging down, it was kinda faded and really torn, but in it was a figure of a great bird. Birds have always taken me over, for some reason. And this bird—I don't know what the bird was doing—it was in some field of grain or something, I couldn't tell what—but there was this very dim, almost lost figure there, and I began to try to reconstitute that figure and imagine what that was." Rolande Ballorain, "Interview with William Goyen," *Delta* 9 (1979): 37.

22. Donald Barr, "Mandolins and Nuns," *New York Times*, July 24, 1955, 17.

23. "Books in Brief," *The Nation*, October 22, 1955, 346–347.

24. "I am primitive," Goyen told his friend John Igo in 1975, "I am impulsive, I work through impulse. And then I find my way through that, I shape it, and work on it after that, but I rely on my folk sense of life and things." John Igo, "Learning to See Simply: An Interview with William Goyen," 273.

25. See Helen Sheehy, *Margo: The Life and Theatre of Margo Jones* (Dallas: SMU Press, 1989), 29.

26. Ibid., 262.

27. Goyen to Dorothy Brett, August 2, 1955 (HRC 49.1).

28. Goyen to Charles and Emma Goyen, August 2, 1955 (WRC).

29. Goyen to Ernst Robert Curtius, December 5, 1955 (*SL* 288).

30. Though the exact date of sale is difficult to determine, it seems likely that Goyen and Glasco sold the house in the summer of 1958. It was on the market then for $8,000 dollars, and Goyen reported to his parents that they had a potential buyer.

Chapter 10: Blood Kindred: 1957–1962

1. Goyen to Charles and Emma Goyen, April 27, 1955 (WRC).

2. His parents' generosity over so long a period was likely due to Emma Goyen's influence. According to Don Gerard, the family was divided over money in general and specifically over whether to continue this kind of support. Goyen's sister Kat was allied with her father against it, and Emma took Bill's side, an echo of her willingness to give him small amounts of cash she secreted for his music lessons when he was a teenager (author interview with Don Gerard).

3. William Goyen, "Unending Vengeance," Review of Flannery O'Connor, *Wise Blood*, *New York Times*, May 18, 1952, 4.

4. "A World of Bad Luck," review of Bernard Malamud, *The Assistant*, *New York Times*, April 28, 1957, 4.

5. "That Old Valentine Maker," review of Truman Capote, *Breakfast at Tiffany's*, *New York Times*, November 2, 1958, 5, 38.

6. Goyen, "That Old Valentine Maker," 5.

7. Quoted in Gerald Clarke, *Capote: A Biography* (New York: Simon and Schuster, 1988), 135.

8. Truman Capote to Goyen, October 12, 1950. *Too Brief a Treat: The Letters of Truman Capote*, ed. Gerald Clarke (New York: Random House, 2004), 139.

9. Goyen to Katherine Anne Porter, March 25, 1951 (*SL* 185).

10. Goyen to Katherine Anne Porter, July 17, 1951 (*SL* 213).

11. Goyen, Review of Truman Capote, *The Grass Harp*, *The Houston Post*, October 7, 1951, 4.14.

12. When Goyen worked in publishing in the mid-1960s, he made use of a similar sort of distinction in a letter to William Inge: "I really think you're on your way towards a marvelous story, but I ask you to re-examine the text with an eye to eliminating any sexual inferences that might be interpreted as just 'queer,' rather than deeper emanations of male sexuality. I ask you to be sensitive to this because I feel the book has a classic quality, a quality of power and universality, and any details that lessens or weakens that quality we would want to clean out." Goyen to William Inge, August 22, 1966.

13. See *SL* ix. The falling-out didn't prevent Doris Roberts from soliciting a blurb from Capote when the twenty-fifth anniversary edition of *The House of Breath* was published in 1975. On that occasion Capote explicitly accused Goyen of treachery towards those who had helped him early in his career, particularly Porter and Spender. Later, at an emotional low

point in 1980, Goyen reached out and the two had a cordial phone conversation. See Goyen to Robert Phillips, August 19, 1980 (*SL* 373).

14. *"House of Breath* at Circle in the Square," *New York Times*, April 15, 1957, 23.

15. Anaïs Nin, *The Diary of Anaïs Nin, 1953–1966* (New York: Harcourt, 1976), 80. Coindreau also saw the production but considered the necessary realization on the stage to be damaging to the book's verbal magic: "The house was there, of course," he explained years later to an interviewer, "and all its inhabitants, but the breath was gone." Maurice Edgar Coindreau, *Mémoires d'un traducteur: entretiens avec Christian Guidicelli* (Paris: Gallimard, 1992), 85.

16. Goyen to Dorothy Brett, April 30, 1957 (HRC).

17. Goyen's brief affair with Dylan Thomas promoter John Malcolm Brinnin in the early 1950s may have given him additional information on Thomas and the results of his early death. See the John Malcolm Brinnin collection at the University of Delaware, 103, Box 8.

18. Though not produced as a film, the screenplay eventually became the play *Christy*, staged in a workshop production at the American Place Theater in 1964.

19. Goyen to Charles and Emma Goyen, September 30, 1957 (*SL* 301). Though Goyen did draft a letter to Coe suggesting revisions for the film, there is no evidence that he actually worked on the screenplay. As he explained to his parents, by the time he flew to California, the film was already finished.

20. The manuscript versions of *The Diamond Rattler* are in HRC 21.1 and 21.3.

21. Goyen to Charles and Emma Goyen, June 7, 1960 (WRC).

22. Goyen to Charles and Emma Goyen, July 15, 1958 (WRC).

23. Goyen to Charles and Emma Goyen, June 11, 1957 (WRC).

24. Goyen to Charles and Emma Goyen, August 11, 1958 (WRC).

25. Brett was puzzled at Glasco's reaction to the death: "Now why did the death of his father so upset him? He hated him, he was so rude, so cruel to him, that the death could have been a release to Joe, of something he could not understand or cope with." Brett to Goyen, August 8, 1961 (HRC).

26. Goyen to Charles and Emma Goyen, May 14, 1961 (WRC).

27. Goyen actually took the name from Dorothy Brett's cat.

28. See Chapter One for discussions of these stories.

29. William Peden, "The Archetypal Situations," *New York Times*, August 7, 1960, 5, 12.

30. Terry Southern, "New Trends and Old Hats," *The Nation*, November 19, 1960, 380–383.

31. Thomas Lask, "Books of the Times," *New York Times*, August 27, 1960, 17.

32. Granville Hicks, "Within the Shadow of Winesburg," *Saturday Review* 43, August 6, 1960, 14.

33. Goyen to Charles and Emma Goyen, February 4, 1960 (*SL* 308).

Chapter 11: "A New Life": 1962–1964

1. See "Playhouse to Premier Original Play by Goyen," *Boston Globe*, April 29, 1960, 41.

2. The manuscript of *Christy* is in HRC 26.6.

3. *Christy* was offered in a workshop production in March 1964 at the American Place Theater, which was housed in St. Clement's Protestant Episcopal Church on West 46th Street in New York. These works-in-progress productions were funded by a Rockefeller Foundation Grant of $15,000. *Christy* was one of three plays by various authors included in the grant.

4. Doris Roberts and Danielle Morton, *Are You Hungry, Dear? Life, Laughs, and Lasagna* (New York: St. Martin's Press, 2003), 253.

5. Ibid., 258.

6. Coindreau, *Mémoires*, 79. He also cites the example of a German professor who visited him at Princeton because he had heard that Coindreau was translating the novel: He "took the trouble to come see me exclusively to tell me about this book that his students were devouring" (79).

7. Ibid., 84.

8. Goyen to Charles and Emma Goyen, February 25, 1962 (WRC).

9. Goyen to Charles and Emma Goyen, June 6, 1962 (*SL* 313).

10. Rolande Ballorain, "Interview with William Goyen," *Delta* 9 (1979): 30.

11. Goyen to Charles and Emma Goyen, June 24, 1962 (WRC).

12. Goyen to Charles and Emma Goyen, January 13, 1963 (WRC).

13. Unedited *Paris Review* interview transcript, HRC 35.14.

14. Ms. of *Christy* in HRC 26.6.

15. Ballorain, "Interview," 30.

16. Roberts, *Are You Hungry*, 261.

17. Goyen to Dorothy Brett, June 6, 1964 (*SL* 316).

18. Goyen to Seymour Lawrence, undated (*SL* 317–319).

19. Goyen to Dorothy Brett, November 15, 1965 (*SL* 321).

20. Robert Phillips remembers Goyen telling him that the lost child was buried somewhere on Long Island. (Robert Phillips to author, September 14, 1999.) The evidence for possible violence, whether physical or emotional, rests with the "Edith" manuscript. Given Goyen's interest during the 1960s in writing a book about his marriage (*Another Man's Son*), it is plausible that he would have attempted to work out this difficult material in somewhat fictionalized form.

21. Goyen to Sam Vaughan, April 4, 1965 (*SL* 320).

22. According to Sam Vaughan's later account, Goyen's agent, Harold Cohen, sent him a manuscript in 1962 that Vaughan rejected before suggesting that Goyen adapt "Savata, My Fair Sister" into a novel. See "For Bill," in *A Goyen Companion: Appreciations of a Writer's Writer*, ed. Brooke Horvath, Irving Malin, and Paul Ruffin (Austin: University of Texas Press, 1997), 182.

23. Interview with Patrick Bennett in *Talking with Texas Writers: Twelve Interviews* (College Station: Texas A&M University Press, 1980), 243. Goyen pronounced the name Sa-vay-ta.

24. Robert Phillips, *William Goyen* (Boston: G. K. Hall, 1979), 78.

25. Robert Gorham Davis, "Sister Ruby and Savata," *New York Times*, September 29, 1963.

26. John C. Pine, Review of *The Fair Sister, Library Journal* 88 (September 1963): 3224.

27. Granville Hicks, "Practicing the Holy Persuasion," *Saturday Review* 46, October 1963, 25–26.

28. Peter Owen, "Light Relief," *Times Literary Supplement*, July 12, 1963, 505.

29. "The Fair Sister," in *Masterplots 1964 Annual: Essay-Reviews of 100 Outstanding Books Published in the United States During 1963*, ed. Frank N. Magill (New York: Salem, 1964), 75.

30. The unexpected failure of support from his publisher clearly played an important role in his diminished ability and desire to write during the 1960s. See Roberts, *Are You Hungry*, 266.

31. Goyen to William Hart, July 10, 1963 (*SL* 314).

Chapter 12: A Living Jesus: 1966–1973

1. Granville Hicks, "Nine Bright Beginnings," *Saturday Review*, August 19, 1967, 23.

2. Elizabeth Spencer, email to author, January 8, 2013.

3. Goyen to Clyde Grimm, July 17, 1970 (*SL* 330).

4. Goyen, *My Ántonia: A Critical Commentary* (New York: American R.D.M. Corporation, 1966), 11, 48.

5. Goyen, *Ralph Ellison's Invisible Man*, (New York: American R.D.M. Corporation, 1966), 10.

6. Robert Phillips has noted the suggestive similarity between this title and *The House of Breath*, which Goyen was working on at the time. See *SL* 80.

7. Goyen to James Laughlin, August 2, 1947. This original project for Laughlin never reached fruition, but in 1949, Goyen was set to work on Cossery's *The Lazy Ones*, which was published by New Directions in 1952.

8. The correspondence related to this project is in HRC 37.1.

9. See Doris Roberts and Danielle Morton, *Are You Hungry, Dear? Life, Laughs, and Lasagna* (New York: St. Martin's Press, 2003), 275. Another dimension of this fear was almost certainly the realization that he was following in the footsteps of his grandfather W. S. Goyen, succumbing to the darker tendencies of his father's family about which he had written so often.

10. Ibid., 276.

11. Mark W. Rectanus, *German Literature in the United States: Licensing Translations in the International Marketplace* (Wiesbaden: O. Harrassowitz, 1990), 91.

12. Goyen to Robert Phillips, December 2, 1971 (*SL* 336).

13. Goyen to Dorothy Brett, August 7, 1968 (*SL* 325).

14. Goyen to Sam Vaughan, April 4, 1965 (*SL* 320). The method Goyen was employing in *Six Women* relied on the same preference for direct address and the re-creation of "talking to" a loved one. Another example of this kind of approach can be seen in the 1978 lecture "While You Were Away," also addressed directly to Charlie Goyen.

15. Goyen was apparently attracted, perhaps from this point on, to small glass figurines of animals. Reginald Gibbons remembers a large collection on the shelf of Goyen's bathroom in the house in Los Angeles (email to author, December 5, 2013), and James White recalls Goyen eagerly buying a "white glass unicorn" from a street person in Hollywood. See "On William Goyen," *Texas Review* 20, nos. 1–2 (Spring-Summer 1999): 49–57, 54.

16. Draft of letter to Phyllis Jackson, undated, in HRC 10.3.

17. Sam Vaughan, "For Bill," in Horvath, Malin, and Ruffin, *A Goyen Companion*, 185.

18. Goyen to Robert Phillips, December 2, 1971 (*SL* 336).

19. There have, of course, been numerous interpretations of Jesus—generally considered heretical—that emphasize his physical nature. Little indication exists that Goyen was aware of this long tradition, but as I have suggested in reference to the "The White Rooster," he likely had read and absorbed Lawrence's ideas on the subject, principally found in "The Escaped Cock" and "The Man who Died." See Chapter Six. More remarkable than any influence, however, is the sense that through his own sensibility and personal experience, he had essentially reproduced in the twentieth century the kind of spiritual transformation of sexuality more commonly associated with the extremes of medieval mysticism.

20. Goyen must have understood that some would see his Jesus as unacceptable when Catherine Marshall painfully refused his request for a blurb. However, this kind of reaction

didn't prevent him from sending copies to anyone and everyone who might help publicize it. In addition to numerous ministers, both locally and nationally prominent, he sent the book to influential old friends like Jack Valenti and well-connected religious and political figures such as Pat Boone, Johnny Cash, and Lady Bird Johnson.

21. "A Book of Jesus," *Catholic Star Herald*, April 20, 1973.

22. "A Book of Jesus," *The Christian Century*, April 25, 1973, 491.

23. Joni Bodart, "Goyen, William. A Book of Jesus," *Library Journal* (September 15, 1973): 2682; Michael Murray, "A Book of Jesus," *Commonweal* (July 13, 1973): 391. Goyen's old friend from San Antonio, John Igo, remembers a very negative reception for the book in Texas.

24. Robert Phillips, "A Book of Jesus," *New York Times Book Review*, May 6, 1973, 30.

Chapter 13: The Restorer: 1974

1. Elliot Norton, "*House of Breath* Rueful, Sad, Solemn," *Record American*, November 11, 1969.

2. R. E. Krieger, "William Goyen Play Tries to Say Too Much," *Evening Gazette*, November 5, 1969, 30. Kevin Kelly, "*House of Breath* Lovely, Loving Play," *Boston Globe*, November 15, 1969, 11.

3. Goyen's note. The manuscripts and notes on *Aimee!* are in HRC boxes 1–3.

4. "New Show in Stock: Aimee!," *Variety*, February 6, 1974, 60.

5. "Aimee!," *Boston Herald-American* (December 11, 1973).

6. "Aimee!," *Worcester Telegram* (December 17, 1973).

7. Goyen to Robert Phillips, May 12, 1972 (HRC).

8. Rolande Ballorain, "Interview with William Goyen," *Delta* 9 (1979): 43.

9. Ibid.," 44.

10. "An Angel, A Flower, A Bird," *The New Yorker*, September 27, 1969, 130–143. Goyen never claimed the article itself as a source for his interest, but no mention of Barbette occurs in his notes prior to the 1970s. In April of 1971, during the period of his spiritual crisis, he recorded his attempts to write about a "wire-walker" at the retreat in Weston (HRC 28.2). From this point on, particularly in the drafts and notes that led to his final novel, *Arcadio*, he referred to Barbette repeatedly as a source for his hermaphroditic title character and sometimes as a version of Folner from *The House of Breath*.

11. Jean Cocteau and Man Ray, *Barbette* (Berlin: borderline, 1988), 5.

12. Ibid., 3.

13. See note 6, Chapter Six.

14. Addis's death in the fork of the tree is another version of Goyen's boyhood fall in the cedar tree in Trinity, recorded in *The House of Breath*: "Then I would turn off at the twisted cedar, in whose branches I had been as often as any bird, that had a forked limb like a chicken's wishbone, where once I slipped and hung like Absalom until Mrs. Tanner came running to save me" (*HOB* 11).

15. Goyen described the process of composition to Robert Phillips: "The book is not being written by me, it is revealing itself—the way all my books have done. I have to wait until the story shows itself. Pieces come—here, there; hang there, manifestly, without any apparent connections. What I write for is the connections." Goyen to Phillips, October 25, 1972 (*SL* 344).

16. "Come, the Restorer," *Publishers' Weekly*, August 26, 1974, 298; Peter G. Kramer, "Come, the Restorer," *Newsweek*, November 11, 1974, 111; Lon Tinkle, "Virtuosic Feast from Bill

Goyen," *Dallas Morning News*, November 24, 1974, 54; Patrice Repusseau, "In the Name of the Father, of the Son, and of the Oily Spirit," *Southwest Review* (Winter 1975): 87–89; Shirley Ann Grau, "Selected Writings of William Goyen: Come, the Restorer," *New York Times Book Review*, November 3, 1974, 73.

17. Perhaps at least in part because of Grau's review, the book did not sell well. Goyen was particularly incensed by Doubleday's failure to solicit blurbs for the cover, an (intentional?) oversight that simply added to his long list of grievances against publishers. See Doris Roberts and Danielle Morton, *Are You Hungry, Dear? Life, Laughs, and Lasagna* (New York: St. Martin's, 2003), 267.

Chapter 14: Precious Door: 1975–1981

1. This tally does not include *The Selected Writings of William Goyen: Eight Favorites by a Master American Storyteller* (New York: Random House; Berkeley, Calif.: The Bookworks, 1974).

2. See Doris Roberts and Danielle Morton, *Are You Hungry, Dear? Life, Laughs, and Lasagna* (New York: St. Martin's Press, 2003), 153–159.

3. Goyen to Robert Phillips, August 13, 1975. Robert S. Phillips Papers, Syracuse University Library.

4. The following account is taken from the unedited transcripts of Goyen's *Paris Review* interview conducted by Robert Phillips in June of 1975, found in HRC 35.14.

5. Goyen to Ellen Garwood, September 13, 1975 (*SL* 351). This letter may have been connected to Garwood's funding of the acquisition of Goyen's papers by the Harry Ransom Humanities Research Center at the University of Texas in 1975. Later, Garwood also offered to endow a chair in creative writing at UT, provided that Goyen was selected to fill it. Though he did give a reading in Austin in pursuit of this possibility, he was apparently opposed by members of the English department. See James White, "On William Goyen," *Texas Review* 20, nos. 1–2 (Spring–Summer 1999): 49–57. Author interview with James White.

6. From notes to "Margo" in *Six Women* material in HRC 29.6.

7. The notebook containing these entries is in HRC 31.1.

8. Goyen to Ellen Garwood, September 13, 1975 (*SL* 351). In his notes to *SL*, Phillips suggests that this letter may not have been sent.

9. Goyen to Ellen Garwood, September 13, 1975 (*SL* 351).

10. According to Gerrard, the impetus behind the volume was primarily the wish to help Goyen during this troubled period of his life. Author interview with Don Gerrard.

11. William Goyen, "Introduction," *Selected Writings*, i–ii.

12. Author interview with Robert Phillips.

13. Richard Rhodes, "William Goyen's world is enormous and enormously minute," *Chicago Tribune*, November 9, 1975, F3.

14. Joyce Carol Oates, "William Goyen's Life Rhythms," *New York Times Book Review*, November 16, 1975, 4, 14.

15. Goyen to Robert Phillips, November 29, 1975 (*SL* 352).

16. In 1978, when Goyen was teaching at Princeton, he developed a warm relationship with Oates and her husband, Raymond Smith. According to Oates, Goyen was "a gracious, soft-spoken, warmly welcoming and sweet-mannered person": "I wish that I could convey Bill's particular sort of southern-masculine gentleness. He had a way of inspiring others,

simply by his example. He was the most 'poetic' of persons in both his writing and in his personality." Email to author, September 24, 2012.

17. Goyen to Robert Phillips, November 29, 1975 (*SL* 352).

18. Goyen to Maurice Edgar Coindreau, February 24, 1975.

19. *The House of Breath*, 2nd ed. (New York: Persea Books, 1986), 178.

20. In the unedited transcript of the interview, Goyen expands upon his critique of Capote: "It's just fake Southern. It's fake sweet and fake naive and fake primitive. To read it is, I mean, it's obvious if one reads it carefully but if one saw it on television you knew then that it was absurd . . ." (HRC 35.14).

21. According to Phillips, because of his role as husband and stepfather, Goyen "would sometimes be very outraged by something that was said in print that he thought was damaging to his image." Author interview with Robert Phillips.

22. Goyen to Robert Phillips, May 16, 1976 (*SL* 353).

23. One potential award was the Pulitzer Prize for fiction, for which Goyen apparently believed he had been nominated. Records for the 1976 award, for which *The Collected Stories* would have been eligible, indicate that the jury (Walter Clemons, Guy Davenport, and Eudora Welty) had a short list that included works by Saul Bellow, Donald Barthelme, Reynolds Price, Diane Vreuls, and E. L. Doctorow. The award went to Bellow for *Humboldt's Gift*. It is possible that Doubleday nominated Goyen's book to be considered on the long list, which may have given him the impression that he was a finalist. According to James White, the failure to receive the Pulitzer haunted Goyen in the years after. In fact, White reports Goyen telling him that he sent the winner of the prize a telegram that said, "You didn't deserve it." If this is true and Goyen did send such a telegram to Bellow, who won the Nobel Prize that same year, it indicates how far his bitterness and disappointment could push him from both rationality and civility. See White, "On William Goyen," 53; and Heinz-Dietrich Fischer and Erika J. Fischer, *The Pulitzer Prize Archive: Novel/Fiction Awards, 1917–1994* (Munich: K. G. Saur, 1997), lxiv–lxv.

24. Roberts, *Are You Hungry*, 276, 277.

25. Ibid., 278.

26. Letter to author from Robert Phillips, September 14, 1999. See also Phillips's "Memories of William Goyen," *Texas Review* 30, nos. 3–4 (Fall/Winter 2009): 103–106, 105.

27. Roberts, *Are You Hungry*, 280.

28. Ernest Kurtz, *Not-God, A History of Alcoholics Anonymous* (Center City, Minn.: Hazelden Educational Services, 1979), 186.

29. Author interview with Eve Caram.

30. Responding to what he called a "self-pitying" phone message from Robert Phillips, Goyen explained how careful he needed to be about indulging destructive emotions: "I am living a different life now, Robert, trying to maintain the Program that keeps me alive, a day at a time. Surely you know this, by now. This requires that I turn away from what is uncomfortable—to save *myself*. It also requires that I be honest and open in my feelings, not sullen and resentful and hidden, as is my nature when rejected." Goyen to Phillips, November 24, 1977. Robert S. Phillips Papers, Syracuse University Library.

31. The image also enters into Goyen's notes on AA: "Runnin down those cold dark streets with God, looking for a door—and finding, suddenly, those two little A's" (HRC 29.6).

32. Paul Tillich, *The New Being* (New York: Scribners, 1955), 20.

33. Tillich, *New Being*, 20, 21.

34. As is clear from *Half a Look of Cain*, Goyen was also accustomed to using the Cain

and Abel story, important in "Precious Door," as a way to frame his relationship to Berns. As the older of the two, Goyen tended to see himself as the discontented, "darker" half who, like the older brother here, had symbolically sacrificed and lost his companion: *"Oh he was bright and I was dark and I gave him all my darkness on that ship; but we joined, for all good things in the world, and to find somethin together . . ."* (*HOB* 36).

35. Goyen's Sunday school books of Bible study exercises are in HRC 54.2.

36. Patrice Repusseau, "Of Two Stranger Hands: A Reading of William Goyen's 'Precious Door,'" *Triquarterly* 139 (Winter/Spring 2011). Online at www.triquarterly.org. Repusseau's reading is the most clarifying and penetrating in the limited critical history of this story.

37. Ibid.

Chapter 15: The Nurseryman: 1976–1982

1. Goyen had been asked to substitute for George Garrett, who later described him as "a great and good influence on some of my best and favorite students." George Garrett, *Southern Excursions: Views on Southern Letters in My Time*, ed. James Conrad McKinley (Baton Rouge: Louisiana State University Press, 2003).

2. Madison Smartt Bell, "A Memory of William Goyen," in *A Goyen Companion: Appreciations of a Writer's Writer*, ed. Brooke Horvath, Irving Malin, and Paul Ruffin (Austin: University of Texas Press, 1997), 156.

3. Ibid., 156.

4. Goyen to Samuel Vaughan and Stewart Richardson, July 19, 1977 (*SL* 357).

5. Goyen to Roberta Pryor, March 26, 1978 (*SL* 359–360). John Igo also remembers Goyen's distress at this experience: "I had to console him." The site of the remaindered books "wounded him." Author interview with John Igo.

6. The insertions in curly brackets {} are Goyen's revisions.

7. This was apparently more than just an imagined gesture. In describing how Goyen "made his peace with Los Angeles," Roberts says that one afternoon she "caught him hugging a palm tree outside our house." Doris Roberts and Danielle Morton, *Are You Hungry, Dear? Life, Laughs, and Lasagna* (New York: St. Martin's, 2003), 281.

8. Ibid., 272.

9. James White, "On William Goyen," *Texas Review* 20, nos. 1–2 (Spring–Summer 1999): 53. Goyen to Eve Caram, March 10, 1980 (*SL* 370).

10. Patrick Bennett, "William Goyen: A Poet Telling Stories," *Talking with Texas Writers: Twelve Interviews* (College Station: Texas A&M University Press, 1980), 233.

11. Roberts, *Are You Hungry*, 272.

12. Erika Duncan, "William Goyen," in *Unless Soul Clap Its Hands: Portraits and Passages* (New York: Schocken Books, 1984), 20, 21.

13. The story was also included in the posthumous *HHM*.

14. In his superb essay on the story, Patrice Repusseau makes this same point: "In many ways it is as if 'In the Icebound Hothouse' were a kind of compression of Goyen's most intimate life and work, which accounts for the amazing intensity of this dozen or so pages. See "Lunar Plexus: On William Goyen's 'In the Icebound Hothouse,'" *Mid-American Review* 13, no. 1 (1992): 9–38.

15. Goyen to Spud Johnson, June 1, 1951 (HRC 49.3).

16. Goyen to Patrice Repusseau, March 18, 1981 (*SL* 377).

17. In his 1983 interview with Reginald Gibbons, Goyen glossed the conclusion of this story in response to a question about returning home to Texas: "When I'd come with my suitcase, saying 'I'm here!', I'd see that figure on that horse saying 'Come in!' and yet 'Don't! It's just pain and darkness.' That house is still there, and so far as I know, that door is still there. A very precious, suspicious, dangerous door" (*GAE* 139).

18. Vance Bourjaily, "Words for a World," *New York Times Book, Review,* June 9, 1985.

19. Goyen to Patrice Repusseau, June 24, 1978. Courtesy of Patrice Repusseau.

Chapter 16: *Arcadio*: 1983

1. Goyen insisted on pronouncing the name with a long "a," perhaps to echo Arcadia or "arcade." John Igo, who read several versions of the manuscript and helped edit the Spanish in the text, objected to the Anglicized (or perhaps Texanized) pronunciation but couldn't get Goyen to change his mind. "Nobody corrects Bill Goyen," Igo explained, "but you can suggest." Author interview with John Igo.

2. Despite Arcadio's male and female attributes, the narrator uses the masculine singular pronoun in those instances when such a reference is called for. Indeed, with the exception of defined moments when Arcadio dresses as a woman, he appears, externally, more masculine than feminine.

3. Goyen to Thomas Hart, August 10, 1981 (*SL* 382).

4. Repusseau convincingly links the *figura* to the high-wire "act" described in *Half a Look of Cain.* See "Lunar Plexus: On William Goyen's 'In the Icebound Hothouse,'" *Mid-American Review* 13, no. 1 (1992): 9–38, 27.

5. John J. McNeill, *The Church and the Homosexual* (Boston: Beacon, 1993), originally published in 1976. Goyen also drew on a number of works about hermaphroditism and gay experience. A list of books in his notes includes Edward Carpenter's *The Intermediate Sex* and *Days with Walt Whitman*; Howard Jones and William Wallace Street's *Hermaphroditisms: Genital Anomalia and Related Endocrine Disorders*; John Money's *Sex Errors of the Body*; Bruce Jackson's *In the Life*; Ambroise Paré's *De monstres et prodiges*; Marie Delacourt's *Hermphrodite: Myths and Rites of the Bisexual Figure in Classical Antiquity*; Jack Kerouac's *Visions of Cody*; and Jane Kramer's *Allen Ginsburg in America*.

6. Goyen to Robert Phillips, May 16, 1976 (*SL* 353).

7. There is some indication that sexual need—perhaps specifically gay desire—functioned like an addiction to Goyen, offering comfort when he felt "pushed down." When he was in France in the mid-1970s looking for a publisher for *Come, the Restorer,* he was deeply insulted by his treatment at the hands of the publisher Gallimard, who had rudely ignored him despite his past successes. According to Repusseau, Goyen's "rage plunged him into a dark pit of anguish and despair clearly tinged with sexual overtones," and he spent the afternoon browsing homoerotica in several sex shops. Patrice Repusseau, email to author, October 8, 2013.

8. Reginald Gibbons, "Redeemed in the Telling: *Arcadio* by William Goyen," *New York Times Book Review,* November 6, 1983, 14, 36–7.

9. Joyce Carol Oates, "Introduction," *HHM,* vii.

Chapter 17: The Wound and the Bow: 1982–1983

1. Goyen to William Hart, March 3, 1937 (*SL* 3–4). See Chapter Three for a discussion of this letter.

2. Anaïs Nin, *The Diary of Anaïs Nin, 1955–1966* (New York: Harcourt, 1976), 79.

3. Edmund Wilson, *The Wound and the Bow: Seven Studies in Literature* (Athens: Ohio University Press, 1997), 228. Originally published in 1941.

4. Ibid., 229.

5. Goyen to Joseph Savino and Mark Zipoli, September 27, 1978 (*SL* 364).

6. In his notes to the *Selected Letters*, Robert Phillips explains that the earlier, 1978 operation was performed to correct Dupuytren's contracture. However, in a letter to Elizabeth Spencer dated May 24, 1980, Goyen describes having undergone "a somewhat ghastly operation on [his] left hand . . . two weeks ago." The 1978 operation apparently required a much longer period of bed rest than hand surgery would typically warrant. It seems likely, therefore, that the earlier procedure, whatever it addressed, was not for Dupuytren's contraction but for something more invasive.

7. James White, "On William Goyen," *Texas Review* 20, no. 1–2 (Spring-Summer 1999): 50.

8. Ibid., 54.

9. Doris Roberts and Danielle Morton, *Are You Hungry, Dear? Life, Laughs, and Lasagna* (New York: St. Martin's, 2003), 285.

10. Goyen to Allen Wier, January 30, 1983 (*SL* 403).

11. See White, "On William Goyen," 54–55. Roberts records a similar reaction when Goyen thought his hospital room was too small (*Are You Hungry*, 290).

12. Letter to author from Eve Caram, April 21, 2013.

13. No relation to Goyen's longtime friend from Houston, William Hart.

14. Goyen to Robert Phillips, August 28, 1981 (*SL* 386).

15. Goyen to Robin Moody, December 5, 1981 (*SL* 392).

16. Goyen to Phyllis Jackson, undated letter (*SL* 375).

17. Goyen to Phyllis Jackson, undated letter (*SL* 375–376).

18. Goyen to Roberta Pryor, February 10, 1983 (*SL* 405).

19. Patrice Repusseau's essay "El Mudo Speaking: A Winged Victory in 'Tongues of Men and of Angels,'" elaborates on these connections: "Charity was the name of the small town where Boy Ganchion . . . was born. And it is also to that same place that Goyen takes us in his very last story. In the beginning was Charity, and Charity we still find in the end. But Love has set these two namesake places pole apart. They do not dwell on the same plane; over the years, and through much pain, the place of nostalgia has become a liberating feeling." See Horvath, Malin, and Ruffin, *A Goyen Companion*, 99.

20. Patrice Repusseau, "Lunar Plexus: On William Goyen's 'In the Icebound Hothouse,'" *Mid-American Review* 13, no. 1 (1992): 18–19.

21. Repusseau, "El Mudo," in Horvath, 115. Repusseau's discussion of the resemblance between this episode and the "miracle of the seven tongues" from the history of Christian martyrdom is also fascinating.

22. Doris Roberts Goyen, "Gifts: A Mosaic," *Mid-American Review* 13, no. 1 (1992): 161–166, 165.

23. Goyen's official death certificate lists "cardio respiratory arrest" as the immediate cause, "hepatic [liver] failure," as the secondary factor, and "chronic lymphocytic leukemia" as the long-term cause of death.

24. HRC 52.3.

Index

Milton Keynes UK
Ingram Content Group UK Ltd.
UKHW012154200224
438149UK00004B/84